Legacy Systems

ISBN 0-13-044927-X

9 790130 449275

90000

MISSION STATEMENT FOR YOURDON PRESS SERIES

In today's hectic, fast-paced economy, IT professionals and managers are under constant pressure to deliver new systems more quickly than ever before. One of the consequences of this pressure is that they're often thrown into situations for which they're not fully prepared. On Monday, they're given a new assignment in the area of testing, or risk management, or building a new application with the latest tools from IBM or Microsoft or Sun; and on Tuesday, they're expected to be productive and proficient. In many cases, they don't have time to attend a detailed training course; and they certainly don't have time to read a thousand-page *War and Peace* tome that explains the theoretical nuances of the technology, no matter how interesting those nuances may be.

Yourdon Press is aimed squarely at these busy professionals and managers. Our mission is to provide enough information for an experienced IT professional or manager to be able to assimilate the key aspects of a technology and begin putting it to productive use right away. We don't cover the historical background or the philosophical nuances of the technology; and in most cases, we don't cover all of the refinements, exceptions, and extensions that a Ph.D. student would want to know. Our objective is to provide pragmatic "how-to" information—supported, when possible, by checklists and guidelines and templates and wizards—that can be put to practical use right away. Of course, it's important to know that the refinements, exceptions, and extensions do exist; and the Yourdon Press books frequently provide references, links to Web sites, and other resources for those who need them.

Over time, we intend to produce books for every important aspect of IT systems development: from analysis and design to coding and testing. We cover project management, risk management, process improvement, and peopleware issues; and we plan to address several areas of new technology, from CRM to wireless technology, from enterprise application integration to Microsoft's .NET technology.

Perhaps one day life will slow down, and we'll be able to spend as much time as we want learning *everything* there is to be learned about IT technologies. But until that day arrives, we only have time for the most essential chunks of pragmatic information. And the place to find that information is the Yourdon Press series of computer books from Pearson/Prentice Hall PTR.

ABOUT THE SERIES EDITOR

Edward Yourdon is an internationally recognized consultant, lecturer, and author/coauthor of more than 25 books, including *Managing High-Intensity Internet Projects, Death March, Time Bomb, The Rise and Resurrection of the American Programmer, Modern Structured Analysis*, and others. Widely known as the lead developer of the structured analysis/design methods in the 1970's and the popular Coad/Yourdon object-oriented methodology in the early 1990's, Edward Yourdon brings both his writing and technical skills as Series Editor while developing key authors and publications for the Yourdon Press Series.

Selected Titles from the

YOURDON PRESS SERIES

Ed Yourdon, *Advisor*

Legacy Systems

Transformation Strategies

William Ulrich

Prentice Hall PTR
Upper Saddle River, NJ 07458
www.phptr.com

Library of Congress Cataloging-in-Publication Data
Ulrich, William M.
   Legacy systems: transformation strategies/William Ulrich.
     p. cm. —(Just enough series)
   Includes bibliographical references and index.
   ISBN 0-13-044927-X
   1. Management information systems. 2. Application software. 3. Business—Data
   processing. I. Title. II. Series.

T58.64.U49 2002
650'.028517—dc21   2002025795

Editorial/production supervision: *Kerry Reardon*
Composition: *Laurel Road Publishing Services*
Cover design director: *Jerry Votta*
Cover designer: *Nina Scuderi*
Art director and interior design: *Gail Cocker-Bogusz*
Manufacturing manager: *Alexis Heydt-Long*
Acquisitions editor: *Paul Petralia*
Editorial assistant: *Richard Winkler*
Marketing manager: *Bryan Gambrel*
Full-service production manager: *Anne R. Garcia*

 © 2002 Pearson Education, Inc.
Publishing as Prentice Hall PTR
Upper Saddle River, NJ 07458

Prentice Hall books are widely used by corporations and government agencies for training, marketing, and resale.

For information regarding corporate and government bulk discounts please contact:
Corporate and Government Sales (800) 382-3419 or corpsales@pearsontechgroup.com

10 9 8 7 6 5 4 3 2 1

ISBN 0-13-044927-X

Pearson Education LTD.
Pearson Education Australia PTY, Limited
Pearson Education Singapore, Pte. Ltd.
Pearson Education North Asia Ltd.
Pearson Education Canada, Ltd.
Pearson Educación de Mexico, S.A. de C.V.
Pearson Education–Japan
Pearson Education Malaysia, Pte. Ltd.

Contents

Chapter 2
Defining the Legacy Architecture Challenge   31

Chapter 3
The Changing Face of Information Technology   65

Chapter 4
Legacy Architecture Management and Transformation Strategies   99

Part II Infrastructure Setup and Planning   131

Chapter 5
Creating a Legacy Transformation Infrastructure   133

Chapter 6
Planning and Justifying a Legacy Transformation Project   161

Chapter 7
Legacy Transformation Technology   189

Chapter 10
Structuring, Rationalizing, and Upgrading Legacy Applications and Data Structures   283

Chapter 11
Logical Data and Business Rule Capture, Redesign, and Reuse   317

Chapter 12
Transformation Project Strategies and Case Studies   359

Appendix
Sample Tool Vendor List   389

Index   417

Preface

This book is about legacy information architectures and the daunting challenges they pose, along with strategies for tackling these problems. Commercial application systems and data architectures, running in production computing environments, are the lifeblood of the modern enterprise. These systems manage business and government operations around the globe. Any organization that believes it can address critical information requirements by replacing, wrapping, or ignoring legacy information assets is headed for a train wreck of monumental proportions.

Legacy application systems are defined as any production-enabled software, regardless of the platform it runs on, language it is written in, or length of time it has been in production. Legacy data structures are defined as the enterprise data that is accessed and modified by these production application systems. Collectively, these systems and data structures form critical information assets that managers and analysts must strive to understand, modify, consolidate, migrate, or otherwise transform to meet critical business requirements.

Despite the vast changes in information technology (IT) in recent years, legacy information challenges have remained. Improvements in business modeling, analysis, design and development, component reuse, and Web-enabled architectures hold great promise. Yet the value of these advancements will be minimal if management does not address legacy architectures under a cohesive, parallel strategy.

Worldwide, there are well over 200 billion lines of software that are fragmented, redundantly defined, hard to decipher, and highly inflexible. These systems, which have been functioning for decades, have survived revolutions in software, hardware, and the Internet. Now, with IT on the cusp of a new era in which handcrafted coding techniques are being supplanted by component-based development and Web Services, organizations run the risk of being mired down by a mountain of legacy code.

Efforts to address the legacy challenge have had limited impact. Over the past few years, stovepipe applications and data structures have been the target of piecemeal integration. While offering some near-term value, middleware and related wrapper-based solutions limit an enterprise's ability to leverage, reuse, and fully incorporate critical business rules and data locked inside of legacy architectures.

Countless companies are struggling to incorporate back-end functionality into front-end applications. Insurance companies would like to Web-enable claims processing environments. Banks would like to fully deploy online banking solutions. Telecommunications firms need to consolidate customer applications to help prepare for entering new markets. Energy companies, health care providers, retailers, and a wealth of other industry sectors must deliver immediate and comprehensive solutions to customers faster and more effectively. Even government agencies have entered the new e-business sector.

Essential legacy functionality and data can be identified, extracted, and reused under emerging information architectures to meet customer and user demands. This will only occur, however, if organizations take a proactive approach to tackling the legacy challenge, and this requires a legacy architecture transformation strategy. This book delivers such a strategy along with practical planning and implementation advice to those haunted by difficult legacy challenges and seeking quantifiable solutions.

Audience for this Book

A variety of readers will find this book of value. Directors, vice presidents, and business managers should read chapters 1 through 4 to gain an understanding of legacy transformation challenges, strategies, and alternatives they may not have known existed. For years, IT has been positioning all-or-nothing rewrite or ERP replacement options as the only way to deal with major information retooling requirements. Senior management should be aware that transformation can lower the costs and risks of planning, development, package selection and deployment, integration, and related information initiatives.

Analysts, project managers, architects, and planning teams are provided with a variety of high-level approaches and detailed planning and implementation techniques needed to document, retool, and transition legacy information architectures. Development teams in particular need to grow a deeper understanding of the role of legacy environments within development initiatives.

Consultants can use this book as a guide to planning and implementing projects involving legacy applications. Outsourcing and insourcing firms can also apply legacy understanding and enhancement guidelines in order to streamline and shrink the scope of effort related to their outsourcing contracts. In fact, anyone tasked with the ongoing management of legacy portfolios will want to carefully review and consider the techniques detailed in Part II and Part III of this book.

Additionally, managers and directors can use this book to craft strategies and detailed plans for project teams on major initiatives involving legacy systems. Analysts can then utilize detailed implementation guidelines on integration, migration, package implementation, CRM, and other major projects.

Finally, anyone interested in learning why corporate and government computing environments are such a challenge to manage, enhance, retool, or migrate should review the first section of this book. This can include investors, business partners, customers, business personnel, and senior executives who have a vested interest in the success and continuity of any corporate or government entities.

Summary of Contents

This book is broken into three parts and an appendix. Part I, "Legacy Transformation: Background and Strategies," contains legacy background information and strategies. Part II, "Infrastructure Setup and Planning," provides insights into establishing a legacy transformation infrastructure and project plans, while Part III, "Transformation Implementation," provides detailed transformation deployment options for implementation teams. The Appendix provides a list of various software products and vendors that can be used to implement transformation projects.

Part I is comprised of chapters 1 through 4 and provides an overview of legacy transformation challenges and strategies. Chapter 1 introduces the origin and evolution of computers along with the software that directs the computing activities. It also exposes the chasm between what people think computers are capable of and how most computers actually function.

Chapter 2 defines the issues organizations face when trying to understand and change the core applications that manage day-to-day business operations. This chapter helps place the significance and scope of the legacy challenge in perspective and refutes the belief that legacy applications can be ignored, easily replaced, or just wrapped in middleware. Case histories demonstrate that failed information initiatives can be traced directly back to the inability of an enterprise to effectively manage change requirements within legacy computing environments.

Chapter 3 discusses new trends in information technology, including the Internet, Java, Web Services, and a host of other emerging disciplines. This modern world of perfection runs in sharp contrast to the world of legacy information architectures. Chapter 4 overviews various strategies for managing, integrating, and transforming legacy application environments. This chapter introduces the concept of business-driven transformation, discusses transformation as a risk management tool, outlines a transformation framework, and provides project planning templates. It also provides an overview of the transformation approaches and techniques that are the foundation for the remaining sections of this book.

Part II includes chapters 5 through 8 and establishes the basis for planning and launching transformation initiatives. Chapter 5 outlines the business and information management infrastructure needed to deliver legacy transformation solutions. This chapter delves into the infrastructure issues responsible for creating the current legacy architecture dilemma and provides organizational guidelines for correcting these issues and avoiding the reintroduction of these problems in the future. Chapter 5 also outlines reuse concepts, project roles and responsibilities, and describes the role of methodologies, repositories, metrics, and software tool options.

Chapter 6 discusses how to plan and justify legacy transformation projects. This includes issues such as total cost of ownership, techniques for determining return on investment (ROI), and ways to redefine the concept of *value* in an ROI effort. In addition, this chapter discusses collaborative planning concepts, project and team formation, the concept of *dual positioning* transformation ROI, how to learn from our failures, infrastructure justification, and project ROI.

Chapter 7 introduces various technologies that an organization can use to plan, analyze, execute, and validate a transformation project. This includes an overview of relevant tool categories. Also discussed are the pros and cons of using certain tools for various transformation tasks and tool identification and procurement strategies. Chapter 8 details the tasks involved in performing the enterprise and project-level assessment. The enterprise assessment forms the basis for creating a transformation strategy or deploying a large-scale transformation initiative—such as a cross-functional package implementation. The project-level assessment begins the detailed analysis required to launch and finalize a transformation implementation project.

Part III, which includes chapters 9 through 12, details implementation approaches and techniques commonly found in a transformation project. Chapter 9 provides a transformation-oriented perspective on various enterprise application, business-to-business, and business process integration scenarios. This includes outlining integration options and approaches that can be pursued over the interim and in conjunction with strategic transformation projects. Chapter 10 provides detailed approaches and techniques for improving application source code and data structures without the need to redesign those structures. These discussions are provided within a context of providing near-term value to the users and beneficiaries of those systems and data structures.

Chapter 11 delves into data and business rule transformation options and techniques. This chapter provides a comprehensive discussion of legacy architecture reverse engineering, reengineering, and reconstruction. This discussion incorporates current-to-target mapping, data and business rule extraction, reuse in target architectures, and related topics. Chapter 12 ties together the strategies, approaches, and techniques presented in previous chapters under case-study-oriented scenarios. These scenarios include application consolidation, multisystem integration, application package selection and deployment, EAI deployment, rehosting, data migration, and component migration.

Finally, the Appendix provides a list of vendors that offer software tools that can help leverage transformation initiatives. Products are organized by the tool categories they support as well as by the vendors that offer those tools.

Acknowledgments

This book could not have been written without the collective efforts of many individuals who have worked long hours during the development and deployment of the actual concepts discussed in this book. First, I would like to thank my family for putting up with long work hours and shortened family time. I would also like to thank my assistant, Mary Dalton, who spent endless hours editing and revising the manuscript as well as helping me with research and fact checking. I would also like to thank Ed Yourdon, who suggested I write a book on a topic that I was both familiar with and passionate about. I also want to thank my publisher, Paul Petralia, for his help and support, and my editor, Kerry Reardon, for her patience.

I additionally want to thank the many individuals who developed bodies of work that allowed me to clarify my message. These individuals include Eric Bush, Dale Vecchio, Frank Kowalkowski, Ivor Jacobson, David Linthicum, James Odell, Paul Harmon, Ken Baskin, Dee Hock, Don Estes, Hina Pendle, Paul Horn, David Marco, Len Erlikh, Kent Beck, Cheryl Traverse, Jim Highsmith, and John Zachman.

In addition to the above individuals, a number of people have played a major role in starting me down the legacy transformation path or worked with me along the way. These individuals include Cris Miller, Al Travis, Pat Casey, John Delmonaco, Peter Harris, Kathy Benson, Ian Hayes, Elliott Chikovsky, Carma McClure, Paul Bassett, Steve Errico, Dan Sullivan, Al Kortesoje, Mary Gould, Susan St. Louis, Julia Laws, Sherrie Merrow, Rob Figliulo, Ravi Koka, John Faulkenberry, Howard Adams, Paul Halpern, Bill Archer, Pat Caputo, Paul Paetz, Peter Witt, and Bill Payson.

Finally, I would like to thank the organizations that served as a source of research including Gartner Inc., Charles Babbage Institute, Giga Information Services, Cutter IT Consortium, Zachman International, UML Partners Consortium, The Standish Group, Netron, Comsys, Micro Focus, Seec, Object Management Institute, The Agile Alliance, Chaordic Commons, Brainstorm Group, ebizq.net, and The COBOL Report.

Part I

Legacy Transformation: Background and Strategies

Part 1 introduces the challenges and opportunities posed by legacy information architectures. Chapter 1 introduces the origins and evolution of computers and the software that directs the activities of those computers. It also exposes the chasm between what people think computers can do and how most computers currently function.

Chapter 2 defines the issues organizations face when trying to understand and change the core applications that manage day-to-day business operations. This chapter helps place the significance and scope of the legacy challenge in perspective and refutes the belief that legacy applications can be ignored, easily replaced, or just wrapped in middleware. Case histories demonstrate that failed information initiatives can be traced directly back to the inability of an enterprise to effectively manage change requirements within legacy computing environments.

Chapter 3 discusses the changing face of information technology by introducing the world of the Internet, Java, Web Services, and a host of other emerging disciplines. This modern world of perfection runs in sharp contrast to the world of legacy information architectures. Chapter 4 introduces various strategies for managing, integrating, and transforming legacy application environments. This chapter introduces the concept of business-driven transformation, discusses transformation as a risk management tool, outlines a transformation framework, and provides project planning templates. It also provides an overview of the transformation approaches and techniques that are the foundation for the remaining sections of this book.

- **Chapter 1** The Modern Enterprise and Legacy Architectures
- **Chapter 2** Defining the Legacy Architecture Challenge
- **Chapter 3** The Changing Face of Information Technology
- **Chapter 4** Legacy Architecture Management and Transformation Strategies

The Modern Enterprise and Legacy Architectures

As businesses and governments greet the new century, they will be relying on technological advancements to deliver a vast array of initiatives across a variety of industries. Institutions charting a course through an increasingly complex and unpredictable future can count on one thing—computers will be their partners in this journey. Unfortunately, many computers carry significant baggage from the past.

This baggage comes in the form of aging hardware, software, and data architectures that prevent organizations from fully exploiting computers and the value they bring an organization, its customers, and its partners. Aging legacy architectures can stymie critical business initiatives while preventing an enterprise from responding to competitive pressures in a timely fashion.

Legacy architectures represent the collective set of application software, data structures, and operational platforms currently running in enterprise computing environments. How organizations deal with these aging legacy architectures will largely determine the depth and breadth of value computers will offer institutions and society in the coming century.

1.1 The Computer of the Future Meets Reality

Computers, for all intents and purposes, have been with us for more than half a century. We are living in a future that was both foreseen and unforeseen by past futurists. It is therefore worth examining where computers fit in relation to today's reality versus the hindsight of history.

The vision of modern computing was originally foretold in science fiction movies of the 1950s, 1960s, and 1970s. Computers had to be small enough to fit on a rocket ship and smart enough to communicate with people. HAL, the computer in *2001: A Space Odyssey*, is a good example. In that movie, Arthur C. Clarke envisioned a very powerful computer that would recognize voices and faces, communicate fluently, and control a wide variety of functions.

Many of these predictions came true to varying degrees. Voice recognition works fairly well, and facial recognition is just now being widely deployed. Computers are smaller, can talk to us and to other computers, and automate transportation and environmental systems.

Of course, the ability for a computer to perform deductive reasoning is still primitive when compared to the human mind. Today's computers can, however, help diagnose diseases, aid research, control airplanes, guide missiles, and process vast amounts of data at increasingly phenomenal speeds, to name just a few of their capabilities.

In spite of these advances, there is another side to this story. With all of these modern wonders being supported by computers, why is it that the following situations are still commonplace?

- Bank balances cannot be updated immediately after a deposit is entered, but must rather be updated during a nightly processing cycle.
- A long-distance provider's computer instructed different service representatives to contact a customer repeatedly because different databases contained the same, inaccurate information.
- A healthcare provider's computer sent out cancellation notices when it was supposed to have sent out payment notices. This continued even after the customer reported the problem.
- Tax payment and tracking systems take well over a year to reconcile statements between what one corporation claimed to pay another corporation and what the receiving corporation claimed.

These may seem like isolated incidents, but I personally encountered these circumstances within the course of doing business over the past couple of years. None of the above scenarios would make good fodder for a science fiction movie, and they are certainly not what Arthur C. Clarke envisioned in his movies about the future. They do bring home the point, however, that many of today's computers are not very smart: They have some major underlying problems.

To a highly valued customer, these scenarios may be a minor annoyance or a major problem. The healthcare scenario in particular was the antithesis of good customer service, and a less than supportive response from the customer service department made the situation even more problematic. This situation also exemplified how humans can magnify computer errors and make a bad situation worse.

When contrasting the challenges above with the promises of modern technology, there is clearly a chasm between the ideal vision of the future and today's reality. The above situations are symptomatic of shortcomings found within "legacy" systems: shortcomings that could ultimately undermine major Information Technology (IT) initiatives across a variety of industries.

If, for example, a bank wanted to deploy real-time banking for customers through the Web, it seems reasonable that it would need to be able to update bank balances in real time. If a long-distance provider wanted to break into local markets or launch new business initiatives that leverage customer data on a global scale, it must be able to store and update customer information in a reliable, nonredundant environment.

Similarly, if a healthcare provider wanted to stay competitive, it would seem apparent that it would stop trying to cancel a customer policy when it really wanted to collect a payment from that customer. With companies in a continuous battle to redefine themselves, which includes shifting toward new markets and offering global services, legacy systems can stifle efforts to undergo strategic transformations to a business.

We are seeing numerous advances, most accompanied by a good deal of hype, in the ability of computers to redefine our lives as we head into the 21st century. The reality of the situation, however, is that there are significant problems within legacy computing infrastructures that must be addressed before many of these visions can become reality.

1.2 Information Technology *Is* Your Business

A few years ago, analysts noted that information technology had shifted from the computer room into the boardroom. Thanks to the Internet, IT has now moved onto the desktop and into the briefcase of customers and business partners around the world. Most executives have come to agree that IT has become essential to the business community. Year 2000 preparations highlighted this fact. To the extent that this has occurred, it has forced businesses into a new paradigm. Organizations are in the business of IT.

Businesses now find that IT has become intertwined with their business infrastructures. If this seems improbable, consider how long an enterprise could thrive or even survive in the absence of critical information systems. Consider an airline's computer systems. These systems are the heart of tracking parts and maintenance schedules, customers, reservations, personnel assignments, destinations, and a number of other business-critical functions. Recent events at United Airlines exemplify this point.

The September 11, 2001, attack on the United States (and a sliding economy) prompted United to furlough almost 20,000 workers. According to *Computerworld* magazine, however, IT remained key to improving customer service and business responsiveness. Less than two months after the attacks, United launched a revamped reservations system with new functionality to handle automated rebookings and new flight schedules. This system helped alleviate reservation staff burdens and made flight transfers easier. A United executive said this was "a revenue-generating mechanism to make flying more convenient" [1].

IT can provide critical revenue opportunities and cost savings during tough times. The above example is just one of many demonstrating how the airline industry is in the business of IT. It is not alone. Financial institutions, telecommunications firms, utilities, manufacturers, retailers, insurance companies, transportation companies, and a host of other industries rely heavily on IT.

Financial institutions have long understood that IT is at the forefront of their business. As these companies respond to market changes, the line between areas such as mutual funds, lending, mortgage, insurance, retail banking, and other categories has blurred. Financial institutions are reinventing themselves. For example, customers can bypass intermediaries and use the Web to obtain a loan or refinance an existing loan. IT has become both an enabling element and a driving force within this rapidly shifting industry as the Web creates new opportunities where none had existed before.

Visa, for example, is expanding its traditional card-based business to be able to process a much wider variety of payments. These include the payment of loans, business (versus consumer) purchases, smart cards, and many other payment types. This is known as *infomoney*, a concept in which financial, transaction, and personal data can be sent anywhere instantaneously. IT in this situation must create a vehicle for deploying a new and revolutionary business model.

Telecommunications firms need to find ways to save money while concurrently shifting from voice services to wireless networks, Web-related hosting and development, broadband networking, and other offerings. IT is at the forefront of this revolution. The telecommunications industry is in the business of IT as much as any industry. Time will tell how effectively it addresses legacy infrastructures as a key component of this transformation.

A utility company's IT organization must ensure that customers get enough electricity and gas by predicting and managing loads across service areas. IT also plays a major role in coordinating power generators, wholesalers, trading firms, and distributors during a period of deregulation. Energy trading firms are almost entirely dependent on real-time information systems to move vast volumes of energy among participants. The result is efficiency and cost savings for all participants.

Numerous other examples across a variety of industries demonstrate why IT has become central to an enterprise's success and survival. This includes retailers integrating online and store-based purchasing environments and manufacturing firms reinventing traditional functions such as supply chain management and distribution. Businesses across the board are relying on IT more and more, to the point where they are now in the business of IT.

Yet each of these industries is facing a major challenge in being mired down by legacy computing architectures that manage critical core functionality and data.

1.3 Public Sector Recognizes Critical Value of IT

The private sector is not alone in moving IT to the forefront of its strategies. Governments are embracing IT as they attempt to reduce costs and streamline services through a variety of initiatives. In many of these cases, it is not survival but cost effectiveness and the ability to respond to constituents in a more timely and effective manner.

One example of this is the *e*Europe initiative, launched by the European Commission in December 1999 with the objective of bringing Europe online. The commission created the following goals [2].

- Improvement of services for users, citizens, and businesses.
- Electronic access to all basic public services for member states by 2003.
- Better working conditions, professional development, and promotion of activities for civil servants.
- Entry of public procurements at the community and national level will be online by 2003.
- Promotion and development of electronic administration.

The Belgian presidency and the European Commission are trying to move this initiative forward across the membership base. They plan to use the following metrics to determine how well e-government efforts are doing [2].

- Existence of public access points to the Internet.
- Percentage of basic public services accessible on the Internet.
- Number of visits to public information sites.
- Percentage of public procurements that can be dealt online.
- Accessibility of public Web sites for the disabled.

On a slightly smaller scale, the state of California is pursuing e-government initiatives. The state's Web site lists certain objectives associated with this effort. Following is a short list of these objectives [3].

- Update the address on a driver's license or on a car registration.
- Update voter registration card and professional licenses.
- Pay tickets, fines, and fees.
- Pay individual and business income taxes.
- Enroll children in school.
- Apply for and receive state procurement contracts.
- Conduct all state budgeting and financial transactions.
- Transmit payment for state employee expense reimbursements.

The U.S. federal government is also supporting e-government efforts. President Bush is providing $100 million for e-government in the 2002 budget.

Key points on the U.S. agenda include development of digital signature technology and broad deployment of e-procurement to lower costs and reduce time and paper use [4].

While e-government is a positive goal in general, most government agencies face more pressing challenges since the September 11, 2001, terrorist attacks. A major issue for the U.S. government is the ability to share data across a variety of disparate agencies. The government faces a massive data integration challenge across a huge information infrastructure involving dozens or even hundreds of databases. According to an *Information Week* article [5], Tom Ridge, Homeland Security czar, sees IT as the vehicle for eliminating the silos that currently separate people and agencies.

With governments around the world taking on more formidable tasks while concurrently trying to manage spiraling costs, IT is clearly a major focal point and priority. Public sector agencies are coming to view IT as being much more strategic than they have in the past. Given that the winners are the individual constituents and businesses relying on services from these government institutions, this is an important goal.

Yet these same governments manage activities at agencies and departments using hundreds of millions of lines of legacy software. Data is not integrated, constituent problems such as errant tax notices are high profile, and replacement project failures are commonplace. Clearly, legacy challenges are commonplace in many government institutions.

1.4 IT Can Disable an Organization

IT, more than ever, has a direct impact on business competitiveness, quality, productivity, the bottom line, and survival. This is true for the private sector as well as for government agencies. As a result, executives can no longer push IT into a corner. Fortunately, IT executives are increasingly moving into positions of power at major corporations. This is important because today's executive must be IT-savvy or encounter difficulty leading an organization through this period of increased innovation. Legacy systems is one area that executives must familiarize themselves with and address as part of this leadership model.

Unfortunately, there is a flip side to the business-enabling, revenue–generating, and cost-saving opportunities IT provides. When problems occur, IT can also be to blame for bottom-line losses. There are numerous accounts of companies suffering lost business, lost revenues, and lost opportunities related to legacy system failures, failed replacement projects, or just a lack of foresight in deploying new IT initiatives. Consider some recent, high-profile reports that have appeared in the press.

- Citibank's 2000 ATM debit and credit systems were down intermittently during a 24-hour period. The outage was blamed on legacy application systems [6].

- JPMorgan Chase & Co. experienced problems in its retail banking systems that impacted transactions at 1900 ATM facilities. The situation was caused by a problem in updating transactions from the prior day [6].
- Kmart planned to take charges of $195 million to modernize its aging warehouse network to improve in-stock management capabilities. This move was necessary to stay competitive with other retail chains [7].
- More than a year after IT had installed new student administration software, Cleveland State University continued to have problems processing financial aid, enrolling transfer students, and recording grades [8].

The ability for IT to trigger problems within an enterprise is not new. What is new is that businesses and governments rely on IT to a much greater degree for business continuity. In doing so, these institutions increase their vulnerability if a critical computer system fails or stays offline for an extended period of time.

Failures come in many varieties. The Citibank and JPMorgan Chase scenarios were failures that resulted in a loss, albeit temporary, of customer confidence. The Kmart situation, on the other hand, reflects a company trying to catch up to retailers that made major IT infrastructure investments well ahead of Kmart to address inventory and customer issues.

The Cleveland State University situation involved a software package being licensed by the university from a major software supplier. This package did not fit the requirements of the university—or so it seems from the media's version of this story. It is quite likely that Cleveland State was able to track students and record grades with the system it replaced. The new package changed this—for the worse. Progress can come with a price, particularly where legacy applications are involved.

Each of the above scenarios involved legacy systems. Whether an organization is just trying to make it through another day's worth of high-profile transactions, is investing in major infrastructure upgrades, or is attempting to transition to a third-party package, legacy systems remain the key to success.

1.5 Rapidly Shifting Business and Technological Requirements

Most corporate and government entities are being pressured to concurrently respond to escalating requirements in four key areas. Shown in Figure 1.1, these four areas encompass industry demands, related internal business requirements, emerging IT technologies, and various IT disciplines that enable organizations to respond more quickly to priority business requirements.

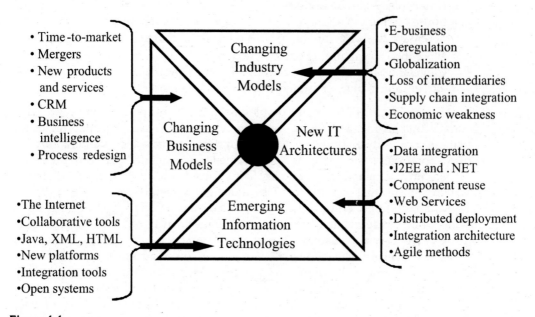

Convergence of Shifting Industry, Business, Technical, and Architectural Requirements

- Time-to-market
- Mergers
- New products and services
- CRM
- Business intelligence
- Process redesign

•The Internet
•Collaborative tools
•Java, XML, HTML
•New platforms
•Integration tools
•Open systems

Changing Industry Models

Changing Business Models

New IT Architectures

Emerging Information Technologies

•E-business
•Deregulation
•Globalization
•Loss of intermediaries
•Supply chain integration
•Economic weakness

•Data integration
•J2EE and .NET
•Component reuse
•Web Services
•Distributed deployment
•Integration architecture
•Agile methods

Figure 1.1
Organizations experience pressure to concurrently respond to rapid shifts in business, industry, technology, and IT architectural climate.

Greatly complicating matters is the fact that each of these four diverse yet interrelated requirements is in a state of flux. Industries are being transformed into other industries, such as the case with insurance companies becoming full-fledged financial institutions. To meet these demands and concurrently address efforts to leverage the Web in these activities, businesses are retooling processes in response to new internal and external requirements.

Industry pressures can also be overwhelming. These pressures include overhauling relationships with suppliers, distributors, and customers to improve efficiency, service, and competitiveness. These changes are rippling through supply and distribution models as well as everything that has to do with customer service.

At the same time, IT has finally begun to settle on a set of languages, standards, architectures, and approaches to systems development and deployment. The problem is that haphazard or poorly planned attempts to deploy these new technologies while trying to respond to shifting business and industry demands have the capacity to throw an organization into chaos.

Industry and business challenges remain key drivers for IT initiatives. Industry drivers include an almost unprecedented attempt to shift from traditional buy-sell models to doing business electronically. The emergence of electronic business (e-business) drove corporations and governments into a mad dash to Web-enable their enterprises. This spawned a series of e-related terms and trends. Many of these common terms, some of which have been short-lived, are described below.

- E-commerce (electronic commerce) is the activity of businesses selling goods or services over the Web.
- B2B (business-to-business) focuses on businesses exchanging goods and services with other businesses.
- B2C (business-to-consumer) is another term for businesses selling goods and services through the Web.
- C-commerce (collaborative commerce) involves business partners working jointly to leverage the Internet to more effectively deliver goods and services.
- W-commerce (wireless commerce) utilizes wireless technology to buy and sell goods and services.
- I-commerce (information commerce) describes a scenario where companies provide information to consumers over the Web.
- E-government (electronic government) is a general term for governments doing business over the Web.
- E-marketplace (electronic marketplace) is the concept of a supply or distribution chain (or both) exchanging goods and services through a Web-based exchange.

Other terms are sure to come and go, but the genie was definitely let out of the bottle when the "e" term and its derivatives began to displace common sense and solid business planning. In spite of the failures of the dotcom companies, the Web is here to stay.

In the meantime, traditional demands on businesses have continued to escalate. Deregulation in the energy industry, for example, is forcing energy producers and distributors to rethink business strategies—and the Web will be a key component of any solution they finally deliver.

Delivering products and services from a global perspective is also forcing many companies to rethink regional business plans. Once a major player in a given industry begins operating globally, others will follow. The ripple effect on corporate infrastructures is significant and requires major integration and retooling of internal and external business processes.

Technological advancements contribute to industry-wide changes as well. The Web can be viewed as disruptive technology because it allows certain industries to bypass distribution or supply chain intermediaries. This is particularly true in distribution models where the auto industry, for example, is beginning to market cars over the Internet. The Web has also changed the way suppliers relate to each other—at least for transactions that do not require extensive human-to-human contact. Electronic marketplaces, such as Covisint within the automotive sector, have allowed entire industries to streamline supply chain management processes.

Over the short term, eliminating intermediaries and streamlining supply and distribution chains will negatively impact certain subsections of a given industry. Distributors, for example, may need to adjust their business models. Economic weakness could force many industries to cut costs. These industries will need to enact and sustain certain initiatives to ensure their survival.

Internally, businesses must respond to industry pressures by bringing new products and services to market in less time and at lower costs. Long-distance providers, for example, are bringing new plans to market every month. Similarly, financial service providers are offering new financial packages on a regular basis. Time-to-market is a critical requirement today, and companies must find ways to respond or fall behind.

Mergers and acquisitions continue to be a factor for many companies. Certain regional Bell operating companies (RBOCs), for example, have reacquired some of the original baby Bell companies spun out from AT&T in the early 1980s. These types of mergers place tremendous integration and retooling pressures on IT. Many companies are also entering or pioneering new markets, such as wireless communications, broadband, smart cards, energy brokering, infomoney, biotechnology, and a host of other areas that are enabled through the evolution of new technologies.

Globalization also places major pressure on IT and a business. Turning a company that is a series of standalone entities into a cohesive, global enterprise is a major challenge for the executive team and requires revamping business processes and systems that once served highly autonomous entities.

Customer relationship management (CRM) focuses on providing more effective and highly automated ways to service customers, which will hopefully differentiate companies from the competition. Organizations must also chart out new business intelligence about the competition in response to increasingly competitive demands from a variety of sources. New software has created new and better ways of achieving these goals.

In the future, disruptive technology will continue to keep many industries and businesses in a state of flux. Consider, for example, the impact that nano technology will have on biotechnology when tiny robots can be sent into humans to fight off plaque in arteries. Or consider how nano technology might impact the energy industry when tiny solar conductors, painted into road surfaces, will provide continuous renewable energy to power cars or generate electric power.

All of these factors are driving organizations to seek new solutions to a wide variety of information challenges. Most of these business-driven factors require retooling business processes—and the computer systems supporting those processes. Yet there is another set of challenges facing IT that stem from emerging IT disciplines and technologies.

While the change in business demands that organizations are facing on a global level are staggering, there is also a revolution going on within the world of IT.

Figure 1.1 depicts a few of the technologies and related disciplines that IT will need to leverage in an attempt to deliver more value to the enterprises they service.

IT is pursuing a series of emerging technologies and improved information architectures. These new technologies include better development environments, new languages (including Java and XML), Web-enabled platforms, enterprise application integration technology, and the open systems movement. In addition, IT is beginning to adopt new approaches to development, which include agile methodologies with the intent of shortening project delivery cycles and improving time-to-market.

New application architectures are also emerging. For example, J2EE and .Net are competing for the future of the IT application architecture where reuse is the ideal, and time-consuming, handcrafted applications will eventually become the exception—not the rule. As reusable building blocks (i.e., components) come into common use, developers will build applications that can seek out predefined solutions across the Internet. This is called Web Services, which is the next level of evolution for information architectures.

IT is changing how it builds, deploys, and manages systems, and this is as important as the emerging technologies that IT now has at its disposal. One major requirement is the need to integrate and purify data as customers and suppliers begin to gain direct access to that data. Most legacy data is typically segregated and lacks a certain degree of consistency and integrity as viewed and used across multiple business units.

Coupled with all of these advancements is the need to distribute applications, integrate existing data and architectures, and accomplish this through collaborative development using agile methodologies such as Extreme Programming (XP). If all of this seems farfetched, it is because the IT industry is still mired in the overwhelming challenges stemming from legacy computing architectures, which stymie new technology deployment.

1.6 E-Business Meets Aging Hierarchies and Infrastructures

Legacy computer systems process the majority of sales, customer service, billing, distribution, inventory management, procurement, and related revenue-generating, cost-saving and accounting tasks. While most companies would not be able to function without these systems, this was not always the case. Examining the evolution of legacy architectures and the organizational infrastructures upon which they were based provides insights into how to leverage these systems to meet time-critical business requirements while concurrently deploying emerging technologies.

Industries and governments across the board use computer systems that are a reflection of the past. The past, in this case, takes the form of management hierarchies pioneered by companies such as General Motors almost 100 years ago. Companies have historically been divided into functional business units. Each business unit performed specific tasks. Traditionally, this included marketing, sales, production, purchasing, accounting, and other speciality functions. Other business units were created to support unique product lines and international functions.

Business units reported up through a hierarchical management command chain based on these segregated functions. It was this environment into which computers first entered the business world during the 1950s and 1960s.

Businesses were wary at first of using computers at all. IBM founder, Thomas Watson, Sr., once said, "I think there is a world market for maybe five computers" [9]. This was a far cry from latter-day predictions that the disappearance of computers, by some accounts, would force over half the female population of the United States to become telephone operators.

In most companies, IT was originally under the accounting department and reported up to the chief financial officer (CFO). This decision was based on the fact that early computer systems typically performed accounting and other financial functions. As IT evolved, more systems were developed to automate tasks for other hierarchical business units. The internal IT department (originally called data processing or automated data processing) reporting structure mimicked the management hierarchies used across the enterprise.

Hierarchical subdivisions were extended further as systems evolved throughout the 1970s and 1980s. For example, a sales system would include order processing, sales tracking, sales forecasting, and various other sales functions. The IT sales team would then be subdivided into these subcategories. Figure 1.2 depicts a systems hierarchy chart that reflects both the infrastructure of the IT organization and the systems supporting hierarchical business units.

The specific functions depicted in Figure 1.2 are not of particular relevance. What is relevant is that almost every IT organization uses such a chart to depict how its systems and its people are organized and aligned with the business. This suggests the pervasiveness of the hierarchical management and information systems model.

The IT organization, and application systems and databases, were segregated silos. Information flow between these systems was at best slow and haphazard. Large mainframe computers would read data from one system and produce files or database updates that could then be processed by the next system. A large-scale legacy environment would repeat this sequential series of steps hundreds of times over the course of a daily or nightly processing cycle.

Hierarchies continued to dominate well into the 1990s as enterprise resource planning (ERP) packages emerged. ERP systems are third-party software packages that became quite popular during the 1990s. These packages were subdivided by the functions they supported, although most ERP systems provided for

Hierarchical Governance Structures and Information Architectures Impede Integration and Agility

Hierarchical organizations

- Do not reflect real workflow
- Do not support e-business
- Hinder collaboration and communication
- Exclude external entities
- Are not self-organizing
- Are not adaptable
- Slow integration at all levels

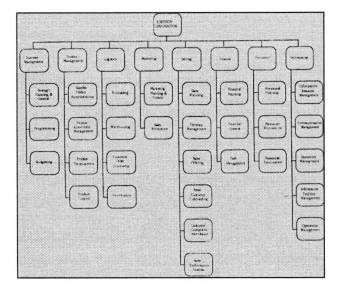

Figure 1.2
Hierarchical information infrastructure and systems definition.

cross-functional data exchange based on a common architecture that was missing from most homegrown legacy systems. Today, ERP systems represent a small but important percentage of the overall population of legacy applications.

When viewing the evolution of legacy systems over the decades, one case study exemplifies how legacy systems have outlived numerous incarnations of the businesses they were built to support.

Many of the original computer systems built by AT&T are still in place as the telecommunications industry enters the 21st century. AT&T developed a number of systems back in the 1960s and 1970s. One of these systems was the Customer Resource Information System (CRIS), which provided billing and related services. When AT&T broke up in the early 1980s, each RBOC took a copy of the CRIS system and enhanced it as it expanded into regional markets and unregulated industries.

Now several RBOCs have been recombined. At the same time, local phone markets are being deregulated. Many of these companies have also gone global and entered a variety of new markets, such as wireless and broadband. Yet multiple copies of the old CRIS system continue to run day in and day out at these companies.

CRIS and other systems survived multiple business retooling efforts over a period of decades. Can global telecommunications providers thrive in global wireless, broadband, and other new markets using segregated customer management systems and databases based on a regional business model that no longer applies? It is unlikely. Is it cost effective to continue to run four copies of these systems within a same company? No. Is there an easy way to address this challenge? The short answer is no, but issues like this must nevertheless be addressed over the long term.

The introduction of the Internet and e-business is driving the need to more fully integrate business processes across old business and IT hierarchical infrastructures as well as across supply and distribution chains. As this occurs, organizations will need to shift to radically different business models. Businesses now have a new set of requirements.

- Business processes must flow from the point where they began in one business unit across other business units in less time than legacy systems allow.
- The transaction-oriented systems that supported segmented business processes should flow from one transaction to another in less time and with less human intervention. This concept is called *zero latency*, where these events are instantaneous.
- Data stored in departmental databases should be integrated with data stored in other departmental databases.
- Cross-functional business process flow, transaction flow, and data flow must occur in a matter of minutes—not hours or days.

As businesses and governments raced to the Web, they began building Web sites to address customer and business partner functionality. Many Web sites and new companies sprung up overnight. The majority of these Web sites had to be rebuilt, which reflected early missteps in assessing how the Web would help businesses expand market share or save money. Little dotcom companies with no infrastructure emerged to challenge established corporations. When they could not sustain a revenue stream, they either folded or were quickly swallowed up by more established enterprises.

In a very short period of time (from 2000 to 2001), the high-tech industry experienced rapid expansion and subsequently rapid compression. All of this was fascinating to watch because it unfolded so quickly, and if you questioned, it you were told that the new economy would be leaving you behind. Then reality sunk in.

As organizations began to Web-enable customers and suppliers, they found that they could not replicate or readily access complex business knowledge embedded in legacy systems and databases. These organizations needed to retool decades of entrenched hierarchical infrastructures in a short period of time. IT is at the earliest stages of this retooling process.

1.7 No Easy Answers to Difficult Legacy Challenge

Businesses have always been very dynamic, and information architectures have remained largely static. Over the years, the gap has grown between how most businesses work and how legacy architectures function. Management is typically aware of this and would like to find an easy solution. H. L. Mencken has been quoted as saying, "For every complex problem, there is a solution that is simple, neat, and wrong." IT has been looking for simple, neat solutions to the legacy systems challenge for decades.

Prior attempts to address this situation have ultimately failed. During the early 1980s, an early attempt to displace legacy systems, and IT in general, drew upon fourth-generation languages (4GL). By the end of the decade, some predicted, we would have no more need for programmers, because users could simply write new systems whenever they needed them. This did not happen.

The Computer-Aided Software Engineering (CASE) solution of the late 1980s and early 1990s would allow analysts to generate systems from business models. The idea was a good one, but the methodology and tools behind the idea were not. This solution also fell flat.

In the early 1990s some IT organizations attempted to rewrite all of their systems in C and put them into workstation-based environments. Mainframes would be gone by the mid-1990s, according to some analysts and executives. This also failed, largely because an enterprise cannot rewrite legacy systems when it does not understand what those systems do.

The most prevalent and innovative solution to date is still under way and will continue to be viewed as a partial or interim solution in years to come. It is called enterprise application integration (EAI).

The EAI concept is simple, although implementation results have grown increasingly complex. EAI can be viewed simplistically as the collective disciplines and technologies used to connect front-end and back-end applications and databases in such a way as to not impact the underlying legacy architecture. In other words, EAI is a "noninvasive" approach to meeting complex integration and business process retooling requirements.

EAI requirements are driven by the need to synthesize disparate systems and data to support various e-business, customer, supply chain, and distribution chain requirements. The industry has tried to subdivide EAI into internal (i.e., enterprise) and external (i.e., supply and distribution chain) integration. This latter category has been termed business-to-business integration (B2Bi). B2Bi is increasingly being viewed as an extension of EAI because the border between internal and external systems, and data and business units continues to blur.

As the IT industry moves toward architectures that utilize Web Services, for example, the issue as to where a given transaction begins and ends will blur to the point where it is no longer relevant. Many of the e-terms and c-terms we use today will likely either merge into a commonly understood discipline or disappear entirely. For our discussion, consider EAI to mean the noninvasive integration of internal and external systems and data structures.

Early on, EAI was simply a series of application programming interfaces (APIs), which evolved into middleware to "connect" applications. These connector-based solutions proliferated. As a result, EAI has been plagued by quick fixes, technocratic thinking, disjointed projects, false starts, inadequate requirements, and a tendency to ignore more strategic integration options.

EAI clearly plays a role in near-term and ongoing efforts to meet critical information integration requirements. Over the long term, however, the connector mentality, regardless of the degree of sophistication the middleware, application servers, and other components achieve, will be viewed as yet another level of hard-to-decipher legacy software.

Interim solutions may have a place in complex business environments as long as they are viewed as such. Noninvasive integration, however, must give way to more strategic and sophisticated thinking over the long term.

1.8 Business Agility and Legacy Systems

If organizational infrastructures had undergone no changes since early computing architectures were designed during the 1960s and 1970s, there would be little need to apply transformation solutions to these architectures. Businesses have changed, however, and as those changes proliferate, driven by the e-business explosion and other major factors, IT will need to respond with more sophisticated solutions.

Because change is the only constant and it appears that it will only quicken, the modern enterprise must be agile. The agile enterprise can be generally defined as having the following attributes.

- Customer information should be readily and accurately available to facilitate the launching of new initiatives or entry into new markets.
- New products and services can be introduced quickly and efficiently.
- Ineffective products and services can be discontinued quickly and efficiently.
- Customer requirements are always handled in a high-priority, rapid turn-around fashion.
- Shifting supply and distribution requirements can be met as needed.
- Change is accepted and welcomed as an ongoing part of the business model.

The need for agility is commonplace across virtually every industry. Automotive conglomerates have divested subsidiaries while merging and moving into foreign markets. Oil companies have undergone global mergers. Media companies are merging with communications providers to synthesize and leverage their offerings. The federal government has redistributed benefit functions to the states. Enterprises are becoming decentralized, deregulated, consolidated, and diversified at a pace hard to imagine just a few years ago.

While many factors contribute to being an agile enterprise, an organization's information systems play a major role. Unfortunately, most legacy systems prevent businesses from being more adaptable to change. As businesses, governments, and entire industries continue to evolve at an increasing pace, organizations will need to find ways to respond to these dynamic requirements. This means transforming legacy architectures into reliable, adaptable assets that contribute to the ability of an enterprise to respond to continuous, fast-paced change.

Consider the electric utility market. Each state used to have one big power company that generated and transmitted energy to homes and businesses. Now, some of these companies handle power generation, while other companies control power distribution. Still other companies are power brokers, buying and selling electricity like a commodity. Consumers can choose who generates their power, but continue to pay bills to a single power distributor.

Many providers have diversified and gone global via joint ventures. The industry is at the early stages of even more changes as new power sources linked to nano technology, hydrogen cells, and other options emerge over the next 20 years. Yet many of these companies still manage numerous functions using the same old systems they created when the utility industry was still a highly regulated, monolithic industry.

Organizations attempting to meet these challenges will quickly discover that legacy systems are the random element in efforts to achieve business agility. In other words, for a business to be agile, its information systems must be adaptable and malleable. Most legacy systems are not adaptable and malleable.

Newer systems, on the other hand, offer more flexibility to an enterprise. If an organization were to create a new company from scratch, management could acquire or build new applications that would be highly integrated and readily adaptable to ongoing change. IT would, in fact, embrace change as opposed to avoiding it. Bridging the chasm between inflexible legacy systems and the near-term need of businesses to be more agile is a challenge that must be met with a multiphased strategy.

1.9 Redesigning Business Processes— Enabling the Agile Enterprise

Historically, organizations sought to deploy new systems without fully understanding the ramifications of how those systems would help their enterprise from a cross-functional perspective. One way of avoiding this problem and concurrently build agility into an enterprise is to redesign, integrate, and automate business processes. The effective deployment of redesigned business processes has a direct effect on business agility because it instills immediate consistency and automation to internal users, customers, and business partners.

Business process redesign (BPR) can be driven by external factors, such as a merger or supply chain management initiative. BPR can also be driven by efforts to make an enterprise more effective and efficient from an internal perspective. BPR gained a bad reputation during the 1990s when it was associated with downsizing. Today, BPR projects focus on integrating and automating internal processes while streamlining supply, distribution, and customer management activities.

One promising aspect of making an enterprise more agile is the advent of business process management and integration (BPM/BPI) tools. These tools facilitate the redesign and integration of redundant, inconsistent processes into well-defined, highly integrated processes. Redesigned business processes along with BPM/BPI tools offer an excellent way to

- Streamline business processes at the point of user, customer, distributor, and supplier contact.
- Provide immediate benefits to internal and external users of a given process.
- Connect and integrate process flows across stovepipe organizational hierarchies and information architectures.
- Extend integration views for internal users, external partners, and customers across the extended value chain.
- Generate a set of business-driven requirements for delivering a phased legacy transformation strategy.
- Establish a long-term model for how legacy systems should ultimately be transformed.

BPR is an important component of any effort aimed at making an enterprise more agile and provides near-term integration value while creating a framework for how target architectures should evolve to support underlying integration requirements long term.

1.10 The Evolution of Legacy Computing Architectures

Legacy architectures are comprised of hardware, software, and data. Old or obsolete hardware is readily replaced, as long as the software can be migrated to another machine and reused. Software portability has therefore been a major consideration since the 1960s. That is when IBM introduced the IBM 360 computer. Prior to that time, most computers were not multifunctional, and the software that ran on one computer would typically not run on a different computer. The IBM 360 changed all of that.

The IBM 360 allowed an enterprise to run multiple applications on the same machine. This made the 360 immediately popular. What sustained its popularity, along with IBM's rise to prominence in the computer industry, was the concept of upward compatibility.

Upward compatibility, pioneered by the IBM 360 along with its successor, the IBM 370, allowed a company to develop software that could be readily ported to the next generation of hardware. As a key component of this strategy, certain application languages were designed to be portable across hardware environments of different manufactures. An application system is used to solve business or user-related problems. This is in contrast to operating system software, which is used to make a computer function at a basic level. The most prominent application programming language to emerge from this era was COBOL.

COBOL, the Common Business Oriented Language, was created in the 1950s by a team headed by Admiral Grace Hopper. COBOL is a third-generation language, meaning it is more understandable to humans than earlier machine and assembler languages. More important, COBOL compilers were built for most hardware platforms so developers could run the same software across any number of hardware environments. Today, there is an estimated 200 billion lines of COBOL software accounting for roughly 60 percent of the total software deployed worldwide [10].

Upward compatibility is a crucial concept in understanding how legacy systems evolved. It allowed most application systems built during the 1960s or thereafter to be moved from an older hardware platform to the next generation of hardware platform without rewriting the source code. The source code is what the programmer maintains. A compiler turns source code into software that the computer can execute. This concept has been the basis for computing languages for the past 40 years.

Many of these application systems are still running in production at countless organizations around the world. Applications have a very long life. In fact, many COBOL applications are older than some of the people working on those applications are. While hardware can be replaced, legacy software and the data processed by that software live on for many decades.

Legacy systems are not defined by age, language, platform, or data structure type. If an application system is functioning in a production environment within an enterprise, it can be considered a legacy system. Today's new system is tomorrow's legacy system. C and Visual Basic applications were once new, but now they are legacy systems. This is not due to their age, but rather to the fact that they are running in a production environment.

Legacy applications include handcrafted systems built inhouse, third-party (leased) software packages, systems generated by other software, and systems managed by third parties. These third parties include outsourcing firms and application service providers (ASPs). Third-party packages represent a minority of legacy applications, but even these packages were mostly handcrafted and therefore pose a major challenge to the vendors responsible for maintaining and enhancing them and companies using them.

Legacy systems run on mainframe, mid-range, or distributed computers and may be written in any one of hundreds of computing languages. COBOL, for example, runs on mainframe, mid-range, and networked computers. COBOL has also been updated to accommodate the latest distributed user interfaces. Other major programming languages include Assembler, FORTRAN, PL/I, C, C++, LISP, Visual Basic, Java, XML, and well over 400 other languages.

The term *architecture* refers to how computer systems were designed and implemented. It also can describe how a system can be invoked or used and how it shares data, interacts with the user, and communicates with other systems. Early software architects lacked the understanding we have today when they originally designed and constructed legacy systems and data structures. This is because, at just over 50 years old, IT is a young industry compared to architecture or engineering, disciplines that are thousands of years old.

Application architecture describes the design and construction methodology, implied or explicit, behind an application. Legacy application architectures typically have the following attributes.

- Humans cannot understand how the system functions.
- The system is hard to modify with confidence that a given change is correct.
- Business logic is hard to distinguish from logic that controls data access, user interface, and environmental management functions.
- Business logic is redundantly and inconsistently defined within and across systems.
- The system lacks functional or technical documentation, or both.
- It is difficult to integrate the system with other systems not built under the same architecture.

Legacy application architectures are not only a major challenge to organizations—they are proliferating at a surprising rate. Each year, more than 5 billion new lines of COBOL code alone are added to legacy portfolios [10]. At the same time, legacy applications are increasingly the focal point for supporting internal and external initiatives. These initiatives almost universally require sharing and integrating functionality and data across barriers built into these early systems decades ago. Legacy applications rarely fulfill these requirements.

Because legacy applications specify access points to legacy data along with the business logic for processing that data, they cannot be eliminated or easily replaced. Most legacy systems do not integrate well with other legacy systems or with new systems because each system tends to access and process data in its own unique way. This is the one main reason that EAI emerged as a means of "triggering" legacy system transactions from Web-based front ends to access and process legacy data.

The data architecture within an enterprise is typically a derivative of the application architecture. In a perfect world, the data architecture would reflect business requirements and facilitate easy access from any application across the value chain, which includes internal business units as well as distribution and supply chains. The term *data architecture* refers to how enterprise data was designed and implemented. Legacy data tends to have many of the following characteristics.

- Data is defined and stored redundantly across multiple stovepipe business units and applications.
- The same or similar data is defined inconsistently across multiple systems.
- The same data terminology may be used to define different data across multiple applications and business units.
- The integrity of the data may be poor and contain information it should not contain.
- Data may not be easily accessible by modern systems or through user-based inquiries.
- Data cannot be readily shared across systems, business units, and organizational boundaries.

Businesses need access to legacy data and system's functionality in ways that legacy architectures cannot support. EAI tools help to a degree, but EAI is a stopgap measure and not a long-term solution. Legacy systems based on stovepipe infrastructures simply cannot support real-time, cross-functional business requirements in zero latency fashion. A Web-based order processing system should, for example, return a customer order confirmation immediately. Back-end procurement systems, however, may take days to confirm a customer order, if that functionality exists at all.

Even if this were the case, legacy data architectures cannot support an integrated, consistent, and readily accessible view of enterprise data on demand. Legacy applications are needed to manage essential business data defined in legacy data structures. Legacy applications accomplish this by applying business logic that most humans have long since forgotten even existed.

Legacy system and data architectures are valuable business assets and should be recognized as such when IT planning takes place. If the role of legacy systems in projects is assessed openly and candidly, executives will discover that they have a better set of options at their disposal for deploying priority business and information initiatives. As this occurs, the enterprise will need to identify more effective solutions to the legacy architecture roadblock than they have found to date.

1.11 The Business Case for Legacy Architecture Transformation

Legacy architecture transformation describes the process of modifying the form, design, and/or function of one or more legacy applications and/or data structures. A legacy architecture transformation strategy defines a commonly agreed upon philosophy that an enterprise can use to reconcile legacy architecture limitations with high-priority, time-critical business requirements.

Many business executives believe that aging legacy architectures will eventually be replaced with new, strategic systems. It would seem logical, so the thinking goes, to simply buy new application systems just as one would buy a new computer. This line of thinking is not unusual for someone not fully apprised of the state of legacy architectures and how these architectures have become intertwined with an enterprise's business model.

Most executives have held the belief for more than two decades that these systems would be replaced. Attempts were made to replace systems on multiple occasions. Initially, 4GLs were going to lead the way. Then it was the CASE revolution. During the early 1990s, IT believed that client/server systems would replace legacy environments. Y2K brought a cold dose of reality. Rewrites were impractical and improbable.

This problem is compounded today because few people can articulate what these systems do. IT has lost many of the legacy skills that developed these systems. This loss of skill extends into the business units as well. Not only are the people who built these systems gone, the users who asked for them to be built in the first place are also gone. Knowledge reclamation of critical software assets is in itself a good risk management policy.

Frustrated with failed rewrite efforts, many executives turned to the "buy" as opposed to "build" mentality. Third-party ERP systems were brought in during the mid- to late 1990s. Some implementations succeeded in part, while others failed entirely. The problem was that the old systems could not be easily displaced, while legacy data created a huge conversion challenge for implementation teams. ERP systems have now joined the ranks of legacy architectures. Many are written using propriety languages, do not support diverse e-business requirements, and have typically ended up running alongside inhouse legacy systems.

Over the past two decades, organizations have spent billions of dollars in failed legacy system replacement efforts. Global Y2K preparation alone cost a half a trillion dollars, and all that did was fix a date problem. Imagine, for a minute, that an organization had unlimited funding for a legacy replacement effort and no delivery deadline—ludicrous concepts, by the way, in today's modern business climate. Such a replacement effort would still fail using traditional rewrite strategies, because the business rules and underlying data could not be replicated through traditional user/analyst re-specification techniques. Organizations no longer know what these systems do.

In spite of all the efforts to replace legacy systems over the years, these systems continue to function and have actually grown in size on an annual basis. Occasionally, a new system is developed to surround or interface with an existing system, but legacy systems are deactivated in only a small percentage of cases.

While politics tend to drive many strategic systems initiatives, including the deployment of a multi-million-dollar ERP application, executives, managers, and analysts should take an objective view of more pragmatic options. Exploring some of the motivations behind failed replacement projects is an important step in this process. Below are some of the rationalizations that have driven high-profile, legacy replacement project failures.

- "The old system does not do what we need, so we must build a new system from scratch, which means that IT should not even look at the old system for ideas on how to build the new system."
- "User requirements have changed, so we are going to just ask the users what the new system should do. They can re-specify it from scratch."
- "A large, multinational consulting firm assures me that a total replacement is the only way to go. If things go wrong, they can take the heat for it."
- "The old system uses old technology and we need to build a new system using new technology."
- "The mainframe has to go—along with the systems that run on it. I want the mainframe gone by the end of next year."
- "We need to buy a package and get these old systems out of here."
- "The best approach is to just leave the old systems alone. We can wrap them with new technology to make them do what they need to do."
- "New technology, such as Java, XML, and HTML, will allow us to rewrite everything in less time."

Politics aside, allowing the advent or promise of new technologies to drive a legacy replacement decision is not wise from a business perspective. Junior programmers are no more likely to succeed in a rewrite than their predecessors did in prior decades using other "new" technologies.

Conventional wisdom has dictated several evolving schools of thought during the past decade. During the 1990s, the from-scratch rewrite approach was displaced by the ERP package implementation approach. The package replacement approach has since been displaced by the EAI approach. Legacy system wrappers, for many of the reasons stated previously, provide only a stopgap measure. This brings executives back to the table to discuss alternative approaches.

If your enterprise's executive team can bring itself to the point where frank dialog replaces political posturing or the promise of technological miracles, here are some questions that you can ask as a first step in crafting a legacy architecture transformation strategy. Can legacy systems be replaced any time soon by rebuilding them? If this were possible, we would have done that already. Remember that these are the same legacy data and application architectures that businesses and governments spent up to half a trillion dollars just to make Y2K-compliant. They did not replace them then and will not replace the bulk of these systems any time soon—at least not using conventional, re-specification methods.

Will buying and implementing an ERP package help address the situation? This should be examined carefully because there are many hidden traps in this approach. An ERP system may not conform to your business requirements or may clash with legacy systems and data to the point where competitive advantage is lost—not gained. ERP implementations can also drag on for years, may succeed only in certain business units, and can cost up to 10 times the cost of the software itself.

Can IT use wrapping or middleware tools to access or trigger the data and transactions embedded within these systems in such a way as to make them more agile and adaptable to business requirements? This can be done, but in limited ways. Many Web-based front-end systems already trigger back-end mainframe transactions, but this approach is limited at best. There are many examples where online banking systems cannot update a bank balance in real time, where an order system could not effectively trigger a procurement process, or where other Web-based interfaces failed to effectively complete many of the capabilities they initially promised. Legacy architecture limitations prevent quick fixes and easy answers. A phased approach, however, could incorporate the best notions from each of the above options and be heavily augmented with a variety of legacy architecture analysis, reuse, and transformation techniques. Most legacy transformation solutions are hybrid strategies that incorporate buy, build, and reuse options over a period of time that provides interim value through phased delivery cycles.

The business case for incorporating legacy architecture transformation strategies is based on the process of elimination. If legacy architectures are preventing you from expanding into new markets, delivering new products and services, fulfilling customer requirements, streamlining supply and distribution chains, going global, or just staying competitive, legacy architecture transformation can help. ERP packages, new development, and EAI may all be a part of this strategy, but legacy transformation may be the missing component to make these other strategies work.

1.12 Crafting a Strategy to Address the Legacy Architecture Challenge

IT or business executives would never actually say, "Let's transform our legacy systems." On the contrary, application projects are driven almost entirely by unique business requirements, with the expectation of near-term results. Occasionally, a strategic project may be funded over a period of more than a year, but this tends to be the exception more than the rule. A legacy transformation strategy recognizes where certain techniques or concepts can be applied to augment traditional IT initiatives to save time, reduce risks, lower costs, and increase the overall quality of the project.

These concepts, which will be explored throughout the remainder of this book, include

- High-level and detailed application analysis and re-documentation.
- Selective application of EAI solutions.

- Program-level and system-wide improvements in legacy systems.
- Language migration.
- Data consolidation, migration, and cleanup.
- Rehosting or migrating legacy systems to modern platforms.
- Applying modern distributed front ends to legacy applications.
- Redesign and reuse of legacy business logic.
- Redesign and redeployment of legacy data structures.
- Package software/legacy application hybrid deployment.
- Augmentation of new development efforts through legacy analysis and reuse.

Any project impacted by or relying on one or more legacy systems or data structures can apply these concepts. The role of the management team is to understand where and how various approaches can be applied and in what combination. To accomplish this, an organization should create a transformation strategy that enables and encourages the use of legacy transformation concepts and techniques on projects. A legacy architecture transformation strategy should minimally include the following items.

- Recognition and concurrence from the executive team that legacy architectures must be considered and accommodated in any type of project impacting or relying on legacy systems or data structures.
- Executive support, senior management sponsorship, and well-placed transformation champions.
- A general understanding or map of legacy architectures, including how systems relate to other systems and data structures.
- An understanding of which systems support which business units and underlying business functions and processes.
- Processes for assessing, planning, improving, integrating, transforming, and testing legacy applications.
- Access to or an understanding of software tools needed to facilitate assessing, planning, improving, integrating, transforming, and testing legacy applications.
- Scenario-based planning guidelines identifying the legacy transformation tasks needed to augment a variety of IT projects, including new development, package selection and implementation, and integration efforts.
- General guidelines for assessing the value to be gained or cost savings associated with incorporating legacy transformation techniques into a project.
- Organizational infrastructure necessary to facilitate and maintain this legacy architecture transformation strategy.

When assessing and developing such a strategy, there are several major factors to be considered. These factors include people and the roles they play, organizational infrastructure, project planning, cost analysis, and third-party participation.

For example, most people in a given IT organization are not predisposed to looking into invasive approaches for addressing issues related to legacy systems or data structures. Legacy transformation may require a shift in thinking. People have a throwaway mentality. Many things we purchase today are inexpensive or designed to be tossed out. My grandfather would be appalled at the thought of tossing out my razor when I finished with it. Throwaway cameras are another example of this concept. The idea of recycling, however, is well accepted, and that is what IT is doing when it seeks to transform and reuse legacy business rules and data.

Organizational infrastructure requires the enterprise to be set up to encourage and enable legacy transformation. This requires examining relationships within IT; between IT and the business units; and between IT, the business units, and third parties. Infrastructure also requires communication and collaboration facilities for knowledge sharing, tool distribution, training, technique deployment, project planning, and support.

Another infrastructure issue must consider prejudices of new development teams against anything that is not technologically state of the art. People working with Java, XML, and a host of newer methodologies and tools are not predisposed to working with anything with the term *legacy* attached. Dealing with these prejudices will need to be done judiciously.

One last infrastructure issue requires the creation of an environment that supports legacy transformation. This includes tools, training, techniques, and preliminary assessment projects. There is, of course, an initial level of funding needed to support such an infrastructure.

Project planning and cost analysis go hand in hand. Traditional development, upgrade, or other types of deployment plans, based on whatever planning methodology is used, will need to be augmented with various legacy techniques if an enterprise wishes to pursue a transformation strategy. This assumes IT does this type of planning in the first place—which it should. It also requires transformation specialists to assist with incorporating these techniques into project plans. Cost analysis is based on augmenting traditional cost models based on these plans.

Finally, third-party participation is a vital component of any transformation strategy. Management may adopt such a strategy, set up the infrastructure, and engage inhouse professionals, but end up having the entire effort sidestepped by a systems integrator, outsourcing firm, ASP, or management consulting firm. Certain consulting firms do not embrace legacy transformation options because it is frankly more profitable for them to apply traditional techniques to most IT projects. I will share a case study on such a project during the cost justification discussion in later chapters.

Third-party consulting or outsourcing firms may just not have the know-how or tool-based experience to engage in discussions about legacy transformation.

This is a matter of education. Executives should be aware that a third-party recommendation not to incorporate legacy transformation into a project could be based on the fact that transformation options would reduce the implementation effort and therefore the fees to be charged for that project. Or it may just be based on a lack of experience with these techniques and related tools. Either way, executives should challenge third parties to incorporate a transformation mindset into their project plans.

1.13 Taking on the Legacy Challenge

Legacy transformation does require a shift in thinking, but it is a slight shift in thinking. The concept of understanding what you are replacing prior to building a new system is not radical. Neither is the concept of reusing established, reliable business logic. Programmers have been doing this on a small scale for years, but that was back when legacy programmers were still building replacement or add-on systems.

Today, however, a 20-something Java programmer would never think to go back and examine a COBOL or PL/I system to determine where and how reuse could be leveraged as part of the planning, analysis, design, and deployment process. A formal legacy transformation strategy would therefore compensate for loss of the legacy expert's insight into these systems.

It takes a person of conviction at the executive level to stand up to peers and incorporate legacy transformation options into more traditional project plans. Over the years, some executives made these commitments, and I will share certain studies outlining how they did.

Legacy transformation tends to boil down to common sense. The business has changed, but the systems have not. Writing a new system is time-consuming, costly, and rarely if ever replaces the need for the legacy system or systems it was supposed to replace. Buying a package makes better sense, but many times companies end up leaving inhouse legacy systems intact even after a package is partially implemented. This is the result of realizing that a package can sacrifice strategic value of inhouse systems that may have been doing a better job in the first place.

Connecting legacy architectures to new Web-based applications has merit, but this assumes that the legacy architecture can mimic the demands of high-speed, Web-based environments. Legacy systems and data were not meant to perform in a zero latency environment, and even the best EAI technology cannot change this situation.

Finally, there are the basic requirements involving the enhancement of legacy systems and data structures required as part of ongoing business operations. Clean, consistent data is a requirement if data is being opened up to customers or business partners or being used as part of a CRM initiative.

Enterprise executives that ignore these factors are more likely than not betting that they will be gone long before legacy systems catch up with them. This may be the case, but legacy systems will catch up with the enterprise as a whole sooner or later. That will be the time when someone will wish that a legacy transformation strategy had been deployed before it was too late.

Notes

1. "Businesses Tap IT after Staff, Budget Cuts," Lee Copeland, *Computerworld*, Nov. 2, 2001.
2. "Resolution on E-Government," www.fonction-publique.gov.
3. "eGovernment Vision for Californians," December 1999, www.ss.ca.gov.
4. "President Bush Backs E-Government," Alorie Gilbert, Digital Signatures, *Information Week*, April 16, 2001.
5. "Safety in Sharing," Rick Whiting & Eric Chabrow, *Information Week*, Oct. 8, 2001.
6. "Citibank Snafu Makes All ATMs Suddenly Seem Much Shakier," Paul Beckett & Jathon Sapsford, *Wall Street Journal*, Sept. 6, 2001.
7. "Kmart Plans a $195 Million Charge," Thomas M. Burton, *Wall Street Journal*, Sept. 6, 2001.
8. "Cleveland State Can't Process Financial Aid Using PeopleSoft Applications," Craig Stedman, *Computerworld*, Nov. 22, 1999.
9. "The Cost of Having Analog Executives in a Digital World," Hal Berghel, *Communications of the ACM*, 1995.
10. "From the Dustbin, Cobol Rises," Stephanie Wilkinson, *eWeek*, May 28, 2001.

Defining the Legacy Architecture Challenge

2

There is a great degree of misinformation surrounding the makeup, impact, and potential contribution of legacy computer systems. Executives have one view of enterprise computer systems, business users have another view, and IT has yet another view. Even within IT, some managers believe that new systems can easily displace legacy systems and that legacy systems can be ignored. Analysts and technicians working on those systems typically doubt these claims because they know that legacy systems are too critical and too complex to ignore.

The fact is that, despite the hype, legacy systems are still here and growing in size. Organizations with an installed base of legacy data and application systems face many of the following challenges.

- Difficulty in responding to rapid shifts in business requirements.
- Inability to deliver industry-wide or regulatory-driven initiatives.
- Risks to customer initiatives due to data redundancy, lack of integrity, and inconsistency.
- Inability to equip e-business initiatives with the richness of functionality found within legacy applications.
- Difficulty in reconciling, integrating, accessing, and sharing critical legacy data.
- Inability to trigger cross-functional transactions in zero latency fashion.
- A lack of skilled personnel needed to maintain older languages, databases, and environments.
- Spiraling costs associated with leasing and maintaining legacy software packages and hardware.

- Dissatisfaction with outsourcing, ASP, or other third-party-related relationships.

- Business failures that at best give the impression of incompetence and at worst can result in lost customers, revenues, funding and market position.

Tackling these challenges, many of which need to be addressed concurrently, requires a highly coordinated strategy. It is also essential for the management team to define and prioritize unique internal and external transformation challenges as a basis for creating a shared vision of how to proceed. Once a shared understanding of the issues is in place, executives can create and deploy an architecture transformation strategy that delivers interim value over phased delivery windows.

This chapter provides insights into a variety of legacy architecture challenges with the intent of coalescing executives, managers, business users, IT personnel, and others around a common understanding of the size, scope, and composition of the legacy architecture challenge.

2.1 Legacy Architectures and the Seven Common Myths

Before detailing various legacy architecture challenges facing organizations, it is important to dispel some common myths about those architectures. Misinformation has always surrounded much of the debate regarding legacy architectures. Misinformation originates from many sources. Most of these sources have little practical experience working with these systems or may have an agenda that is furthered by avoiding or downplaying the role of legacy systems within the enterprise. Below are seven common myths associated with legacy architectures.

- **Myth #1: Legacy applications provide little or limited business value.**

  Legacy applications are the lifeblood of an enterprise because they process critical enterprise data. As discussed in Chapter 1, the majority of legacy systems are written in COBOL. COBOL applications process 85 percent of all global business data [1]. If these applications suddenly disappeared, enterprises would find themselves at a major loss. Recognizing legacy systems as important organizational assets is the first step in crafting a strategy to address related challenges.

- **Myth #2: Web-based systems are rapidly displacing legacy systems.**

  Web-based front ends may appear to be displacing legacy applications, but legacy online transaction volume continues to grow. The predominant online transaction processing facility is IBM's Customer Information Control System (CICS). CICS handled 20 billion transactions per day in 1998. This was more than the total number of hits per day on the Worldwide Web at that point in time. If legacy systems were being displaced, one would expect that this number would shrink over time. Two years later, however, IBM reported that the number of daily CICS transactions jumped to 30 billion—an increase of 50 percent. The number of customers has also grown. Gray & Reuter reported 30,000 CICS systems in use in 1993. This number jumped to 50,000 CICS mainframe licenses by 1999 [2]. It is clear that legacy systems continue to be the mainstay of the majority of business environments.

- **Myth #3: COBOL is a dead language and is no longer being enhanced or upgraded.**

  Universities that dropped COBOL from their curriculum propagated the myth that COBOL was a dead language. To the contrary, there are more than 200 billion lines of COBOL globally, representing more than 60 percent of the world's software. COBOL applications are also expected to grow by 5 billion lines of code annually. Fifteen percent of all new application functionality over the next 5 years will be written in COBOL [1]. COBOL is also being Web-enabled. It is a good thing that a few universities have kept teaching COBOL, because it will be around for a long time. COBOL is alive and well.

- **Myth #4: Legacy data stores can be left intact and made accessible to Web-based applications.**

  Legacy data is redundantly and inconsistently defined, hard to integrate, and lacks integrity. Standalone legacy data structures typically define the same data differently, while a data element as simple as a customer or phone number may mean different things to different business units. These issues, coupled with the fact that some of this data contains invalid values or no information at all, makes the process of creating direct interfaces to this data from external Web sites a risky proposition. Legacy systems have built-in safeguards to deal with these issues, while many new systems do not.

- **Myth #5: Legacy system functionality is no longer valid.**

  This is perhaps the greatest misconception about legacy systems. Legacy functionality may be hard to decipher, hard to invoke (outside of a normal processing cycle), or redundantly defined, but legacy business logic is also very reliable. In other words, most legacy systems contain accurate and relevant business logic, but they do not typically invoke this logic in a way that is conducive to dynamic business requirements.

- **Myth #6: Web-enabling legacy systems will satisfy new business requirements.**

  Functional fragmentation, a condition caused by the hierarchical or stovepipe evolution of legacy systems and data structures, has created a situation where legacy systems fulfill tasks in a piecemeal fashion. Each system performs a step in a larger process and then relies on other systems to continue the cycle or process. Between many of these steps, a human or batch job stream typically triggers a subsequent step until a point when the processing cycle is completed. This approach is in direct conflict with the need for an e-business system to trigger rules and access data on demand. Web-enabling legacy architectures can fulfill certain near-term requirements and is a legitimate activity for application teams. This approach will not, however, fulfill long-term requirements to Web-enable key functions within an enterprise. A more comprehensive transformation plan is needed to meet this goal.

- **Myth #7: Organizations developing new systems can ignore legacy systems.** Studies (most notably one performed by Gane and Sarson) have shown that replacement systems typically retain up to 80 percent or more of the functionality of the existing system. Even if this figure is only 40 to 50 percent, the business rules that are in legacy systems tend to be difficult to reproduce to any degree of accuracy. Any effort to rebuild or replace a legacy system, in whole or in part, should do so with an understanding of the systems being replaced. Legacy understanding is a minimal requirement to determine which portions of the legacy system need to be replaced.

Subscribing to these myths will dangerously skew an organization's ability to deliver time-critical business solutions. Underestimating the value of legacy architectures and their complexity will result in the delay or failure of a wide variety of business initiatives. Recognizing these challenges, on the other hand, is the first step toward creating a legacy architecture transformation strategy that will deliver critical business solutions in the timeframes required.

2.2 Evolving Hardware Architectures

Over the past 50 years, room-sized computers that were basically giant calculators shrunk to the size of tiny chips that fit inside devices of every kind. Modern computing devices perform functions that early computing engineers never would have envisioned. Predictions that computers would shrink to fit on a desktop were laughed at by many in the industry. Yet today, computer chips are small enough to be inserted in countless devices from cell phones to wristwatches.

Moore's law explains the phenomenal advances in hardware computing capacity over the past few decades. According to Intel cofounder Gordon Moore, "Chip complexity (defined by the number of active elements on a single semiconductor chip) will double about every device generation, which is usually around 18 calendar months [3]. This law has been valid for more than three decades, and it appears likely to be valid for several more device generations. As a result, computers keep getting faster, gaining greater memory capacity, becoming physically smaller, and getting less expensive.

During the late 1940s and early 1950s, computers took up entire rooms and were based on vacuum tube technology. The invention of the transistor made the reality of Moore's law possible. The first computer that I worked on was the IBM 360/50. It was powerful compared to very early systems, yet the entire system had to be fully dedicated to running the PL/I compiler. Most of today's calculators, typically costing just a few dollars, are more powerful than that old 360/50.

Moore's law is the reason most hardware, at least in mainstream business environments, is replaced or upgraded every couple of years. The concept of upward compatibility, where software can be ported to the next generation of hardware, made hardware upgrades an easy decision. This is the reason that many of the applications originally developed for systems such as the 360 are still running in production today in many organizations.

In general, upwardly compatible software has enabled most organizations to avoid getting tied down to a given piece of hardware, but this is not universally true. There are still quite a few older UNIX machines, Digital Equipment Corporation PDP 1100s, Hewlett-Packard HP 3000 systems, and other environments running around the world. Some of these systems can be difficult to upgrade or replace because the software is proprietary or lacks certain upward compatibility because the vendor stopped supporting the operating environment.

Even recent hardware advancements can cause challenges for software technicians. For example, the upgrade from the 32-bit to 64-bit hardware environment, driven by Intel's release of the Itanium chip, is one major scenario that organizations will face over the next two to three years.

The Intel Itanium architecture provides an improved enterprise-computing infrastructure by changing the way the hardware processor interacts with compilers, applications, and memory. In doing so, the Itanium offers sustainable increases in application throughput through Explicit Parallel Instruction Computing (EPIC). Itanium offers 64-bit addressing to increase database memory support. This in turn increases throughput for e-business applications, promising increased compatibility for Java applications. It will also expedite encryption and authentication processing for security systems.

The main benefit of increased processor speed and memory capacity is that it will expedite efforts to port applications and databases from mainframes into distributed environments. In spite of these advancements in distributed computing capacity, the mainframe is not going anywhere soon. A Cutter Consortium survey [4] of 35 global enterprises found that 40 percent of respondents felt the mainframe would be around for 10 to 15 years or more. Yet 61 percent of respondents plan to migrate applications off of the mainframe.

Other hardware platforms are being discontinued, however. Hewlett-Packard, for example, told users of its HP e3000 server that they should switch to other systems because it's discontinuing that line. The phase-out period is expected to last five years, but will affect up to 70,000 customers. Whenever a hardware platform is discontinued, an operating system can also become obsolete. In this case, customers will need to migrate to the MPE operating system. HP claims that it wants to move customers to open systems, but this move will require a major migration for applications running on that platform [5].

IT can be assured, however, that increases in computing power will continue to drive mainframe and other hardware upgrades, which in turn will increase software migration requirements. In the case of moving to new distributed environments, this means changing data and application architectures as well as simple rehosting activities. Rehosting simply moves the data and application architecture to a new platform with minimal changes.

Moore's law is predicted to taper off in a few years. Other advancements will continue, however. These new advancements promise to be even more dramatic. The ability to store, back up, and transmit massive amounts of data over high-speed communication lines will make computing ubiquitous. These advancements are expected to deliver mobile-computing devices, for example, that fit into a pocket and are always connected to the Internet.

As this technology emerges, it will put even greater pressures on those responsible for software and data architectures to deliver better migration, integration, and transformation solutions. One important point to remember is that hardware architectures rarely stifle business initiatives to the same degree as software and data architectures. Hardware can be readily replaced, but the software and the data cannot. The remainder of this chapter and this book, therefore, focuses on addressing legacy software and data architecture challenges.

2.3 A Brief History of Software Architectures

In spite of the vast differences between the original computers built decades ago and today's networked and distributed devices, they all have one thing in common. People must find a way to tell them what to do by programming them. This concept gave birth to the software industry.

Early programmers had to program computers using machine language, which was basically a series of ones and zeros. The first computer programmers were women. In 1945, the U.S. Army recruited a team of 80 female mathematicians. Their job was to program, at the machine level, the first all-electronic digital computer called the Electronic Numerical Integrator and Computer (ENIAC). The ENIAC (see Figure 2.1) was 80 feet long, 9 feet tall, and required the use of 18,000 vacuum tubes.

The ENIAC computer had no stored programs, which meant that the machine had no operating system or other software running on it that you could use to communicate with it. The creators of the ENIAC received high praise, while the ENIAC programming staff went unheralded for decades. From the beginning, the job of the programmer (versus that of the electrical engineering team) was overlooked and underappreciated. To this day, the role of the software professional is a huge challenge that is often taken for granted by many executives and business professionals.

After the ENIAC, higher-level languages emerged. One language that was slightly more sophisticated was called the Assembler language. Assembler was a

The First Computer Programmers

Figure 2.1
Women mathematicians programming ENIAC—the first electronic computer used
by the Army from 1945 to 1955.
(Source: Charles Babbage Institute.)

higher-level embodiment of machine language, but was still a low-level
(second-generation) language and therefore difficult for humans to program and
interpret. There are still many business systems along with numerous operating
systems written in Assembler.

Third-generation languages increased programming productivity during
the 1950s and 1960s. Women from the original ENIAC programming team helped
design several third-generation languages, including FORTAN and COBOL.
These languages are still commonly used today. Given that hardware has come so
far, it's incredible that software languages designed almost 50 years ago still
power the bulk of today's business environments.

The basic makeup of how computers are programmed remained, until very
recently, the same as it was during the early days of computing. Virtually every

commercially viable computer since the 1950s has had an operating system that handles basic communication with the hardware. Various "compilers" are installed on a given computer to translate higher-level languages such as FORT-AN, COBOL, or C into a series of commands that the computer can perform. A software programming language consists of syntax or symbols and symbol group-ings that form commands and semantics (the meaning of the commands).

Computers can work in a foreground or a background mode. Older com-puters called background computing *batch processing*. Batch processing was the only way to communicate with a computer in the early days of programming. Newer computers use online environments, meaning that the user can interact directly with the computer. Batch processing, for example, is used to update bank accounts hours after the initial transaction was put into the system. This is why some bank receipts have a notice that states, "Funds added to your account may not be available until tomorrow."

Large-scale computers can process hundreds of nightly update cycles in batch mode. They also process month-end, quarter-end, and year-end batch jobs to update records on a periodic basis. Online processing emerged during the early 1970s when IBM introduced CICS and online processing capabilities for its cus-tomers. As a footnote to this story, Burroughs (now Unisys) Corporation intro-duced online computing prior to the introduction of CICS, but IBM won the mar-keting battle.

Online processing allowed users to enter information directly into a comput-er. This allowed avoiding filling out forms, having the data keypunched, and load-ing the punch cards into the system to await a batch-processing cycle. Yet even today, many basic business functions, such as updating a bank account or balanc-ing inventory levels, must wait until a batch job updates that information. Our real-time world is, in many cases, actually an illusion or a "batch mode simulation."

Based on this foundation, application software proliferated during the late 1960s and throughout the 1970s and 1980s. Many of today's legacy systems have roots from this timeframe. During the early 1980s, software was introduced that would generate other software. Much of the generated software resulted in COBOL programs that performed various business functions. Programmers could generate code more quickly than they could write it by hand. Unfortunately, gen-erated business applications were poorly structured, had cryptic naming conven-tions, and were difficult to read and harder to enhance when business require-ments changed.

Poor program design and construction was the hallmark of countless legacy application systems. This was true for software written by humans as well as soft-ware generated by other software. In other words, the compiler and hardware could correctly interpret the code, but another programmer could not figure out what the original programmer was trying to accomplish. As this problem came to light in the late 1970s and early 1980s, the industry came to realize it had created a "software maintenance problem."

Various solutions emerged to address the maintenance challenge. Structured programming was introduced during the 1970s to make programs more readable, but this did not address the haphazard design that proliferated across and among many legacy applications. Poor design means that two programs might have overlapping functionality, define data inconsistently or redundantly, or implement a solution in a nonobvious way.

The rank-and-file programming community did not immediately adopt structured programming and structured design. Other competing methodologies just confused the situation. Information engineering, for example, seemed to get stuck in endless analysis and design cycles and rarely produced concrete results. The deployment of increasingly onerous methodologies during the 1980s caused a backlash against methodologies in general by the early 1990s.

As a result, programmers during the past decade bypassed formal planning, analysis, and design activities in lieu of just writing code. This is akin to a construction company beginning work on a building without having any plans or design specifications drafted by architects or engineers. This abandonment of formal methodologies resulted in modern-day legacy systems, written in languages such as C, C++, and Visual Basic, that introduce a whole new legacy architecture challenge on top of older legacy systems.

Many new systems, written in these "modern" languages, are no more maintainable than older COBOL systems. In fact, year 2000 remediation teams discovered that COBOL was easier to fix than many other computing languages because COBOL language pioneers did a good job designing a maintainable, yet somewhat cumbersome, language.

There have been some major changes in the world of software programming over the past several years. Procedural or block-structured languages, such as C, FORTRAN, COBOL, and other older dialects, apply an explicit series of steps to achieve an intended result.

The introduction of Java and the concept of component reuse have changed this programming paradigm. Older programming languages are considered structured languages that work based on the premise that custom code is written to flow procedurally from one statement to the next in order to act upon global data elements. Newer languages, such as Java and C++, are object-oriented (OO) languages.

In an OO language the data is defined as an object, and that object is responsible for performing its own actions. In other words, OO languages reduce the level of explicit programming requirements and only need to request, for example, an inventory balance. The object "inventory balance" would do all of the work needed to calculate and return an up-to-date balance. A procedural language, on the other hand, would need to actually calculate the balance with specific programming logic.

The applicability and characteristics of OO-based languages are discussed in more depth in Chapter 3.

IT is slowly beginning to adopt OO analysis and design techniques along with component-based development. While far from being fully accepted by the vast majority of programmers and analysts, the IT industry is beginning to head in the right direction. Changes in how programmers design and construct new application systems have a direct impact on transformation strategies because the target architecture involves a paradigm shift from the legacy architecture. As Dorothy said to Toto, "We're not in Kansas anymore."

2.4 Embedded and Non-IT Systems

Most IT departments and business units, working in conjunction with IT, manage and utilize application systems that run on "traditional" mainframe, mid-range, and networked computers. Many organizations utilize other systems that function outside of these traditional computing environments or run on embedded devices. The majority of these systems can be considered legacy systems. The applicability of legacy transformation techniques depends on whether or not the software is "embedded" within the hardware.

Applications generally considered non-IT systems include embedded systems as well as a wide range of applications that have been acquired or built by engineers, plant managers, or other non-IT professionals. These systems run in plants or other decentralized locations and can be written in Assembler, FORTRAN, Pascal, C, or more obscure languages.

Embedded systems monitor, control, or facilitate functions within a component device, piece of equipment, or work environment. The term *embedded* means that it is an inaccessible black box. Embedded chips residing inside of electronic devices or equipment rely on hard-wired programming combined with certain types of software. Hard-wired programming is burnt into computer chips. The software may or may not be modifiable.

For example, Ladder Logic is used to program programmable logic controllers (PLCs). The PLC is an embedded device, but the code developed to program it is considered "low-level" application software. In many cases, it will be difficult to distinguish the embedded device and the software that was used to program that device.

Embedded systems and the software that interfaces with these systems can play a role in the operation of the machine, component device, or environment. Embedded technologies are typically concealed and difficult to identify. Embedded technology tends to function on an ongoing basis without anyone really knowing that it exists.

Many non-IT or embedded systems are integral assets within an enterprise, and interface with application systems. Some examples of non-IT systems that a company might use include telephone switches, PBX equipment, voice mail, global positioning systems (GPSs), switching equipment, credit card systems, and point-of-sale systems.

A bank might also be using ATM machines, safes, or vaults. Utilities or manufacturing firms might also use systems embedded in power station grids, pipelines, refineries, storage facilities, metering devices, and location equipment.

Organizations embarking on a transformation project will want to recognize the existence of these systems and identify any interfaces to business applications that may rely on data produced by these systems. These systems should not be ignored by architecture planning teams because they could have an impact on mainstream application systems or important enterprise functions.

In addition to this, many of the techniques described here and in subsequent chapters can be used to assess and transform higher-level, non-IT software if it is not directly connected to an embedded systems function.

If an enterprise is trying to modernize or replace these systems, it may require contacting the manufacturer of those systems. It is particularly important to include any non-IT or embedded systems in an assessment if it impacts, is impacted by, or in some way interfaces with a legacy architecture transformation project.

2.5 Legacy Application Architectures— An Archaeological Dig

Application architectures are based on stovepipe hierarchies of past generations. Figure 2.2 depicts how application hierarchies mirror organizational hierarchies. It is this infrastructure that generations of programmers have built upon.

Trying to decipher legacy application architectures is comparable to an archaeological excavation. Software has been applied in layers over the years. Early application systems were primarily comprised of one or two languages, such as Assembler and COBOL, and the basic runtime environment needed to make those systems function. Over the years, more software and interfaces were added. Applying major changes to these systems today requires untangling these layers.

Decades later, thousands of changes have been applied to legacy systems. These changes tended to shield the original intent and design of a system. For example, the Saber System, which is a reservation system started by American Airlines and spun off into its own company, was developed during the 1960s. It has been enhanced and upgraded countless times to the point where the original developers would no longer recognize it.

Decades of quick fixes, functional enhancements, technology upgrades, and other maintenance activities obscure application functionality to the point where

Stovepipe Infrastructures, Processes, and Architectures

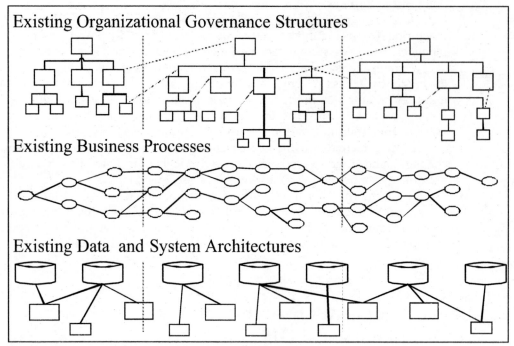

Figure 2.2
Business processes, applications and data structures mirror hierarchical governance
structures in stovepipe or silo-based fashion.

no one can understand how a system functions. In most cases, the original authors of these systems are long gone, and countless programmers with varying styles and skills have maintained them. New or less experienced programmers cannot fully understand how the application functions. In these cases, technicians tend to take a path of least resistance by creating workaround routines to ensure that the changes they apply will work.

For example, assume that I want to add tax exemption logic to a government tax system to ensure that anyone involved in the war in Afghanistan would automatically get a filing extension. Now assume that this same approach was used to extend file deadlines for people involved in numerous other wars dating back to the 1960s. If a programmer along the way built a table that could be updated to accommodate this, all I would need to do is incorporate my new requirements into that table.

Because there is no documentation for this system, however, I may not understand how the table works. This leads me to work around the existing table routine by writing new logic that examines certain dates and other data needed to trigger the exemption. I must work around the old solution and numerous other fixes because I do not understand how they work. This situation is commonplace and happens as programmers update billions of lines of code on a year-to-year basis.

This phenomenon may explain, at least in part, why the amount of COBOL in the world today is increasing at the rate of 5 billion lines of code per year. Programmers do not have the time or skill sets to fully ascertain what legacy applications are doing, so they add new, extraneous code to the system. This problem can be extrapolated to the system level. Some analysts add entire programs, new data structures, or even entire subsystems to work around a program or system they do not understand.

In a worst-case scenario, entire systems have been created to work around legacy applications that people are either afraid to change or simply cannot change with any degree of certainty that the changed system will still work correctly. Few systems have reliable documentation. The only way to figure out what these systems are doing is by looking at the code or running the system to see what happens.

Two examples highlight the depth and impact of this problem. The U.S. air traffic control system is old, large, and very complex. It is also a mission-critical system because it deals with human life. The Federal Aviation Administration (FAA) has spent many years and billions of dollars trying to replace this system to no avail. This system is shaky on its best day based on the number of failures reported that have forced air traffic delays. The system clearly needs to be reengineered.

Rewriting the air traffic control system from scratch is an unlikely option because the system has been fine-tuned for decades in real-life scenarios involving high air traffic volume. I for one do not want to be a test case on a new system that has not undergone extensive, real-life fine-tuning. Yet the FAA will need to take some action in coming years as air traffic continues to rise over the next decade.

During the 1990s, the Internal Revenue Service (IRS) spent billions of dollars on a tax systems modernization project with limited success [6]. IBM Assembler applications, written during the 1960s, still process U.S. taxes today. Of course, the IRS has added new code and additional systems to augment the original system. Other applications were built on a Unisys mainframe and on a variety of distributed environments. The IRS kept these systems functioning through the year 2000, which is a credit to technical skills. Yet the core system, along with all of its legacy baggage, remains intact. As of this writing, yet another tax systems upgrade is under way and over budget.

One challenge found within legacy environments like the one at the IRS is consistency. When multiple systems give different answers to the same question, users are at a loss to respond. One option that has been used in the past is to take the answer from the system that is hardest to understand or fix. This is called "de facto" correctness and is a common strategy when a company is running multiple legacy systems with overlapping functions. This is particularly true in situations where new layers of redundant logic have been added to augment the original system.

Another layer of application complexity was added to legacy applications using fourth-generation languages (4GLs). Over the years, business users decided that IT was not as responsive as the users needed them to be, and the business community needed to address this problem. One limitation of many legacy languages is the time it takes to update the software to add a new report feature. Most legacy applications provide users only with a fixed view of enterprise data. If a user needs to see different information or view that information differently, a new report would need to be created.

The business community used 4GLs, such as Mark IV, RAMIS, FOCUS, SASS, and Easytrieve, to extract legacy data and create special reports. Programs using these languages proliferated during the 1980s and 1990s. One healthcare provider found that users, over a period of years, had created more than 6,000 4GL programs to handle "special requests." There was no documentation or any other indication as to what these programs did, what data they accessed, or what kind of reports they produced.

Financial institutions have a similar challenge in user-built application layers, but these companies typically use Microsoft Excel to build special reports and inquiries. This is an example of how the business community can add a layer of complexity to legacy application architectures outside of the traditional IT infrastructure.

Other layers of software have spawned from the introduction of mid-range or distributed systems meant to replace certain legacy functionality. In reality, most application upgrade or replacement projects fail to actually displace legacy application functionality. At best, these projects replicate existing logic in part. One telecommunications company spent $80 million with a consulting firm on such a project. Its business users were then forced to reconcile results from the new system with output from the legacy system. These types of projects may deliver some near-term value, but also create layers of complexity on top of already complex application architectures.

The latest layer being added to the legacy puzzle uses EAI software to create interfaces between Web-based applications and legacy applications and data structures. These API and middleware tools introduce another layer of legacy software that organizations must dig through to determine how a system is really functioning. If we think programmers are having a hard time determining what an old COBOL system is doing, consider the difficulty in deciphering hundreds or even thousands of new interfaces being built on top of legacy architectures.

EAI and other solutions, including application packages, can provide business value when applied properly. Applying these solutions, however, without understanding what they will ultimately do to complicate or further entangle existing application architectures is problematic—particularly when executives have little knowledge of the existence or the ramifications of these projects.

2.6 Packaged Applications—Falling Short of Expectations

Packaged application software performs business functions. This should not be confused with operating system or environmental software such as IBM's MVS operating system, the CICS transaction processing monitor, or Windows NT. Operating system packages indirectly impact the business, but the code is almost always inaccessible and shielded from application teams. Many of these operating environments have legacy tendencies as well, but software companies tend to rewrite them or release significantly upgraded versions of these systems. CICS was re-architected in 1985, for example. Most important is that fact that while operating or environmental software upgrades are typically transparent to the business community, application package upgrades are not.

Packaged application software first became available during the mid- to late 1960s when financial accounting and payroll software was made available for lease from companies such as Information Science Inc., McCormack & Dodge, and FORTEX [7]. This was the beginning of a new option for IT that allowed them to lease versus build application systems. Early application packages focused on accounting or financial solutions. Application packages eventually offered manufacturing, human resource, and a variety of other functions to organizations.

Many of theses systems were designed using the same principles as inhouse legacy applications. Early packages focused on a single function within a corporate or government hierarchy, such as accounting, and were built using legacy application languages and programming techniques. These systems are also hard to maintain and decipher.

Application packages, on the other hand, perform business functions and must therefore be integrated into inhouse application architectures. In many cases, inhouse programming teams have modified application package source code and, as a result, could not reintegrate vendor upgrades back into those applications. This has become a major challenge for a number of organizations, but the year 2000 forced many enterprises to upgrade their package software to the latest release or abandon vendor support.

During the 1990s, a variety of ERP packages were released. ERP systems seemed quite appealing to executives frustrated with inadequate responsiveness from inhouse programming teams struggling with legacy application enhancements. Many times, the decision to acquire and install these packages was driven by the CEO or CFO based on promises from vendors that the ERP package would address or eliminate their legacy architecture problems. In theory, ERP systems sounded appealing based on many of the following promises.

1. An ERP system would replace legacy applications in their entirety and therefore eliminate most of the headaches and personnel associated with those systems.
2. The ERP system would integrate cross-functional areas, including order entry and sales, inventory management, manufacturing, accounting, and human resources.
3. Organizations could customize ERP applications by manipulating user-driven parameters and reduce or eliminate the need to make software changes.
4. The vendor would issue new releases with new functionality and reduce the need for inhouse support teams.
5. Later versions of ERP software ran on distributed environments, and this would speed an enterprise's migration away from the mainframe.

In reality, the challenges associated with the introduction of ERP systems were more than executives anticipated. A few of these challenges are as follows.

1. Many ERP applications did not conform to organizational business models and requirements, which meant businesses had to change the way they worked to conform to the package.
2. Lack of support for certain business functions meant that certain legacy systems had to remain intact and that certain package components were not implemented.
3. User customization was table-driven, difficult to perform, and almost impossible to decipher from a maintenance perspective.
4. Because legacy data did not conform to the ERP environment, migration efforts required rationalizing, integrating, cleaning up, and redesigning that data. This proved too great a challenge for some enterprises.
5. Moving from a series of stovepipe applications and data structures to an integrated ERP package while concurrently forcing a company to change how it did business was untenable for many enterprises.
6. Most ERP systems, until very recently, did not support e-business requirements.

As one might expect from the above list of challenges, ERP projects struggled to succeed under any definition of the term. Cost overruns, cancellations, and the inability to deliver anywhere close to the functionality envisioned by the buyer are commonplace. A Standish Group study found the following levels of success and failure for ERP implementation efforts [8].

- Of the total ERP projects undertaken, 35 percent were canceled outright.
- Another 55 percent of the projects experienced cost and schedule overruns.
- Cost overruns ran, on average, around 178 percent of original cost estimates.
- A worst-case cost overrun was close to 300 percent of the estimated budget.

- Project delivery schedules were, on average, 230 percent longer than originally estimated.
- A worst-case schedule overrun was over 325 percent longer than originally estimated.
- The average level of implemented functionality was around 40 percent of what was originally anticipated or promised.
- Only 10 percent of ERP projects came in on time and on budget.

Of all the above statistics, the most problematic is the level of functionality implemented. IT projects are almost always late and typically run over the planned budget. While this is a problem and management should be concerned about this late projects in general, when a project is eventually completed it should ultimately meet its goal. In the case of numerous ERP projects, the level of capability or functionality was, on average, well under half of what management anticipated.

Many articles have cited ideas on how to avoid ERP problems, and many of these are valid. Businesses should rethink their processes before jumping into a new software package that forces them to change how they function. An enterprise should also ensure that they have the skills and time needed to customize ERP parameters. ERP projects also require a champion, buy-in from the implementation team, and strong project management. Addressing each of these requirements, however, is not enough.

A strategy to accommodate, transform, and integrate legacy applications and data must be an integral part of any package implementation project. If this is not done, organizations will encounter many of problems highlighted by the Standish Group study. Because most application packages are interwoven with homegrown applications, what once was viewed as an easy answer to an application development effort is now just another piece in the legacy architecture puzzle.

To fully appreciate this, consider the latest ERP-related project being undertaken by companies that actually implemented portions of an ERP package. These organizations are applying EAI technologies to build front end to back end interfaces between ERP systems, legacy systems, data structures, and Web-based front ends. This maze of package, inhouse, and legacy interfaces will evolve into the next generation of legacy application architecture challenges.

2.7 Application Architectures—A Myriad of Challenges

Legacy applications, introduced over the decades as a series of increasingly complex layers, can complicate business initiatives relying on these applications. The underlying challenge involves understanding the underlying legacy application architecture and how it is preventing an organization from achieving the agility it requires in today's dynamic markets.

Small Cross-Section of Daily Run Cycle for Edit, Update, Sorting, and Reporting Sequence

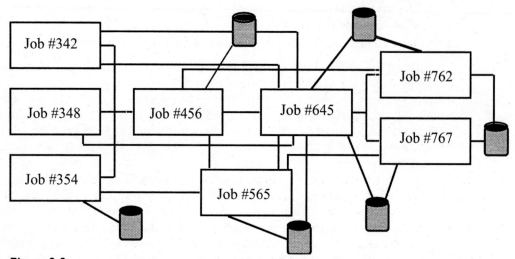

Figure 2.3
Multiple business units run dozens of jobs with hundreds of steps on a daily and nightly basis.

Figure 2.3 depicts a small cross-section of a series of batch jobs that might execute on a daily or nightly basis. Batch jobs typically receive and process data from online programs. Within each job step, many steps may need to execute to complete the sequence of tasks required by that job. These steps typically include a mixture of application edit, update, sorting, and reporting steps running throughout a system. Many companies have dozens of business units with dozens of systems that execute hundreds or even thousands of job steps every day.

Online architectures are even more difficult to track. While batch systems run on a planned schedule, online programs run on demand. If this was all there was to it, the management, enhancement, and transformation of these architectures would not be a big deal. Several factors, however, further complicate legacy information architectures.

- **Fragmentation**

  Functions are split across multiple legacy online and batch processing environments. This means that there are multiple systems that deal with differing aspects of customer issues, supply and distribution management, administration, and a host of other business functions. It often requires humans or special reconciliation jobs to consolidate or rectify discrepancies found across different applications. Some enterprises do not even bother to reconcile non-mission-critical results.

* **Redundancy**

  Different application systems perform the same or similar functions against the same or similar data in different business units. This can result from mergers, mismanagement, or any number of other historic factors within business units or IT. These redundancies may get reconciled within executive reporting systems, but typically they are left to the business user or even the customer to decipher.

* **Technical Diversity**

  A given company may be using dozens of different pieces of hardware, languages, databases, teleprocessing monitors, and utilities within the same computing environment. Technical diversity results in interface challenges in addition to the need to staff a cross-section of projects on different platforms. Technical diversity can also spawn design diversity.

* **Design Diversity**

  Differing designs are actually more problematic than technical diversity. For example, one application may key activity on a customer, while a second system with similar functionality may key activity on the product being used by that customer. This is one of the underlying inflexibilities that complicate integration and enhancement efforts.

* **Timing**

  Legacy systems do not reflect changes in a timeframe that is conducive to user business requirements. Most legacy systems started as batch environments that were enhanced to incorporate certain online functions. These online functions, however, still rely on a any number of batch jobs to run in the background to edit, update, reconcile, and report on activities from the prior day, month, quarter, or year.

* **Size**

  Many legacy application architectures are very large. Most companies disclosed the size of their application software portfolios during year 2000 preparations. A small enterprise may have up to 10 million lines of software, while mid-sized companies may have up to 50 million lines of code. It is not unusual for a large company or government agency to have hundreds of millions of lines of code. General Motors, for example, has stated that it had over 1 billion lines of software. These are numbers that most humans have difficult envisioning.

When one couples all of the factors within a given enterprise, the legacy application architecture challenge becomes very difficult to manage. The combination of issues in a large application software portfolio, combined with differing cross-functional business demands, drive many executives to the point where they want to see the legacy issue disappear entirely.

Many of the above issues deal with design and structural issues within the architecture when viewed from a cross-functional perspective. One of the biggest challenges at a more granular level, however, is the separation of program logic into three main areas based on the role that logic plays within an individual program.

- **Presentation Handling Logic**

  Presentation logic is responsible for controlling all program input and output processing. In a new system, for example, this would be isolated to special routines that would clearly handle any user interface functionality. In legacy systems, presentation-handling logic is typically embedded in the application program. A CICS program, for example, dedicates major portions of source code to building screen content, issuing screen input-output (IO) calls, and checking to see if the screen issuance process worked correctly. While cumbersome, CICS programmers can typically find their way through this type of logic. Junior programmers have a much harder time. Older UNIX systems, the Unisys V Series, certain Bull systems, and many other legacy source programs can contain even more convoluted logic that is strictly dedicated to communicating with the user of the system.

- **Data Access Logic**

  Another type of logic found in legacy programs deals with obtaining or updating data. Data can be stored in a permanent data file or database, or it can be written to a temporary file. Extensive data manipulation logic can be found in application software using the IBM IMS database. Legacy programmers think nothing of making multiple calls to access a given segment (record) of this hierarchical database. IMS is very common, very efficient, and processes billions of dollars of transactional data everyday. Data access logic is strewn across numerous programs, including those that access relational databases. IMS, by the way, is not a worst-case scenario. Other environments can be even more confusing and do not always use the readily recognizable naming conventions found in IMS programs. Relational data access routines, along with their error handling routines, are also embedded in most legacy programs—although relational systems are a little easier to decipher.

- **Business Logic**

  Program logic that impacts business data is called a business rule or business logic. By varying estimates, business logic comprises up to –30 percent of the source code in a given system. Some programs have very little business logic, while other programs have a higher percentage. Differentiating business logic is difficult because it can be interwoven with data access or presentation logic. It is also difficult because a programmer may not be able to differentiate business data from data used by data access logic or presentation logic. This is particularly true in lower-level languages like Assembler. In a worst-case scenario, business logic might be buried in a combination of complex tables, where interlocking values from different tables drive business decisions.

Business logic may determine whether or not to even invoke a program. This occurs when program Calling logic, job control language (JCL) or a similar facility is set up to determine when other programs, batch jobs, or online transactions should be triggered. When this occurs across diverse technical environments, such as a distributed network application triggering a CICS transaction, analysts can very quickly lose track of what is happening.

Unfortunately, differentiating what constitutes presentation handling, data access, and business logic is difficult because it is all mixed together within large, complex programs and systems. When coupled with fragmentation, redundancy, design and technical diversity, and size factors, it can be difficult to discern business rule logic across even smaller operating environments. In other words, deciphering legacy application architectures is difficult in the best of circumstances.

2.8 Data Architecture Challenges

To this point, I have discussed hardware and software architectures, with an emphasis on the complexities found within legacy application architectures. The other factor to be considered when discussing legacy architectures involves data. Data tends to be more static than the applications that act upon that data and is defined in large databases or older data structures called files. While senior analysts can decipher the meaning of a specific data element based on how it is used within a given system, many data architectures are complex and highly diverse when viewed from an enterprise perspective.

As shown in Figure 2.2, legacy data stores evolved in parallel with legacy applications. As such, legacy data shares many of the diverse challenges found within legacy application architectures. Early data was not even stored on traditional disk drives but was rather placed on punch cards, paper tape, or other ancient media. As storage technology evolved, data was placed onto magnetic storage media. Files were stored on magnetic tapes, on cartridges, or on early disk drives. Many file formats still use the old 80-byte (a unit of computer storage) record format, reflecting restrictions that originated with the 80-column punch card.

Data management has evolved considerably over the decades. File management grew more sophisticated during the 1960s and 1970s. Early files could be read only in a sequential order—beginning to end. Later file formats allowed programs to access specific records through the use of a key—such as a customer number, part number, or order number. Indexed files became very efficient, but business requirements drove computer scientists to devise more flexible ways to store data. This research resulted in the concept of the database.

Databases are large collections of data arranged in a way that makes information more accessible to the business user. Data in a database is keyed in varying ways so business users and programs can access data on demand. Databases can be hierarchical, like the IMS database; networked, like the IDMS database; or organized based on other design principles or access methods. Data in a database is typically designed so that it aligns well with a variety of business requirements. Early databases did not achieve this goal to the degree that modern databases have.

For example, an IMS "parent segment" might define data unique to an order, while its children would define data items or elements subordinate to that order. A single order, for example, may encompass multiple order items, each of which in turn becomes a child under that order parent. While this data design may work well for the order entry system, it is unlikely to work well for other systems or business units. The order database, for example, probably does not communicate very well with the inventory or customer database.

The majority of older databases are not flexible enough to accommodate a wide variety of future, highly unpredictable user requirements. The introduction of relational databases changed how data could relate to other data and introduced more flexible ways to store and access business data. Relational designs tied information together in ways that reflected real-world relationships and allowed systems to access that data in very flexible ways using sequential calls in a structured query language (SQL).

In spite of the fact that SQL has become a universally agreed upon data access language for relational databases, countless legacy data structures, using archaic and highly inflexible design and implementation styles, continue to run in organizations today. The main reason for this is that a great deal of enterprise data is aligned with legacy application designs and therefore is inaccessible to other systems that do not share those designs. Some programs even define data using internal, hard-coded tables unique to that program. This is a common phenomenon with location codes, part numbers, or other data that programmers felt would not change very often. A number of programmers even embedded hard-coded data within the program logic. These are worst-case examples of how data can be locked into the application architecture.

Other data designs in old file structures may be implied. Many sequential tape files, for example, store multiple record types. Deciphering record types can be impossible without examining the program logic that can determine one type of data record from another. Much of this data represents critical enterprise knowledge that is needed to fulfill various customer and other core business functions.

Data architectures in any given enterprise are made up of a wide variety of legacy files, databases, and embedded data. Data is typically scattered across multiple hardware platforms and physical locations, and stored in proprietary or cryptic formats. Data architecture challenges are summarized as follows.

- **Redundancy**

  Legacy data tends to be redundantly defined across a labyrinth of applications, hardware platforms, and business units. A major bank had 11 major implementations of customer data across various business units. Each database contained unique and overlapping customer name, address, history data, and related information. Mobilizing special customer programs was extremely difficult given that the level of redundancy was both significant and undeterminable.

- **Fragmentation**

  Legacy data in many organizations has historically been maintained in piecemeal fashion. Order data relies on accurate inventory data, but this information may be defined in separate and incompatible data structures. Fragmentation, coupled with incompatibility, complicates integration efforts essential to e-business, customer, and related initiatives.

- **Integrity**

  If a data element contains data that is not valid in any business scenario, the data has an integrity problem. An assessment of telephone numbers at a directory company determined that the phone number field contained thousands of records with spaces or other invalid values. Phone number integrity was the mainstay of this company's business. When IT was notified of the problem, it was not concerned about it. When the invalid phone numbers were brought to the attention of the business team, however, they were quite upset. IT tends to ignore data integrity issues until business users, customers, or business partners demand resolution.

  E-business, for example, is opening data up to third parties that never had direct access to internal information. If this data is wrong and a third party makes a decision that results in harm to its company or to another third party, an enterprise may face potential legal risks. Data integrity is a major problem in organizations today that executives need to focus on or face very serious downstream consequences.

- **Semantics and Consistency**

  Ensuring that data is consistently used across an enterprise and through relationships that now extend to customers, distributors, and suppliers is a major challenge. There are numerous examples of situations where different business units or third parties apply different meanings to the same data. A bank could not agree on the definition of a customer, a phone company could not agree on the definition of a phone number, and a hardware manufacturer could not agree on the definition of a unit sold. A lack of concurrence on the meaning of data across the virtual enterprise is a major roadblock to data integration and architecture consolidation.

- **Accessibility**

  In many cases, disparate customer and supplier data cannot be accessed, rationalized, and consolidated quickly enough to accommodate the speed of the Internet without significant back-end retooling. Customer, supplier, and new market requirements have elevated the need to address legacy architecture accessibility. Organizations will need to consider ways in which they can improve cross-functional data accessibility as e-business and other requirements continue to grow.

- **Flexibility**

  Fragmentation, redundancy, a lack of integrity, and inconsistency have resulted in inflexible data architectures that impede strategic business initiatives. This lack of flexibility is also driven by data design and platform inconsistencies common in legacy environments. Projects aimed at increasing data flexibility must be driven by and based on the criticality of the business requirements using that data.

- **Security**

  One area gaining increased attention involves multiple sign-on windows and passwords for security clearance. This is common in enterprises with multidimensional systems, networks, Internet environments, and users. Each user may need five to six passwords, causing them to have to sign on many times to get to a given system. While this problem appears to be a security issue, this is really a directory services, data management problem that should be addressed as such.

Many efforts to address each of the above data architecture challenges tend to focus on only one aspect of the problem or be limited to a specific business unit or project need. Data architectures have broad impact across an enterprise, and that is why any project addressing a data-related requirement should view each of these challenges in aggregate.

CRM is one high-profile business initiative that relies extensively on the consistency, integrity, and accessibility of enterprise data. According to one recent study, more than 75 percent of enterprises engaged in CRM initiatives cannot combine a comprehensive view of a customer with actionable, personalized advice to customer service and sales agents [9].

Other studies also cite CRM data integrity and reliability issues. These concerns reiterate the fact that data architectures lack the consistency, integrity, and accessibility required by business-driven initiatives such as CRM. If organizations continue to sidestep serious data architecture issues, particularly issues related to integrity, consistency, redundancy, and fragmentation, it will impact their ability to attract and retain customers.

2.9 Systems Management, Maintenance, and Outsourcing

Managing and maintaining legacy applications and data structures involve numerous, seemingly mundane activities. Maintenance can be considered the "care and feeding" of legacy systems. Just as a car needs regular oil changes due to ongoing use, legacy architectures require periodic fixes or enhancements to keep them current with ongoing business requirements.

Transformation, on the other hand, focuses on more strategic activities. Much of the analysis gathered and the tools used by a transformation project can also be applied to leverage maintenance activities. Managing, maintaining, and outsourcing application systems preserve the status quo within an IT environment. Transformation's goal, on the other hand, is to reach beyond the status quo.

Software maintenance has been going on since the first system hit production and required a change of some sort. Decades of changes by countless IT professionals have made many systems harder to understand and maintain. These are the same factors that complicate transformation projects.

The main issue with software maintenance involves people. Retaining and keeping personnel resources with the ability to understand, change, and test legacy systems is becoming a major issue for IT. Gartner Inc. estimated that the total number of COBOL professionals in the United States stood at 90,000 in early 2001. This number was estimated to be shrinking at a rate of 14 percent annually [1]. If this estimate is anywhere close to accurate, organizations will see continued attrition in the skills and related ability to effectively maintain and transform legacy application architectures.

Executives have always been unhappy with the time and cost associated with software maintenance. In response, numerous projects have been undertaken to replace systems with new systems or packaged applications. These efforts have not made a major dent in the maintenance challenge, so executives have outsourced application management and maintenance to third parties.

IT and application outsourcing is escalating with a focus on shifting application management to vendors while utilizing inhouse personnel on new projects, such as those deploying e-business initiatives. Executives should consider that outsourcing can complicate e-business integration and legacy transformation initiatives. Integration and transformation projects can be accommodated, however, if careful thought is given to how the outsourcing contract can facilitate architecture integration and transformation. For example, outsourcing can be incorporated into overall transformation strategies with work being divided between inhouse and offsite project teams.

One issue that transformation should ultimately help address is the difficulty of managing and maintaining application systems. Executives should keep this

in mind when initiating new development projects because application maintenance will always be a fact of life regardless of the type of system deployed or
technology used in a given development effort.

2.10 Application Architecture's Impact on Business Initiatives

Legacy application and data architectures can have a direct impact on an organization's ability to thrive and survive in highly competitive, fast-moving markets.
The following examples cite just a few of the challenges facing various industries
and government sectors.

- **Financial Institutions**

  Chapter 1 cited some of the high-profile problems encountered by Citibank
  and JPMorgan Chase. To enhance customer confidence, companies such as
  Charles Schwab, Wells Fargo, Morgan Stanley, and USB PaineWebber are
  spending millions of dollars to update computer systems. Lower-profile
  problems at SunTrust Banks and TD Waterhouse respectively have impacted
  balance of accounts statements and customer service [10].

  Financial institutions, particularly as they continue to merge or be acquired,
  are facing tremendous pressures to integrate, Web-enable, and upgrade
  legacy applications and data structures. As discussed in Chapter 1, a great
  deal of this activity is being driven by the push for these companies to move
  into new and more dynamic markets. Because financial institutions understand that these systems cut to the core of their business, they are willing to
  invest in these initiatives. But money alone will not correct fragmentation,
  redundancies, and other issues associated with 20- to 25-year-old legacy
  architectures.

  A legacy transformation strategy is needed to create a phase reconciliation of
  these applications and databases and begin to move them into an architecture that is more conducive to the changes impacting 21st-century financial
  markets.

- **Telecommunications**

  Telecommunication firms are as susceptible to the impact of legacy architectures on business initiatives as any industry. Telephone companies introduced computers into their business early in the cycle, and regulated industries tended to have more convoluted and less structured information architectures than their unregulated counterparts. With the 1983 AT&T divestiture,
  recent consolidation of a number of RBOCs, and the move to broadband and
  wireless technology, these architectures will become a major obstacle.

Redundant billing, customer information, maintenance, and a host of other systems will slow many firms from being able to access and redeploy data assets under a host of new marketing and product initiatives. These companies may seek easy answers, such as just moving every region to the same customer information system, but the RBOCs have applied extensive customization at the state and regional levels to make this solution work.

While some executives may believe that the cost of maintaining and upgrading these legacy architectures is the biggest problem they face, the real challenges lie in how to invest in and transform these systems to make them valuable assets while evolving into integrated, global providers of telecommunication services.

- **Energy and Utilities**

  While the energy industry undergoes the efforts to deregulate, one unforeseen situation arose recently to highlight some of the challenges facing this industry. The Texas Electric Reliability Council, a nonprofit overseen by the Public Utility Commission (PUC) of Texas, collects and maintains all customer data. This company, which is the broker for wholesale electricity buyers and sellers, created an application and database to manage this process and is now facing integration problems with third-party systems [11].

  The fact that this organization is facing these problems is curious given that the specifications for this system should have accommodated integration as an essential function. This "new" legacy system (it is in production and therefore meets the criteria for being a legacy system) is facing the same data exchange issues many other legacy systems face.

  As the utility and energy industries undergo many of the changes cited in Chapter 1, they must ensure that legacy applications and data structures do not stifle efforts to create, move, and deliver energy more effectively. Because some power providers are facing significant financial problems, particularly where deregulation resulted in unforeseen rate fluctuations, they may slow IT investments needed to streamline and leverage legacy applications and data. Legacy data structures and applications, created when a power producer also delivered that power to the customer, are likely to slow deregulation and other market shifts into more specialized aspects of this industry. Management must therefore evaluate and pursue strategic investments in legacy architectures commensurate with ongoing industry requirements.

- **Healthcare**

  The Health Insurance Portability and Accountability Act (HIPAA), which went into effect in 1996, is a major challenge for healthcare organizations. The Administrative Simplification provision, for example, is aimed at streamlining the healthcare system through electronic data interchange

(EDI) and protecting the confidentiality of a person's healthcare information. Failure to comply could result in penalties, which include fines up to $250,000 and imprisonment for willful intent to sell healthcare information. Compliance dates begin coming due in 2002 and run out through 2004. Some of the impacts include

- Requirement for unique identification numbers for individuals, employers, health plans, payers, and providers of healthcare.
- Increased security, encryption, and audit capabilities of patient information.

The ability of the healthcare system to respond to bioterrorism threats also puts IT to the test. Patient data, for example, contains much of the intelligence needed to spot trends by comparing symptoms across a base of patients. The collaborative tools are not in place, however, to share this information across a national base of healthcare providers. Much work is still required to upgrade infrastructures to deal with these issues [12].

Other factors facing the healthcare industry include reliability of critical patient information. For example, the average hospital has 25 different record systems, most of which are unique to a given department. Data spread across these systems has, on average, a 10 percent error rate [9]. Data errors at a hospital can be a very serious problem, given that a person's health may be at stake. Healthcare providers face a wealth of other legacy challenges, including widespread proliferation of nonstandard and departmental systems that need to be standardized to accurately reflect patient and payer information.

- **Retail and Travel Industries**

The retail industry and the travel industry have a few things in common. Both must deal with consumers, were hit hard in the recent economic downturn, and must find new ways to gather customer intelligence. One example of these requirements comes from Hyatt Hotels. Hyatt is attempting to achieve greater recognition of the customer across the enterprise, improve marketing based on customer-driven preferences, and increase customer convenience through online access to special offers [13].

Both industries also need to upgrade and integrate field-based computing environments and ensure that data being collected and distributed is effectively consolidated and of the highest integrity. With cost cutting occurring at many of these organizations, they will be looking to IT to streamline business processes through better data integration and better access to online information. IT remains key to the success of these industries.

- **Manufacturing**

Corning was running nine incompatible manufacturing systems, each of which stored information on various products and processes. Difficulties in creating a consolidated view of this information caused one engineer to use the term *data jail* [14]. Manufacturing companies face many of the same legacy architecture limitations as other industries and need to find solutions as margins get tighter and competition gets tougher.

Supply and distribution chain management activities are forcing manufacturers to invest in integration efforts driven by larger conglomerates or industry consortia. These initiatives, which require sharing information over the Web, require major data integration, redundancy and inconsistency elimination, and potential data clean-up efforts. Consolidating and streamlining the systems and databases in many manufacturing firms, particularly those that grew through acquisition strategies, are a major legacy transformation undertaking. Some integration tools offer interim support for these activities, but taking shortcuts to achieving consolidated views of high-integrity data will eventually fail to achieve the business requirements driving these efforts.

One other major factor facing manufacturing firms is the integration of legacy systems and partially deployed ERP systems. Most companies that battled through an ERP implementation (versus those that just canceled their projects entirely) achieved only partial deployment. One high-profile failure occurred at Hershey, where a $112 million ERP implementation resulted in shipping delays and deliveries of incomplete orders. This in turn caused Hershey's profits to drop 19 percent in one quarter [15]. Companies deploying ERP systems will need to seek new transformation options for assessing and deploying these systems while creating new hybrid architectures where inhouse and packaged applications can coexist with e-business applications.

- **Small- to Mid-Size Companies**

  Small-to-mid-sized enterprises (SMEs) are not exempt from legacy architecture issues. While IT infrastructure investments at these organizations have traditionally been smaller, many of these companies are still running older applications on small mainframes, mid-range systems, or network environments. Even these smaller applications can manage relatively large legacy data structures. Challenges for these companies include

  - Integrating redundant functionality across standalone locations.
  - Creating interface formats for exchanging information with suppliers or distributors.
  - Mining knowledge from legacy databases to launch new customer programs.
  - Migrating from unsupported hardware and software platforms due to cost considerations.

- Transforming systems from older, proprietary languages to systems that support more flexible business requirements.

Solutions for the SME may vary due to budgetary or resource considerations, but a smaller enterprise can still be hurt by the limitations imposed by legacy architectures.

- **Governments**

  Federal, state, and local governments are probably facing some of the greatest legacy architecture transformation challenges. This includes integrating information across agencies, consolidating operations from multiple command and control environments, migrating from highly proprietary computing environments and databases that have limited flexibility, and cutting costs while leveraging existing resources.

  Complicating this situation is the fact that most civilian and defense agencies evolved as large, stovepipe bureaucracies, each possessing a unique management and computing infrastructure. Cost-cutting measures are forcing an ongoing consolidation of many agencies. In addition to this, a number of intelligence agencies are under extreme pressure to consolidate information in an attempt to coordinate their operations more effectively.

  Projects to share and consolidate intelligence data among the U.S. Department of Defense (DOD) and various security agencies are either planned or under way. Transformation strategies will be required to control the level of expenditures, reduce the risks, and increase the potential of success associated with each of these efforts.

2.11 Historical Attempts to Address Legacy Architecture Issues

Frustration has been the primary result of numerous projects associated with efforts to replace, redesign, integrate, or upgrade legacy application and data architectures. Many of these issues stem from ill-conceived deployment plans that ignored the need to understand, migrate, reuse, or in other ways accommodate legacy architectures. Below are a number of the options that organizations have pursued to limited success.

- **Application Rewrites**

  The industry is rife with stories about failed replacement projects, although few organizations choose to air their failures in public. These projects have typically attempted to rewrite complex legacy applications using 4GLs, CASE tools, C, C++, and most recently, Java. The vast majority of these efforts failed to examine the intelligence embedded in legacy architectures. Results included

- Systems that did not come close to what the user needed.
- Partial implementations that replicated but did not eliminate a portion of the legacy system.
- Systems that missed the vast majority of functionality that the users assumed would be carried over from the existing applications.
- Missing data that was never included in the new design and discovered during the system implementation.
- Total failure to implement any type of replacement system.

Most IT organizations now try to avoid total rewrites because of the inability of current staff to replicate core application and data functionality that support critical business operations on a daily basis. Replacing a system is a conceptually valid concept, but doing so without recognizing and reusing legacy architectural components as input to the design process is not. Ways to achieve strategic information architectures that incorporate legacy reuse and phased deployment will be addressed in later chapters.

- **Business Process Reengineering (BPR)**

BPR has been deployed to streamline business processes within and across business units. While the goal was worthy, IT was brought into the project too late. Ironically, while businesses found that retooling legacy business processes was a useful endeavor, IT never pursued the retooling of legacy applications that needed to accompany these projects for them to succeed.

BPI offers new tools, new approaches, and new opportunities that allow BPR efforts to leverage legacy transformation tools and techniques. This will ensure that business process retooling is synchronized with the retooling of legacy application and data architectures.

- **ERP Application Implementation**

Buying and installing a package may be a good approach to migrating away from legacy applications. This strategy only works, however, if there is

- An analysis of the current environment.
- Determination of strategic system requirements.
- A mapping of the requirements and the legacy system against the ERP system.
- Determination if the ERP option is valid.
- A deployment plan based on the delta between the selected package and the legacy information architecture.

Ultimately, an ERP deployment project must know which functions to implement, which legacy functions to reuse, which ERP functions should not be implemented, which legacy functions need to be deactivated, and how the data should be transformed.

- **Data Warehouse Deployment**

  In an effort to make a wide range of legacy data available to a greater number of users, organizations created data warehouses. The data warehouse concept collects and consolidates legacy data into user-friendly formats and offers greater data accessibility to a wider number of users. This is all accomplished without requiring the redesign of a large number of legacy data structures and application systems. Data warehouses are useful and will be discussed as part of a transformation option in later chapters. The data warehouse does not eliminate the need for having or deploying a transformation strategy to deal with legacy data architectures.

- **Adding New Front Ends to Legacy Systems**

  Putting new user front ends on legacy applications was an attempt to make legacy systems more palatable to business and external users. This approach has been compared to putting a new coat of paint on a rusted out car. The theory behind this concept was to link or mimic poorly integrated system functionality and data under distributed, pull-down/pop-up menu systems. Many of these efforts provided interim value by allowing users to access legacy functions and data, but only offered the illusion of integration.

  This is because legacy applications only perform a subset of a given function from the view of that particular system. The legacy system itself is not integrated, and neither is the data being accessed by that system. Another problem is the ripple effect of future changes on this new composite system. When legacy functions or data undergo a structural change, these interfaces will be disrupted. This will in turn increase the maintenance burden for people working on this system.

- **EAI Projects**

  As discussed in Chapter 1, EAI projects use a noninvasive approach to creating an integrated view of a legacy environment. This approach has value if there is a near-term need to add back-end functionality to a Web-based application. EAI does not replace the need to build and deploy a legacy transformation strategy, but could provide a model from which a Web-enabled architecture might best serve the business community.

There are variations on the above projects that have been used in the past to address the legacy challenge. Outsourcing was not included in the above list because it does not actually impact the legacy environment other than to keep it functioning while IT seeks other options. Any or all of the above options could be valid under certain conditions, but most of these approaches need to leverage legacy architectures as a part of the solution—if those projects want to increase their odds of success.

2.12 Addressing the Legacy Architecture Challenge

The modern enterprise relies on aging software built before the emergence of the Internet. These architectures embody core business knowledge that is hard to decipher, difficult to enhance, and impossible to replicate. This presents a direct challenge to organizations that must continually enhance, integrate, and transform information architectures to thrive in a competitive climate.

Historically, little formal analysis of legacy environments has been applied to the planning and analysis of replacement projects. If a new system actually does make it into production, it usually ends up running in parallel with one or more mainframe systems that already perform many of the same functions. Manual reconciliation of replicated functions and redundant data have added additional tasks to already complex IT environments. The end-user situation, in this scenario, degrades, and executive management then responds by renewing discussions to outsource IT to a third party.

If management wants to change this situation, it should begin to examine transformation strategies to augment critical IT projects. This requires an understanding of legacy architectures and a plan of how to proceed. Ultimately, organizations relying on legacy systems must employ a coordinated approach to managing, integrating, and evolving them—otherwise, they will fail to meet critical business requirements and leverage powerful new information technologies.

Notes

1. "From the Dustbin, Cobol Rises," Stephanie Wilkinson, *eWeek*, May 28, 2001.
2. "The Evolution of CICS: 30 Years Old and Still Modern," T. Scott Ankrum, *The COBOL Report,*
3. "21st Century Semiconductor Manufacturing Capabilities," Eugene S. Meieran, *Intel Technology Journal*, Q4 1998.
4. "Cutter Statistics Newsletter," Vol. 3, No. 1, Jennifer Lichtman, Feb. 27, 2001.
5. "HP Discontinues E3000 Servers," Martin J. Garvey, *InformationWeek*, Nov. 14, 2001.
6. "Aging Technologies," Kathleen O'Connor, *oreview.com*, Vol. 3, No. 2, Mar. 1997.
7. "Partial List of People Important to Software History," [Online], *http://www.softwarehistory.org/people.htm*, 2001.
8. "Who Is to Blame for ERP Failure?" Barry Calogero, *serverworldmagazine.com*, June 2001.
9. "CRM Plagued by Data Quality Issues," Paul Krill, *InfoWorld*, Oct. 5, 2001.
10. "Financial Giants Push to Revamp Their Outdated Computer Systems," Jathon Sapsford and Paul Beckett, *Wall Street Journal*, Sept. 7, 2001.

11. "IT 'Hiccups' Could Slow Energy Deregulation in Texas," Rick Whiting, *Information Week,* Sept. 10, 2001.
12. "Get Well, Fast," Marianne Kolbasuk McGee, *Information Week,* Nov. 19, 2001.
13. "Hyatt Opts For All-in-One Approach," Cheryl Rosen, *Information Week,* Sept. 10, 2001.
14. "Corning Plans to Free Information from Data Jail," Tone Gonsalves, *Information Week,* Sept. 10, 2001.
15. "Failed ERP Gamble Haunts Hershey," Craig Stedman, *Computerworld,* Nov. 1, 1999.

The Changing Face of Information Technology

IT is on the cusp of a new era. The way in which we define, build, and deploy application systems is changing, and the implications are significant. Distributed architectures, object-oriented design, component reuse, modern languages, the open systems movement, collaborative development, agile methodologies, and improved tools open up new opportunities for IT.

Successfully deploying emerging technologies and development disciplines promises to expedite an enterprise's ability to deliver more value to customers, internal users, and suppliers. If deployed effectively, businesses and governments will benefit significantly from e-business deployment, retooled information architectures, improved design and development processes, reuse, better collaboration, and an increasing acceptance of industry-wide standards.

The success of these new technologies and disciplines relies on maximizing business involvement and synchronizing deployment with a legacy architecture transformation strategy. The business community, including third-party participants, must be fully engaged in architecture design and deployment. Legacy architectures must also be incorporated into a long-term deployment strategy because the bulk of revenue and data still flows through legacy applications. Legacy transformation tasks, depending on the scenario, must be built into analysis, design, construction, reuse, and implementation activities.

This chapter discusses the breadth of new technologies and related opportunities that IT and business units have at their disposal and will need to incorporate into strategic transformation initiatives.

3.1 The E-Business Movement—Driving New Technology Deployment

E-business is here to stay. According to Strategic Focus research findings [1], over 37 percent of all software applications used Internet technologies in the year 2000. This number was projected to rise to over 41 percent by 2002. We should not read too much into these statistics. While Web-based applications are growing in number, most new applications still rely on legacy systems and data to deliver value. A better measure of the Web's impact on application architectures is the amount of revenue flowing through or resulting from Web-based versus legacy applications.

Related findings from the Strategic Focus study provide additional insight into the impact of the Web on IT and business. The study found that corporate priorities are focused on customer service, order processing, e-commerce, and manufacturing. Customer service and revenue generation continue to be the focus as e-business spreads throughout a cross-section of industries. These findings indicate that Web-based applications are proliferating while customer and revenue-driven initiatives are increasingly important to most organizations.

A second study emphasized the impact of e-business based on corporate spending. According to a Cutter Consortium study, 73 percent of respondents said that e-business spending has remained steady or increased. Another 87 percent felt that e-business was critical to the long-term success of their business. Over half the companies in a related Cutter survey stated that their e-business development plans were on the rise [2]. With e-business priorities likely to remain strong, the push to create more Web-based applications will continue over the long term.

Many organizations are seeking answers as to how this will be accomplished. The answer lies in how well they can link business requirements to their IT strategy—and this relies on their information architecture.

3.2 The Information Architecture Framework

An enterprise's information architecture is the framework through which IT defines and deploys hardware, communication capabilities, application systems, integration technologies, and data. Architecture has several key components that include the functional architecture, the data architecture, and the technical architecture. All three are important, yet IT teams have a tendency to focus on the technical architecture to the exclusion of creating a framework for the functional and data architectures. A comprehensive architecture strategy ensures that

- Applications are designed to interact effectively and efficiently to support current and unforeseen business requirements.
- Data is organized in a way that facilitates an infinite variety of business demands within a flexible business model.

- Technology supporting the functional and data design is appropriate within the context of the environment.
- Software, communication, network, and hardware infrastructures fully support functional objectives.
- Processes and standards are defined and utilized where appropriate.
- The overall architecture is flexible enough to withstand ongoing changes in business requirements and emerging technologies.

Historically, information architectures were limited by the bounds of the enterprise and were more implicit than explicit. The complexities in today's IT organization have changed all that. Strategic information architectures must now accommodate internal and external users, applications, networks, and data. They must also be flexible enough to incorporate dynamic shifts in external and internal business and technical requirements.

Just as an architect creates plans for engineers and construction personnel who are building a physical structure, information architects provide a similar service to IT designers and builders. Having a formal framework that defines the enterprise information architecture provides

- Shared understanding of business functionality and data usage across the virtual enterprise.
- A baseline from which applications can be deployed or integrated in a coordinated fashion.
- Context for performing business-driven process and information modeling.
- Understanding of how business models drive the creation of functional IT and data models.
- The capability for planners and business owners to communicate and exchange requirements with IT.
- The ability for IT to understand and respond to dynamic business impacts on the IT environment.

A general framework for strategic information architectures has existed for years, although few organizations have deployed this framework with any degree of long-term commitment. This is due to a lack of collaboration across business and IT units, as well as shortsightedness among executives who feel that "techies" should solve strategic information problems on their own. This must change if an enterprise wishes to successfully leverage emerging technologies.

The Zachman framework (see Figure 3.1) defines a series of views describing how business planners and owners envision IT requirements as well as how designers and developers view a logical or physical implementation of those same requirements.

Note that this framework does not suggest a return to the idealistic vision of information engineering (IE) imposed on IT during the 1980s and 1990s. IE promoted a "plan-based" approach to information environments that assumed the

Enterprise Architecture—A Framework™

	DATA *What*	FUNCTION *How*	NETWORK *Where*	PEOPLE *Who*	TIME *When*	MOTIVATION *Why*	
SCOPE (CONTEXTUAL)	List of Things Important to the Business	List of Processes the Business Performs	List of Locations in which the Business Operates	List of Organizations Important to the Business	List of Events/Cycles Significant to the Business	List of Business Goals/Stratgies	SCOPE (CONTEXTUAL)
Planner	ENTITY = Class of Business	Process = Class of Business Process	Node = Major Business Location	People = Major Organization Unit	Time = Major Business Event/Cycle	Ends/Means = Major Business Goal/Strategy	*Planner*
BUSINESS MODEL (CONCEPTUAL)	e.g. Semantic Model	e.g. Business Process Model	e.g. Business Logistics System	e.g. Work Flow Model	e.g. Master Schedule	e.g. Business Plan	BUSINESS MODEL (CONCEPTUAL)
Owner	Ent = Business Entity Reln = Business Relationship	Proc. = Business Process I/O = Business Resources	Node = Business Location Link = Business Linkage	People = Organization Unit Work = Work Product	Time = Business Event Cycle = Business Cycle	End = Business Objective Means = Business Strategy	*Owner*
SYSTEM MODEL (LOGICAL)	e.g. Logical Data Model	e.g. Application Architecture	e.g. Distributed System Architecture	e.g. Human Interface Architecture	e.g. Processing Structure	e.g. Business Rule Model	SYSTEM MODEL (LOGICAL)
Designer	Ent = Data Entity Reln = Data Relationship	Proc. = Application Function I/O = User Views	Node = I/S Function (Processor, Storage, etc) Link = Line Characteristics	People = Role Work = Deliverable	Time = System Event Cycle = Processing Cycle	End = Structural Assertion Means = Action Assertion	*Designer*
TECHNOLOGY MODEL (PHYSICAL)	e.g. Physical Data Model	e.g. System Design	e.g. Technology Architecture	e.g. Presentation Architecture	e.g. Control Structure	e.g. Rule Design	TECHNOLOGY MODEL (PHYSICAL)
Builder	Ent = Segment/Table/etc. Reln = Pointer/Key/etc.	Proc.= Computer Function I/O = Data Elements/Sets	Node = Hardware/Systems Software Link = Line Specifications	People = User Work = Screen Format	Time = Execute Cycle = Component Cycle	End = Condition Means = Action	*Builder*
DETAILED REPRESEN- TATIONS (OUT-OF- CONTEXT)	e.g. Data Definition	e.g. Program	e.g. Network Architecture	e.g. Security Architecture	e.g. Timing Definition	e.g. Rule Specification	DETAILED REPRESEN- TATIONS (OUT-OF- CONTEXT)
Sub- Contractor	Ent = Field Reln = Address	Proc.= Language Statement I/O = Control Block	Node = Address Link = Protocol	People = Identity Work = Job	Time = Interrupt Cycle = Machine Cycle	End = Sub-condition Means = Step	*Sub- Contractor*
FUNCTIONING ENTERPRISE	e.g. DATA	e.g. FUNCTION	e.g. NETWORK	e.g. ORGANIZATION	e.g. SCHEDULE	e.g. STRATEGY	FUNCTIONING ENTERPRISE

Figure 3.1

The Zachman framework maps business and IT views of the enterprise.
(Source: John A. Zachman, Zachman International.)

existence of a "right" way to build systems based on an "end-state" vision. This end-state vision is continuously disrupted by the fluidity of changes in business processes and requirements determined by the ongoing impact of customers, distributors, and suppliers [3].

An architectural framework, unlike IE, provides the *context* for defining and deploying business, data, and technical design models; it does not tell an organization *how* to build and deploy those models. Another difference between architectural frameworks and IE is that a framework does not imply or assume that everything will be interconnected at an enterprise level. This is important because no organization that adopted IE ever achieved the end-state vision promoted by IE idealists well over a decade ago.

While architectural frameworks are not idealistic visions, they also have not been emphasized as a major business-IT theme. One impediment to successful architecture deployment is legacy infrastructures built in a non-architected, nonintegrated fashion [4]. Information architectures must therefore incorporate the following considerations.

- Representations used by business analysts must be separate and distinct from those used by application and data analysts.
- Broad recognition of the value of reuse must permeate all representations of the functional, data, and technical definitions of the information architecture.
- An understanding of virtual data requirements is needed along with knowledge of how those requirements map to or translate into current and future data structures.
- A general understanding of how application functionality should be deployed to meet business requirements is essential to ensure individual project success.
- A means for reconciling legacy environments with the ideal information architecture is required and must include mappings between legacy data, functionality, and technical deployment.
- Flexibility is needed so new technologies and functional requirements do not invalidate the architectural framework but only result in revisions to definitions within that framework.

Modern functional, data, and technical architectural requirements differ from past requirements because of changes in business demands and Web-driven technologies. This magnifies the present need for information architectures.

3.3 Data Architecture—Defining the Essence of the Enterprise

Data defines the essence of the enterprise. Business rules or logic act upon data. Data is also the core of a business object—discussed later in this chapter. Without the data, systems and the enterprise could not function. The ability to understand and manipulate enterprise data is essential to business continuity.

Business owners are responsible for defining business entities within an enterprise. An example would be a customer or an order. Business and IT analysts can then drive these definitions down to an implementation level. In a perfect world, business entities would end up in an integrated relational database. In most enterprises, however, the de facto data architecture is typically a myriad of legacy and modern data structures, defined redundantly across a variety of business units and application environments.

The challenge facing a typical enterprise is how to reconcile an ideal data structure with the imperfections of the real world. This challenge will be an ongoing one because few organizations are willing to undertake the rationalization and normalization of enterprise-wide data structures because it has proven to be too impractical over the near term. This leaves the enterprise with the challenge of managing an imperfect world of data redundancy and inconsistency.

Some of the data architecture challenges facing enterprises include

- Developing an understanding of overall data structure, usage, and relationships across the virtual enterprise.
- Understanding cross-functional data integration requirements.
- Mapping logical views of business data back to physical implementation views.
- Abstracting data representations and incorporating them into the design of business objects.
- Mapping object-oriented implementations back to legacy data structures.
- Addressing interim data requirements to ensure that redundant, fragmented, and inconsistent data is recognized and accommodated from a business perspective.
- Mapping the use of enterprise data to the functional architecture.

Understanding enterprise data requirements from a business and logical perspective requires a commitment from business planners and owners as well as from data architects. Having a high-level model in place that depicts which business entities are used by specific business units and applications is essential for ongoing planning and application implementation activities. Legacy transformation plays a key role in this mapping process because it requires an understanding of the existing environment.

Establishing a cross-functional understanding of enterprise data architecture can also involve the use of a thesaurus. In the context of data architecture, a thesaurus is used to translate semantic meaning across business units for data that is called one thing but means something else.

For example, a hardware manufacturer's domestic and international divisions meant two different things when they referred to a "unit" sold. When a sale occurred in the domestic division, they counted a package containing a PC, a mouse, manuals, and related peripherals as a single unit sold. In the international division, a sales log on this package would show four units sold, with each item being logged as a unit. The accounting department did not know this and therefore had difficulty reconciling unit sold data at an enterprise level.

Data entities such as a customer or buyer are terms that one would think should be commonly understood but are not universally agreed upon within a given enterprise. Any organization that has a fragmented and redundantly defined data infrastructure should consider the need for a thesaurus.

Data architecture is a basic building block of an organization and its IT strategy. Data architecture discrepancies, which can occur among business units as well as between business units and IT, drive legacy architecture transformation and integration projects. A Brainstorm Group survey [5] of 105 user organizations listed data integration as the number one integration issue—ahead of security, privacy, supply chain management, business-to-business integration, and application integration. Understanding enterprise data architecture is also essential to deciphering and defining a functional enterprise architecture.

3.4 Functional Architecture—Delivering Information Requirements

Business requirements, now more than ever, need to be communicated effectively and efficiently to IT analysts. One way to accomplish this is to use a model-driven approach in creating these requirements. Referring back to Figure 3.1, business requirements are defined in the first two rows of the Zachman framework. At the most abstract level (first row), this includes stating what the business does, how it functions, where it operates, who it works with, when events occur, and business goals. This may sound trivial, but not every business has articulated this information or kept it current.

At the enterprise model level (second row), business owners maintain a list of business entities, processes and process relationships, logistics, workflow, schedule of events, and business objectives. One issue that has confounded business owners is the fact that IT analysts have taken over their role and substituted third-row models for second-row requirements [6]. This compression of business owner input has reduced the business community's ability to impact business architecture requirements. Business owners and analysts must reengage in these activities to ensure that new architectures are valid from a business perspective.

One company that maintains a business model that is separate and distinct from its technical model is Wells Fargo, the fourth largest bank in the United States, with a market value of $85 billion. The Wells Fargo Business Object Services (BOS) group created a business model to reflect a technology-independent view of its enterprise. Wells Fargo has a variety of business units, hardware and software platforms, applications, and data structures. Many of its packaged applications are legacy systems that use legacy data structures. The business model normalizes disparate environments through a common logical view that allows Wells Fargo to more effectively respond to dynamic business requirements [7].

One e-business requirement is the growing need for a zero-latency enterprise. This describes an environment where all parts of the enterprise can respond to events as soon as they become known to any other part of the enterprise. This concept implies an ability to exchange immediate communication among multiple, independent distributed systems [8]. Zero latency will likely remain a goal to strive for rather than ever fully achieve. In either case, architecture plays a big role in the pursuit of this goal.

An example of this pursuit can be seen in Wells Fargo's objective to understand and be able to quickly determine the impact of a transaction as it occurs across disparate business units and application environments. Event-driven architectures play a role in achieving zero latency. According to a presentation by Gartner, business events should be "explicitly defined and managed in a way that enables them to be shared by multiple people and applications." [8] Events are also incorporated into the Zachman framework under the concept of Time.

In general, the creation and maintenance of a functional architecture incorporate business processes and goals at the top row of the Zachman framework, and programs and business rules at the detailed representation (the bottom row) of the Zachman framework. Organizations may believe that developing architectural models at each of these levels is extraneous to getting their jobs done, but it is important given the continuous miscommunication that occurs between business owners and information technology deployment teams.

3.5 Business Processes Modeling

In Chapter 2 we discussed the importance of understanding application architectures in legacy and modern application environments. The application architecture is a component of the functional architecture within an enterprise. The business owner's view of this architecture is the business process model. Creating a process model was typically the first step in a business process reengineering (BPR) project.

There have been a number of debates regarding BPR in recent years, but in general it has had a positive effect on streamlining organizational efficiency and effectiveness. The original goal of BPR was to document and then improve how a business functioned. A depiction of a business process model is shown in Figure 3.2. BPR has been pursued by a number of organizations both internally and in connection with third parties whose processes interact with internal business processes. The next logical step in this process involves business process integration (BPI).

BPI has become a vehicle for achieving sustainable value for organizations that have redundantly defined business processes across business units, supply chains, and distribution environments. BPI projects foster revenue growth, increase customer satisfaction, facilitate e-business deployment, and meet cost reduction targets because they take a business-driven, not a technology-driven, view of functional fragmentation. BPI, therefore, is also an important step in the development of a business-driven architecture. Two key elements in this process involve business process management (BPM) and business process automation (BPA).

BPI delivers these benefits by reaching beyond traditional departmental retooling of processes to address a more comprehensive set of solutions. Specifically, the integration, management, and automation of business processes

- Enables functional integration across segregated business units.
- Extends vertical process management into supply and distribution chains.
- Provides companies with e-business integration capabilities.
- Creates a framework under which application architectures can be transformed to support retooled business processes.

BPI allows previously segregated business units to work in synthesis, enables business units to integrate processes with external entities, and consolidates

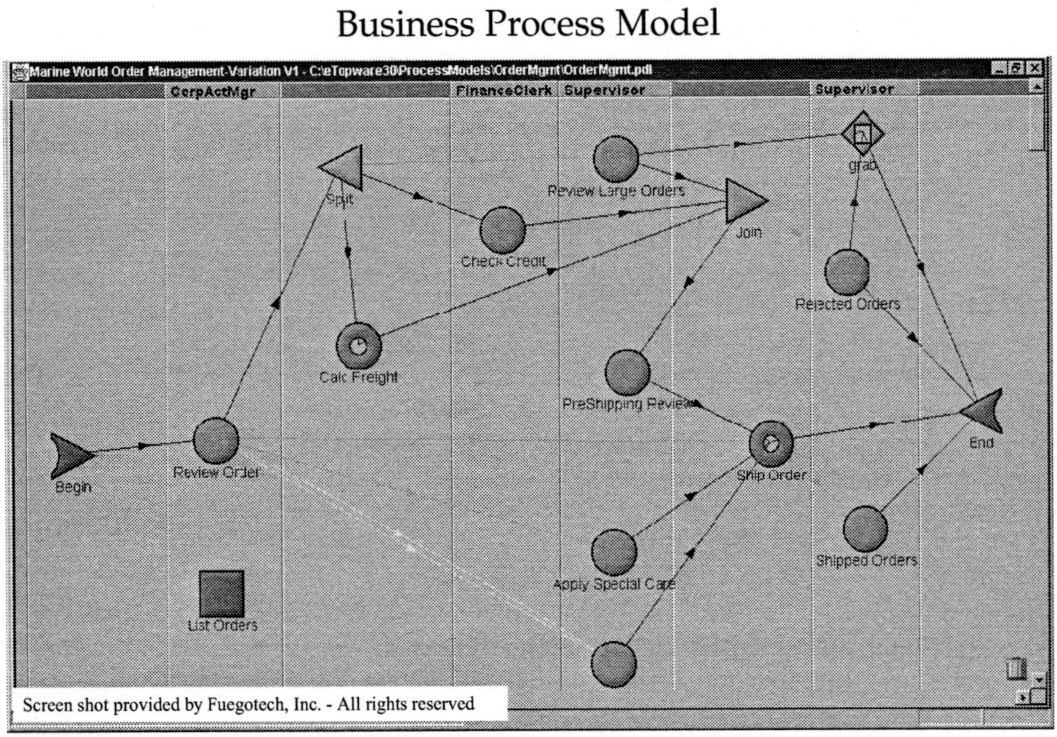

Business Process Model

Figure 3.2

Sample business process model of a cross-functional order process.
(Courtesy of Fuegotech, Inc. All rights reserved.)

redundant processes across functional areas. The last bullet is the key to defining an integrated application architecture. Otherwise, an enterprise will subscribe to a future in which layers of middleware end up wrapping layers of convoluted application functionality and data ad infinitum.

The Function column of the Zachman framework shows how the business process model reflects the business owner's view of the application architecture. If an enterprise wishes to incorporate the business owners' requirements in the application architecture, then a transformation strategy should be crafted to facilitate the integration of business processes.

BPI is always business-driven, which is why the business process model is the most effective way of communicating application architecture transformation requirements. The telecommunications industry, for example, contains numerous time-consuming business processes that hinder its ability to improve customer sales and service. One telecommunications firm, Nextel International, decided to address this challenge through a multidivisional BPI initiative [9].

Nextel had the objective of growing international digital subscriber units to the 1,000,000 mark and beyond. The goal was to empower markets with faster order processing times, improved network provisioning, lower operational costs, and a faster sales cycle. Clearly, near-term business value can be achieved and cost-justified under a BPI initiative.

BPI initiatives are increasing across a number of industries. The enterprise that recognizes the need for documenting, integrating, and automating business processes well positions itself for creating an application transformation strategy that it can implement. For example, if five business units have integrated and automated business processes associated with a customer service function, the application transformation activities might involve integrating the five disparate systems that enable those processes.

Any enterprise with a defined set of BPR/BPI projects is laying the ground-work for defining the application architecture at the design and implementation level. If an enterprise is ignoring business process management, it is missing a key component needed to more fully align its business model with its information architecture.

3.6 UML—The Unified Modeling Language

The Unified Modeling Language (UML) is the generally accepted language for specifying, visualizing, and documenting software systems and related require-ments. UML was the result of a collaborative effort among a number of object-ori-ented methodologists. UML emerged during the mid- to late 1990s and was a product of the UML Partners Consortium, formed by Rational Corporation [10].

UML is widely accepted as a specification and design standard geared at providing users and IT with the ability to build and exchange models that repre-sent application requirements. UML is independent of any given programming language and supports the development of object-oriented systems. UML sup-ports nine different modeling diagrams.

- Use Case Diagrams
- Class Diagrams
- Object Diagrams
- Sequence Diagrams
- Collaboration Diagrams
- Statechart Diagrams
- Activity Diagrams
- Component Diagrams
- Deployment Diagrams

An example of a Use Case diagram is shown in Figure 3.3. This depiction shows how the user views a particular business process, fully independent of the implementation of any given system. While Use Cases are useful for IT analysts to communicate with business users, they do not eliminate the need for business users to create the higher-level requirements definitions shown in the first two rows of the Zachman framework.

Class diagrams are the blueprints for the creation of objects in an implementation of an application. Sequence diagrams depict the timing of events, while Collaboration diagrams depict the roles of various objects. State diagrams address the data portion of an object, while Component diagrams define a unit of reusable code for a system. Deployment diagrams define the software and hardware to be used in the new system.

UML is methodology-independent, but works well with various development processes. The core of UML is the metamodel, which represents an abstraction of the problem solution, and the modeling language itself. Because it was developed through a consortium, UML is an open language that can be applied to

Business Modeling with Use Cases

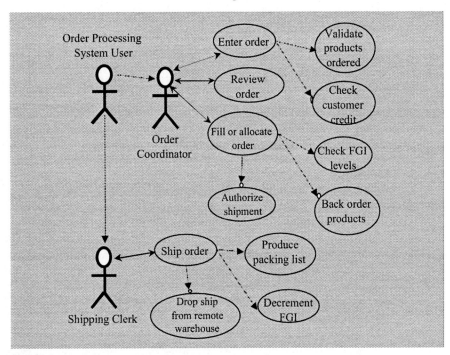

Figure 3.3
Business modeling with Use Cases captures user's view of a process.

the design of many different types of systems, including real-time systems, system software and tools, and business systems.

UML displaces a variety of legacy modeling techniques, many of which had little relationship to other models. For example, IE always struggled with ways to connect certain data flow models and process diagrams because they emerged from unrelated disciplines. UML is not subject to this handicap, because it was created as an integrated set of diagrams that have gained significant support from the Object Management Group and other industry associations and vendors.

Vendor support is evidenced by the growing number of software products that can generate source code from UML diagrams. Changing the system, in many cases, just means changing the UML diagram. Conversely, a change to generated source code within certain development tools triggers a change to the original UML diagrams. This bidirectional change ability was never achieved in previous generations of development environments and should help reinforce the value of UML in the ongoing applications development and maintenance process.

3.7 Modern Technical Architectures

The technical architecture tends to be where IT spends a good deal of time—and for good reason. There are numerous changes afoot in the area of technical architecture design and deployment. It is important to recognize that technical architectures can be quite volatile, but also that the industry appears to be heading toward a subset of acceptable architectures supported by a collective of standards bodies.

Technical architectures were originally quite simple. Companies had a mainframe computer that ran all of their applications and held all of their data. Everyone was connected to the mainframe through a character-based terminal. Mid-range systems followed a similar architectural pattern, but networks introduced the concept of client/server architectures. Client/server was the next step in architectural evolution. The client was the piece that controlled the user interface, while the server ran on another piece of hardware or across a network.

Client/server architectures came in the two-tier variety with a client front end, which used a graphical user interface (GUI), and a back-end server that contained both the business logic and the data. Client/server was also deployed in a three-tier variety, where the client interfaced with a logic server that in turn interfaced with a third tier that contained the data.

The server component may have been a network computer, mid-range system, or even the mainframe. The client may have very little application logic (a thin client) or a greater amount of application logic (a fat client). These architectures are all still in use at organizations, but are now being augmented through the use of Web-driven front-end clients.

Web-driven architectures are multitiered or n-tiered, meaning that the presentation layer, business layer, and data access layer are split into various applications that run across virtual machines. Web-based architectures are distributed because people use the Web from anywhere on the planet. The interface is based on the Hypertext Markup Language (HTML), which has become the standard user interface facility for Web-based applications. Web-based architectures challenge technology architecture teams because they need to conform to the following requirements.

- Infinite scaleability—the number of users is difficult to determine.
- Continuous operation—applications must function 24/7.
- Unknown user base—systems must be intuitive because you cannot determine who will be using the system.
- Back-end integration—Web-based systems must interface with back-end environments to connect into legacy data and functionality.
- Portability—users have numerous and undefined hardware and software environments.
- Personalization—Web users expect application personalization based on user preferences and history.

Web-based applications have unique requirements, but there are a number of industry-accepted deployment options that facilitate the development of Web-based architectures. The following considerations must be incorporated into planning and development of modern technical architectures.

- Object-oriented analysis, design, and development paradigms.
- Component-based development.
- Modern computing languages.
- Open systems.
- Integrated development environments.
- Agile methodologies.
- Collaborative development.
- Web Services and standards.
- Information portals and user-driven integration.
- Distributed transactional architecture platforms.
- Integration technology and interim architectures.

Modern technical architectures are becoming increasingly complex from a variety of potentially conflicting and competing positions. This increasingly complicated scenario demands a closer level of attention from executives than has been exercised in the past. There is a real risk of software computing environments becoming so convoluted that they gridlock an enterprise in an inflexible and unresponsive environment.

3.8 Object-Oriented Analysis, Design, and Development Paradigms

Object-oriented analysis, design, and development provide a more effective mapping of the real world to applications and data systems than older techniques such as data flow diagramming or process modeling methods. "An object is an entity that is able to save a state (information) and which offers a number of operations (behavior) to either examine or affect this state" [11]. Object-oriented languages, covered later in this chapter, are coming into their own in commercial use, with Java leading the way. An object model defines relationships among objects.

Anyone who has come from the world of legacy architectures and is just now entering the world of object-oriented computing may need a roadmap. Basic object terminology, useful for anyone working in these environments or needing to transform legacy systems into these environments, is explained in layman terms below [11].

- State—information or data stored within an object.
- Attributes—a grouping of common data items that define information within an object.
- Behavior—operations that an object can perform, upon request, on its own data.
- Encapsulation—a concept describing the fact that information and behavior are self-contained within an object.
- Class—a template of characteristics that can be used to create a new object. Many objects can belong to an object class.
- Instance—an object created from a class (template) of objects.
- Inheritance—an object can inherit the attributes and behavior of other objects. For example, a *discount book order* would inherit the attributes and behaviors of a *book order*.
- Polymorphism—when something stimulates an object, the stimulus does not need to know how the responding object fulfilled the request. An object can decide, for example, if it should fulfill a request using a *book order* object or a *discount book order* object.
- Persistent Data—data that is stored in a permanent database.

These concepts form the basis for object-oriented analysis, design, and development. They are very powerful, but are not new: They originated during the early 1970s.

In an object-oriented world, an application environment would be defined as a collection of objects, each with its own unique set of attributes and related behavior. When an application wishes to accomplish a task, it stimulates one or more objects to get what it needs or to accomplish a series of tasks.

For example, an order object has the attributes of order type, order status, item ordered, and various other attributes. Behavior for an order object might include issuing an order, checking order status, determining order age, and so on. An order might aggregate with another object, such as a customer, to form a new object. This can get complex, but it offers developers a great degree of flexibility.

The benefits of object-oriented approaches from a development perspective are significant. Programmers would ultimately write less code in favor of manipulating a series of objects. Efforts related to delivering maintenance and major revisions would be reduced exponentially. Another benefit is that because objects more closely resemble the real world, the implementation using this approach would change less frequently than procedural systems. While object-oriented techniques have been around for many years, they have only recently become commercially viable for building large-scale applications.

Legacy applications are almost entirely procedural systems that act upon redundantly defined, non-object data. Object-oriented programming differs from procedural programming in several ways. Procedural programming is based on writing detailed instructions for programs that perform action against certain data. In other words, procedurally developed systems are based on data flow. If requirements change in how data is flowing through a system, which is quite common, the program has to be modified. Objects, on the other hand, perform actions or behaviors on themselves.

The fact that objects mimic the real world also makes systems built using this approach more easily decipherable by humans. Procedural systems are harder to figure out because they work against data that is "disconnected" from the behavior of the system. This disconnection means that other programs or systems can act on the same data in ways that are unknown to a program or programmer. There is limited confidence in determining how a given set of data evolved or might be impacted by various systems without in-depth analysis.

A major object-oriented benefit is the concept of reuse. Object-oriented analysis and design approaches are predicated on creating reusable objects that become building blocks for new systems. Reuse is a given. In procedural programming paradigms it is not. Reuse is likely to become more common now that the IT industry is working with component technology. Objects are fine-grain, self-contained chunks of data and action. Building applications with fine-grain objects has been difficult, which has led to the creation of reusable components.

3.9 Component-Based Development

Components are self-contained, single-function applications consisting of a related set of data and logic (code). A component could also be considered a course-grain object. Components adhere to the same basic principles as objects, but have been prepackaged in a way that makes them ready to use within a component-based architecture.

Components streamline the development process by reducing the number of pieces needed to create an application while retaining the basic concepts of object-orientation. Components

- Are self-contained pieces of software and data that perform a unique function within application architectures.
- Reside in component containers, such as JavaBeans or the CORBA component model, that offer various services to manage component deployment.
- Have well-defined interface points to enable component management.
- Are event-driven, given that a component subscribes to be notified.
- Can trigger other components.

There are several different types of components, including

- GUI components to manage user interfaces.
- Utility components that perform functions such as accessing a database or generating a report.
- Business components, which contain business logic along with GUI and utility logic.
- Client components, which manage user interfaces.
- Server components that provide business functionality, especially at an enterprise level.

In addition to the above categories, components can be black box components or white box components. A compiled component is immediately reusable and considered a "black box" because the source code is hidden from the user of the component. When component source code is provided, as is the case in a white box component, developers can customize the component for reuse [12].

While white box components may offer more flexibility, the concept of reuse could be transformed into replication and redundancy—and this is not the goal of a development organization. Redundancy is a major problem in legacy application environments already and adding more redundancy would make the problem worse.

In spite of competing standards, performance challenges, and platform compatibility, components are gaining a strong foothold in the commercial market. According to PricewaterhouseCoopers, the commercial component market is expected to grow to around $4.4 billion by 2002, with $3.4 billion of this revenue being generated by services [13].

Components can be obtained or derived from an application server, accessed via Web Services, developed by Java programmers, or derived from legacy environments. While component-based development is likely to continue to grow, business rules that need to be turned into components are locked inside of legacy applications. Legacy transformation can be used to unlock these components. Whatever form components ultimately take or wherever they come from, they are very likely to become the standard building blocks for new applications and enhancements to existing applications.

3.10 Modern Computing Languages

Advances in computer languages have taken the evolution of software from cryptic, low-level languages to procedural computer dialects to the object-oriented languages of today. Java, HTML, and XML (Extensible Markup Language) have taken center stage in today's IT development environment, yet these languages comprise a mere fraction of the computer software in use. They promise, however, to bring a degree of reuse, portability, interoperability, and standardization to software development that has been lacking in the past.

Programmers tend to gravitate toward the latest technologies. When a new computer language enters the scene, it tends to be greeted with much hype. IT professionals gravitate toward that language because it implies that they can command better positions and better salaries. Java is one such language and has emerged as a very popular facility for building e-business applications.

Java originated as a pre-Web programming language called Oak [14]. Sun Microsystems repackaged this language and released it as Java in 1995. Today Java is positioned as an enterprise programming language as well as a vehicle for programming microdevices and embedded systems. There is a major push, for example, to utilize Java in hand held computers, wireless applications, and consumer devices using Sun's Java 2 Micro Edition (J2ME) architecture. Java is making an even greater impact, however, as an enterprise application programming language.

Java comes with a comprehensive set of prebuilt components that support a variety of basic utilitarian functions, such as GUI handling. One major benefit of Java is that it is highly portable. Once Java code has been compiled, it can be ported and run on a multitude of environments without needing to be recompiled. Languages such as COBOL, C, and C++ typically need to be recompiled prior to being executed on a different type of platform. Java programmers, on the other hand, can write an application, compile it, and run it on any machine that supports a Java Virtual Machine.

Java technology enables the development of concurrent multithreaded programs. Classes may be loaded dynamically, even from across the Internet. The language itself is very secure in that you cannot "forge pointers" to arbitrary areas in memory. Memory management is done automatically, thus freeing the developer from the mundane and often error-prone tasks of explicit memory management. Some basic Java terminology is defined below.

- Applications are standalone programs that perform some technical or business function.
- Applets are applications that cannot run standalone but rather run under a Java-compatible browser stored on an HTML page.
- A Java Servlet is a server-side application that can access enterprise databases and make that data available to Web applications.
- JavaServer Pages are Java components that also run as a server platform.

Enterprise Java deployment, which primarily relies on the Java 2 Platform Enterprise Edition (J2EE) platform, additionally incorporates the following capabilities.

- An enterprise bean is a component that defines and implements a business task or business entity and resides in an Enterprise JavaBean (EJB) container.
- Entity beans define data that is stored in a database. Entity beans are identified by a primary key and may manage its own persistence or delegate this function to a component container.
- Session beans capture the interaction between the user and the system, perform tasks such as calculating information or accessing a database, and do not save data.
- Enterprise JavaBean provides a specification for a server-side component model for building and deploying enterprise applications.

Data in an enterprise Java application is managed in a way that is similar to the way other applications manage data, but programmers must establish entity beans to map to persistent data. Entity bean referenced data is stored in either a relational or an object-oriented database. Commercial Java applications primarily use relational databases to store data. Entity beans are transactional, which means that changes to the state of that data occur within the context of a transaction.

J2EE and enterprise platforms are discussed in more depth later in this chapter. While object-oriented programming is not new, Java has become the object-oriented programming language of choice for the development of application systems. Another language that has been developed by Microsoft is called C#. It is very similar to Java, but contains Microsoft specific extensions.

Java and other object-oriented languages can accomplish a given task using fewer statements than a procedural language would use to accomplish the same task. For example, solving a programming task might require many lines of COBOL code, but require very few lines of Java.

Java does suffer some limitations. It does not run as quickly as many other languages, such as C or COBOL. Java and other object-oriented languages are also restricted to accessing either relational or object-oriented databases. Performance and data accessibility limitations along with the sheer volume of data processed by legacy applications will limit Java's ability to displace legacy applications for quite some time.

Other languages that have taken on important roles in the development of application software are HTML and XML—along with various offshoots of these languages. Each of these languages performs very specialized functions within the context of Web-based application architectures.

HTML is the universal tool for representing information on Web sites. It is an industry-wide standard, which is something that the IT industry had not previously deployed at any significant level. When one considers that the typical enterprise has not even standardized inhouse applications and data structures, the fact that HTML is the universally accepted interface for Web front ends accessed billions of times a day is astonishing.

HTML emerged from an early language called the Standardized Generalized Markup Language (SGML), which was developed by the World Wide Web Consortium (W3C). HTML is good at displaying data, but not for interpreting the meaning of that data. A Web browser, for example, can display content between HTML tags, but does not care where the data comes from, what that data means, or how it is formatted [14]. Fortunately, XML can address this requirement.

XML is a generalized language for data interchange. XML makes all information "self-describing" through a standard tagging protocol. XML allows content to be described in a very specific way and therefore enables automated data interchange without the need for extensive, customized programming. XML will ultimately

- Dramatically reduce the need for custom data exchange solutions common in electronic data interchange (EDI) environments.
- Increase the capacity to exchange data across networks of suppliers, distributors, and customers.
- Streamline internal communication and exchange of information across an enterprise.
- Expedite the ability of countless industries to reduce the overhead and increase the efficiency and quality of information flowing throughout those industries.

There is a good deal of effort being put forth to ensure that XML plays a major role in trading partner information exchange. For example, the Organization for Advancement of Structural Information Standards (OASIS) announced electronic business XML (ebXML) in December 2000. The ebXML standard will establish transport, routing, and trading partner protocols for businesses looking to trade with one another over the Internet [15].

XML is no panacea to the data interchange problem and is unlikely to replace the vast number of legacy EDI systems over the near term. There is a wealth of work to be done in this area before XML can achieve its true potential. Standards are still being created, reviewed, and revised across dozens of vertical industries. In spite of this, XML will increasingly serve as the glue for a wide variety of initiatives, including Web Services, a topic discussed later in this chapter.

It is worth noting that Microsoft has extended XML to support intercompany communications and EAI with a framework called BizTalk. BizTalk offers some additional business-to-business benefits, but was created by a single company as opposed to an industry standards body or consortium of participants [16].

In addition to Java, C#, HTML, and XML, languages such as C++, Visual Basic, various scripting languages, and even COBOL continue to support distributed Web-based deployment. Java and XML are currently the most popular enterprise application languages and will likely continue in that role in the future.

3.11 Open Systems—Collaborative Software Development in Action

It is difficult to discuss modern computing languages and tools without commenting on the open systems movement. Open systems is a concept in which software circulates through the public domain, is updated by various teams and individuals, and in come cases is resynchronized with a product baseline. A basic version of an operating system, development environment, or runtime tool could, for example, be circulated to business partners over the Internet. Various software teams could then enhance the software in a modular fashion.

The LINUX operating system is a good example of the open systems movement in action. The product is free and the source code can be updated by third parties. Sun has also used the open systems model for a number of products. Sun would release a version of a tool, such as Forte, into the public domain. At some point, Sun and other vendors would reincorporate public domain changes into a baseline version of the product and add features and functions that do not reside in the open version of the software. The enhanced version would then be offered as a licensable tool by Sun.

The open systems concept flies in the face of the closed model, where software was protected like the crown jewels. The value is self-evident. If enough developers add value to a product, everyone benefits—including the vendor. The product also retains a level of peer input that has been lacking from closed system software products. Open systems are here to stay and will likely provide Sun and its allies an edge over Microsoft, who has not embraced open systems with a great deal of enthusiasm.

3.12 Integrated Development Environments (IDEs)

Historically, CASE technology promised to streamline and improve the software development process. First- and second-generation CASE tools never lived up to their promise. The modern IDE, however, can synchronize e-business design, development, and deployment activities across a spectrum of business users, analysts, third parties, designers, developers, and implementation personnel.

Synchronization of development activities helps ensure that businesses get what they want from IT. An IDE provides access to design and development tools, component libraries, and external resources. This environment, depicted in Figure 3.4, enables individuals, with proper clearance, to visualize task flow and readily exchange project-deliverable data across the application development and maintenance life cycle.

When users, developers, and third parties openly collaborate through an IDE, the result is a highly streamlined development delivery cycle that retains the integrity of business requirements through the implementation phase. Development project

Integrated Development Environments

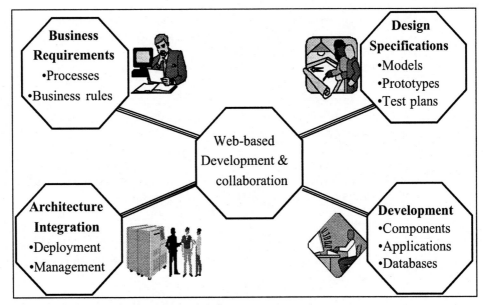

Figure 3.4
An IDE lets users, analysts, and developers exchange plans, designs, and related deliverable items over the Web.

plans, status reports, and abstract representations include business models, design specifications, test plans, code, test results, integration plans, and implementation results. This information may be shared within a project team, which includes business participants, or across project teams spanning physical locations, business units, and enterprise boundaries. Sharing information within a single project team for a development project facilitates iterative development concepts where development is a cycle of continuous improvement. Analysts can specify requirements using UML and share these requirements with design teams.

The design team uses these requirements to draft a set of designs and test plans to communicate how they envision implementing those requirements. Business users would in turn review and comment on these designs and return them to the design team. Designers submit these designs to developers, and developers share their comments with the designers and business users. This process continues throughout the delivery cycle. All participants stay in the loop as the system evolves through a series of iterative refinement cycles—which includes post-implementation updates.

The IDE also allows project teams to share information across multiple design and development initiatives. One project team might have a dependency on work being done by a second project team. This is common in large IT environments.

Developers tend to be too busy, however, to share detailed project status and related information with other business units.

The IDE is particularly useful in situations where large development teams are broken into subteams based on project functions and subfunctions, distributed across multiple locations. Users, designers, developers, and managers could examine the work being done at each stage of one or more parallel subprojects from remote locations.

IDEs are deployed using Internet and intranet environments, which allow teams to virtually align themselves and include external resources as well as internal participants. The IDE facilitates the creation of large-scale, component-based applications by streamlining the specification, design, programming and code generation, testing, and integration tasks. As previously discussed, UML facilitates the creation of design specifications in a neutral format. Through the IDE these designs can then be passed to code generation facilities to ensure that the code resulting from these designs reflects the integrity and intent of those designs.

IDEs facilitate the generation and editing of Java, XML, HTML, and other modern languages. Code-generation technology works by interpreting design models and creating code that meets the specifications set forth by the design. A commercial IDE should support

- Integrated design, development, and code generation.
- Application and component editing and application generation.
- Component assembly to ensure proficient, broad-based reuse of components.
- Bidirectional synchronization of design level and code-level changes, which ensures the integrity of both designs and applications.
- Testing and debugging of components and applications.
- Change control tracking and application asset management.

The ability to integrate development technologies under an IDE is important for development teams with a strong commitment to the collaborative development process. Development teams must also consider the importance of maintaining a level of discipline while not dictating how development teams should do their jobs. This requires the use of agile methodologies.

3.13 Agile Methodologies—Balancing Rigor and Flexibility

To application developers, the term *methodology* conjures up images of form-filled, multistep procedure guides and manuals. Old-style methodologies can elongate development projects to the point where nothing is ever delivered. This is why many companies abandoned methodologies. In abandoning formal processes and methods, however, development teams sacrificed the degree of rigor needed to keep projects in line with their goals and objectives.

Business and IT development teams still require an appropriate degree of rigor to ensure that critical steps are taken at the appropriate stages of the development cycle. This includes deliverable coordination for all project participants across the analysis, design, coding, testing, and deployment phases of the project. Agile methodologies should also be synchronized with the use of an IDE.

Table 3.1 lists a set of principles drafted by the Agile Alliance [17], a group of methodologists who promote minimal rigor to keep projects on track. Under these principles, customers receive ongoing value in the form of functioning systems delivered over interim periods of time. Managers focus on enabling teams to deliver quality software for indefinite periods of time while the team focuses on technical excellence. This avoids unproductive activities and increases the odds of delivering quality work.

One example of an agile process is called Extreme Programming. The concept of Extreme Programming is to accelerate up-front design activity and spread design work throughout the development cycle. This in turn reduces the time it

Table 3.1
Principles of Agile Methodologies

Slanted Toward Customers	Slanted Toward Managers	Slanted Toward the Team
• Our highest priority is to satisfy the customer through early and continuous delivery of valuable software. • Welcome changing requirements, even late in development. • Deliver working software frequently, from a couple of weeks to a couple of months, with a preference to the shorter timescale. • Business people and developers must work together daily throughout the project.	• Build projects around motivated individuals. • The most efficient and effective method of conveying information to and within a development team is face-to-face conversation. • Working software is the primary measure of progress. • Agile processes promote sustainable development. Sponsors, developers, and users should be able to maintain a constant pace indefinitely.	• Continuous attention to technical excellence and good design enhances agility. • The best architectures, requirements, and designs emerge from self-organizing teams. • At regular intervals, the team reflects on how to become more effective, then tunes and adjusts its behavior accordingly.

(Source: The Agile Alliance.)

takes for a development team to move from the design phase to the point where they deliver a working system. Extreme Programming promotes the goal of performing tasks concurrently wherever possible. For example, if part of the business design has been completed, developers may begin implementing the system while uncovering additional business requirements.

Extreme Programming also introduced the concept of *pairs-programming*. This fosters the idea of programmers working as two-person teams. This concept reduces or eliminates the need for post-development code reviews—a process that has always had questionable value, even when it was actually used. Pairs-programming allows strong technical talent to transfer skills to more junior personnel and is based on the idea that two heads are better than one. The goal is to catch errors during the coding cycle and allow for a broader range of implementation techniques.

Iterative development is another important concept for development teams trying to employ an agile approach. Under iterative development, a system subfunction is created, tested, and delivered to the user. Additional system subfunctions can then be added on an ongoing basis. Changes to previously implemented subfunction designs are called *refactoring*. The concept of "scope creep" is eliminated, because scope is set in increments that can be implemented in a period of weeks or months, but not years. Changes in requirements are an accepted and welcome part of this process.

A major conceptual shift in Extreme Programming is the idea that testing is performed throughout the development cycle and not at the end of the project. One precept is that a line of code is not developed unless a test case has been written for the function being automated by that line of code. Spreading out testing tasks also increases the stability of the resulting application because it captures errors early in the delivery cycle.

Extreme Programming and other agile processes should be deployed under a larger framework to ensure that it can be effectively deployed on larger projects. This includes melding the use of agile processes with the deployment of an IDE. Linking agile processes with an IDE ensures that protocols are followed based on standards set by architecture and related infrastructure teams. Under this approach, disparate development teams are more likely to conform to corporate data models, language guidelines, data exchange formats, hardware standards, and other architecture requirements.

Extreme programming has not been used extensively on very large projects. Large development teams still require the rigor, however, that Extreme Programming provides. The alternative, using no methodology at all, is a poor one. Use on larger projects is therefore likely to increase.

Development processes must by definition be agile enough to be deliver value to customers on an ongoing basis, be accepted by development teams, provide enough rigor to keep projects on track and be incorporated into an IDE, and leverage related development technologies. The use of agile processes also provides project teams with the flexibility needed to incorporate transformation deliverables into projects at interim points.

3.14 Collaborative Development

Technological advancements in the IT industry have not eliminated the challenge of ensuring that functional requirements are turned into functioning business systems in an acceptable timeframe. Deploying new technology and processes must go hand in hand with deploying a collaborative approach to the development process.

For example, a telecommunications executive hired a large consulting firm to replace a billing system. Tens of millions of dollars and years of effort went into building a system that not only failed to replace the old system, but also increased user workloads to reconcile outputs between the old and new systems. Business users did not get what they wanted. This is an example of an executive who did not know how to build a collaborative team of IT and business professionals to define a set of requirements and act upon those requirements.

In this example, numerous project participants knew that the project was doomed to fail. They never told the executive sponsor, however, because a collaborative environment was never established to enable this type of communication. In other words, subordinates will not challenge poor decisions by executives if there is no vehicle in place to do so.

IT must deploy new business systems in a fraction of the time spent on development projects during prior decades. They also need to ensure, however, that the functionality requested by the business community is the functionality that gets implemented. Various solutions have attempted to address e-business time constraints. Agile methodologies, for example, encourage collaboration of the people on the team, but do not necessarily build collaboration into the executive, management, and third-party relationships that a project relies on.

To reduce or eliminate communication failures between business users and development teams, an enterprise must improve and streamline collaboration among all participants at every level and across organizational infrastructures. This requires that project participants create a shared purpose and set of principles, develop a common set of specification models, and deploy collaboration tools through which they can freely exchange requirements and results.

Project participants include representatives from any group impacted by or responsible for creating or changing the systems affected by the project's requirements. This includes business users, analysts, designers, developers, testing personnel, customers, and business partners.

Representatives from each participant category must then collectively create a project purpose and set of principles to guide the actions of the participants. For example, a project purpose may involve creating an e-business system that allows customers to order products without having to interface with a human being. A principle may state that "any participant can view any requirements, specifications, test cases, prototypes, or other results at any stage of the project life cycle."

Agreeing on common specification models is more important than the types of models being used. Any participant should additionally be able to view system specifications and determine how those specifications will impact the resulting system at any point in the life cycle. This capability increases the likelihood of a business user catching problems early in the development cycle, before the cost of fixing those problems increases exponentially.

Web technology facilitates the open exchange of ideas, requirements, specifications, prototypes, test cases, and related information. Online meeting and development tools allow participants to collaborate more frequently and more freely than face-to-face meetings. These tools should link all participants at every stage of the life cycle and be integrated with the use of an IDE.

Collaboration is not a difficult concept, but can be hard to implement based on historic barriers between the business community, third parties, and IT. New technology will not solve problems such as the one found in the telecommunications example. Only collaborative thinking and actions will address these issues.

3.15 Web Services and Standards

Web Services provide a way for organizations to build and deploy applications using a virtual set of business logic services that extend beyond the bounds of their enterprise. Web Services allow collaborating enterprises to exchange information or business logic over the Web using XML based on the Simple Object Access Protocol (SOAP). There are many variations on the definition of Web Services, but it has been described as "an interoperability standard" that will unleash "a flood of user and developer creativity" [18].

Exchanging application logic and information over the Internet is a radical approach that makes one wonder if this is a reality that can be accomplished in any practical way. SOAP provides the exchange protocol, so that part of the problem is being addressed. Using SOAP, developers can layer an interface over a piece of code to allow other applications to access that capability.

How can applications find this information? The answer to this question lies in the Universal Discovery, Description, and Integration (UDDI) facility. UDDI is the directory that facilitates the search and find component of Web Services. The interface definition for a service is defined using another standard called the Web Services Description Language (WSDL).

Are Web Services for real? SOAP and UDDI have been broadly adopted by most industry heavyweights, including IBM, Sun Microsystems, and Microsoft. Additional encryption, digital signing, and message routing standards are in progress along with the deployment of a variety of software packages to support Web Services. A large number of companies also subscribe to the UDDI directory.

There are some early examples of how Web Services work. A business portal, for example, may wish to display weather, stock quotes, and other information. That portal application accesses another application that already contains the logic needed to obtain that information and request the weather forecast or stock quote.

In reality, most applications are not ready to communicate with other applications. They were never designed that way, so Web Services will rely on either new applications or the componentization and Webification of legacy business logic. Unless legacy business logic can be transformed to support remote Web access, Web Services will likely hit a usage plateau as it is more widely deployed over the next couple of years.

There are some positive signs regarding the potential of Web Services. Major companies are buying into it and, conceptually, it has the potential to radically change how applications are built and maintained. Most organizations have a difficult time, however, in just attaining a reasonable level of reuse on an internal basis, let alone trying to accomplish this across intercompany boundaries. The Web Services model is a good one, however, and may help force IT organizations to enact better disciplines within their own organizations.

3.16 Information Portals—Business-Driven Information Gateways

In large-scale computing environments, information is scattered across numerous physical files, databases, directories, and user environments. This information is further distributed across multiple business units and physical locations. Complicating this situation is the deployment of a multitude of first- and second-generation Web sites that have emerged at the departmental level over the past few years.

Organizations have created a legacy of distributed information and Web-based entry points to that information. These information gateways need to be consolidated, and information portals are being used to organize this information. Portals provide

- Simplified information access for customers, suppliers, distributors, employees, and the general public.
- Access to multiple Web sites, including Internet, Extranet (secured third-party Internet access), and intranet (internal internet) sites.
- A basis for securing access to certain information based on the user.
- The foundation for creating consolidated, single sign-on user entry to simplify and improve security protocols.
- Business integration capabilities at the point where the users enter an enterprise domain.

In order to succeed, information portal initiatives require participation from a cross-section of business units and collaboration with third parties. Portal utilization provides a singular and effective entry point to enterprise information environments. Portal planning should be incorporated into architecture planning and jointly coordinated by business planners and owners along with IT personnel.

3.17 Distributed Transactional Architecture Platforms

A number of commercial platforms are available for enterprises pursuing the creation and deployment of distributed transactional architectures. These platforms facilitate the management and distribution of component-based applications and allow a developer to build, share, and manage components. A distributed transactional architecture, shown in Figure 3.5, runs on multiple hardware platforms and accesses enterprise data.

Distributed transactional architectures focus primarily on runtime environments. This is in contrast to the IDE concept discussed earlier. The IDE services the analysts, designers, and programmers building or maintaining a system. Runtime environments, on the other hand, service users of the system and take control once an application is released to production. Runtime environments are where a distributed transactional architecture platform delivers real value.

One key piece of the runtime environment is the application server. In early legacy architectures, the runtime environment resided on a single machine, which was typically a mainframe. The machine may have been partitioned into multiple

Typical Transactional Architecture

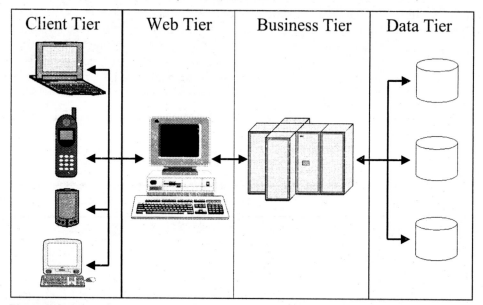

| Client Tier | Web Tier | Business Tier | Data Tier |

Figure 3.5
Distributed transactional applications run on any machine and access and update back-office applications and data.
(Source: J2EE™ Technology in Practice.)

virtual machines, but that was about as complicated as it got. Middleware and client/server architectures complicated things further by introducing numerous point-to-point system and data communication links. The application server has emerged as a means of more effectively coordinating the different pieces of a run-time environment. Application servers, which originally grew out of the age-old concept of the TP monitor, provide many of the following services.

- Facilitates transaction handling.
- Provides a component processing environment.
- Centralizes business processing capabilities.
- Interfaces with the Web server, which in turn manages Web-based interfaces.
- Communicates with back-end applications and databases.
- Communicates with ERP packages.
- Provides development support for assembling components.

A number of commercially available application servers run under various distributed transactional architecture platforms. This is particularly true for Java-based environments. Each of the four main platforms for deploying distributed transactional architectures is summarized below.

- **CORBA—Common Object Request Architecture**

  CORBA is an object model standard created and maintained by the Object Management Group (OMG). CORBA provides an object request broker (ORB), object services, application objects, and common facilities. The ORB is an engine that provides standard objects that developers can use to communicate with other objects. Companies supporting the early development of CORBA included IBM, Apple, and Sun. CORBA has had difficulty gaining traction in the marketplace due to a lack of commercial tool support from a wide variety of software vendors. The challenge with ORBs is that "they don't perform garbage collection functions, load balancing, or concurrency control. This means they don't scale well." [19]

- **COM—Common Object Model**

  COM is the Microsoft component model for various Windows platforms. COM was based on the Microsoft object linking and embedding (OLE) facility and comes with development tools such as Visual Basic. The ActiveX facility within COM supports the development of Web-based interfaces and provides facilities for building reusable user interface components. The main benefit of COM is that Microsoft distributes it across a widely used development platform—Windows. COM does not support inheritance and relies on DCOM to distribute COM-enabled ORBs [19]. COM will eventually be displaced by the Microsoft .Net architecture.

- **.Net**

  Microsoft offers .Net as a product suite that enables organizations to build enterprise class Web Services. The .Net product suite is a rewrite of Windows DNA. DNA was an early attempt by Microsoft at creating an enterprise application platform. .Net is hosted in a container that provides transaction management, security, and messaging services. It also offers a business layer, which performs business processing and contains data access logic. .Net facilitates Web Services using various Internet standards [20].

- **J2EE—Java 2 Platform Enterprise Edition**

  The J2EE platform was developed by Sun Microsystems. J2EE blends technologies such as Java Servlets, Java Database Connectivity (JDBC) and the CORBA Interface Definition Language (IDL) under a common environment. J2EE provides a unified programming model and a standard set of APIs that expedites development, streamlines performance, and creates an upwardly compatible environment for Java development and deployment [21]. J2EE essentially blends and integrates the best ideas from a variety of sources under a cohesive deployment platform. For example, J2EE uses an OMG-specified communication protocol for CORBA-based systems to facilitate interoperability between systems written in different programming languages. J2EE allows clients to simultaneously run applications written in C++, C, Cobol, Java, and other languages. Most important is that J2EE reduces the ability of a single vendor to control the Java runtime market. In addition to Sun, J2EE participants include IBM, Oracle, Borland, and a number of other major players in the software field.

One major challenge for larger organizations is the task of managing multiple versions of commercial component architectures within the same enterprise. In many cases, companies are divided as to which "standard" to pursue. This situation is quite common in multidivisional companies that subscribe to a Microsoft strategy within one business unit and believe in open systems in another business unit. There is some work being done to integrate these competing platforms, but this is not the ideal scenario for an enterprise.

Coexistence of J2EE and .Net, for example, means that developers will need to rewrite parts of one application in the competing environment. This will result in redundant programming and multiple systems that perform the same tasks [22]. This is an important consideration and can ultimately cause great confusion and further stymie the ability of IT to support a more agile business environment.

Unfortunately, because of its technical nature, little senior executive attention is being paid to this battle. Ignoring platform deployment decisions like .Net versus J2EE will only decrease IT's ability to respond to critical business requirements. It will also complicate IT's ability to dig out of the legacy architecture situation it is currently trying to address.

3.18 Integration Technology and Interim Architectures

When discussing the future of information technology, it is important to consider the challenges along with the possibilities of that future. Modern technologies support a long-term vision for IT environments that standardize concepts such as component reuse, object orientation, Web Services, collaborative environments, as well as concepts pointing in many other positive directions. We must acknowledge that this future is by no means close to reality, given the prevalence of legacy architectures.

We must also acknowledge that there is an alternative view of future information architectures that is being shaped by the proliferation of middleware and wrapper technology. No single middleware solution is in and of itself bad, and many of those solutions provide positive value over the near term. There are even middleware solutions for regulatory requirements such as HIPAA. It is the collective impact of middleware from multiple vendors, aimed at addressing multiple challenges and deployed over a period of years, that is troubling.

Figure 3.6 depicts what typical information architectures might look like in the near future. In EAI vendor circles there is a mantra that says "change nothing and integrate everything." This quote subscribes to a theory in which legacy architectures are left untouched while Web-based applications wrap and invoke legacy functionality for decades to come. Given that legacy architectures are unlikely to go away anytime soon, the proliferation of EAI and other middleware solutions begins to paint a bleak picture for application management teams.

Executives must step into this situation and request an accounting of middleware proliferation. It will be much more difficult to apply legacy architecture transformation strategies to the architecture depicted in Figure 3.6, because changing a legacy application or database will trigger a series of unforeseen events across various APIs and interfaces. An enterprise must deploy middleware solutions carefully, with full knowledge of the consequences, and under the auspices of an overall architecture strategy.

3.19 Beyond the Immediate Future

Looking beyond the mid-term to the long-term evolution of computing systems offers additional insight into potential transformation strategies. The concept of autonomic computing has recently been introduced to address many of the challenges of maintenance, enhancement, and ongoing request backlogs [23]. Autonomic computing is based on the premise that someday IT will be able to develop applications that are capable of maintaining themselves in response to ongoing changes in their environment.

These systems would accomplish this by continually adjusting to real-world circumstances. Such a system would need to understand its role in conjunction

The Future of EAI Architectures

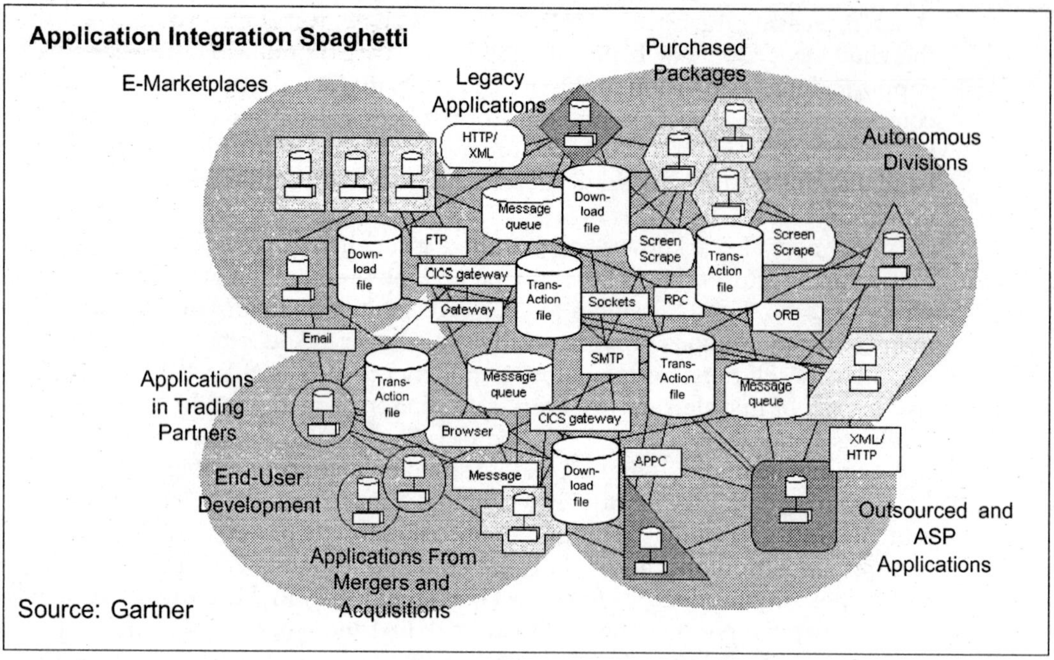

Figure 3.6
Vendor-driven integration solutions create layers of legacy chaos across information architectures.
(Source: Gartner Forecast Newsletter, Issue 3, 2001.)

with other systems. The autonomic systems would also reconfigure and protect themselves while adhering to open standards. According to Paul Horn [23], work leading to such an environment is already under way in the fields of artificial intelligence, control theory, catastrophe theory, and cybernetics.

While these types of systems are likely to be developed and deployed in commercial environments in the near term, enterprises must keep an eye on long-term shifts in technology in order to continuously adjust future strategies.

3.20 Emerging Disciplines and Legacy Transformation

Prior chapters reviewed the legacy architecture challenges facing today's enterprise. This chapter provided an overview of a number of emerging information technologies and disciplines that offer IT new ways of specifying, designing, building, and deploying information architectures. An enterprise must maintain a realistic perspective, however, on its ability to displace entrenched legacy architectures. This is particularly true in terms of the near-term viability of deploying new technologies in complex production environments.

Planning teams must recognize that legacy architectures are not immovable objects and that EAI is not the only legacy option available. The organization that concurrently leverages emerging technologies and legacy transformation will deliver real value in a timely fashion to the bottom line.

Notes

1. "Legacy at Web Speed," Rich Seeley, *eAI Journal*, Feb. 2000.
2. "Companies Stand by Their E-Business Guns," Cutter Consortium Business-IT Strategies E-Mail Advisor, Sept. 5, 2001.
3. "What's Wrong with Information Engineering," JS and HCS, *eAI Journal*, Sept. 2001.
4. "Zachman Framework and Enterprise Portals," Clive Finkelstein, *DM Review*, April 2000.
5. "Brainstorm Group Survey," Brainstorm Group, Nov. 2001.
6. "The Row Three Squeeze," Frank F. Kowalkowski, ZIFA Conference, Aug. 23, 1999.
7. "Wells Fargo's Business Object Services: A Case Study in Model-Driven Architecture," Paul Harmon, *ebizq.net*, Oct. 15, 2001.
8. "The Event-Driven Enterprise: Mixing Messages, Objects and Data," Gartner Application Integration Conference Spring 2001, Roy Schulte, May 16-18, 2001.
9. "Critical Success Factors in a Business Process Integration Initiative," William Ulrich, *ebizq.net*, December 2001.
10. "UML 2001: A Standardization Odyssey," Cris Kobryn, *Communications of the ACM*, Oct. 1999, Vol. 42, No. 10.
11. *Object-Oriented Software Engineering*, Ivor Jacobson, Addison-Wesley, 1998.
12. "Black Box vs. White Box," Sharon Fay, *ebizq.net*, Nov. 26, 2001.
13. "Creating Commercial Components," Andrew Pharoah & Faiz Arni, Jan. 5, 2001 [Online], Available: www.componentsource.com.
14. "XML: Solving Business Problems," George Reese, *Cutter Consortium Executive Report*, Vol. 3, No. 3, 2000.
15. "XML Trading Standard to Debut in March," Michael Meehan, *Computerworld*, Dec. 18, 2000.
16. "Don't Discount BizTalk," David S. Linthicum, *eAI Journal*, April 2001.
17. "Agile Alliance Manifesto," Agile Alliance, 2001 [Online], Available: www.agilealliance.org.
18. "Web Services: A New IT Ballgame" Debra Donston, *eWeek*, Sept. 10, 2001.
19. *Enterprise Application Integration*, David Linthicum, Addison-Wesley, 2000.

20. "J2EE vs. Microsoft .NET," Chad Vawter & Ed Roman, 2001 [Online], Available: www.middleware-company.com.
21. *J2EE Technology in Practice*, Rick Cattell & Jim Inscore, Addison-Wesley, 2001.
22. "Integrating EJB and COM Using the J2EE," Mark Hansen & Peter Mamorski, white paper from Javector Software, 2001.
23. "How Autonomic Computing Will Reshape IT," Paul Horn, *Tech News at CNET.com*, Oct. 15, 2001.

Legacy Architecture Management and Transformation Strategies

Aging information architectures are an entrenched reality in organizations because legacy applications and data structures are highly intertwined with enterprise business models. At the same time, there remains a continuing need for organizations to provide more effective and efficient computing solutions to an increasingly demanding and diverse set of customers and users. Yet few organizations have a strategy that reconciles the limitations of entrenched legacy architectures with high-priority, time-critical business requirements.

In order to manage costs, deliver new products and services more quickly, respond to competitive pressures, streamline supply and distribution efforts, capitalize on e-business opportunities, and improve overall customer responsiveness, an enterprise must craft a strategy that leverages complex legacy information architectures. The executive team must drive this strategy and ensure that it considers and synchronizes ongoing business and IT requirements and activities under a common approach.

Understanding enterprise requirements, assessing legacy environments, examining various scenarios, and crafting a cohesive approach to the legacy challenge are essential elements in a legacy architecture transformation strategy. This chapter discusses basic requirements and business-driven scenarios that form the basis for developing such a strategy.

This chapter also discusses justification for creating a legacy transformation strategy and provides examples of what can occur in the absence of an agreed-upon approach for addressing the legacy architecture challenge. This strategy becomes the foundation for a coordinated set of business and IT initiatives that deliver bottom-line value to an enterprise on a continuing basis. Note that this chapter presents a high-level approach to legacy transformation and that detailed project planning guidelines, tool overviews, and transformation techniques are presented in later chapters.

4.1 The Legacy Triangle—Management, Integration, and Transformation

There are three main topic areas that managers should consider when creating a strategy to address legacy architectures. Figure 4.1 depicts the three sets of activities that can be applied to legacy information architectures. These three focal points address management and maintenance, enterprise application integration (EAI), and legacy architecture transformation.

Architecture management involves maintaining legacy systems in a cost- and time-effective manner that delivers small-scale, ongoing upgrades and enhancements to the business community as needed. There are a number of transformation tools and techniques that help IT perform legacy architecture management and maintenance tasks more effectively. For example, rationalizing legacy data definitions allows application teams to apply data-related changes more quickly and reliably. Management should therefore make every effort to leverage transformation tools and techniques within the context of ongoing application management and maintenance efforts.

Enterprise application integration, or EAI, involves connecting legacy data and applications with Web-based applications, using noninvasive techniques. EAI, which was introduced in prior chapters, is an industry-accepted approach for

Legacy Architecture Strategy Components

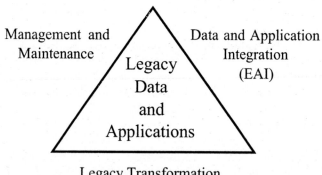

Figure 4.1
IT will need to use a combination of maintenance, EAI, and transformation options to address legacy challenges.

addressing the near-term need to deliver enterprise data and functionality to the Web. The noninvasive approach taken by various EAI solutions provide near-term value, but as discussed in Chapters 1 and 2, EAI can also result in a legacy architecture that stymies future business agility and continuity. This is due to the fact these interfaces, once incorporated into the fabric of legacy architectures, can become a maintenance burden if they need to be changed based on new business requirements.

The final focal point for legacy architectures involves the transformation of legacy data and application architectures. This last approach differs from EAI because it is invasive and changes underlying legacy applications and data studies. Transformation options include a wide variety of data and system-level activities that examine, modify, and migrate legacy applications and data.

Legacy application management, integration and transformation can be incorporated into a single, multi-phased strategy that is blended with various package deployment, consolidation, data warehouse, platform migration, and new technology deployment initiatives. Executives should remember to not ignore any of these issues when considering a legacy architecture strategy and be sure to consider how these three critical issues impact one another and the ability to deliver rapid value to the business community on an ongoing basis. The remainder of this book addresses how to define and apply these disciplines based on requirements-driven scenarios.

4.2 Legacy Architecture Terminology

Because the remainder of this book is solution-oriented, I wanted to clarify certain terms that may not be commonly understood within a typical enterprise. These terms are based on numerous transformation projects and the development of formal disciplines to support those initiatives.

- **Legacy Architecture**

  This term describes how one or more existing applications and data structures have been assembled. This includes how data is stored and accessed; how a system communicates with users; how applications interface with each other; how functions are distributed; and the design, construction, and implementation techniques applied. Legacy architectures tend to be implicitly defined rather than explicitly defined. Three main aspects of a legacy architecture include the functional architecture, the data architecture, and the technical architecture.

- **Application Maintenance**

  Maintenance is the ongoing process of applying small-scale functional or technical upgrades to an application and related data to keep it working in a production environment. Maintenance does not include structural or architectural changes applied across a spectrum of programs, applications, and data structures.

- **Assessment**

  An assessment is the first phase of a transformation project, used to determine transformation requirements at a high level or detailed level. High-level assessments may be used to define requirements for more detailed assessment transformation projects. An assessment is business-driven, can use a phased approach, clarifies requirements, and documents applications and data structures of interest.

- **Business Process Redesign (BPR)**

  BPR is the analysis and subsequent modifications applied to streamline or improve how a business user does his or her job. This typically includes the integration (BPI) and automation of business processes through the use of business process automation (BPA) tools. This has also been called business process reengineering.

- **Enterprise Application Integration (EAI)**

  EAI involves the noninvasive API-driven approach used to connect front-end systems with back-end legacy applications and data structures. EAI commonly uses middleware as the main vehicle for connecting front-end and back-end environments.

- **Legacy Architecture Transformation**

  Legacy architecture transformation describes the process of applying changes to the form, design, and/or function of one or more legacy applications or data structures. Legacy transformation can be applied to a program (i.e., structuring and redesign), an application, multiple applications, and data structures. It may involve structural, design, language, and/or platform changes to applications or related data structures.

- **Legacy Architecture Transformation Strategy**

  This defines a commonly agreed-upon philosophy and general approach that the management team in an enterprise has agreed to use to reconcile legacy architecture limitations with high-priority, time-critical business requirements.

- **Rationalization**

  Rationalization is the consolidation and redeployment of physical data definitions or business logic within the legacy application architecture. Rationalization is commonly applied at the front end of any project relying on consistent, succinct definitions of the data or logic representations within one or more application systems.

- **Rehosting**

  Rehosting is the process of moving one or more applications and data structures from one hardware platform to a different hardware platform, while minimizing design-level changes. Rehosting typically involves a language upgrade and can also be a first step in a more comprehensive transformation project.

- **Restructuring**

  This term describes improvements made to an application program without changing the architecture of the application in which a program functions. Restructuring has generally been used to describe the process of taking a poorly written, "unstructured" module and transforming it into a module that uses a commonly accepted, more easily understood form of programming.

- **Software Reengineering**

  Software reengineering is the use of tools and techniques to facilitate the analysis, improvement, redesign, and reuse of existing applications and related data structures.

- **Systems Redevelopment**

  Systems redevelopment describes the process of significantly modifying or rebuilding applications in order to replace portions of or the entire application through the use of software reengineering tools and techniques. Redevelopment has also been called a rewrite, but relies in part on the legacy applications being replaced as input to the design and development of the new application.

- **Target Architecture**

  This term describes a newly designed environment that is the target of a transformation project. This new environment differs from the legacy environment in terms of the functional, data, and technical architecture being deployed.

- **Transformation Scenario**

  A transformation scenario is a project-oriented assessment and implementation project template or approach that incorporates legacy architecture analysis, improvement, migration, and/or integration tasks. Transformation scenarios are almost always phased in and customized to fit a unique set of business and technical requirements.

While it is useful to have a common understanding of various transformation technologies, project teams should not dwell on these terms. These terms are not essential to the underlying objectives of a given project, particularly when communicating with executives or business users who are sponsoring or funding a transformation initiative. Project teams should alternatively focus on a clear statement of requirements and business-driven project scenario defining how transformation will be applied to meet those requirements.

4.3 E-Business Initiatives Drive Transformation Requirements

Companies are seeking ways to integrate the Web with legacy data and application functionality. Having built or rebuilt Web sites to address customer, supplier, or distributor requirements, companies are seeking to enrich Web-based applications with business functionality ranging from order handling to procurement. The functionality they need, however, is embedded in legacy systems. The solution to this challenge will be achieved in stages based on a growing understanding of long-term requirements.

The Web has opened up new opportunities to businesses wishing to streamline relationships with customers, distributors, business partners, and suppliers. To make these opportunities a reality, critical enterprise data and legacy functionality needs to be Web-enabled. Because legacy applications are the gateway to enterprise data, these systems have become targets of a series of recent IT initiatives. These initiatives can be broken into four stages, shown in Figure 4.2, that address the need for enterprise data evolution, legacy functionality, accessibility and reuse, and Web-based architectures.

Stage 1: Build and deploy new Web sites.

Stage 2: Integrate Web-based front ends with legacy systems, using middleware technology.

Stage 3: Web-enable legacy systems using semi-invasive technology.

Stage 4: Extract, consolidate, and reuse legacy data and business logic under newly defined information architectures.

The first stage is mostly in place, although organizations will be retooling Web sites for an indefinite period of time. The second stage has been under way for the past several years. Middleware is an accepted form of linking Web-based

Four Stages of E-Business Deployment

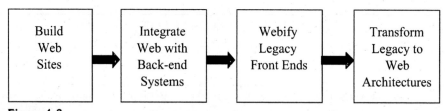

Figure 4.2
These four stages of e-business deployment are applied concurrently in most enterprises.

front ends to legacy applications. For example, a customer or business user may place an order through a Web site that triggers a back-end CICS transaction that actually places the order. To the customer or user, it looks like this was done by a Web-based system as opposed to an old legacy system.

While this is a good first step, the horizontal customer business process, including order confirmation, inventory maintenance, procurement functions, billing, and shipping, cannot be triggered through a single legacy transaction. It would be ideal to make this process work seamlessly, but legacy systems do not work this way. Much of the processing in a legacy environment is done at night during batch-processing cycles through a series of stovepipe systems.

An alternative approach is to Web-enable the legacy application. This allows the legacy system to interface with the Web-based front end directly. Transformation tools, for example, allow IT to migrate "green screens" to Web-based front ends and update legacy programs to access these screens. While this is a better approach than that used by older middleware software, legacy architectures remain a series of stovepipe transactions that rarely accommodate Web-based requirements. Even though underlying architectures remain intact, the approaches described in stages two and three are generally believed by industry experts to provide bottom-line business value.

According to Dale Vecchio of Gartner, "While the organizational impact of e-business initiatives are many and varied, existing systems continue to deliver value to most organizations. These systems, built for high performance, speed, and reliability, were designed for internal constituents familiar with the organization's business process. Mission-critical, industrial-strength systems can be e-business-enabled without the risk of package replacement or complete transformation. Companies that develop a plan for determining the business value of existing systems and use them as important building blocks of their e-business initiatives will significantly reduce the technological risk of change."

The second and third stages of Web deployment create hybrid or "composite" systems made up of old and new technology. Composite systems will always have clashing architectures that IT will find onerous to enhance and manage. More important, composite systems rarely fulfill the business requirements idealized in the first place.

In the future, IT teams will need to define new Web-driven architectures, under J2EE or .Net, for example, and migrate data and business rules into this new environment. This fourth stage of legacy-to-Web integration requires vision, careful planning, phased deployment, and patience. In the meantime, IT will need to Web-enable systems under the second and third stage while keeping a close eye on long-term Web-driven requirements.

The challenge for IT as they undertake efforts to build and deploy these new technologies to support Web-based environments is translating business requirements into functioning systems. Project track records have been less than stellar, however, and this reinforces the need for a risk-adverse approach.

4.4 Past IT Project Failures Shape Strategy

Conventional wisdom has drawn executives toward one of two lines of thinking: Applications can be rebuilt from scratch or they can be licensed as part of an application package. While both new development and packages will continue to play key roles in ongoing IT strategies, both approaches have been plagued with significant failures.

ERP package implementation efforts, as discussed in Chapter 2, have resulted in a large percentage of package deployment project failures. As a result, only 10 percent of these projects came in on time and on budget, 35 percent were cancelled outright, and of the projects that went forward, only 41 percent of the package functionality was deployed [1].

IT projects in general have also not faired well. A Standish Group study found a great majority of IT projects are not implemented on time or within budget and that 31 percent are cancelled outright. Consider the following track record for IT projects [2].

- Only 16.2 percent of projects finish on time and within budget.
- A total of 31.1 percent of projects are cancelled outright.
- Of projects completed by large companies, the resulting applications only contain 42 percent of the proposed functionality.
- In 1995, companies spent more than $81 billion on projects that were cancelled outright.
- The number one reason for project failures, according to this study, was "incomplete requirements."

Incomplete requirements translate into situations where companies spend millions of dollars, struggle through multiyear projects with no interim deliverables, and, if the project is not cancelled outright, end up with a system that does not perform the functions promised. Organizations continue to attempt to create new application functionality but do not know how to specify what those systems should do. Consider some of the following approaches taken by IT and their long-term impacts.

- A CIO at a major financial institution demanded that all mainframe applications be replaced with new, from-scratch client/server applications within a two-year window. This never happened, and the architecture team wasted two years trying to deliver.
- A large insurance company CIO wanted the IT organization to completely redesign every application to move from IDMS to DB2 as part of its Y2K project. Because this project would have taken five to seven years in the best of circumstances and the company was already behind on its Y2K remediation work, the entire Y2K team resigned.

- A federal government agency tried to replace a complex human resource system by hiring a large consulting firm to interview thousands of users as a way to rebuild the system from scratch. This was in spite of the fact that the government agency had a phased redevelopment strategy in hand from another firm. The from-scratch rewrite was halted two years into the project and has resulted in a major lawsuit.

- Executives at an RBOC that had undergone several recent mergers decided to eliminate three billing systems by moving users and customers to a fourth system—without considering or incorporating functional discrepancies. Fortunately, this project idea was squelched before it was turned into action.

- A U.S. federal agency decided to replace a cross-section of its legacy architecture with a new system. Because the cross-section being replaced contained replicated functionality, the actual processing problem it was trying to solve would not have been addressed. A million dollars was wasted on this project—even though the management team was warned in advance of its potential for failure.

- A transportation company hired a firm to perform a quick and dirty IDMS (networked) database migration to a DB2 (relational) database without redesigning the database or the applications using the database. The new relational database did not improve the organization's ability to access or manipulate the data because it was never redesigned to take advantage of the relational data architecture.

- Manufacturing executives attempted to replace complex legacy distribution systems with an ERP package without considering the functionality that would be lost in the process. This resulted in a serious delay in product distribution that lasted for many months.

- Y2K project team members decided to create a bit-manipulation routine to fool a system into processing the correct century date information. At some point in the future, this is likely to blow up, particularly the next time some unsuspecting maintenance programmer tries to upgrade the data and logic in this application.

- An HIPAA project team examined a middleware solution to reconcile payer identification numbers on the fly without changing underlying data structures. Before moving forward with this approach, they carefully documented the impact on future maintenance, data migration, or application management initiatives. In doing so, they discovered that this middleware-oriented solution was not in the best interest of the enterprise.

- A major financial institution planned to use a COBOL-to-Java conversion tool to "convert" its legacy applications into Java. Moving directly from a procedural language to an object-oriented language will deliver unmaintainable Java applications that are likely to cripple IT's future ability to support ongoing business requirements. They have since reconsidered this approach.

The above examples are only a few of the many scenarios that demonstrate the need for clear-headed thinking and a holistic approach when it comes to launching a project that involves legacy application and data architectures.

4.5 Holistic Thinking Is Essential

Three major issues emerge when legacy challenges are not addressed from a holistic perspective. The largest of these issues is the lack of project coordination from an enterprise-wide project perspective. The second problem is the tendency to gravitate toward quick and dirty solutions to complex problems, which typically demand a more comprehensive approach. The third issue stems from the absence of collaborative thinking, which results in executives mandating oversimplified and unfeasible solutions.

Holistic thinking must guide legacy transformation planning efforts. Taking a big-picture approach is essential for crafting a transformation strategy because numerous projects impact legacy architectures. Unfortunately, most enterprises have not established the collaborative infrastructure needed to coordinate multiple project goals, teams, and deliverable items across multiple business units, third parties, and IT groups. Chapter 5 provides additional insights for executives attempting to introduce collaborative infrastructures into their enterprise.

Legacy application and data architectures are highly intertwined. In other words, it is difficult to separate or discern business, presentation, and data access logic within a system. In addition to this, a business process may be implemented through a complex series of steps that cuts across multiple applications, data structures, and business units. A business-driven transformation project must incorporate each of these applications and data structures into the assessment and, as a rule, the implementation phase of a project.

This is the main reason that piecemeal approaches to any project involving legacy architectures are prone to fail. Taking a holistic approach to the planning process ensures that piecemeal approaches are avoided. Since multiple business and IT teams have differing agendas and motivations, collaborative approaches tend to encounter resistance. Logically speaking, one would think that management would persist in coordinating project plans and impacts to ensure that

- Common tasks can be leveraged and cost-justified across multiple projects.
- Projects can be synchronized and prioritized based on the dependency of deliverable items.
- Tactical deliverable items can be reused where appropriate in later phases.
- One project is not at cross-purposes with one or more other projects.
- Competing projects do not cancel each other out.

- Project work products can be staged appropriately so that application and related data structure changes can be delivered in incremental units, each of which deliver business value.

One example of where projects can be leveraged against other projects can be found in certain Y2K initiatives. Most Y2K projects gathered a great deal of data about applications and related data structures during the initial inventory phase. Because this information was gathered and loaded into tools and repositories, it could be used as input to related projects. These projects included data migration and data warehouse initiatives as well as application integration and migration projects.

In addition to treating most projects as standalone operations, which rarely leverage other projects, IT also has a penchant for pursuing the quickest, dirtiest solutions possible. Poorly coordinated projects along with widespread use of shortcuts are the two main reasons that legacy architectures are so convoluted. This is not always the fault of IT, and many times businesses push IT into these directions. Often, the business community has little or no appreciation for what really must be done to

- Enact solutions that have long-term value.
- Create systems that do not have to be reworked over and over again.
- Create a foundation solution that can be used to achieve subsequent value over the long term.
- Deliver broader value to other business units than initially perceived.

Application architectures, for example, are already riddled with countless legacy languages, half-baked implementations, middleware, replicated software patches, emulators, and point-to-point solutions that apply specialized coding for the same problem over and over again. Most quick and dirty solutions are the underlying cause of long-term problems. I have actually spoken to some IT professionals who think these approaches are fine because they plan on leaving their company long before their ineffective, piecemeal implementations are discovered.

The executive mandate is another source of narrow solutions that have a high failure rate. A number of IT professionals have shared similar stories about being ordered to do something they knew would fail. These mandates have included

- Eliminating all inhouse mainframes for a multibillion dollar financial institution.
- Redesigning hundreds of IDMS applications as part of a Y2K project in an absurd timeframe.
- Moving tens of millions of lines of COBOL code into a now defunct CASE tool.
- Converting every line of code in the company to Java.
- Spending billions of dollars to modernize a legacy portfolio with no real plan.

A phased approach that recognizes the need to incorporate an understanding of complex legacy business logic and data usage is the risk-adverse strategy that executives should consider as they continue to build new functionality to meet Web-driven and other critical business requirements.

4.6 Risk Management Requires Phased Deployment

Legacy transformation strategies and scenario-driven projects must be based on a phased approach. The reason for this is that assessing legacy architectures is a lot like peeling an onion. As project teams move beyond the technical assessment to expose the underlying architecture and functionality of legacy applications, more information is discovered that may shift the approach applied during the implementation stage of that project.

A second reason for phasing in a legacy transformation project is purely pragmatic. Legacy transformation involves the application of a variety of techniques that address physical and logical aspects of a system, at the program and system level, from both a business logic and data perspective. This multidimensional set of techniques and related tasks should be applied through a series of staged delivery windows, each of which delivers value in its own right. A phased approach

- Provides ongoing and interim value to the customers and users of the system.
- Reduces the risk of an all-or-nothing project approach common with a from-scratch rewrite or package deployment project.
- Can be cost-justified in stages as well as in aggregate.
- Successively moves an enterprise toward its final deliverable through a controlled series of value-added project phases.
- Can be cancelled at any number of defined checkpoints without losing the value delivered during previously completed project phases.

The phased approach can also help alleviate conflict inherent in the systems planning process. Managers who find themselves torn apart by individuals in varying camps are likely to be in this situation because multiple correct solutions have been proposed. In these cases, the team as a whole did not exercise a collaborative approach that considered each project option as a step in a multiphased project.

For example, an executive team may be seeking ways to consolidate a customer-order handling and procurement situation that has been fragmented across multiple business units for a period of years. Many of the business units have common customers, and these customers want their orders consolidated for tracking and billing purposes. Different individuals have offered the following proposed solutions.

- Document, integrate, and automate order-handling and procurement business processes across disparate business units using business process automation software.
- Create a data warehouse of summary-level information for customers so they may access the status of any order, by customer, through an online interface.
- Consolidate back-end data structures and modify the existing systems to access these structures as a way to integrate the customer view.
- Create a new, integrated order-handling and procurement tracking application that replaces the individual applications currently in place.

Each of these options may appear on the surface to contradict the other options. Planning participants may have taken strong positions and be unwilling to listen to alternative arguments. The BPI team sees the first approach as the best one from a business perspective. The data warehouse team sees the second approach as the only way to go, while the application team wants to try the third approach so that they can retain control of the project. Certain managers may, on the other hand, view the fourth option four—new development—as the "right" option.

The irony of this situation is that, depending on the business requirements and underlying architecture, each of the above options could be incorporated into a phased transformation strategy. Consider a strategy that applies the following steps as a multiphased approach to addressing this issue.

1. The BPI/BPA team can collect requirements, draft a schedule, define the costs, and prototype a set of business process automation solutions. The new front end could be deployed to users while triggering access to back-end legacy applications. This may involve using certain middleware on an interim basis to accomplish this.
2. Data architecture and application personnel could concurrently create a plan to document, extract, rationalize, and populate a warehouse with the data definitions from disparate applications.
3. Application team members could then connect a Web-based query capability to the data warehouse for customers or for the customer help desk. This project phase would provide essential information to the customer without impacting the underlying architecture.
4. In some cases, the application team may decide to implement a new data model based in part on the work done in step 2 above. They would then rework existing applications to use this new data model. This interim deliverable step may or may not be feasible based on the structure of the original data and applications that use that data.
5. The new data model (created in step 2) could be reconciled with the business process model built in step 1. Using this information, an application design team could define the new target architecture that integrates required functionality under a new, object-oriented design. Design efforts would be augmented through the analysis of legacy application and data structures.

6. Finally, the new design could be populated with legacy application business logic. Developers can apply differing techniques to accomplish this, including defining reusable components from legacy business logic or populating an alternative design model.

The above sample scenario offers executives the option of delivering phased value to customers while avoiding an all-or-nothing approach by trying to rewrite this system from scratch. If the team decides to exit this strategy at any point before proceeding to a subsequent step, customers and users will still have gained value from the work delivered to that point.

While the phased approach intuitively appears to be the lowest risk and most pragmatic, there is a philosophical reluctance to use such an approach or attempt to sell it to the individuals funding the project. There are a number of reasons behind this reluctance. Many times, executives do not want to hear the details of a project plan. Because of this, the phased approach, which involves multiple versions of an application being introduced into production over a phased period of time, may be too much information or appear too complex.

Another reason is that large-scale consulting firms, particularly those that sell to the CFO and CEO, may not buy into a phased approach. This is due in part to the belief that the consulting firm would need to resell each subsequent phase of the project in increments. If that consulting firm can convince the CFO or CEO to sign up for the entire, multi-million-dollar project, then that project is theirs in its entirety through the implementation phase.

These same consulting firms also find it more profitable to interview hundreds of users than to leverage the knowledge built into the legacy systems that define the rules that currently run the business. Executives also shy away from new ideas if they do not feel a comfort level with those ideas. The tendency in these situations is to gravitate back to a traditional strategy that involves an all-or-nothing approach to the application replacement or package deployment concept.

In spite of a reluctance to pursue a phased approach, logic dictates that a series of smaller, low-risk projects—each of which can be cost-justified in its own right—makes more sense than one big project with few or no interim deliverables. The phased approach can be applied to any type of data or application migration, redevelopment, package deployment, or smaller-scale project involving legacy architectures.

4.7 Transformation Strategy—Putting a Framework in Place

An enterprise must complete certain tasks as part of the creation and deployment of a transformation strategy. Legacy transformation does not represent a "business as usual" solution for IT, and it therefore requires more direct involvement of the executives than they may have had in the past. Initiating executives into this process normally requires an orientation session along with ongoing communication updates. These sessions are geared at shifting the IT planning process away from all-or-nothing approaches and toward a phased deployment approach that leverages legacy application and data assets.

One precursor to building a legacy transformation strategy involves assembling a team that can lead the development and subsequent deployment of a legacy transformation strategy. If there is an architecture team with executive level sponsorship and cross-functional business unit, third-party, and IT representation, they are the ones that should create and monitor a transformation strategy and deployment program. If this team is not in place, readers should refer to the infrastructure discussion in Chapter 5.

Another point that the management team should emphasize is that legacy transformation is enacted under a program and not through a one-time project. Legacy systems will always be around, so a transformation program must be enacted as an ongoing effort. The following steps form the basis for establishing and deploying an enterprise-wide transformation strategy.

1. Gain concurrence on the need for a legacy transformation strategy from the executive team. This process should utilize legacy architecture discussions presented in Chapters 1 and 2. This step also requires establishing an executive program sponsor within IT and various business units.
2. Establish additional communication and support infrastructures, as discussed in Chapter 5. These infrastructures include solidifying the architecture team that will head up the program.
3. Determine the availability of inhouse or third-party metrics, measurement criteria, and project planning facilities.
4. Examine the ability to perform cost, benefit, and value analysis on projects based on the maturity of inhouse cost-justification programs.
5. Identify potential software tools and, as needed, tool budgets. Various software technologies that can be used to support transformation projects are covered in depth in Chapter 7.
6. Indoctrinate inhouse project or program offices so they can begin to support transformation projects. This should include third-party program offices managed by outsourcing or consulting firms.
7. Launch a series of transformation communication sessions, but avoid using hype to promote the transformation concept. Most people do not appreciate hype, and it has been the death knell of good and bad ideas alike.
8. Create a list of major business initiatives that impact legacy architectures. The list should define the business impact, business owner, time constraints, business benefits, budgetary constraints, and impact on legacy applications and data structures where possible.
9. Identify potential scenarios that can benefit those initiatives. Build a suggested set of scenarios that could be deployed to fulfill these project requirements.

10. Build the resulting work product from the above steps into an executive summary, detailed documents, and presentations—incorporating inhouse standards as needed. Avoid squeezing the transformation strategy into waterfall or similar templates, as this will confuse people. If a manager demands this, you may be working at too low a level in the enterprise.

The following scenarios summarize how legacy architecture transformation strategies can be incorporated into selected business–IT initiatives to support certain business requirements. The project planning, cost analysis, tool requirements, and detailed techniques for deploying these scenarios are discussed in later chapters.

4.8 Transformation Scenarios—Project Planning Templates

Because most business professionals and IT executives have little time or inclination to sit around and discuss the fine points of varying legacy transformation disciplines, executive-level discussions of this topic must be driven by business scenarios. In other words, transformation, whether employed on a small scale in a maintenance upgrade or on a larger scale in relation to a redevelopment or consolidation project, should always be couched in terms of the business problem it is solving.

For example, a database consolidation and redesign project is more readily understood when positioned as a customer service improvement project. A legacy application gap analysis is more readily understood if it is positioned in terms of a larger initiative, like an ERP implementation. Similarly, a data definition rationalization project is more effectively sold if it is part of an HIPAA, data migration, or replacement project.

Transformation projects should not be positioned or justified as standalone efforts that are not connected with a business requirement. While this may appear evident to executives and the management team, rogue software reengineering projects have been launched over the years to extract business rules, rationalize data structures, fix poorly structured programs, and migrate to new technologies.

If these kinds of projects are not connected to and positioned primarily as business-driven scenarios, project initiators will likely have a hard time gaining executive sponsorship, project funding, business unit support, and cross-functional participation.

Another lesson learned over the past two decades of working on these projects relates to the concept of "dual positioning" transformation activities. Dual positioning ensures that the benefits and related tasks are positioned as having near-term and long-term benefits. This concept also refers to how various tasks can be applied to multiple business-driven scenarios.

An example of dual positioning is the identification and rationalization of redundant data definitions across one or more physical applications. This process can be cost-justified only if it is positioned as part of a bigger effort—such as an HIPAA initiative. Even then, management may erroneously assume that it can just go in and update payer identification fields by hand in the hundreds or thousands of physical record definitions where those fields are defined.

Further analysis may determine that these same data definitions have been targeted by data architecture teams as the basis for an integrated data design model. This model is to serve as the basis for a new data warehouse as well as the foundation for a new, target data architecture. These near-term, mid-term, and long-term projects could all benefit from the same task—rationalization of legacy data definitions—but it must be positioned this way from the start to effectively communicate the dual benefits of such an effort.

Scenarios, in practice, take the form of project templates that can be used and customized by various project team members. Scenario templates are modular, which means they can be combined, plugged into each other, or strung out in a multiphased project. For example, data migration and consolidation templates could serve as a subset of the application consolidation scenario.

Scenario templates are the basis for project plans that define the cost of a transformation project. The cost can then be compared to the value the project will deliver—which is typically a front-end planning task for the business, third-party, and IT personnel on the project team. Creating and delivering scenario-driven transformation solutions will occur only if executives establish an overall strategy that synchronizes legacy architectures with a cross-section of business information requirements.

The scenario discussions that follow are starting points for transformation planning teams. Scenarios can be combined, embedded, split, or executed in a specific sequence to meet a given set of business requirements. For example, a human resources (HR) system may reside on an outdated DEC platform and be using an older version of DEC COBOL. A planning team may decide to rehost the system, upgrade the language to Windows-compatible COBOL, rationalize the data definitions, standardize (i.e., structure) the source code, and integrate the system with a related HR application.

This example combined five scenarios to deliver a new HR system that was integrated with another HR system. Flexibility and out-of-the-box thinking are important factors to keep in mind as you build familiarity with various transformation scenarios.

The following sections overview generic scenarios that can be customized for specific projects. Scenarios should be renamed to reflect the project objective. For example, an application consolidation project would be called the HR consolidation project if it targeted multiple HR systems. Planning teams must remember to communicate transformation scenarios in business terminology or they will lose their audience and their funding.

4.9 Application Management Requirements and Scenario Overview

One of the first places to start applying legacy transformation principles is in the management and maintenance of legacy applications. A large number of applications have been outsourced to third parties to manage and maintain. Application outsourcing differs from facilities outsourcing. Outsourcing of facilities involves running a data center, operations, and other physical tasks. In application outsourcing, an outsourcing firm takes ownership of application maintenance, enhancement requests, late-night problem calls, and related support functions.

Turning over the ownership of one or more application systems to a third party provides benefits to an enterprise but also has a downside. The benefits include reducing application management costs, streamlining the time it takes to deliver upgrades and enhancements to users, and freeing up inhouse staff to work on other critical projects. The downside is that the application knowledge and software assets have been moved into a third-party domain, outside the control of application teams that may need access to that software. This is a major consideration if IT plans to use that application as part of a transformation project.

For example, assume that an order-processing system has been turned over to an application outsourcing firm. Now assume that a phased redevelopment initiative requires access to that application during a series of project steps that include

- Assessing the current system for potential reuse and integration purposes.
- Building EAI interfaces from a Web-based order-processing system.
- Extracting data usage and business logic from the application as input to the replacement system.

In other words, the legacy application has certain processing capabilities that a project team may need to invoke and serve as the source for additional information useful in the redevelopment of a replacement system. The need to have access to legacy applications that have been outsourced is likely to grow. Management should therefore review package replacement, multisystem consolidation, integration, data migration, and a variety of other projects involving legacy environments prior to finalizing an application outsourcing initiative.

Application outsourcing agreements should be structured in a way that facilitates access to the applications being outsourced. The agreement might state, for example, that inhouse personnel would receive a backup copy of the application source code on a periodic or upon-request basis for their review. Another option involves working with the outsourcing firm as a partner that can participate in one or more transformation projects.

Another aspect of an outsourcing agreement to consider is the ability to build an application improvement clause into the agreement. Some of the techniques discussed later in this book, such as rationalizing data definitions to use consistent names and definitions across the application, could be applied to these systems as a value-added service by the outsourcing firm. This is particularly useful in situations where the application is not being retired, has been targeted for integration with a Web-based front-end application, or is being used as a basis for data and business rule extraction for a new system.

Surfacing these challenges was not meant to dismiss outsourcing as an application management option for legacy architectures. This is a decision management must make on a case-by-case basis. It does suggest, however, that management should consider outsourcing requirements within the context of their legacy architecture transformation strategy.

Regardless of who is managing and maintaining your legacy applications, there are certain scenarios that can be applied to those applications and related data structures that can streamline efforts to upgrade them. These same scenarios also prepare applications for subsequent transformation scenarios, depending on the plans for those systems. Maintenance and management facilitation scenarios, highlighted in Figure 4.3, include

- Application documentation is a multiphased process for extracting data usage and process flows from systems. This scenario provides system planners, analysts, and programming teams with a better understanding of the application.
- Application improvement enhances the overall maintainability, understandability, and structure of an application as the basis for streamlining enhancements or related initiatives.

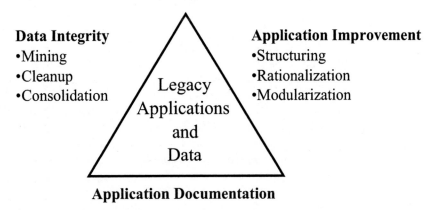

Application Management and Maintenance Facilitation Scenarios

Data Integrity
- Mining
- Cleanup
- Consolidation

Legacy Applications and Data

Application Improvement
- Structuring
- Rationalization
- Modularization

Application Documentation

Figure 4.3
Documentation, improvement, and data integrity scenarios streamline management and upgrade tasks.

- Data integrity improvement enhances data quality and reduces data redundancy.

Analysts can draft variations on each of the above scenarios and incorporate them into specific business-driven initiatives. Planning teams should determine the need to launch one or more of these initiatives from business and application enhancement plans and requirements.

4.10 Architecture and Application Documentation Scenarios

Attempting to understand the existing application architecture and source code is a challenge maintenance and enhancement personnel face daily. Whether fixing a bug or applying a multi-application upgrade, knowing where certain data and functions exist across application architectures reduces the cost and time associated with these tasks. For example, projects have shown that the process of applying a data or logic change on a legacy application could be improved up to 20 percent to 40 percent through the use of certain documentation technologies.

Y2K projects applied tools to help find certain data and related logic needing correction. Yet many of these tools were abandoned because Y2K teams were disbanded, because the tools were too specialized for general analysis tasks, or because a third party performed the work. One or a combination of the following application documentation scenarios may be applied based on the requirements of the team supporting those applications.

- **Cross-Functional Architecture Documentation**

    Many large-scale projects require an understanding of large cross-sections of the enterprise application architecture. While documenting the entire application architecture is a rare requirement, understanding major cross-sections of an application architecture provides useful insights into planning more detailed projects. High-level documentation defines which applications access major data stores, which applications perform certain functions, the flow of a transaction across related applications, and summary-level metrics. Transaction analysis is a common requirement for large-scale enhancements to stovepipe application architectures because it is difficult to tell where a given transaction begins and ends. These high-level scenario options typically require cross-functional collaboration, but can yield beneficial results from application planning and enhancement perspective. In addition to high-level cross-reference information, this analysis also delivers a list of unused or "dead" programs, data definition language models, screen maps, and data structures. These items should be excluded from future analysis efforts.

- **Application Flow Analysis and Mining**

  Application flow analysis and mining performs more detailed analysis on a smaller subset of the enterprise application architecture. This scenario is typically used by design analysts who need to drill down into a system to identify specific modules impacted by a given change request. Understanding how an application processes various transactions, which data structures are used by that application, and the program execution sequence provides basic documentation that can be used for planning a variety of maintenance or enhancement projects. This documentation includes job control or online screen flow charts, data structure where-used reports, screen mockups, summary metrics, and transaction flow analysis.

- **System- and Program-Level Data Definition Usage Analysis**

  Data documentation discussions must differentiate between the "cup" versus the "contents." In the case of application data usage, the source code, data definition languages, and screen maps define the cup that holds the data. The data (i.e., the contents) is addressed in a subsequent scenario. This level of documentation is useful for small-scale or large-scale changes impacting any data definitions that cross a program boundary—which by definition is virtually all data. This scenario delivers information that shows where physical data is used by various application programs, the level of redundant definitions across programs and systems, definitional inconsistencies, and possible candidate elements with conflicting semantics. This information is useful for maintenance, but essential for cross-application data initiatives.

- **Program Logic Flow Documentation**

  Complex legacy programs, written in various procedural languages, can be confusing to programmers not familiar with a given piece of software. Logic analysis tools depict the logic flow of a program, which can be quite convoluted in some cases. Certain source programs can contain 10,000 or even 20,000 lines of source code and can cause a programmer's eyes to glaze over. This level of documentation can be generated in a highly automated fashion and can be readily cost-justified for small-scale maintenance tasks.

- **Functional Documentation**

  Much of the information derived in the prior scenarios can be augmented with functional analysis of the applications and modules within a given business area. Analysts can augment physical cross-reference data about one or more applications with functional documentation. This requires gathering input from business and IT analysts and loading this information into an metadata repository (discussed in Chapter 7). Functional documentation can take the form of a general description of the functions supported by an application, program, or data structure, or it can utilize business rule data extracted from various programs. Functional documentation should be placed within a framework that has been built on one or more of the above architecture-, system-, or program-level documentation scenarios.

Leveraging the above scenarios to streamline application management requires justifying documentation tasks based on a reduction in maintenance or outsourcing costs. Another justification factor is the ability to use less experienced programmers on applications where senior professionals have moved on.

For more specific and extended projects, such as an HIPAA initiative, each of the above scenarios should be incorporated into specific project plans that support those initiatives. This process requires the creation of phased project plans that integrate tasks from each of the above scenarios at key points within the overall project. Project planning and related cost analyses are discussed further in Chapter 6.

4.11 Application Improvement Scenarios

Application improvement enhances the overall maintainability and structure of an application as the basis for streamlining enhancements or related initiatives. These improvement scenarios may be driven by the need to

- Improve an application to make it more understandable at the onset of an outsourcing project.
- Implement a data-oriented initiative or other cross-functional upgrade.
- Prepare application data definitions for a data migration and/or consolidation project.
- Help less experienced programmers navigate the application more efficiently and cost-effectively.

The following scenarios summarize basic application improvement options for legacy planning teams. These scenarios would typically be embedded in a scenario with specific business-oriented objectives.

- **Program Structuring and Modularization Improvements**
  The concept of using software tools and related techniques to impose a new structure and improved design on application programs was popular during the 1980s and early 1990s. When IT attempted to rewrite their applications using CASE, C, and now Java, interest in structuring and slicing tools and techniques dropped off. If an application is to be kept around and maintained over a period of two or more years, and the people working on that system are not familiar with it, structuring the source code, splitting up large programs, and recombining small programs is a justifiable activity. The benefits

include a reduction in how long it takes to apply changes, the ability to use less experienced programmers on the system, more confidence in the changes that are applied, reduced testing time, and lower maintenance costs. This scenario is also useful when used in conjunction with an application consolidation project.

- **Data Definition Rationalization**

  Rationalizing systemwide data definitions is valuable if there are plans to upgrade or reuse those definitions within the context of a larger initiative. It is important to remember that data definitions hold, but are distinct from, the actual physical data. Rationalization reduces the number of redundant, disparate, and conflicting references to physical data across one or more applications. An insurance company, for example, was able to reduce data definition redundancy within the claims area by 80 percent. This allowed them to change a data element in one place instead of in the hundreds of places where the data definitions had been hardcoded into the system. Data definition rationalization can be incorporated into a cross-functional data initiative or front-end data consolidation and migration scenarios.

4.12 Data Integrity Analysis and Improvement Scenarios

Data integrity analysis and improvement scenarios introduce consistency, improve the quality, and reduce data redundancy in physical data structures. Many organizations have countless data structures that are filled with invalid information or are redundantly defined across different applications. In addition, companies are seeking ways to extract information across these structures without actually changing them, and this is called data mining. The following data scenarios improve the quality of the data, but do not change the underlying data architecture.

- **Data Mining**

  Companies are finding it difficult to discern how certain data is being used across different physical data structures. Mining customer data, particularly across disparate data structures that contain the same data types with different data attributes, is a process that companies are using to support new marketing and customer research programs. Data mining uses tools to examine, compare, and extract related data and present it in a way that is useful to a business or marketing analyst. The benefits include the ability to make business decisions based on an improved understanding of implied data relationships.

- **Data Cleanup**

  Prior chapters provided some examples of where bad data can enter a production environment and hamper customer service, information tracking, and other critical business functions. Cleaning up enterprise data requires ascertaining valid values for the data in question, comparing these values to what is actually in the data, and replacing that data with valid values. Sometimes this is difficult because the business user does not know what the data should be. This scenario requires close coordination with business analysts and could be structured so that it becomes an ongoing process involving customer input and participation.

- **Data Redundancy Consolidation**

  Consolidating physical data redundancies, within this scenario, does not change the underlying data architecture. This is accomplished in a later scenario. This scenario combines existing physical structures into a single structure and typically involves reconciling format discrepancies. The value of data reconciliation is that it can reduce ongoing data maintenance tasks, serve as an interim step to future data migration efforts, or be combined with an application consolidation scenario. Management may also use this scenario to facilitate application rehosting, performance improvement, or auditing requirements.

These scenarios can be combined with functional data upgrade tasks, data definition rationalization, or related data migration scenarios. For example, a company may want to add a new customer, patient, or client identifier to legacy file structures. A combination of the documentation, data definition rationalization, and data cleanup scenarios could serve as a prerequisite to application and data file upgrade projects.

4.13 EAI: Front-End/Back-End Integration Scenario

A Morgan Stanley survey of 225 CIOs, completed in November 2001, identified application integration as their number one priority—tied with security [3]. EAI defines a multifaceted approach to noninvasive integration of Web-based environments and back-end applications and data. This scenario applies various middleware solutions to connect these front ends with legacy environments. The application server is becoming the main vehicle for accomplishing this objective.

The goal is to provide access to functions and data that Web applications do not have access to today. The important thing to consider when deploying an EAI scenario is that it should be coordinated closely with transformation planning teams who need to document these interfaces and assess how they impact related projects. An EAI environment can provide useful clues as to which Web applications require access to certain functions and related data. This information can provide a transformation map for future data and business rule extraction teams that need to enhance front-end applications with core business functionality.

4.14 Language and Platform Migration Scenarios

Moving an application from one platform to another or changing the language or language level being used by that system are transformation projects that require no logical redesign because it is merely a physical conversion. Language conversion and platform rehosting are the two main scenarios in this category.

- **Language-Level Upgrade and Conversion**

  A language-level upgrade moves an application from an older or obsolete version of that language to a modern or standardized version of that same language. Upgrading a system from an obsolete version of DEC, Hewlett-Packard, or Wang COBOL to a Windows version of COBOL that can run in a distributed environment is one example of a language-level upgrade. A language conversion, on the other hand, converts a language like Assembler to a more acceptable language, such as COBOL. Planning teams should be careful not to attempt to "convert" a procedural language, such as COBOL, to an object-oriented language, such as Java or C++. The result of such a project would produce unmaintainable Java code that would be essentially worthless. Logical transformation scenarios, on the other hand, involve modeling the target environment and migrating to those logical models. The value of standardizing on a common language or language level is portability, reusability, and maintainability.

- **Platform Rehosting**

  Platform rehosting involves moving an entire application and related data from one hardware platform to another. This typically requires a language upgrade or conversion along with the migration of the job control language, data definition language, screen definitions, and data to the new platform. The benefits of such a scenario include standardization, the elimination of obsolete or undesirable hardware, and the creation of an interim version of the application as a stepping stone to a consolidation or migration scenario.

4.15 User Presentation Migration Scenario

Migrating presentation views can be viewed as a scaled-back version of EAI. This scenario category is invasive because it modifies the user interface and, in some cases, the legacy application to create a Web-based or distributed front end on an existing application. The benefit of this approach is that it provides the user with a modern front end on a system that contains core legacy functionality and enterprise data access. The restriction on this scenario is that the resulting application remains locked into the stovepipe legacy architecture. It provides value, however, by taking an existing online legacy application and making it Web-enabled, which in turn makes the application more palatable to users and customers.

4.16 Data Migration and Consolidation Scenarios

The goal of the data migration and consolidation scenarios is to make data accessible in a relational or object-oriented format, which can then be accessed by Java and other modern applications that cannot access legacy files.

- **Data Migration**

  Data migration moves data representations from one logical data definition to a different logical data definition. For example, an organization can migrate a hierarchical, networked, or flat-file structure to a relational database. There are quick and dirty approaches to this scenario that do not adequately apply relational redesign techniques to the new database, but these are not recommended because they introduce poor data flexibility and promote inaccessibility—which is what this scenario is meant to correct in most cases.

- **Data Warehouse Development**

  The data warehouse scenario is a variation on the data migration scenario. This scenario does not impact existing data structures, but creates an extracted relational view of operational data. This operational view is then used for customer inquiries and other functions that could not be accomplished using operational data because it is too fragmented and splintered across disparate physical file structures and locations. A data warehouse project can also serve the dual purpose of creating a relational data model for an application and/or data migration and consolidation scenario.

- **Data Migration and Consolidation**

  This scenario migrates legacy data to a relational architecture while merging multiple physical data structures in the process. For example, assume that an inventory application has six "part management" databases of differing formats across six business units. This scenario reconciles each of these databases to create a combined view of the aggregate data from each of these systems. This scenario is normally associated with an application consolidation or migration scenario because it impacts operational data. For best results, this scenario should be combined with the data definition rationalization and data cleanup scenarios.

4.17 Application Consolidation—Reengineering in Place

The application consolidation scenarios apply a concept called "reengineering in place." This scenario is in contrast to the component-based architecture migration scenario (see below) because it does not attempt to re-create applications and data within a totally new paradigm (i.e., component architectures). This approach assumes that the same language and platform will continue to be used for the resulting consolidated application and data structures.

- **Multisystem Consolidation**

   One example of this scenario involved an organization that wanted to take standalone payroll, insurance, and pension applications and create a new, integrated HR application. The new application would contain all the basic functionality and data defined in the old systems, but also contain some new features. The new HR application would be designed around a consolidated relational database, which would be created using the data migration and consolidation scenario. This scenario involves business rule analysis, consolidation, and reuse. Benefits provide users of the system with a fully integrated application, not the old piecemeal systems that contained redundant, fragmented data and business logic.

- **Redundant Systems Consolidation**

   This scenario is very similar to the multisystem consolidation scenario, but involves consolidating multiple systems that are essentially the same. For example, the earlier example of the RBOC with several of the same billing applications would be a good application of this scenario. The fundamental approach in this situation is to identify overlapping logic, modules, or submodules, map them to a common set of consolidated routines, reconcile discrepancies, and create subroutines or tables to address unique regional requirements.

These scenarios provide approaches for an enterprise seeking a low-risk, phased approach to addressing application and data architecture fragmentation and redundancy challenges. They also serve as stepping-stone projects for an enterprise considering a migration to component architectures. The reengineering-in-place strategy is particularly valuable when the systems involved have a major impact on customers who have been putting up with inconsistent customer support due to fragmented information architectures.

4.18 Package Assessment and Implementation

ERP applications will continue to be the predominant option for enterprises looking for ready made software solutions. However, application packages rarely offer a total solution to an enterprise's unique business requirements. The two package scenarios below help an enterprise make sure that it selects the right package, which has not always been the case, and then crafts a pragmatic implementation approach once that selection process has been completed.

- **Package Analysis and Selection**

  The most important task in a package analysis and selection process is that of ensuring that the package meets the requirements of the business. This scenario involves a "gap" analysis to determine if one or more packages meet the business requirements. The value of this scenario to the business is that the right package is selected and the wrong package or packages are eliminated from consideration. In other words, the enterprise uses concrete analysis to avoid the costly mistake of selecting the wrong package based on vendor claims or personal relationships.

- **Package Implementation**

  Once a package is selected, analysts will need to perform additional gap analysis, shown in Figure 4.4. Gap analysis determines which pieces of the package should be implemented, which legacy applications must remain intact, how the package will need to interface with the new environment, where new functions need to be added, and how the data needs to be migrated. Historically, package-to-legacy architecture reconciliation efforts have not been formally defined and have been unnecessarily time-consuming and costly. This scenario streamlines package deployment and ensures that the appropriate mix of business functionality is derived from the package, legacy environments, and customer development efforts.

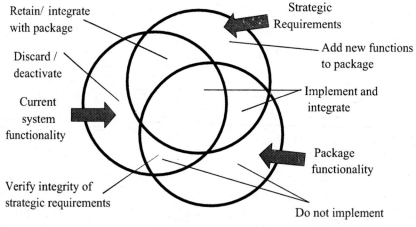

Figure 4.4

Package implementation scenario determines role of legacy systems and data, package, and new development.

4.19 Component-Based Architecture Migration

If an enterprise has made the decision to deploy component-based architectures, as discussed in Chapter 3, there are valid and invalid approaches for achieving these architectures. Transforming legacy business logic and data to a component-based environment is a logical transformation, not a conversion. Component-based migration scenarios can be used to help capture legacy business logic, reconcile redundancies, deploy a new data model, and redeploy these rules and related data attributes within a new component architecture.

The benefit of this scenario is that it moves selected business functionality and data from a legacy environment to a component environment that can begin to leverage reuse, Web Services, distributed platforms, new technologies, and modern architectures.

4.20 Transformation Strategy Summary

Determining overall business requirements and incorporating these into a business-driven perspective are critical tasks in building a transformation strategy. These requirements must drive the strategy, but are not the only consideration. New technologies, as discussed in Chapter 3, are being introduced into information environments at an astonishing pace, and the use and migration to these new technologies must be interwoven into a transformation strategy.

Another requirement is to understand management's position when it comes to dealing with legacy architectures. Digging into the history of failed projects is one way to do this. Some IT executives have given up trying to understand, realign, replace, or even upgrade legacy architectures with business requirements, while others continue exploring scrap-and-replace options that have not worked in the past and continue to show little promise. Communicating the value of legacy architecture transformation to the economic buyers within an enterprise is essential to the success of such an initiative.

Table 4.1 shows the impact of various transformation scenarios on legacy and target architectures. This impact analysis can be used to communicate differences in proposed project scenarios during management feasibility planning sessions.

One hidden element of transformation is the fact that departmental teams have used a variety of piecemeal legacy management, analysis, upgrade, and transformation tools over the years. Most of these projects fell under the executive "radar screen," rarely applied cross-functional disciplines, and have not been connected to an overall enterprise transformation strategy. These efforts may be beneficial to build upon, or they may have created a belief that these projects are not worth the effort. The latter is typically attributable to a lack of executive sponsorship for these projects.

Table 4.1
Scenario Architecture Impact Summary

Impact Scenario Category	Documentation	Legacy Application and/or Data Impact	Target Architecture Impact
Architecture and Application Documentation	X		
Application Improvement	X	X	
Data Integrity Analysis and Improvement	X	X	
Enterprise Application Integration (EAI)	X		X
Language and Platform Migration	X	X	
User Presentation Migration	X	X	X
Data Migration and Consolidation	X	X	X
Application Consolidation	X	X	
Package Assessment and Implementation	X	X	X
Component-Based Architecture Migration	X	X	X

Finally, the scenarios discussed in this chapter require a variety of infrastructure setup tasks, project planning and cost-justification activities, implementation techniques, and transformation tools. Many of the topics involved in a transformation strategy are basic elements of a good information management program—but an organization may not see it that way. Seeking ways to spread the benefit of these approaches to all relevant and affected parties is a good way to help gain acceptance at all levels of the organization. Deploying transformational disciplines will also improve the overall information management infrastructure within your enterprise.

Notes

1. "Who Is to Blame for ERP Failure?" Barry Calogero [Online], *serverworld-magazine.com*, June 2001.
2. "Chaos," The Standish Group [Online], *www.standishgroup.com/chaos.html*, Jan. 1998.
3. "Surveys Reveal Application Integration Is a Key Issue for CIOs in 2002," Ken Vollmer, *Idea Byte—GIGA Information Group*, Nov. 1, 2001.

Part II

Infrastructure Setup and Planning

Part 2 establishes the basis for planning and launching transformation initiatives within an enterprise. Chapter 5 discusses the business and information management infrastructure needed to deliver legacy transformation solutions. This chapter delves into the infrastructure issues responsible for creating the current legacy architecture dilemma. It also provides organizational transformation guidelines needed to address the legacy systems challenge and avoid re-creating it at some point in the future. Chapter 5 also outlines how to create a culture of reuse, project roles, and responsibilities, and discusses the part that methodologies, repositories, metrics, and software tools play in a transformation effort.

Chapter 6 discusses how to plan and justify legacy transformation projects. This includes issues such as total cost of ownership, techniques for determining return on investment (ROI), and ways to redefine the concept of *value* in an ROI effort. In addition, this chapter discusses collaborative planning concepts, project and team formation, the concept of *dual positioning* transformation ROI, how to learn from our failures, infrastructure justification, and project ROI.

Chapter 7 introduces the various technologies that an organization can use to plan, analyze, execute, and validate a transformation project. This includes the underlying foundation and various approaches used by these tools as well as an overview of various tool categories. This chapter also discusses the pros and cons of using certain tools for various transformation tasks and tool identification and procurement strategies. Chapter 8 details the tasks involved in performing the enterprise and project-level assessments. The enterprise assessment forms the basis for creating a transformation strategy or deploying a large-scale transformation initiative, such as a cross-functional package implementation. The project-level assessment begins the detailed analysis required to launch and finalize a transformation implementation project.

- **Chapter 5** Creating a Legacy Transformation Infrastructure
- **Chapter 6** Planning and Justifying a Legacy Transformation Project
- **Chapter 7** Legacy Transformation Technology
- **Chapter 8** Enterprise and Project-Level Assessments

Creating a Legacy Transformation Infrastructure

5

Albert Einstein once said, "We can't solve our problems using the same mind we used to create them" [1]. This is particularly true when it comes to addressing the legacy architecture challenges currently facing business and government institutions. Addressing these issues requires examining the cause- and effect-relationships that gave rise to the shortcomings inherent in these architectures. "Changing our thinking" in this case involves looking beyond quick fixes to address the underlying infrastructure weaknesses that spawned these architectures in the first place.

In fast-paced business environments driven by quarterly returns, infrastructure investments get shortchanged. Infrastructure also gets neglected within government sectors, although in these cases it results from a reluctance to tamper with entrenched political hierarchies. One commonality found across the private and the public sectors is that people gravitate toward shortcuts when they should be focusing on long-term solutions to complex information challenges. The rapid and explosive rise of EAI is one example of an interim tactic that has been positioned as a long-term solution. In addition to contributing to the creation of convoluted legacy architectures, shortcut solutions also stymie efforts to realign data and application architectures with business infrastructures and requirements.

Legacy architecture transformation is an alternative to the quick fix because it promotes a series of tactical steps that collectively establish more agile and more effectively aligned information architectures. Selling executives on the value of a phased solution to a problem as an alternative to the quick fix is difficult because it challenges "business as usual" thinking. To overcome this difficulty, planning teams must instill a more open-minded philosophy and certain disciplines to facilitate cross-functional, business-driven transformation initiatives. This philosophy and related disciplines are embodied within the transformation infrastructure.

The infrastructure provisions detailed in this chapter establish a foundation for creating, applying, and sustaining a legacy architecture transformation strategy. Employing these infrastructure recommendations will also help ensure that future information architectures are more agile and more effectively aligned with current and future business requirements. Infrastructure topics include organizational alignment and collaboration, process and methods, measurement, software tools, and skill building.

5.1 Business–IT Alignment Requirements

In *The Biology of Business* [2] Andy Clark states, "Markets, companies, and various forms of business organizations can all be usefully viewed through the lens of complex adaptive systems." He goes on to say that a market or a company is self-organizing where "crucial interactions are not controlled or orchestrated by an overseeing executive, a detailed program, or any other source of strict hierarchy." A growing number of management theorists, consultants, and futurists have echoed this view. In other words, institutional structures are becoming more organic and less mechanistic. IT must be able to adapt to these changes.

As introduced in Chapter 2, legacy information architectures were patterned after hierarchical organizational models pioneered by Alfred Sloan of General Motors [3]. These hierarchies are slowly giving way to organic networks of individuals that require an increasingly open and rapid exchange of information flow across and beyond enterprise boundaries. As these hierarchies give way, IT will need to retool relationships with customers, business units, and suppliers. Addressing this evolutionary shift in organizational structure is a key component of a legacy transformation strategy, and IT can take a leading role in this process.

Business–IT alignment is a recognized industry challenge. According to a Cutter Consortium survey, respondents overwhelmingly reported that the top two limitations to their e-business initiatives were vague business objectives (41 percent) and lack of integration between business and IT (39 percent) [4]. These two findings suggest that IT needs to discover new ways to collaborate and communicate with the business entities that it supports.

The onus is on IT to drive this integration and alignment process because business units do not have a clear understanding of the challenges faced by IT. In other words, IT must initiate business, third-party, and IT alignment discussions or continue to turn poorly defined requirements into functionally inadequate applications.

To meet this objective, IT and business planning teams should review and incorporate the following organizational principles into an overriding information management philosophy. These principles form the foundation for strategic IT initiatives as well as a legacy architecture transformation strategy.

- Seek out ways to improve collaboration among third parties and business units that have been segregated by traditional organizational models or hierarchies.
- Ensure that IT redefines its relationship with customers, business units, distributors, and suppliers to remain synchronized within an increasingly organic organizational model.
- Assess and adjust IT, business unit, and third-party relationships as the basis for creating collaborative solutions to the transformation of legacy information architectures.
- Examine ways to realign legacy architectures to more closely reflect the reality of loosely coupled networks of business units, customers, suppliers, distributors, and IT teams.

While many of the above infrastructure principles may seem tangential to a legacy architecture transformation strategy, they are not. If IT is misaligned with business units and third parties, IT initiatives will remain poorly synchronized with the needs of those business units and third parties. In addition to staying aligned with the business, an IT organization must be aligned with its own goals and objectives.

Most important, the execution of a transformation strategy is prone to failure in a poorly aligned organizational structure. Transformation efforts are unlikely to be launched or could get cut short if a project team cannot effect changes on business processes, applications, and data structures that cross corporate hierarchies. IT will also have difficulty determining if a legacy transformation strategy is on track if that strategy has not been aligned with the business infrastructure and related information requirements.

To accomplish these goals in conjunction with an overall transformation strategy, IT will need to address the issue of centralization versus decentralization, collaboration through a virtual community structure, organizing principles, and related roles and responsibilities.

5.2 Looking Past the IT Centralization/ Decentralization Argument

One alignment challenge is the argument over IT centralization versus decentralization. Unfortunately, this is the wrong question. The real issue is determining how well business, IT, and third parties have aligned responsibilities for the effective management of information to support time-critical business requirements. This is an accountability issue—an issue that gets lost every time executives attempt to rearrange the boxes on the organization hierarchy chart.

Before discussing ways to achieve business–IT alignment, it is useful to provide some background on how IT functions have historically been distributed across an enterprise under various centralized and decentralized management models. In a centralized IT organization, information management reports up through a single chain of command. Decentralized IT, in contrast, distributes the management of IT through a multitude of command chains. A hybrid approach involves centralizing some functions, such as facilities management, while decentralizing others, such as application management.

Arguments for centralization focus on coordination, standardization, and consolidation of facilities and equipment, processes, technology, and customer and vendor management. Centralization also provides economies of scale, reduction of redundancies, and improved management efficiencies. Arguments for decentralization center on allowing business units to make and implement autonomous decisions about business supply chain, distribution chain, and customer-driven information requirements.

Over the years, IT has centralized, decentralized, and recentralized again and again in an attempt to fix a more systemic problem: the inadequacy of hierarchical governance structures as a vehicle for managing information infrastructures. Continuous reorganizations tend to make things worse. Anyone who has undergone multiple reorganizations, driven by the need to trim costs or suit the fancy of the new CIO, knows that rearranging the boxes on an organizational hierarchy chart tends to do more harm than good. It demoralizes people or makes them more cynical about management's ability to govern.

One major healthcare provider underwent three such decentralization and centralization efforts within a three year span. People actually doing the work in the lower half of the organizational hierarchy either ignored these goings on or found ways to work around it within the informal channels that emerge in most enterprises. These informal channels allow real work to get done—until people encounter an organizational hurdle they cannot circumvent.

Lost in the centralization and decentralization battle is the issue of accountability. Legacy transformation solutions rely on institutionalizing accountability for the quality of the information management function across the virtual enterprise. A comparable level of accountability is already in place in the financial management practices of an enterprise, because the legal system and accounting principles mandate accounting practices. Until this level of accountability and discipline is imposed upon information functions, it is up to the management team to monitor and self-correct poor information practices and related architectures.

5.3 IT Realignment—Forming Virtual IT Communities

The reorganization trend must give way to a more measured strategy that combines the most effective elements of centralized and decentralized IT without the need to rebuild the organization over and over again. New collaborative organizational structures must be adaptive and be able to self-organize so internal and external dynamics do not trigger yet another reorganization.

Information management has become an increasingly virtual practice because IT-related tasks are distributed across a growing number of business users, partners, and customers. This is evidenced by the proliferation of Web sites, distributed systems, outsourcing, portals, and supply chain consortiums that expose enterprise information environments to the outside world. This level of exposure dramatically increases the need for a governance structure that is more collaborative and can adapt to the increasing demands of highly distributed and less predictable business environments.

The emergence of the virtual enterprise suggests that IT can no longer funnel information management tasks through a hierarchical infrastructure in a business climate that is becoming increasingly permeable. As an alternative, IT should establish a loosely coupled, collaborative infrastructure that allows business, third-party, and IT professionals to self-organize into virtual communities, as needed, to accomplish a given set of tasks or in pursuit of a common purpose.

IT virtual communities provide for a working infrastructure that is more collaborative and conducive to building and deploying a legacy transformation strategy. The following steps outline a high-level process for creating such a virtual community among relevant and affected participants in the information management process.

- Establish an organizational design team with cross-functional business and IT responsibilities to realign current IT activities.
- Identify various functions that IT performs or should be performing and review this with people from each of these functional areas.
- Develop a self-describing purpose for each of these function areas.
- Formalize a virtual community that is responsible for fulfilling each purpose within each functional area.
- For each virtual community, establish a set of principles that will guide that community in achieving its purpose.
- Allow individuals from various business units, third parties, and IT to associate themselves with these new virtual communities.
- Create a constitution stating that individuals associated within these virtual communities will abide by their stated purpose and principles [5].

This newly aligned virtual IT community can coexist with the existing organizational model. In other words, people may still report to an individual in a business unit, but work toward the purpose and abide by the principles established for each IT community they have self-selected. Figure 5.1 depicts a high-level view of various functional IT communities [6]. Under this structure, individuals can physically remain in their same location, but they are virtually tied to the purpose and principles of the IT community (or communities in some cases) they self-selected.

Sample Virtual IT Community Model

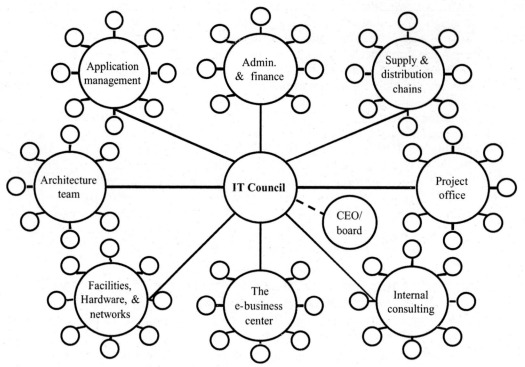

Figure 5.1
Major or inner community groups form as a result of smaller or outer groups coming together under
a common purpose.

Under this governance structure, traditional IT functions such as network coordination or communications management evolve into a series of virtual communities comprised of representatives from across the enterprise. These centralized communities may mirror formal IT units, but also incorporate personnel from other business units. Some of these individuals may be third-party participants. Application teams, under this model, may reside in multiple business units but share a common purpose and operating principle.

For example, assume that a multidivisional RBOC has established a new IT governance structure and that IT personnel from various business units and central IT are participating in this new structure. A customer resource information system (CRIS) community, for example, may define its purpose as follows: "Increase the efficiency and effectiveness of all customer and related business activities managed or impacted by CRIS applications across the enterprise."

This purpose would need to be supported by a set of principles that bind the virtual team responsible for managing multiple CRIS applications and related data. A brief subset of these principles could, for example, include

- Focus on the customer as a top priority in all CRIS application-related decisions.
- Collaborate on all CRIS application decisions with cross-functional impact.
- Involve representation from all relevant and affected business and IT units in these decisions.
- Seek a coordinated strategy to create a consolidated set of CRIS applications and data structures.

The above purpose and related principles can be used to establish a "constitution" that participants commit to as part of their role within the extended enterprise. Anyone working within a business unit, IT role, or third party that participates in the planning or evolution of any CRIS application would commit to this list of principles to guide their actions in fulfillment of their agreed-upon purpose.

Other application teams and various specialty functions, shown in Figure 5.1, would form communities around a common purpose and create a set of principles to guide their actions in accordance with that purpose. As related communities found the need, they could form and send representatives to common communities. For example, application teams could form a community to which they send representatives to discuss package selection, integration, or consolidation option on an enterprise scale.

It is important to note that application communities are formed locally and join together to form "inner" communities. Inner communities are an assemblage of outer communities around a common purpose. Centralized functions, such as hardware management, are more likely to form centrally and enlist participants from distributed units later. Each of these inner communities could join to form an IT council. This council would be responsible for major IT decisions that impact an aggregate of various communities across the enterprise.

This self-organizing infrastructure incorporates IT, business, and third-party professionals. Communities can form or disband based on the establishment or fulfillment of their purpose. Inner communities form as needed to address common issues.

Under this adaptive and collaborative infrastructure, new concepts can be quickly tested and shared. Mistakes are also communicated more quickly and therefore less likely to be repeated by related communities. Areas where new strategies could quickly take hold include the proliferation of new IT infrastructure components, such as agile methods or new technologies, as well as the deployment of a shared transformation strategy. One community that is required for the creation and deployment of a transformation strategy is the architecture team.

5.4 The Architecture Team—Synchronizing Enterprise IT Initiatives

Legacy information architectures continue to grow in sophistication and complexity. One of the main contributors to convoluted legacy architectures are piecemeal approaches taken by one project team that conflicts with and greatly complicates the ongoing efforts of other teams or departments. This lack of coordination is common, yet problematic from a long-term architecture perspective.

One project team could, for example, create an order processing subsystem that fulfills the immediate needs of one business area, but should have been incorporated into a more comprehensive effort to streamline order processing across multiple business units. This order processing subsystem may even create functional redundancies that would complicate data reconciliation activities for users and stymie more comprehensive solutions that could benefit the enterprise as a whole.

The diversity of development and management platforms, standards, processes, data architectures, and software technologies creates decision-making scenarios that should be considered from an aggregate perspective. Efficient and effective selection and deployment of strategic information architectures, along with the planning, integration, and transformation of legacy architectures, require the coordination and focus of an IT architecture team.

In the absence of this type of coordination, individual technology teams, business units, application areas, and third parties will be on their own to stumble through a series of trial-and-error technology selection and abandonment scenarios. The aforementioned health care provider that reorganized three times in three years disbanded its central technology assessment and coordination center during one such negotiation. This resulted in the loss of scarce architectural knowledge, the replication or disbursement of critical architecture skills, and the proliferation of poorly coordinated projects.

While lost productivity, wasted resources, and misuse of funds are enough to justify an architecture team, cross-functional coordination presents an even a stronger case for such a team.

The uncoordinated propagation of technologies, applications, and data creates an environment that stymies cross-functional integration—an essential component in virtually every e-business and business-to-business initiative. Business units wonder why systems cannot communicate, why user requests take so long to fulfill, and why Web-based applications cannot communicate with legacy systems. The answer lies in poorly coordinated technical and information architectures.

Forming a virtual architecture community, as shown in Figure 5.2, allows an enterprise to achieve architectural "synergy." This community would function throughout the enterprise in the form of local individuals working within various business, IT, and third-party teams. Other than establishing a small core team to facilitate and coordinate activities, no significant reorganization is required to create a virtual

Architecture Team Virtual Communities

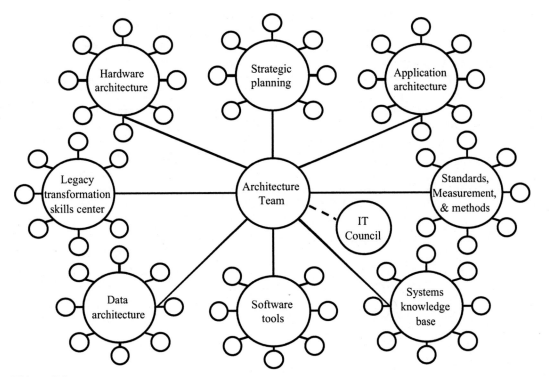

Figure 5.2
An architecture team supports enterprise-wide and localized technical and functional planning along with method and tool deployment.

architecture community. This is because the team would be comprised of IT, business, and third-party professionals, bound by a common purpose and operating principles, in a common effort to synchronize enterprise information architectures.

An architecture team's purpose may, for example, be stated as follows: "Create an environment where all business applications, data, and users can readily and effectively communicate with related applications, data and users." The important concepts to remember when forming such a team is to ensure that it embodies the needs and desires of all relevant and affected parties in the community affected by architectural decisions. This objective can be achieved by creating this team through a bottom-up, versus a top-down, approach.

Figure 5.2 depicts various communities that an architecture team may include in its charter. Each community includes representatives from relevant business units, IT, and third parties—bound by a common purpose. The application architecture community, for example, represents individuals from application areas that focus on cross-functional consolidation, replacement, or package deployment initiatives. This group would send representatives to participate in a central architecture team whenever collaborative decisions are required that incorporate other functions, such as data or hardware architecture planning.

A virtual architecture community provides a vehicle for project teams to band together to pursue common goals and collaborate on broader initiatives. Participants joining the architecture team should be empowered to make decisions that impact hardware, software, application, and data architecture. These individuals also participate in the process of identifying, selecting, procuring, and distributing software technologies, methodologies, and other facilities that can help streamline information-related projects.

Operating principles define how participants in the architecture team act in pursuit of their purpose. A principle may state, for example, that technologies counter to the architecture team's recommendations can be adopted if they do not run counter to the architecture team's purpose. Virtual community operating principles provide a degree of latitude for participants because they describe an end result and never tell people how to do their jobs.

Establishing and empowering an architecture team will likely meet political resistance. If the team has proper, sponsorship, representation, a commonly accepted purpose and clear operating principles, the odds of their success will increase dramatically. The architecture team plays an important role in the development, communication, selling, support, and implementation of a legacy architecture transformation strategy.

5.5 Creating a Culture of Reuse

Legacy transformation is based on establishing an appreciation for the value inherent in leveraging legacy architectures in the creation and deployment of new information initiatives. Legacy transformation is based on the principle of reuse versus rebuilding. Reuse is a powerful concept if positioned and implemented effectively. The concept of reuse involves

- Seeking data and business logic that already exists as an alternative to building those components from scratch.
- Creating an infrastructure that supports and encourages reuse across the virtual information enterprise.
- Establishing a culture that rewards reuse and creates disincentives to the pursuit of needless redundancy.
- Adopting and leveraging emerging reuse models such as component architecture and Web Services.

The concept of reuse was introduced in Chapter 3 during the discussion of component-based architectures. These architectures, particularly Web Services, are the ultimate manifestation of reuse. If an enterprise buys into the concept of reuse, it would seem logical that its first step would be to seek opportunities where reuse can be applied and leveraged across legacy architectures. Legacy transformation offers IT the opportunity to build credibility in the area of reuse. An organization should, for example, consider legacy reuse versus paying for less complete functionality from an application vendor.

Building a new piece of code or an application is costly and time-consuming regardless of the technology being used. Rebuilding an interest rate calculation, order-handling capability, or account posting logic that must interface with existing customers or partners is also risk-prone because that logic may no longer function within previously agreed-upon specifications. Reusing existing logic, particularly if that logic is going to be used in a replacement or complementary application that needs to synchronize with existing processes and business rules, reduces the cost, time, and the risk of building, testing, and implementing new applications.

The concept of reusing legacy applications serves as the foundation from which application development, integration, and package selection and deployment projects can be launched. Reuse should be used to either augment or displace application package procurement and new development options wherever possible. Reuse of legacy data and business logic

- Can streamline application design and deployment by augmenting the task of building new functionality.
- Provides software solutions that are already proven to work in production environments.
- Establishes a foundation for new applications and, at a minimum, a basis for design analysis.
- Can augment application packages that deliver only part of the required application functionality.
- Offers a rich source of potentially reusable components that can be redeployed under component-based architectures and Web Services delivery models.

The concept of reuse extends well beyond its role in a legacy architecture transformation strategy. Reuse is central to the deployment of components and Web Services. If the management team does not buy into reuse, then they also do not buy into component-based development or Web Services. Efforts to sell the concept of legacy transformation should leverage the IT industry's newfound predisposition toward reuse.

In Chapter 4, I discussed the importance of phased deployment for transformation projects. Phased deployment complements reuse because the process of determining reusability requires the phased discovery of reusable data, designs, interfaces, and components. Reuse coupled with the concept of phased deployment creates a basis for risk aversion and cost and time reduction in transformation projects.

5.6 The Sponsor, the Champion, and the Evangelist

Gaining support for a legacy architecture transformation strategy requires imparting basic values and a level of understanding within an information management infrastructure. This requires building support for such a strategy on multiple levels. A sustainable transformation strategy requires instilling the concepts of risk aversion and cost reduction through reuse and phased deployment at an executive, management, and implementation level. This multitiered support structure manifests itself in the form of the sponsor, the champion, and the evangelist.

A transformation sponsor should be an executive that can fund and cajole fellow executives into supporting alternative approaches to IT initiatives. Initial funding, which is discussed along with cost justification in Chapter 6, is required to establish an infrastructure, license software tools, and create a support system for various projects.

Just as important, however, is the need for a sponsor to sell the idea of transformation within the executive team. Sponsorship must be established across vertical business boundaries. It is not enough to just have executive IT sponsorship, although this is important. In many cases business unit sponsorship is also required because the business owner of an application typically provides project funding. Gaining sponsorship can be accomplished through the following steps.

- Identify historic failed projects, cost overruns, or missed deadlines that occurred over the past few years.
- Find commonalities in these failures that could have been prevented through a program of transformation, reuse, and phased deployment.
- Highlight planned information initiatives that compare in scope and type to the failed initiatives.
- Gain approval to supply a detailed cost analysis for a transformation approach versus historical approaches currently being planned or under way.
- Selectively pilot these approaches on candidate projects.

Planning teams should also review projects in progress that might also be candidates for a transformation approach. Many times projects in progress can still benefit from applying certain elements of a transformation approach because of the phased nature of this approach. For example, if a project is under way to rebuild one or more applications and the team is struggling with that project, consider how an assessment of the current data structures or applications could be used to augment requirements analysis. This may not be politically viable, but it should be presented to the executive team as an option.

In addition to developing IT and business unit sponsorship, transformation programs require champions and evangelists. A champion is typically a manager who understands and is willing to promote the concept of transformation. An early champion is probably a member of the architecture team and behind efforts to initiate the transformation strategy and obtain sponsorship. Additional champions are useful as well because a solo champion can retire, change job titles, or leave for varying reasons. Losing a champion effectively ended a number of successful transformation programs.

The evangelist is a highly respected technical individual who is known within the enterprise for delivering on projects when needed. The champion will need to pair up with an evangelist because it will be difficult to sell the concept of transformation without support from a respected analyst within the inner circle of various application domains.

Many Y2K projects succeeded because there was a champion and an evangelist who drove these projects forward. Building sponsorship, establishing champions, and recruiting internal evangelists provide a strong foundation for ongoing transformation initiatives within an enterprise.

5.7 Role of Third Parties in a Transformation Strategy

Third parties play a major role in ongoing architecture transformation efforts. In many cases, third parties need to be involved because they have taken an ongoing role in the management of information-related tasks. In other cases, third parties can help deliver key initiatives because inhouse IT professionals may not have the skills or the tools needed to accomplish certain tasks.

Outsourcing firms and application service providers (ASPs), for example, have responsibility in many organizations for managing significant segments of the application and data architecture. In these situations, it is likely that these third-party-managed applications may be involved in transformation planning and implementation efforts. The best way to include these organizations in these efforts is to have third-party representation within the virtual architecture communities that have input to cross-functional transformation plans.

For example, assume that a customer billing system has been outsourced to a third party and that a new ERP application is being implemented to displace this billing system along with a dozen other applications. Existing billing data and application functionality will need to be assessed as an integral part of the package implementation process. The replacement of one application along with the migration of legacy data structures requires in-depth understanding of the legacy applications.

If the outsourcing firm is not engaged in this effort as a partner and a participant, the migration to the ERP package could encounter major delays and cost overruns. Ultimately, the effort to displace outsourced applications may fail and only a subset of the ERP functionality would end up being implemented. These types of package deployment problems, as discussed earlier, are common within the IT industry. Not engaging third-party application management teams increases the odds of package deployment failures.

Third parties also play a role in providing planning and implementation skills, processes, and tools to legacy architecture transformation projects. Consulting firms, for example, can be used to supplement inhouse skills in the planning, analysis, and implementation of these projects. It is important that organizations view these relationships as partnerships. A consulting firm should not work unilaterally on a project, but in conjunction with application and architecture teams toward a common set of objectives.

This has not always been the case. One large consulting company created a subsystem that was both functionally and technologically incompatible with the existing information architecture. The CIO commissioned this project without conferring with relevant and affected architecture and application support teams. These teams could have prevented the implementation of an incompatible subsystem that did nothing to address critical business requirements—if they had been included in the decision process.

It is important to coordinate legacy transformation projects with relevant third parties on an ongoing basis. Incorporating third-party input into legacy transformation efforts early in the cycle helps ensure that these projects reflect a comprehensive approach based on participation from all affected parties. The best way to accomplish this is to establish a continuing dialog with these third parties by incorporating them into virtual IT communities shown in Figures 5.1 and 5.2. The architecture team, in particular, provides a good forum for maintaining this level of ongoing dialog. Executing conflicting or poorly coordinated strategies without involving third parties is a sure way to disrupt phased legacy transformation initiatives.

5.8 Agile Methodologies and Collaborative Project Management

One challenge that transformation and development projects face is the need to manage complex and decentralized projects. In Chapter 3 I reviewed agile methodologies with a specific focus on Extreme Programming as one example of an agile method. Extreme Programming provides rigor for analysis, design, development, and testing tasks. A project management process, on the other hand, addresses project coordination and delivery and is a key element within a transformation delivery infrastructure.

Managing diverse tasks in highly distributed development environments with interim delivery windows demands new approaches to the discipline historically known as project management. Project management includes the ability to deliver required functionality, at specific project intervals, for an agreed-upon cost. An organization's project management capabilities will either increase the odds of success—or increase the possibility of failure.

Project management impacts legacy transformation in two important ways. Transformation projects rely on the coordinated efforts of IT, business, and third-party professionals, and therefore require good project management skills. Long term, the delivery of functionally acceptable applications will reduce the need for future legacy transformation projects because the applications being deployed reflect a cross-functional set of requirements.

Project management may be viewed within the context of virtual communities. Under this view, there is a recognized need to increase participation from relevant and affected parties and place a greater focus on collaboration of distributed teams. This approach is augmented by a shift away from tightly controlled project management practices and focus on a deliverable based project management practice with distributed project teams. The project office community, shown in Figure 5.1, provides oversight for these projects.

Project management challenges can be met through more effective collaboration. Consider this familiar scenario. A group of business unit managers wants a system replaced, but cannot articulate why or how. In response, executives have hired consultants to define a set of from-scratch requirements for a new replacement system. The consulting firm, however, is not coordinating its efforts with the corporate architecture group. To complicate the situation, the existing maintenance team thinks a redesign effort without their input will fail. Yet repeated replacement efforts have ignored their potential contributions. Complicating this already impossible situation is the fact that the entire initiative lacks executive sponsorship.

Consider some of the challenges facing this project versus those cited by participants in the previously referenced Standish Group study [7]. Top issues found in this study include (1) a lack of user involvement, (2) inadequate executive support, (3) no clear requirements statement, (4) improper planning, and (5) unrealistic expectations. This study and the prior project scenario point to the fact that many project teams lack the cohesion needed to bring major initiatives to a successful and timely conclusion. The inability to collaborate with disparate groups of participants is problematic for legacy transformation projects and most other cross-functional initiatives.

Jim Highsmith wrote, in *Adaptive Software Development: A Collaborative Approach to Managing Complex Systems*, "Approaching software development as an adaptive process, and viewing the project team itself as a living organism rather than an impersonal machine, provides a better model for managing extreme software projects" [8]. Highsmith argues for applying collaborative approaches to software projects. Collaborative approaches are what a virtual community embodies from an organizational perspective. Project virtual communities follow the same collaborative model as more permanent IT community structures.

A project office community, shown in Figure 5.1, incorporates roles such as enterprise resource integration, planning support, methods, measurement, reporting, tools, and outreach. A sample statement of purpose for the project office might say, "Foster an environment where projects are routinely delivered on time, within budget, and within the level of quality required for that project and business unit." Sample principles supporting this purpose might include

- Each project should raise the level of customer satisfaction.
- Every project should enjoy the resources needed to succeed.
- Project management should have current data regarding skill availability for internal and external resources.
- Internal and outsourced projects should live up to a predetermined level of quality.
- Tracking and reporting on project progress should be done in a fully open manner.
- Troubled projects should be corrected or halted before too much time, money, and value are lost.
- All projects should contribute to and benefit from a feedback loop based on historic successes and failures.

Launching a project requires gathering all stakeholders contributing to or benefiting from the project, determining each participant's stake in the effort, surfacing and resolving conflicts, and agreeing on a common purpose. Stakeholders include sponsors, users, customers, designers, developers, and support teams for the proposed system and any systems it may replace. Ignoring this requirement can doom a project to ongoing false starts, design delays, and cancellation.

Refocusing distributed project management on a deliverable-oriented plan versus a task-oriented plan streamlines the overall management of cross-functional projects. The concept involves each team taking responsibility for a set of deliverable items that they will deliver within a fixed timeframe. Combining this with the Extreme Programming concept of delivering value in short intervals creates a more agile project management model for large projects.

Transformation projects should therefore focus on delivering interim value under a phased strategy, take a deliverable-oriented instead of a task-oriented approach, not attempt to micromanage distributed teams, and ensure that all relevant and affected stakeholders are involved in the planning and project oversight.

5.9 Transformation Methodology

Using a transformation methodology is recommended for organizations applying a cross-section of transformation scenarios, techniques, and tools to multiple projects. The scenario, technique, and tool overviews provided in this book provide a framework for transformation projects. A formal transformation methodology additionally offers project-estimating models and detailed technique and tool guidelines.

As an enterprise embarks upon and continues to build its transformation knowledge base, it will want to document useful techniques within an internal Web site or repository that it can draw upon based on various scenarios. A commercial transformation methodology is organized around the concept of drawing upon certain techniques based on the project scenario being pursued by the project team. This is very similar to concepts presented in the remaining portions of this book where project planning guidelines drive the need to apply certain transformation techniques to a variety of project scenarios.

A commercial transformation methodology incorporates planning and estimating guidelines, detailed tool and technique guidelines, commercial tool recommendations, metrics, forms and project planning, and process management tool links. Certain consulting companies can provide a transformation methodology as part of their project commitment. Commercial transformation methodologies are listed in Appendix A.

5.10 The Transformation Repository

Transformation planning teams need to determine the scope of applications, data structures, and functions involved in various transformation projects that can cross business unit or enterprise boundaries. A related difficulty involves identifying relationships, redundancies, and impacts across business units, functions, data structures, and applications. The ability to track this type of information across projects and environments is most effectively accomplished with the help of a transformation repository.

Mapping and understanding the scope of the information enterprise are essential for many transformation projects, particularly when they cross application boundaries. Because many transformation analysis and implementation projects cross functional boundaries, this repository provides a basis for understanding a legacy environment that few individuals or existing documentation can articulate with any degree of depth or accuracy.

For example, a government project needed to track a tax transaction from the point that it entered the system to the point where it was registered. Because a given transaction was handled by a series of stovepipe applications that passed data across a number of hardware platforms, data types, and systems, there was no documentation in place as to how this occurred. Capturing and loading this type of information into a repository was a powerful vehicle for communicating how a tax transaction flowed across disparate legacy environments.

Figure 5.3 is a repository model similar to the one used on the tax agency project. Note that business processes are linked to application functions. These functions are in turn linked to the source programs that automate them. Business processes can also be associated with the business unit or units performing them

Detailed Legacy Transformation Repository

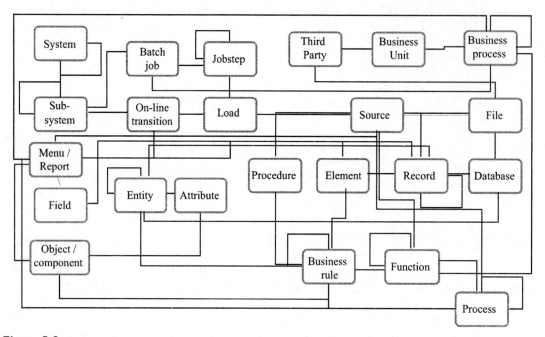

Figure 5.3

The detailed transformation repository depicts legacy and target system components and relationships to support transition planning and management.

as well as the online transactions or batch jobs that trigger the execution of the functions that enable those processes.

A significant portion of the repository model in Figure 5.3 can be derived from the physical application environment using automated analysis tools. The identification and documentation of business processes and related application functions must be derived and added by humans. The collective set of information in such a repository represents a knowledge base of the enterprise information environment. This repository can be used to

- Document applications for strategic planning, upgrade, or replacement efforts.
- Detail where application upgrades impacting specific business processes or functions need to be performed.
- Provide the basis for mapping legacy functionality to required functionality for migration projects.

- Represent data and functional redundancies as the basis for creating an integration or consolidation plan.
- Delineate where legacy data and functionality can be mapped to an application package and deactivated or integrated into the application environment.
- Provide the foundation for configuration management, security planning, or other infrastructure projects.
- Document as-is application and business environments to streamline the transition to an outsourcing project.

While not all business processes may be automated, analysts should still document them in this repository because they represent future automation requirements for application upgrade or package implementation efforts. The repository model shown in Figure 5.3 is too granular to represent a sizeable enterprise in its entirety. This particular view is geared toward a single business unit or major application area. Business executives or strategic planning teams will want to work with a higher-level view of this information, such as the model depicted in Figure 5.4.

Enterprise Transformation Repository

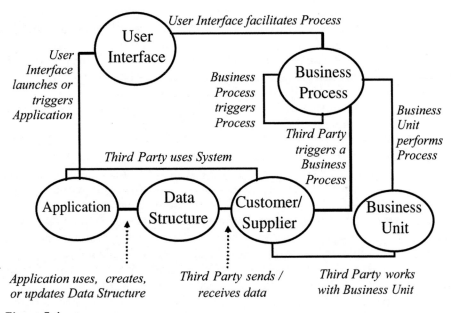

Figure 5.4

Transformation repository maps data and application architecture to business units, business processes and third parties.

The enterprise-level transformation repository is an aggregate view of information collected at a more detailed level. This high-level repository can also be created through a series of interviews and refined over time. The concept of creating tiered repositories suggests that analysts could create application, business unit, divisional, or enterprise views based on ongoing needs analysis.

The transformation repositories shown in Figures 5.3 and 5.4 are structured as many-to-many relationships of current and target business, application, and data objects. Both repository examples represent information that can be stored and cross-referenced as required by various transformation projects. These repositories need to be extensible and flexible to support multiple initiatives and can be implemented using any commercial repository or relational database.

In the tax agency example cited earlier, this repository depicted a business process, such as issuing tax receipt, and linked that process to a physical application that performed the function that supported that process. This relationship was carried down to the individual source code that automated this function. The source code was also cross-referenced to the load module name, the job that executed that load module, and the data that was used by that program. At a very basic level, application teams could use this information to quickly identify the programs and data involved in any type of tax processing change request.

Strategically, the repository allowed transformation planning teams to discern the scope and validity of replacement initiatives. One such project attempted to replace a subsystem involved in tax receipt processing. Viewing the information provided by the repository allowed planning teams to determine that replacing this subsystem without accommodating related and redundant subsystems was an unworkable solution to a tax-handling issue. While this recommendation was made, the replacement project moved forward anyway due to political commitments. Needless to say, it was a very costly lesson for this agency, its management, and, unfortunately, the tax-paying public.

Because development paradigms may vary to a great degree across an enterprise, organizations can utilize the transformation repository to allow different business units to create a generic mapping of functions, business processes, and implementation metadata. For example, a business unit using object technology could map its object models to a business unit using more traditional design models. In this way, enterprise planners can see that different business units are actually performing related or even redundant functions.

Building and populating a given repository can be justified on multiple levels. If management can sell the concept of incorporating this type of documentation into an enterprise-funded initiative, this is ideal. Much more expensive documentation efforts have produced significantly inferior results. Individual projects can also build the repository requirement into their funding model. This is particularly useful when a current-to-target gap analysis is required.

The task of updating one or more repositories can be performed by the architecture community shown in Figure 5.2 called the "systems knowledge base." This team can establish and manage tiered repository structures as a service to business units and application teams. Individual application and business areas could build these models and the knowledge base team could roll this information up to an enterprise level. This approach provides central tracking of valuable enterprise knowledge that, in most cases, does not likely exist in any understandable format. While this may have been acceptable in the past, transformation projects have a way of highlighting missing infrastructure items that should have been in place long ago.

5.11 Metrics and Measurement— A Transformation Yardstick

Historically, IT organizations have not applied formal measurement principles to the quantitative evaluation and analysis of various IT initiatives. The lack of solid measurement programs in the vast majority of modern enterprises creates a significant challenge for transformation planning teams because there is no yardstick in place to determine the best approach for a given scenario.

Consider, for example, a retailer evaluating whether to consolidate and upgrade inhouse HR applications, acquire an application package, or use some combination of these approaches. Each project should be evaluated on the ability to deliver required functionality within a specified timeframe for a given cost. The package option may have been estimated as the $1 million cost of the software and a $1 million implementation cost. Studies have shown, however, that five to ten times the cost of an application software purchase will be expended on implementation. User experiences indicate that these figures may be conservative [9]. If management will not acknowledge these costs, transformation planning teams will have a hard time justifying alternative or hybrid approaches.

Another important consideration is that cost is not the only factor in assessing a migration or replacement option. If the application package does not provide the requisite level of functionality required for this business unit, the project will not succeed at any cost. Metrics can be derived to help quantify the percentage of functionality a package contains when compared to a set of functional requirements. Metrics can also be derived to assess the level of functional conformance the current applications contain versus strategic requirements. These measurements can then be combined with the cost of one approach versus other options to create hard data upon which management can make more informed decisions.

The typical enterprise may not have a measurement program in place, however, so the depth of knowledge needed to perform this type of analysis may seem difficult to achieve. Executives may be in a hurry to acquire and implement an application based on a vendor sales pitch and unwilling to perform the analysis that identifies the best approach. Establishing measurement expertise through a virtual community of specialists within the architecture team is the best way to ensure that a measurement program is in place to avoid major missteps in these types of initiatives. General measurement categories include

- Functional conformation of legacy and/or package applications in comparison with functional requirements.
- Technical and architectural conformance of legacy and/or package applications in comparison with strategic requirements.
- Current and projected maintenance expenditures.
- Application failure, downtime, and problem backlog metrics.
- Metrics that assess the overall quality and maintainability of an application.
- Cost of implementation based on an assessment of the tasks involved in various approaches or combination of approaches.
- Total cost of ownership based on historical and projected figures for the existing and resulting application solutions.

I will provide more insight into these types of metrics and measures in the chapter on project planning and cost justification. Historically, metric and measurement programs have been shortchanged by executives and eliminated when budgets are tight. This type of program supports IT planning, assessment efforts, and transformation projects.

In the absence of a coordinated measurement program, the basic knowledge required to critically assess various options for pursuing IT initiatives is either ignored by project teams or too time-consuming to perform. These types of programs should be reconsidered as organizations fine-tune their ability to apply quantitative analysis to various transformation options.

5.12 Software Tools and Technology Center of Excellence

IT organizations that do not leverage software tools to accelerate and enhance the quality of their work are analogous to the shoemaker whose children have no shoes. IT professionals automate everything except their own work. Leveraging automated software tools to improve the time-to-market and overall quality of mission-critical software projects will allow an enterprise to achieve improvements in productivity while controlling or reducing related costs.

The architecture team should incorporate a software tools center of excellence. Such a center, shown in Figure 5.2, would support tool assessment, procurement, and implementation across the enterprise—with local expertise within local IT and business units. The following guidelines could be used to help this software tools center develop its charter.

- **Determine the best way to leverage tools within the enterprise.** If an enterprise is performing an extensive amount of development work, it should deploy an integrated development environment (IDE) to streamline those tasks. If, on the other hand, most of the work involves legacy maintenance, then application analysis and testing tools should be a higher priority.

- **Expand the use of tools to business analysts and designers.** Ensuring that requirements are transformed into viable, robust application systems requires maintaining the integrity of these requirements throughout the development process. Business analysts can use simple tools to diagram their requirements and provide these to IT analysts. IT analysts can use these business specifications to specify UML models that clarify the needs of a given set of business users. A number of IDE products can then transform UML into functioning systems, which helps ensure that resulting applications do what business analysts require.

- **Invest in tools that address legacy systems.** Much of the work being done by application teams is on legacy environments. Using software tools to help analyze, enhance, and transform these applications increases the productivity and quality of the work being done in the area of maintenance, enhancements, integration, and transformation. Companies unaware of the value of legacy software tools will need them as they embark upon legacy assessment, integration, and transformation projects.

- **Leverage software tools already in place.** Most companies already own a variety of software tools that can accelerate and improve the quality of application design, development, enhancement, and project management tasks. Architecture teams with cross-functional responsibility should inventory and communicate the availability of these tools. Leveraging existing investments in software tools provides the quickest path to achieving tool-related benefits.

- **Use integrated frameworks to streamline software tool training and deployment.** If tools are integrated under a common framework, the potential users of those tools can more readily assimilate them. Ongoing training and mentoring also streamline tool deployment and simplify and encourage tool utilization.

Chapter 7 provides an in-depth look at various software technologies that can help the technology center of excellence pursue the above objectives. Applying a comprehensive set of integrated software tools to accelerate the delivery of quality information management solutions should be a key goal for every IT organization.

5.13 Legacy Transformation Skill Center— Training, Education, and Support

The architecture team model shown in Figure 5.2 depicts a legacy transformation skill center. This virtual team is comprised of individuals that reside within various business and IT units who have the capacity to identify how legacy transformation options might be applied to fulfill business-driven requirements.

While the skills listed below may appear to require a great deal of training, this is not the case. Much of the work involved in legacy transformation projects is based on common sense tempered with a willingness to see beyond traditional scrap-and-replace philosophies. Instilling these alternative approaches in individuals with solid application management skills will create a foundation needed for a variety of transformation projects.

The capabilities described below should be distributed across various inhouse and third-party teams that play key roles within the management and evolution of application and data architectures. The following transformation skills will need to be developed or acquired as this team is organized.

- **Strategic Transformation Planning**

  One essential requirement for a skill center is to educate managers in the transformation analysis and planning process. This will enable management to spot situations where transformation techniques can augment traditional projects to provide more cost- and time-effective solutions.

- **Transformation Assessments**

  Transformation assessment skills require the ability to examine strategic requirements and develop a gap analysis to determine how legacy applications and data architectures need to be transformed to fill those gaps.

- **Enterprise Application Integration**

  EAI embodies a unique set of disciplines that the skill center should be able to provide. EAI skills include the ability to assess the need and define an approach for various middleware and related EAI solutions.

- **Data Architecture**

  Most organizations already have skilled data analysts with the ability to analyze, upgrade, and redesign legacy and modern data structures. These analysts will need to ensure that this includes the ability to support legacy data analysis, rationalization, redesign, consolidation, integrity improvement, and migration work.

- **Application Improvement**

  Analysts will need to be able to upgrade application structure and design. This includes the ability to structure, slice, reaggregate, and generally improve the overall quality of the application source code.

- **Rule Capture, Reuse, and Componentization**

  In situations that require the identification, consolidation and reuse of legacy business rules, analysts will need to be able to capture and migrate these rules into target environments and architectures.

- **Testing Infrastructure**

  A key element in a transformation project is the ability to validate and verify that transformed applications conform to business specifications. Keeping in line with Extreme Programming precepts, test cases need to be established during early stages of a transformation initiative.

- **Transformation Tool Knowledge**

  The transformation skill center requires a basic understanding of available transformation tools. The software tool center, on the other hand, has people with detailed tool knowledge, training, and implementation skills. These tools are unlikely to be used, however, if the transformation center does not know where or when to apply them. Many good software tools have been installed, but never used, because project teams did not know about them.

- **Transformation Training, Facilitation, and Implementation Support**

  The transformation skills center should also offer training sessions or project skills transfer. These skills are likely to be distributed across project teams but centrally tracked and enhanced through a core team.

- **Executive Education**

  Executives will require an overview and ongoing updates on how legacy architecture transformation can help reduce costs, improve quality, and speed time-to-market. The skill center should maintain people, typically other managers, who can discuss these benefits.

- **Project Planning, Oversight, and Quality Reviews**

  Project planning teams will need to augment basic skills with an understanding of transformation planning templates. They also provide project oversight and quality reviews. These individuals are likely to be existing project managers or part of the project office shown in Figure 5.1.

A core team of transformation specialists should organize individuals that are already working in various application areas. This team should consider setting up a skill-tracking database that could be used to track inhouse and third-party individuals with transformation skills. These individuals could be loaned out to perform specific transformation tasks on various projects. This group, which could function as a small core staff of three to four individuals, depending on the size of the enterprise, is the core enabling capability for transformation planning and project tracking.

5.14 Launching a Transformation Awareness Initiative

The best approach for building awareness of a legacy transformation capability is to seek out candidate initiatives that could be augmented by various transformation scenarios. This approach will allow executive teams to apply transformation principles in actual scenarios as opposed to considering them in the abstract.

The launch point may be formal or informal. Transformation concepts do not lend themselves to hype. A better approach is to sell transformation as the ability to augment existing projects with an improved understanding of legacy systems. A second selling point is the concept of reuse—discussed at some length earlier in this chapter. Reuse is the basis for reducing the costs and risks associated with package implementation, integration, replacement, and other initiatives.

The list of project candidates should include opportunities to apply transformation techniques and scenarios to any or all of the ideas outlined in the transformation strategy discussed in Chapter 4. Candidate projects should be mapped to one or more potential transformation scenarios that can benefit each of those projects. The next step involves identifying application areas and business units to become a pilot project. A pilot project should

- Verify the existence of a sponsor for the project.
- Begin with an assessment based on the requirements of the project.
- Augment transformation planning and implementation skills with third-party expertise to ensure that the pilot does not fail based on inexperience with the tools and techniques.
- Focus on augmenting existing project plans.
- Consider simple concepts such as improving an application that is heavily maintained or providing gap analysis for a package implementation effort.
- Apply a phased approach to prevent use of a big bang approach from dooming the pilot project.
- Ensure that the project has buy-in from all relevant and affected business unit, IT, and third-party professionals.
- Utilize appropriate tools and techniques to increase the efficiency of the project team and odds of success.
- Document the cost and time improvements associated with each step of the project.

As pilot project phases are completed, the transformation skill center should document the experience, build a knowledge base of lessons learned, and communicate the success of the project. This could be posted to an internal transformation Web page or in various other communications media to business and IT professionals. Over a period of time, successes should increase the awareness of transformation alternatives throughout the enterprise.

5.15 Transformation Infrastructure— An Essential Foundation

Creating a transformation infrastructure may be accomplished in phases, particularly the knowledge and skills transfer process typically required in a larger enterprise. An infrastructure coordinator can reside in the legacy transformation center to coordinate efforts to deliver various infrastructure components. This individual should create an infrastructure deployment plan and keep management up to date on ongoing efforts and developments.

Ignoring transformation infrastructure issues complicates the deployment, cost justification, and ability to sustain these types of projects. It also increases the likelihood that subsequent project phases will lose funding and support. Finally, lack of a transformation infrastructure will dramatically enhance the odds that legacy problems will proliferate through the continued application of quick fixes to highly complex information requirements.

Notes

1. "Collected Quotes from Albert Einstein" [Online], *http://rescomp.stanford. edu/~cheshire/EinsteinQuotes.html*, 1995.
2. *The Biology of Business,* John Henry Clippinger III (Ed.), Jossey-Bass, 1999, p. 47.
3. *Corporate DNA*, Ken Baskin, Butterworth Heinemann, 1998, p. 146.
4. "Enhancing the Business-IT Relationship," Chris Pickering, Cutter Consortium Business-IT Advisory Service, Vol. 4, No. 19, 2001.
5. *Birth of the Chaordic Age*, Dee Hock, Berett-Koehler, 1999, pp. 7–9.
6. "Organizational Metamorphosis: Becoming the Hub," Hina Pendle and William Ulrich [Online], *www.systemtransformation.com/organizational_articles.htm*, 2000.
7. "Chaos," The Standish Group [Online], *www.standishgroup.com/chaos.html*, Jan. 1998.
8. *Adaptive Software Development: A Collaborative Approach to Managing Complex Systems,* James A. Highsmith III, Dorset House, 1999, p. 11.
9. "ERP: Time for a Rethink," Richard Todd [Online], *http://www.max-international.com/PAGES/NEWS/Whitep.htm*, June 1998.

Planning and Justifying a Legacy Transformation Project

Project planning and justification are important steps in launching and sustaining a successful transformation initiative. Determining ROI on any IT-related project is difficult and has never been an exact science. Applying sound planning principles, augmenting traditional approaches with transformation options, and applying unbiased analyses to alternative scenarios can, however, provide justification for a variety of transformation initiatives.

Transformation planning scenarios serve as the basis for determining a project's value, related cost, and subsequent justification. Scenario-driven planning couples situation-specific project requirements with the transformation strategies described in Chapter 4. This chapter discusses transformation planning and deployment planning along with value and cost justification for these projects.

6.1 The Transformation ROI Dilemma

Transformation project justification is similar to justification efforts for other IT projects. This is good news and bad news. The good news is that if IT can justify new development and package replacement projects, then it can apply similar concepts to justify transformation projects. The bad news is that, according to Computerworld ROI, 83 percent of companies do not track or measure return on investment (ROI) in technology projects. Those that do measure ROI track timelines and costs, but not value [1].

With ROI being, at best, an inexact science and, at worst, totally ignored, planning teams face significant challenges when trying to justify a transformation project. Transformation planners who propose a solution that is counter to "conventional wisdom" will find themselves in the position of having to "prove" their case, while opposing, more traditional views are accepted at face value. This has occurred time and again in executive sessions in a variety of industries.

For example, assume that a manager has proposed the use of legacy application analysis and transformation as a way to create a consolidated billing application. Another manager has suggested a counter proposal that requires the acquisition and implementation of an ERP system with a billing component. Management may require the transformation team to create a detailed cost analysis that demonstrates how the transformation approach is more cost-effective. The transformation team reworks their analysis over and over again, but in the end, executives select the package option.

The majority of project decisions are made based on personal relationships, politics, or gut feeling as to which approach is best. These decisions occur or go unchallenged because there is no vehicle in place to evaluate multiple ways for IT to achieve a common business goal. This needs to change. The way to make this transition is to introduce transformation analysis, integration, consolidation, and/or migration options into the mix.

6.2 Transformation Introduces New Options and Opportunities

In the above billing application example, management gravitated toward a solution that it considered less risky. Many times the transformation team is, at least in part, at fault for driving management back toward traditional solutions. This is particularly true when those individuals promoting a transformation solution propose an all-or-nothing approach.

Individuals promoting the use of legacy transformation techniques should present the variety of project options that can be applied to lower costs and risks while meeting the business requirements of the project. Table 6.1 depicts how package selection and implementation can leverage or ignore legacy architectures. Outlining variations on a traditional package replacement discussion addresses a number of the challenges involved in introducing legacy transformation into a strategic planning discussion.

- Transformation is not an all-or-nothing approach and should never be presented as such. Presenting variations on how transformation can help meet a given goal broadens a planning team's vision of how transformation options can be applied to meet a variety of information requirements.

- When a planning team is presented with multiple replacement options, it improves their level of critical thinking and increases the likelihood of selecting the best solution.

- Legacy analysis techniques augment traditional rewrite or package replacement projects. Selling this capability to executive planning teams is easier than selling the concept of full-scale legacy architecture migration.
- Because traditional replacement projects can be blended with transformation scenarios to deliver more functionality in less time and at a reduced cost, selling transformation becomes a matter of comparative cost justification.

One way to avoid unilateral decisions by an individual or biased team is to introduce multiple approaches for achieving a common goal and opening up the dialog at the executive level. In the example in Table 6.1, transformation analysis and reuse options provide an opportunity for planning teams to make better decisions about a project and reduce the tendency to gravitate toward quick and easy options. Sharpening the cost justification debate requires drafting and agreeing to two key principles.

- Do not assume that the "cleanest" or least sophisticated solution (i.e., buy and install a package) is always the best solution.
- Avoid unilateral decisions made by a single executive or individual with little or no objective assessment of alternative options.

Evaluation teams can rally around a shared purpose and principles similar to the ones listed above. Executives who try to sidestep this process should be reminded that IT project failures tend to be the result of quick decisions made without the necessary level of analysis.

Table 6.1 Basic Package Replacement Options
Package selection and replacement options can leverage or ignore legacy architectures. Option 5 uses the legacy architecture as the baseline for the new application as an alternative to licensing and implementing a package.

Replacement Option	Utilizes Legacy Analysis Techniques	Reuses Legacy Application in Target Architecture
1. Standard Package Selection	No	No
2. Package Selection with Gap Analysis	Yes	No
3. Standard Package Implementation	No	No
4. Package Implementation with Gap Analysis and Legacy Reuse	Yes	Yes
5. Legacy Consolidation and Migration to Target Architecture	Yes	Yes

6.3 ROI Challenges: Cost of Ownership and Shifting Business Priorities

Total cost of ownership (TCO) is a new buzzword being used within the IT industry. The TCO concept involves calculating how much an enterprise is spending on IT and breaking that figure down by business unit and application area. While controlling or reducing IT costs is admirable, it is more important to focus on the value being delivered by IT to the business as a whole.

For example, a Gartner study showed how the total cost of ownership for an ERP package on a per-employee basis increased after the installation of an ERP application [2]. While this provides useful insights to executive teams considering application package options, it does not address the value being provided by that package in terms of bottom-line savings or revenue generation. Just because a package costs more to maintain from an IT perspective, it may be more than justified if it streamlines customer, inventory, and procurement management to the point where it increases revenue.

In other words, the IT TCO differential of $2,300 per employee (taken from the above study) would be almost irrelevant if business revenues jumped by $10 million as a result of this new system. If the company in the above study had 500 IT professionals and the cost per employee jumped by $2,300, the resulting annual increase in costs would amount to just over $1.1 million. The company would still be ahead by almost $9 million in revenue on an annual basis.

The bottom line is that information systems provide leverage for a business, and most entities could not function in the absence of these systems. While this is clear to most executives, it may not be clear as to how much value a given application delivers to the bottom line. It may also not be clear as to how much incremental value an upgraded application or replacement system might provide. Determining this value for a project is the challenge that business and IT professionals must address.

An executive team that focuses exclusively on reducing TCO while ignoring the value IT can deliver in terms of cost reduction or increased revenue does not appreciate the value IT brings to an enterprise. Cost justification under this situation will be very difficult, and IT will need to lay the groundwork for value-based project assessments.

Determining business value may seem like something that could be readily attained from business unit and IT executives based on research into the requirements and proposed benefits of the project under evaluation. Unfortunately, the perception of what constitutes value can be skewed by difficult economic times. An AMR Research survey [3] exemplifies how the financial services industry, widely believed to be the most progressive in terms of IT utilization, shifted its priorities.

The top four IT spending priorities in 2000 were customer relations (37 percent), competition (18 percent), cost savings (14 percent), and efficiency (10 percent). By mid-2001, as the recession began to take hold, these same financial services firms shifted their IT spending priorities to cost savings (32 percent), efficiency (29 percent), available market share (23 percent), and customer demands and requirements (15 percent). The most notable change between the 2000 and 2001 surveys is that cost savings moved from fourth to first in priority, while customer-related issues moved from a top priority to fourth place.

Surveys like this should concern IT management because a project may have been funded based on improving customer relations, but then finds itself in danger when priorities shift. Because it is unlikely that customer relations are no longer important to this particular business, this surfaces a serious underlying problem within the enterprise. A CEO who has been ordered by the board to lower costs to drive up quarterly profits was forced to place renewed emphasis on cost cutting over and above customer satisfaction and revenue generation.

While shifting priorities, driven by short-term thinking by directors and investors, are cause for concern, they are beyond the scope of this discussion. IT can, however, respond to shifting priorities by creating a project delivery model that includes a phased ROI approach.

6.4 Determining ROI—A Multiphased Process

Planning teams must consider the value of a particular project based on an agreed-upon approach. While an enterprise may already have a project justification process, it is important that the approach examine all project alternatives and ROI options. The ROI process should

- Identify various project alternatives for addressing a given set of requirements. This allows planning teams to evaluative more than one project approach or option.
- Estimate the revenue increase or cost savings that would be delivered to the business community for each proposed approach.
- Include, as one option, the cost of doing nothing or other scaled-back options.
- Determine the cost of delivering each approach. Cost includes the cost of implementing the project along with the projected annual net operating costs for the resulting solution.
- Estimate the "net value" for each option by subtracting the cost of the project and annual costs from projected annual revenues. (Future projections and related accounting issues should be based on inhouse accounting procedures.)
- Present the net value of each alternative to the executive sponsors and other planning team participants for a decision.

The above ROI approach appears to be fairly straightforward but can involve numerous variables that are difficult to discern. The level of effort that should be dedicated to detailing a given alternative depends on the level of detailed cost analysis needed by management prior to selecting an approach.

Phasing ROI analysis to mirror the phased deliverable stages of a transformation project is a good way to address rapidly shifting and highly unpredictable business priorities. When each phase of a project can be justified as a standalone effort, then an enterprise can achieve partial value even if a project is canceled after completion of that phase. This may not always be possible. Certain project stages tend to involve setup tasks for subsequent phases. Where possible, however, project-planning teams should attempt to quantify the value to be derived from each phase of a given project.

For example, an ERP package implementation effort has historically been pursued as an all-or-nothing, big bang implementation option. An alternative approach, presented in a paper by Richard Todd [4], includes the phased implementation steps listed below.

- Migrate legacy applications to an industry-standard database.
- Migrate application front ends to a client/server environment.
- Add core ERP functionality to that environment.
- Integrate additional package features with alternative best-of-breed solutions.

The concept presented in the above scenario is one in which the business community can achieve near-term value from a consolidated view of manufacturing data, a distributed interface, and core ERP functionality that implements only the most useful portions of the application package. This type of multiphased approach to achieving ROI is a fundamental consideration for projects incorporating legacy transformation scenarios.

Another example of justifying a project based on phased ROI involves supply chain package deployment. In a supply chain ROI article [5], Ram Reddy suggested that implementing the 20 percent of the most commonly used features in a supply chain package provides 80 percent of the value. Later phases can add more functionality, but the greatest ROI would be delivered in earlier project phases.

Assessing the business value, related costs, and annual projected TCO for a project should be incorporated into a cost model that quantifies ROI by project phase. Doing so ensures that if a project is put on hold or canceled due to a "shift in business priorities," that project will have delivered some value prior to being cancelled. If the project is resurrected, the project team can pick up where it left off. Phased ROI is supported quite effectively by the transformation principle of delivering interim value through a staged set of project deliverables.

6.5 Motivating Factors in Transformation Projects— Defining Value?

Operational cost control or reduction, revenue generation, and profit improvement are yardsticks for success that planning teams should consider when evaluating a project's value to the business community. Unfortunately, many executive decisions, particularly those that decimate the IT infrastructure needed to ensure a project's success, have focused on cost reduction. Lowering IT costs to increase corporate profits is akin to a construction company saving money on building costs by placing 80 percent of the required support beams in place. Eventually, the building will collapse.

IT departments can grow oversized and inefficient, but eliminating essential IT personnel and related functions impacts the bottom line in very marginal ways. In some cases, executives have depleted IT units to the point where they can barely perform their jobs. Short-term thinking has won out over value-driven ROI. Establishing an IT project that allows a business to collapse three redundant billing teams into one, consolidates the balance of accounts across disparate business units, or reduces customer response time by 30 percent is an example of value-driven project objectives. Executives should consider business value as the main ROI motivator for IT projects.

Value-driven projects should take precautions to incorporate the following questions into the planning process as requirements begin to synthesize.

- Can the project be tied to cost-reduction efforts such as business unit consolidation, lower inventory levels, streamlining of supply chain management, reduced labor costs, improved revenue management, or similar cost-driven factors?
- Can the project be tied to revenue-generation efforts through customer service improvements, delivery of new product or service offerings, synthesis of distribution functions, or related revenue-driven factors?
- Are there regulatory requirements that justify this project, and if so, what are the deadlines for completion?
- Does the project enable another project that can be justified based on cost savings, revenue growth, or regulatory requirements?
- Can cost, revenue, or regulatory value-driven requirements be clearly articulated to the project planning team?
- What factors could cause the project to change priorities or be canceled, and when might this occur?
- How can the project team phase the project in a way that delivers partial value in interim steps that move the business community closer to meeting their requirements?
- If there are no clear cost, revenue, or regulatory requirements driving this project, can the business community state any other reason why the project team should move ahead?

Unfortunately, the type of value-driven ROI outlined in this series of questions is rarely performed. As cited previously, 83 percent of companies do not track ROI. Those that do, track costs as opposed to value. Many projects have actually been initiated by IT managers who believe that there is business value to be gained by translating COBOL applications to Java. Technology-driven projects are the antithesis of business-driven, value-based projects, although business-driven projects may have strong elements of technological change.

For example, a cross-functional project to add a new patient identifier to every file containing patient data may contain tasks to rationalize disparate data structures as a first step. In this situation, however, the business objective, not the technology objective, drives the project. Communicating the need to take an interim technological step to business executives may not come across clearly because IT and business professionals do not always communicate effectively.

Two major obstacles can derail project-planning teams. The first is the fact that many IT professionals lack the functional insights or operational knowledge needed to articulate business-driven requirements. The second obstacle is that business executives know less about technology than IT professionals can fathom. This is why establishing a project driven by business value requires planning teams comprised of individuals with business and IT knowledge. Building trust, communication, and collaboration within planning teams is essential to the success of that project.

6.6 Collaborative Project Planning—Team Formation

Project team stakeholders must function as an integrated unit and work toward a common goal to achieve their collective goals. Stakeholders include relevant and affected customers, sponsors, business users, designers, developers, support teams, and third-party participants such as suppliers or distributors. Ignoring the need for creating a collaborative project team can doom a project to misinterpretation of business requirements, conflicting objectives, false starts, infighting, design delays, cost overruns, and, ultimately, cancellation.

Turning a disparate group of project participants with conflicting goals into a cohesive work unit requires that stakeholders work through two distinct planning phases. The first phase establishes the project team framework or governance structure, while the second phase establishes the framework for the project itself.

As a rule, most project teams skip the governance structure development phase and move directly into project planning. This results in a project team with the inability to govern its own actions, communicate effectively, collaborate, and deal with conflict. Formalizing a project governance structure is geared at nullifying the challenges highlighted by the Standish Group study cited in Chapter 5. Primarily, project governance removes the "us versus them" attitude that afflicts so many IT projects. A governance structure also streamlines communication and helps ensure that users get what they need as well as what they requested.

Various stakeholders contributing to or benefiting from the project gather to determine each participant's stake in the effort, surface common and conflicting objectives, and agree on a common purpose. The purpose is a clearly articulated statement of the value the project will provide to the enterprise. A sample project purpose might be to deliver a customer information system that allows business and IT units to effectively and efficiently coordinate and fulfill common customer requirements. A purpose may take time to develop, but should be agreed upon by the entire team of stakeholder representatives.

The creation of a project purpose paves the way for the team to create a set of operating principles to govern the actions of the team and create a project infrastructure that adheres to these principles. The following sample project team principles can be used to govern the actions of a project team [6].

- Put the customer first in all project decisions, with a focus on the prime purpose of the project.
- Meet the collective needs of the marketing, sales, and customer business units.
- Integrate functional requirements from a business, data, and technical perspective.
- Utilize, as appropriate, off-the-shelf solutions.
- Incorporate legacy data and business rules into the design and development function.
- Allow any relevant and affected party to join the project if they comply with project purpose and principles.
- Proactively address integration with related business areas that will not directly utilize the target system.
- Position the development feedback cycle to allow input from all relevant and affected parties.
- Create a phased design and implementation plan that delivers interim project value to the sponsoring business unit.
- Allow any party requesting project status access to this information as long as it does not compromise privacy or security constraints.
- Create a system that can be maintained effectively and efficiently for a minimum of three to five years.
- Vest decision-making powers at the lowest level within the project team possible. This means that decisions are rolled up to a higher level only if input from that level is essential.
- The project can be canceled at any time by an 80 percent vote of all project participants.

This last principle may seem unusual, but having participants determine if a project should continue at various checkpoints is a valuable strategy. A number of high-profile project failures, in my experience, could have been avoided if the executive sponsor would have asked team participants if the project had a chance of succeeding. Project cancellation in these cases would have saved millions of dollars for the enterprises involved.

Role, responsibility, and project infrastructure definition is critical to the success of large projects. A typical project infrastructure, which should be established prior to launching a project, is shown in Figure 6.1. Management should not assume that a single project manager can assume responsibility for all of the task categories below. Large projects are too complex to leave this up to a single individual. The following roles and responsibilities, as appropriate to a given project, should be addressed as part of the project infrastructure [6].

- **Project integration and oversight.** This group manages the project, resolves conflicts, seeks compromises, and verifies that the team adheres to purpose and principles.
- **Funding team.** This group is responsible for obtaining project funding from executives and managing against a fixed budget. Any changes to cost structures or funding issues must coordinate through this team.
- **Architecture oversight.** The architecture team ensures that the target business, data, and technical design approach maps to institutional or preferred standards as well as to the requirements of the project.
- **Business unit requirements definition.** This functional analysis team defines business requirements based on stakeholder input obtained from representatives from each business unit. The team's approach should focus on articulating, integrating, and reconciling requirements and functions across business units.
- **Data specification and integration team.** This team assesses current and target data requirements and then designs a common data architecture to be used by the target system. This step would accommodate legacy data migration issues.
- **Target specification design team.** The target specification team turns business requirements into a target system specification document that reflects the ideal target system design.
- **Legacy architecture assessment and mapping team.** Legacy expertise, centered within this group, identifies, inventories, assesses, maps, and performs related work on legacy architectures involved in a given project.
- **Technical specification team.** This team defines the technical environment for the work in progress and resulting application. They identify tools and skills needed on the project, as well as perform application development and testing.

Division of labor utilizes the virtual community model shown in Figure 6.1 and mirrors the virtual community models discussed in Chapter 5. The only difference, in the case of a specific project, is that a community has formed around a project purpose as opposed to a more permanent information management function. The teams described are virtual subcommunities. Each subcommunity should establish a purpose to ensure that it fulfills its respective role.

Virtual Project Community

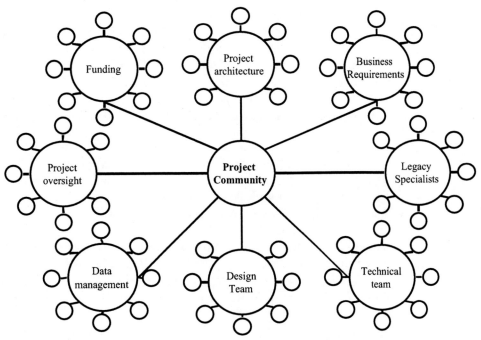

Figure 6.1
Project community is comprised of a variety of virtual teams united in pursuit of a project's purpose.

Finalizing the project infrastructure defines a process for managing group dynamics, a communication infrastructure, and a plan for ensuring that the team can function within the constraints of the enterprise. Enterprise constraints may involve adhering to formal chains of command that govern various stakeholders. For example, if a chain of command structure prevents informal and ongoing communications among project stakeholders, the project team will want to resolve this limitation prior to proceeding with the project.

6.7 Collaborative Project Planning—Project Formation

The second phase of project initiation encompasses more traditional project planning activities and establishes project tasks, deliverable items and timelines. To accomplish this, the project team will need to document and formalize the following deliverable items in a project specification document.

- **Impacted business units and third parties.** Project teams need to take a cross-functional view of the impact of the project to ensure that participation and requirements include all relevant and affected parties.

- **Legacy systems to be impacted or replaced.** Project teams have a tendency to ignore the applications and support teams impacted or being replaced by a project. Legacy transformation scenarios require participation of these teams as well as identification of the applications being replaced.
- **Specific methodologies guiding project activities.** Based on the type of project, the team may want to consider the use of Extreme Programming concepts, transformation processes, various testing methods, and adaptive project management techniques.
- **Alternatives for meeting the project's purpose.** The project team will need to draft alternative approaches to meeting the project's purpose and objectives. Alternative selection will hinge on delivery schedules, the perceived value of those deliverables, and related costs. Management may require deliverable details, schedule data, and cost analysis for more than one approach as input to selecting an approach.
- **Business value expected from each alternative.** One approach may yield more business value than another approach. It is important for the project team to articulate this to executives so that a fair assessment can be made as to which approach is better suited to meeting the project purpose.
- **Deliverable schedule and cost structure for the selected approach.** Unless the unusual strategy of dual design is pursued (where two teams work toward the same goal using different approaches), one of the proposed approaches will need to be selected. The team will need to provide more detail for the selected approach, including a detailed schedule, cost structure, deliverable assignments, and project timeline.

The cost analysis for any project is a result of determining the required tasks, time estimates associated with those tasks, the labor costs for each task, and nonpersonnel expenditures. Labor is a calculation of the estimated hours each deliverable will require. Labor estimates may be associated with a deliverable or with the task required to create and provide that deliverable. Nonpersonnel costs include items such as hardware, networks, third-party software, rent, and other items.

Project formation coupled with the work completed during team formation will help ensure the project infrastructure is resilient yet flexible enough to withstand a variety of ongoing business and technical challenges.

6.8 Transformation Project Augmentation and Dual Positioning

Two important concepts should underscore the use of transformation scenarios within an IT project. Transformation scenarios can augment a wide variety of business-driven projects by providing analysis, improvement, and/or reuse of legacy architectures. The second concept is that a single set of transformation tasks could benefit more than one business-driven initiative. Planning teams should consider the concepts of transformation augmentation and "dual positioning" within the context of projects impacting legacy architectures.

Transformation projects should never be positioned or cost-justified as standalone efforts. Transformation augments business-driven projects. While this may appear evident to any manager keeping a close eye on a limited budget, a number of rogue software reengineering projects have been launched over the years to extract business rules, rationalize data structures, fix poorly structured programs, and migrate to new technologies. If these are not connected to and positioned primarily as business-driven scenarios, project champions will have a hard time obtaining executive sponsorship, project funding, business unit support, and cross-functional participation.

Business planning teams have the responsibility to set project objectives that serve the business, while project delivery teams have the responsibility of meeting them. Part of this responsibility involves leveraging each project to support the broadest number of business requirements.

One lesson learned over the past two decades of working on transformation projects relates to the concept of dual positioning, discussed in Chapter 4. Under this concept, certain project tasks provide near-term and long-term benefits across a spectrum of requirements. In other words, the same set of transformation activities may lead to benefits for more than one business-driven project.

The example cited in Chapter 4 involved identifying and rationalizing redundant data definitions in preparation for an HIPAA initiative. From a project planning and justification perspective, this task would need to be estimated and cost-justified based on the reduction in effort needed to deploy new payer identification fields across the applications of interest.

Additional justification could then be developed based on the need to rationalize data definitions in preparation for a data architecture redesign effort. The key requirement here is the need to identify the cost of rationalizing data usage and balancing that against the savings to be accrued during the payer identification update phase of the project. Additional savings related to the long-term redesign of application data structures should then be projected and added to the cost justification document for the project.

6.9 Learning from Project Failures

Most executives do not like to discuss failed project initiatives unless they are looking to place blame. Unfortunately, because major project decisions are often made unilaterally by a lone executive, large-scale failures frequently get swept under the corporate rug. Little failures, on the other hand, allow executive teams to place blame on a low-level manager as a way to demonstrate a commitment to project integrity. A failed project presents an enterprise with the opportunity to expand its collective wisdom and is not a time for placing blame.

Failures fall along a scale. A large-scale failure may involve a canceled project with no deliverable. A smaller-scale failure may involve a cost or budget overrun. A more subtle failure may involve the deployment of a system that does not meet requested user requirements. Big or small, all project failures should be documented and communicated to ensure that the same pattern of failure is not repeated in the future.

Avoiding the repetition of the same mistakes is important because project failures can have a negative ROI impact. Large-scale supply chain implementation failures, for example, can drive down a firm's overall valuation [5]. In addition to this, the lost revenue on the project, the lost benefit to the business community, and the cost of retrenching create a negative ROI scenario for organizations. To avoid future negative ROI scenarios from project failures, a peer review should be scheduled for all failed projects.

The medical profession, for example, does a peer review of any situation where a patient does not make it and there is a question that the competence of the team resulted in that patient's death. When a project dies, a peer review is more than warranted. Peers in this case include project managers from business and IT areas other than the one where the failure occurred. Issues to consider in such a postmortem review include

- What was the nature of the failure (cancellation, cost overrun, time overrun, missing functionality, incomplete solution, etc.)?
- In which phase of the project did the failure begin to manifest itself?
- How far beyond the manifestation point did the project team continue working on the project?
- What could have been done differently to avoid the failure?
- What quality checkpoints, project principles, or other safeguards can be built into other projects in the future to avoid repeating the same mistakes again?

In addition to performing a project postmortem, the review team should determine how the final decision to proceed was made. If it was a unilateral decision, this should be communicated as part of the failure analysis. The results of the peer review would then be posted and shared (names omitted, of course, where confidentiality is required) for other project teams to consider as they move forward. Internal project management training should incorporate these peer reviews into project management training classes.

Increasing an enterprise's collective intelligence based on past failures works, of course only, if management is willing to examine and consider past mistakes within the context of planning the next project. If a new CIO enters the scene and is unwilling to leverage the postmortem knowledge base because he or she "knows better," then the value of failure analysis is lost. Establishing a basic project principle that requires reviewing postmortems of similar projects prior to planning the next project will help ensure that past mistakes will not be repeated over and over again.

6.10 Justifying Transformation Infrastructure Funding

The first transformation justification requirement typically involves infrastructure funding. In Chapter 5 I outlined fundamental infrastructure requirements needed to support transformation initiatives. Basic requirements include training, support functions, skilled personnel, a process, and software tools. These requirements may be derived from from inhouse sources or from third parties.

The alternative to building and funding an inhouse transformation infrastructure involves obtaining skills, tools, and project support from external consultants. This is certainly an option, but as discussed in earlier chapters, there is no guarantee that a given consulting firm can support a transformation strategy. Consultants may not be motivated to save time and reduce costs on major client initiatives. Having an inhouse function in place, on the other hand, allows start-up, support and technology costs to be distributed across the infrastructure and IT budget.

Another argument for establishing an inhouse transformation support capability is that the absence of such a support function means that project teams will be unaware of transformation options for various projects. The benefits of transformation will remain largely unknown to those project teams that need it the most. Even if consultants are used for all major IT projects, transformation specialists should still be maintained inhouse to develop requests for proposals and create third-party work requests. The absence of such a function translates into the absence of transformation benefits for the enterprise as a whole.

The transformation champion should clearly communicate these issues to the executive team who can provide infrastructure funding. Assuming that executives are willing to fund transformation infrastructure costs, the project champion should identify minimal requirements needed for a support center. This typically includes

- **Transformation center personnel.** For a medium to large enterprise, three full-time employees will need to be funded on an annual basis. At least two of the individuals in the transformation team should be full-time employees, while the others may be contract personnel. The number of individuals may vary, but they will need to have and be able to transfer transformation planning, implementation, and tool usage skills to project teams. Part of this team's role is to manage a transformation lab where they can test and implement software tools, train project participants, and process code through analysis and transformation tools. In a smaller company, two people might be able to launch such a function.
- **Transformation software tools.** Transformation software tool usage depends heavily on the environments found within an enterprise. Basic requirements include software that can analyze, cross-reference, and document the most commonly found computing language within the enterprise. If this is COBOL, for example, the team should procure a COBOL analysis

tool that can analyze, cross-reference, and depict data and procedural flows across the system. A handful (three to five) of copies might be obtained for under $50,000. These tools could then be applied to many systems across the enterprise. Refer to Chapter 7 for more information on software tools.

- **Hardware for a central transformation lab.** The team will need to be able to run various software products, support training, and communicate with other teams over a network. This will require a hardware budget. If the hardware is already be in place, no additional investment may be required.

- **A training capability.** Training material involves the distribution of vendor software materials and inhouse developed procedures. If the support center wants to replicate the ability to support and enable projects in remote locations, which is likely, they should consider integrating guidelines, processes, tools, and other supporting materials online. This will ultimately keep the central transformation team small, reduce travel costs, and allow for the infiltration of support personnel into application and business units.

- **Consulting support.** The team should set aside a small consulting budget to be used to hire transformation planning, implementation, and tool specialists for various projects.

I recommend drawing funds for a transformation support center from various business units or from a central budget if this is available. The center should also consider setting up a charge-back system when its personnel are used on projects. One approach is to provide free training and planning support to application and business units, but charge for any consulting time required on an actual project.

6.11 Determining Legacy Application Asset Value

In order for planning teams to cost-justify legacy application reuse, they should have some basis for assessing the value of both legacy and new applications. This analysis is useful in assessing build, lease, and reuse alternatives along with variations on those options. Valuing legacy assets can be done in several different ways.

One way to value applications software is based on that software's contribution to the business. Business valuation of legacy application assets is difficult because there is no clean link between a given piece of code and its business contribution.

Valuing software based on its replacement cost is more pragmatic. If the application disappeared tomorrow, how much would it cost to replace that application? Historically, application replacement costs have been estimated to be around $25 per fully debugged line of production software [7]. This would be interpreted to mean that a 1-million-line system would cost $25 million to replace.

A Standish Group study found that less than 30 percent of the code in a given application contained business logic, while the remaining source code supported infrastructure-related activities [8]. This could be interpreted to mean that replacing only the business logic while ignoring the infrastructure logic would lower replacement costs by a factor of 70 percent. This assumes that a replacement team could figure out what the system did in the first place, but that is a different issue.

A conservative figure for application replacement costs could be stated as follows.

- Total lines of code $\times$ .30 (percentage of business logic) $\times$ \$25 (replacement cost per line)
- In other words, a 1-million-line application would cost \$7.5 million to replace.

The above calculation may produce a conservative estimate because all applications require some degree of implementation dependent logic to address data handling, user communications, and related functionality. In addition, re-specification of complex business logic is extremely difficult and this factor could elongate analysis and design efforts to the point where the replacement cost exceeds \$25 per line of code.

One factor that could lower the replacement cost, however, is that newer, high-level languages allow technicians to build more functionality into an application using fewer lines of code. A line of Java, for example, would translate in 10 or more lines of COBOL. This factor could also decrease comparable productivity levels and drive up per-line of code costs.

Historic precedence is probably the best source of project estimating guidance. Many organizations have 10, 20, or even 100 million lines of application software. These same organizations have attempted to replace portions of their application portfolio. In reality, many replacement projects have spent far more than \$25 per line and delivered nothing. Application package implementation efforts have run up costs in the tens of millions of dollars—and that software was already written.

In other words, replacing an application is as much a matter of time and difficulty as it is an issue of cost. Most application teams ignore these statistics when they estimate what it will take to build a new system. While per-line figures are just broad estimates, they offer development teams a reality check. Previously cited Standish Group research suggests that replacement projects, whether being built from scratch or through a package acquisition, have been derailed for many reasons unrelated to the amount of money spent on the project.

Another consideration in fine-tuning legacy asset valuation involves examining how much money is spent supporting or maintaining legacy applications. The Standish Group found that maintenance costs for application code (i.e., business logic) range from 10 percent to 20 percent of the original development expenditure. The maintenance cost for infrastructure code falls in the 15 percent to 25 percent range [8].

At the low end, assuming that only the application code is being changed, an enterprise may be paying \$100,000 per year to maintain a \$2 million application. This figure would be higher, however, because infrastructure software is likely to change as well when databases, screen, or other access logic needs to change. Maintenance costs are a factor when assessing TCO for a planned application, and the Standish Group figures are useful for performing those types of calculations.

6.12 Preliminary Project Planning—Transformation Option Selection

Planning teams will want to review various business-driven requirements and related initiatives to ascertain how they might apply certain transformation options to augment those initiatives. Table 6.2 shows where one or more transformation options can augment a number of commonly occurring business-driven projects.

If management is developing an enterprise information strategy, it will require a high-level inventory of the existing information architecture as the foundation for that plan. This is based on the adage that "if you don't know where you are, a map won't help." The inventory also forms the basis for subsequent transformation work because it identifies high-level, functional boundaries that are key to defining the scope of various IT projects. Leaving an application, data structure, or related substructure out of an application assessment or deployment effort can result in an incomplete solution. The inventory ensures that this will not occur and is essential for scope definition.

Subsequent transformation options may be applied in combination or as standalone tasks. For example, if a business unit is performing a business process integration and automation (BPI/BPA) project, they will want to know which systems perform certain high-level functions as input to possible architecture retooling tasks. If architecture migration is not envisioned, a scaled-back BPI effort may just apply user interface and integration tools to link front-end business processes with back-end environments.

Another example involves a CRM project. Dirty, redundant, and highly fragmented data has been the downfall of more than a few CRM projects. Data mining, selective data cleanup, redesign, and consolidation can go a long way toward ensuring a successful CRM implementation. CRM teams struggle with data issues all the time, but management may be reluctant to apply formal transformation techniques to enterprise data. A transformation team could formalize this effort, lower related project risks, and improve the overall results of the project.

While most projects benefit from high-level inventory and application-specific documentation, the remaining transformation options are applied much more selectively. Architecture migration may or may not be required for a package deployment effort depending on the legacy applications being reused and the package application architecture. Similarly, consolidation tasks may or may not be required during a component-based development project, depending on the level of legacy reuse and underlying redundancy within the legacy architecture.

Table 6.2 Business Project/Transformation Mapping
Transformation options that can be applied to various business projects over a phased timeframe.

Transformation Option / Business Project	Enterprise Inventory	Application Documentation	Application Cleanup	Data Mining/ Cleanup	Data Redesign/ Migration	Language Upgrade/ Conversion	EAI & User Interface Upgrade	Application Modularization	Architecture Migration
Strategic IT Planning	X								
Outsourcing Initiative	X	X	X						
Maintenance Upgrades	X	X	X						
BPI/BPA	X	X					X		X
Rehosting	X	X							
Package Assessment	X	X							
Package Implementation	X	X		X	X				X
HIPAA (data upgrade)	X	X	X	X					
Web-to-Host	X						X		
CRM Initiative	X	X			X		X		
Data Warehouse	X	X		X	X		X		
Application Consolidation	X	X	X		X		X	X	
Component Development		X	X		X			X	X
Web Services Migration		X	X		X			X	X

The preliminary project planning phase is an important step for planning teams as they begin to leverage transformation options on actual projects. A summary of how various transformation options can be applied to business projects is provided in the following sections. Note that transformation options are aligned slightly differently than they were under the strategy discussion in Chapter 4. This is because the following tasks are being presented strictly as transformation options that augment business-driven project scenarios. In Chapter 4, the emphasis was on the types of scenarios an enterprise might initiate that leverage transformation options.

6.12.1 The Enterprise Inventory and High-Level Assessment

With a replacement cost in the tens or hundreds of millions of dollars, one would think that legacy architectures would be well documented. Most are not. An enterprise should maintain an enterprise-level inventory of legacy environments, regardless of the size and scope of the projects planned for those applications.

The transformation assessment provides a map of the legacy application environment and can be applied to a wide variety of maintenance, integration, and transformation projects. The depth of analysis depends on the information required for a given project. Application inventory and cross-reference information provide basic intelligence needed to proceed with subsequent documentation, upgrade, or transformation projects. Assessment tasks generally include

- Building an inventory of the legacy application and data-related components.
- Creating a cross-reference of the legacy application and data-related components.
- Loading this information into a repository for future reference and use.

Because this assessment is typically performed on a large number of enterprise applications, the analysis is limited to high-level items, including business unit, application, major data structure, and third-party interface. The level of effort associated with such an effort varies based on the size, distribution, and diversity of the enterprise, but one to two analysts could gather this information, in a period of a few weeks.

The high-level transformation repository introduced in Chapter 5 should be used to track this information. Once the information has been gathered, procedures should be established to update it on a regular basis.

6.12.2 Architecture and Application Documentation

Documentation is one task that IT tends to leave until last and apply halfheartedly. One government agency paid summer interns to document changes that had occurred over the course of the prior year. When that documentation was checked for accuracy, it was discovered that it was wrong in every instance.

Creating automated documentation that points to the actual source code is much more pragmatic and manageable. This information is typically collected for an application or related group of applications as opposed to an enterprise-wide inventory.

Capturing application cross-reference information, shown in the detailed transformation repository in Chapter 5 (Figure 5.3), requires documenting each component in one or more applications along with their relationships to other components. Tracking information down to a program level or below that is typically part of a more detailed modularization or architecture migration effort. This level of documentation supports outsourcing, upgrade, replacement, or any other type of transformation project. It is also a prerequisite to subsequent legacy analysis or transformation efforts.

Data definition usage analysis depicts where and how data is used across applications and is key to most upgrade, integration, and transformation efforts. Analysts attempting to assess a systemwide migration, integration, or redesign effort without adequate knowledge of that system's data usage are at a disadvantage. Data usage analysis is typically justified if a data-related project is planned. This includes data upgrade, redesign, consolidation, and package implementation.

Program-level documentation is mainly driven by maintenance or specific program upgrade requirements. Application programmers can typically run this level of documentation themselves if they have the tools available. Program-level documentation is also useful for analysts assessing potential application consolidation or migration effort.

Finally, the functional assessment documents high-level application functions. This type of analysis is a derivative of system and data flow analysis and requires input from application analysts who know what the system does. The results of this assessment can also be represented in the detailed transformation repository by adding business function and, if available, business rule definitions that map to the physical system. In this way physical application attributes can be coupled with analyst generated functional documentation and stored within the transformation repository.

As a general rule, application documentation can be used to leverage outsourcing and maintenance projects and provides a basic foundation for the remaining transformation tasks depicted in Table 6.1.

6.12.3 Application Upgrade and Improvement

The premise behind application upgrade and improvement is that applications are easier to maintain and migrate if they contain easily understood data definitions and process flows. A number of case studies from the 1980s and early 1990s support this premise, but the application of these disciplines stagnated as companies pursued Y2K and Web-based development efforts.

Program structuring streamlines application understanding and maintainability. The structuring process standardizes program flow by applying structured disciplines to "spaghetti" code. This is particularly useful if an application is to be modularized to reflect a more functional, cohesive structure—a common requirement for an application consolidation project. Additional tasks include program slicing and re-aggregation, which realigns physical applications to make them more functionally cohesive.

Data definition rationalization is a key transformation task for any project that requires a consolidated picture of cross-functional data usage for a legacy environment. This includes data warehouse or other data redesign projects as well as more tactical initiatives such as an HIPAA or related data upgrades.

Application upgrade options may be added to project plans as prerequisite tasks or applied as a way to streamline maintenance and outsourcing activities. Using the proper tools, the effort to complete these tasks can typically be justified as a way to improve the integrity of the resulting solution.

6.12.4 Data Mining, Cleanup, and Consolidation

Data mining is a commonly applied discipline that analysts may not consider a transformation activity. When analysts dig through legacy data structures or applications to support a strategic project, however, they are performing legacy transformation analysis. Mining supports CRM projects as well as other business initiatives relying on high-intensity data.

If a mining effort uncovers invalid data types within physical data structures, the project team may want to apply data cleanup or cleansing techniques. Data cleansing is a very valuable, yet often ignored step in a CRM effort. Data cleansing can also be applied as a standalone project to improve the integrity of application processing results. The process of consolidating physical data redundancies may be used within application consolidation projects or any project needing to reduce physical data redundancies.

Data mining, cleanup, and consolidation should be selectively reviewed and added to projects whenever there is a need to ensure that a common view of high-integrity data is needed to support customer-related or other priority business requirements.

6.12.5 EAI and User Interface Upgrades

EAI is typically driven by the need to link front-end, Web-based applications to back-end systems through a data or message-driven interface. User interface upgrades, on the other hand, apply semi-invasive techniques to legacy applications by replacing legacy interfaces with distributed GUI views.

Web-enabling legacy architectures and creating distributed user interfaces increase user and customer satisfaction on a near-term basis while facilitating BPI and B2B projects. EAI and user interface upgrade tasks can also be positioned as interim ROI deliverables within the context of more strategic projects. Interim ROI is achieved because the user gains Web-based access to back-end functions. Over the long term, new user interfaces serve as design input to subsequent architecture migration projects.

Positioning EAI and user interface upgrades as part of a larger architecture migration initiative can be useful if executives are looking for a longer-term solution to replace the existing architecture. It is also useful to remind executive planning teams that EAI is a tactical approach to integration and should be considered as such.

6.12.6 Language Upgrade and Conversion Scenarios

Language conversions are not as common as they used to be, but are still selectively included in comprehensive projects that address application rehosting, consolidation, and migration. As mentioned previously, moving a procedural language (e.g., COBOL) to an object-based language (e.g., Java or C++) is not a valid conversion option due to the architectural difference in these languages. Language-level upgrades are, however, more common within the context of a rehosting effort.

Rehosting typically forces a project team to change compilers, and this entails modifying code constructs within the primary language being used in the original application. Project teams also need to convert application or job control procedures, data definition language, and screen definitions to rehost an application. Rehosting itself can be positioned as an interim deliverable within a larger project aimed at consolidating and/or migrating the existing application architecture.

6.12.7 Data Migration and Consolidation Scenarios

Data migration entails a redesign and, almost always, some degree of consolidation. This concept involves taking multiple physical data structures and consolidating and migrating these structures to a new database that can be used by emergent systems written in languages such as Java. Tasks to create a redesigned, consolidated view of operational data can be incorporated into data warehouse projects as well as more strategic architecture migration efforts.

Data warehouse projects require consistent, consolidated views of high-integrity data that has been extracted from legacy data structures to support user and/or customer inquiries. The same front-end legacy analysis and bottom-up redesign work inherent in a strategic architecture consolidation or migration project is required during the design and creation of a data warehouse.

The difference between a data warehouse project and application consolidation or migration project is that the warehouse does not replace operational data structures. The data warehouse itself may be viewed as an interim step in moving toward a consolidated operational data architecture that can be accessed directly by emergent, Web-based applications.

Coupled with data cleanup tasks, legacy data analysis, extraction, redesign, consolidation, and migration can be embedded in various projects geared at delivering a new application architecture solution. While analysts may not reuse application business logic in a replacement solution, legacy data must be incorporated into any major migration or replacement initiative.

6.12.8 Application Modularization

Application modularization facilitates the consolidation of multiple related and/or redundant applications. Modularization is based on the concept that certain functions within applications are either unnecessary, redundant, or defined in the wrong physical module. The business driver behind eliminating, consolidating, and redefining application logic on a small scale can be to improve maintainability—although this is rare. On a larger scale, however, modularization can be very useful for major application consolidation projects.

Application consolidation projects merge multiple redundant applications like those found in the previous billing application examples within regional telephone companies. Another business driver may involve consolidating related systems, such as found in the example of the three standalone pension, payroll, and insurance applications that needed to be combined into a single, integrated HR application.

Consolidation can also play an interim role in an architecture migration project. In this case, the project team would define several interim deliverables, each with its own ROI. Project phases could include

- Requirements analysis and target architecture definition.
- Legacy data definition analysis and documentation.
- Legacy data definition redesign.
- Legacy data migration and consolidation.
- Application modularization, including consolidation of redundant functions, creation of common routines, and isolation of unique functionality.
- Retooling of data access logic layer.
- Testing and redeployment.

These steps may be positioned within a larger functional upgrade, as part of an architecture migration effort, or as a standalone effort. Standalone consolidation can facilitate major operational downsizing by eliminating redundant user roles and business units while streamlining customer interfaces. As part of a larger project, application consolidation lays the groundwork for moving toward a component-based or Web Services architecture.

6.12.9 Architecture Migration

Architecture migration entails reusing selected data and business rules from one or more legacy applications and data structures into a new design and development paradigm. This can include a component-based or a Web Services architecture. Many of the legacy options employed to this point, including data migration and application consolidation, support architecture migration as interim deliverables.

For example, if a project's purpose is to move to singular, reusable components that could be deployed to eventually replace sections of the legacy architecture, then consolidation of reusable business rules is a step in that direction. Because application consolidation collapses redundant business logic into common application modules, deploying the consolidation option as an interim step can make sense from an ROI perspective.

In the previous billing system example, assume that three billing systems underwent consolidation. This would have created the following consolidated application infrastructure.

- Shared modules for common billing and customer functions.
- Unique modules or table-driven logic for regional billing differences.
- Consolidated data structures wherever possible.
- Consolidated user front ends for special-case scenarios.

With this consolidated architecture as the baseline, the architecture migration project tasks could focus on delivering

- Redesigned application architecture where certain functions would be Web-enabled while other functions would remain running in a background environment.
- Relational database design and migration plan.
- Consolidated relational customer database.
- Common business rule components for common billing functions that could be deployed in Java or in COBOL.
- New functionality built using components developed in an emergent language such as Java.
- New Web-driven front ends.
- Selectively deployed business rules that would allow customers and users real-time access to data and application functionality.
- A newly deployed billing infrastructure, likely using a hybrid application architecture that utilizes the Web and back-end mainframe architectures.

Migrating to a Web Services architecture would be a next step. All of this assumes that there are valid business drivers behind this type of migration project. If there are not, the project team should focus on other activities.

6.13 Building the Project Plan

Building a project plan that incorporates transformation options into broader, business-driven initiatives is fairly straightforward. One aspect of this, which will be covered in more depth in Chapter 8, is the use of various metrics to aid the estimating process. The concept involves determining certain counts and derived scores in a variety of areas and using these to estimate how long the next set of tasks might take.

Environmental metrics provide baseline counts, collected during the enterprise inventory process, that can be used to derive other metrics and estimates. For example, if 3 applications use 5 databases, 30 front-end screens, 5 additional data files, and decompose into 20 major functions, analysts can assign time estimates to assess, upgrade, and/or migrate certain portions of the application. As additional information is gathered through detailed documentation and subsequent tasks, these estimates could be refined further.

The project planning process that infuses transformation options into a business-driven project scenario is summarized as follows.

- Review the comprehensive set of business requirements, including related impacts.
- Establish various proposed solutions and settle on an approach. (Note that the following steps may need to be repeated for each approach to settle on a single alternative.)
- Create a standard plan that incorporates requirements, design, implementation, and testing tasks.
- Verify that the enterprise assessment is built into preliminary analysis and planning tasks.
- Where any task relies on a legacy application, incorporate one or more legacy analysis and/or transformation options into the project task structure.
- Create a phased deliverable structure that produces quantifiable value for the users and customers being addressed under this project.
- Estimate personnel and nonpersonnel costs for each phase based on level of effort, and compare this to the value proposition for that interim deliverable to determine interim and total ROI.
- Be sure to use standard project planning tools to formalize the deliverable-based plan and include deliverable dependencies for virtual teams.

This approach will require deployment of the virtual project team, discussed earlier in this chapter. It will also need to be customized to accommodate project planning requirements unique to a given enterprise.

6.14 Selling Legacy Transformation—Leveraging Legacy Assets

Selling legacy transformation is a subtle task that must focus on augmenting the phased delivery of business-driven requirements. Transformation must be positioned carefully because there are many misconceptions about legacy transformation. Some people think it means converting COBOL to Java. Others believe that it means restructuring old programs. The best approach is to focus on business-driven ROI, project augmentation, phased delivery of ongoing value, and risk reduction based on incorporating legacy asset value into projects that previously ignored that value.

Notes

1. "Building and Measuring ROI for Application Integration Projects," Julia King, presentation of Computerworld ROI, Brainstorm eBusiness Integration Conference, Oct. 29, 2001.
2. "IT Spending Budget Practices Beyond Service Level Agreements," Gartner Inc. [Online], *www.gartner.com*, 2001.
3. "Budget Season Is Here: Financial Services IT Spending Is in for Big Changes," John Hagerty, AMR Research, May 2001.
4. "EAP: Time for a Rethink," Richard Todd, white paper [Online], *www.max-international.com*, June 1998.
5. "ROI From Supply Chain Technology Investments: Is It Real?" Ram Reddy, Cutter Consortium Business–IT Strategies Advisory Service, Vol. 4, No. 17, 2001.
6. "Chaordic Development: A New Direction for Large-Scale IT Initiatives," William Ulrich, Cutter Consortium Technology Trends [Online], *www.cutter.com*, 2000.
7. "Remember COBOL? If You Don't, Get Reacquainted," William Ulrich, *Computerworld*, May 22, 2001.
8. "The Internet Goes Business Critical," Standish Group white paper [Online], *www-4.ibm.com/software/ts/mqseries/library/whitepapers/internetbc/*, 1997.

Legacy Transformation Technology

7

Software tools leverage and enable a wide variety of information management tasks. While technology continues to mature in a variety of software tool categories, much of the technology needed by business and IT professionals is readily available for use on projects today. Identifying and deploying these tools are steps in the process. Convincing business and IT professionals to use these tools, however, remains an obstacle to leveraging technology in order to meet critical business requirements.

Organizations have not leveraged software tools to the degree possible to increase the efficiency and effectiveness of IT-related tasks. IT professionals have failed to employ a wide variety of software technologies to the point where they have been dubbed the shoemaker's children. This is in part due to a lack of knowledge of available software tools and in part due to a reluctance to change the way people perform their jobs. This is unfortunate because IT and business professionals could streamline a variety of information management tasks through the use of software tools.

This chapter introduces various tool categories that facilitate legacy analysis, integration, and transformation. It also outlines strategies for identifying, justifying, procuring, and deploying these technologies. Because transformation projects incorporate various analysis, design, development, and management tasks, I have included a summary of these tool categories as well.

7.1 Transformation Technology Concepts

Before discussing transformation technology categories, readers should be familiar with some basic concepts. These concepts place transformation technology options into a broader context for tool evaluators and users. Understanding these concepts helps position tools within general categories. This is useful because certain tools may perform one function well, but not support a seemingly related function.

For example, static program analysis tools do not track live data through a program or system and therefore are not as useful for enhancing test execution coverage as tools that execute dynamically. Unfortunately, analysts have used static analysis tools for this purpose because they were unaware of the availability of dynamic analysis software. This supports the old saying "When all you own is a hammer, every problem looks like a nail." The following concepts will help the enterprise tool center position and communicate tool options to management and product users.

- **Dynamic Versus Static Tools**

  Dynamic tools are invoked when a program or system is actually executing in a production or test environment. A dynamic program analyzer, for example, will depict all program paths executed based on the data run through that program during a given execution or transaction cycle. A static tool, on the other hand, analyzes source or object code while the program is not being executed. The most common static tool example is a product that outlines all possible logic paths that flow through a source program.

  Static tools tend to mimic the execution of a program, while dynamic tools track actual execution. Dynamic analyzers are useful for developing test data, while static source code analyzers are useful for understanding how a program works. The important point to remember here is that dynamic tools and static tools each have a role in a software portfolio but tend to be used at different points within the software development, maintenance, and transformation cycle.

- **Source, Object, and Data Tools**

  Most transformation tools accept one of three kinds of inputs: source code, object code, or data. Source code tools analyze and/or change one or more program, job control, user interface, and/or data definition source objects. Object module tools are mostly limited to basic analysis capabilities. Software that reads user data can analyze, modify, redesign, merge, or in other ways manipulate that data. A few products, such as a comparison tool, can accept source code, object code, and data as inputs.

- **System versus Program Level Tools**

  Software products can analyze and/or modify source code from a program perspective or from a systems perspective. Certain program analysis tools can summarize program-level information from a systems perspective, but this is not the same as being able to analyze source code from an application perspective. For example, a program analyzer may create complexity scores and summarize these scores for an entire application in a management report. The tool, however, is still limited to a single program view for analysis purposes.

System-level tools, however, understand relationships among programs, job control logic, user interfaces, and data structures. Both system-level and program-level tools are useful on projects depending on the tasks involved. For example, a project involving analysis or changes to global data structures would benefit from using a tool that performed system-wide data definition analysis.

- **Production versus Development Tools**

  Some products are used in a preproduction environment, while other products are used in a postproduction environment. A preproduction tool would include most static analysis tools as well as dynamic analyzers used during the testing phase of a project. Production software includes diagnostic tools built into a production compile step as well as certain integration technology that runs in a production environment. This second category includes middleware and related software that becomes part of the production application architecture.

- **Open versus Closed Products**

  The concept of open software implies that any tool that captures information about a system should have a facility for exporting or sharing that information. Closed software does not facilitate the sharing of tool-captured metadata, while open tools make this information accessible in various formats. Open tools share information through standard export formats or through the use of XML interfaces. All things being equal, analysts should try to employ open software as opposed to tools that do not make information available through an export capability or open repository.

- **Integrated Workbench Technology versus Standalone Tools**

  Software can be delivered as a standalone tool or as part of a workbench environment. Standalone tools tend to be limited to a single set of related functions, while workbench environments deliver multiple tool features and functions. The main differentiating factor between a standalone or "point" tool and a workbench is a workbench's ability to integrate point tools into a cohesive user environment. Workbenches are very useful because they streamline the deployment and acceptance of multiple software products once the targeted user community becomes accustomed to that workbench environment.

- **Packaged Software, Inhouse Tools, and Consulting Technology**

  Software tools can originate in one of three places. Tools may be licensed from a third-party software company, inhouse developed, or brought in under a consulting agreement. Software products from tool vendors are typically the most desirable because they are documented and supported by software professionals. Inhouse-developed software is typically undocumented and unsupported, but may be the only option available. Software built by consultants tends to be less robust than packaged software, is typically undocumented and unsupported, and may carry certain restrictions. Consultants may, for example, allow only their own staff to use their tools.

  When reviewing the tool categories outlined within this chapter, it is important to remember that a given software product may fall into multiple tool categories. A systemwide cross-reference tool, for example, may also have business rule capture capabilities. Planning, outsourcing, and maintenance teams could use the cross-reference capabilities to set project scope, ascertain upgrade requirements, or perform a variety of other tasks. Transformation analysts, on the other hand, employ business rule capture capabilities to detailed analysis and migration tasks.

  Another example of a product that contains multiple, disparate features can be found in integrated development environments (IDEs) that have the ability to reverse-engineer Java components into UML models. Reverse engineering is a modeling function feature that is distinctive and indirectly related to other IDE tool capabilities.

  For the sake of clarity, I have divided various tool types into major tool categories. Commercially available software products mix and match various features and functions into one product or under an integrated workbench environment. Commercially available software product examples for various tool categories are listed in Appendix A.

7.2 Business Modeling Technology

Business planning tools aid in depicting basic business processes for the purpose of modifying those processes and as a way to facilitate the creation of functional requirements from a business user's perspective. Business modeling tools also allow an enterprise to document, revise, and improve how an enterprise functions from a business process perspective. Two general software tool categories support business modeling requirements.

- **Business Analysis and Knowledge Management**

  Documenting business processes and related enterprise knowledge allows users to create their view of how the business works as opposed to relying on IT's interpretation. Business analysis and knowledge capture tools also allow the user community to communicate requirements to information professionals in a technology-independent format. Many times, IT places a technological spin on business requirements that taints the information being gathered. A business analysis and knowledge management tool should allow users to depict processes via simple flow diagrams and matrices that link these flows with data and related business areas.

- **Business Process Integration and Automation**
  BPI/BPA software, also known as business process management (BPM) technology, facilitates the documentation, consolidation, standardization, synchronization, and modification of business processes. BPI/BPA software allows users to diagram, integrate, and automate business processes and incorporates menu-driven software features to trigger manual and automated processes through user notification and authorization.

  These tools can also trigger back-end application transactions through process-to-application integration. The main difference between the BPI/BPA approach to integration and the EAI approach is that BPI/BPA software integrates business processes at the point where the user interacts with a business process. EAI integrates applications only after the user has actually triggered a transaction to occur within an application system.

  BPI/BPA software provides a powerful capability for business units needing to streamline, integrate, and automate business processes. This technology also creates a roadmap for information planning teams who need to design a target architecture for aligning information architectures with retooled business processes. This target architecture becomes the driving force in a transformation planning initiative.

Business knowledge capture, analysis, planning, integration, and automation technology are not being deployed and utilized to a great degree. Process integration provides significant benefits to business units attempting to streamline internal and external processes. Business units would also benefit from taking the initiative for communicating information requirements to IT in a more formal and therefore effective way than has been the case in the past.

7.3 Analysis and Design Modeling Tools

Analysis and design modeling tools, which are typically bundled into integrated workstations, provide a mechanism for specifying a variety of application and data models. The latest modeling tools tend to fall into the UML category, which supports a variety of specification models, and standalone data modeling tools.

- **UML Modeling Tools**
  Because UML is an industry accepted standard for specifying system design models, UML modeling tools play an increasingly important role in

development and transformation projects. Reverse engineering legacy functionality into UML models allows analysts to manipulate that functionality in design models. This approach is a more effective method of leveraging legacy business data and logic in target architectures than a straight migration to Java because it interjects reusable functionality into the target architecture at the design level. Doing so adheres to a model-driven systems management and maintenance strategy that many enterprises envision as a long-term goal.

A UML modeling tool should allow analysts to create and modify Use Case, Class, Object, Sequence, Collaboration, Statechart, Activity, Component, and Deployment diagrams. In addition to this, certain UML tools have the capacity to reverse-engineer Java classes into UML models. Reverse engineering tools will likely continue to mature to the point where they can populate UML models with input captured from legacy environments. UML tools should be able to accept these legacy representations as a step toward redesigning legacy architectures. Modeling tools have not been employed to the same degree as Java code-generation tools. This suggests that too much emphasis has been placed on the coding portion of a project, while too little emphasis has been placed on the analysis and design stages of a project.

- **Data Modeling Technology**

  Data modeling tools continue to play a role in the design and deployment of enterprise data. Relational data modeling tools, for example, have been in use for many years. In addition to this, a number of IDE tools transform relational models into object models and object models into relational models. These are used during the creation of object models and deployment of component-based applications that need to interface with relational databases. Some data modeling tools also support the reverse engineering of nonrelational views into relational data models. This is very useful for transformation projects where migrating application data to a relational data environment is required.

7.4 The Environmental Analyzer

Environmental analysis is a term used to describe the inventory and cross-referencing of physical application environments. The ideal tool can parse all physical application objects, identify relationships among these objects, produce summary-level reports of this information, and deliver environmental counts or other metrics. A sample environmental cross-reference analysis report for a mainframe system is depicted in Figure 7.1.

Environmental metrics should minimally include total counts of each object type, including source program, object model, screen definition, job control member, copy member, data definition language members, and other relevant items.

Dataset to Source Cross-Reference

DATASET NAME	SOURCE PROGRAM	SOURCE LIBRARY	DDNAME	LAYOUT COPY MEMBER	OPEN MODE
PROD.LEDGER.FILE	GLREAD	PROD.SOURCE.COBOL	INDD1	LEDGERIN	INPUT
	GLUPDATE	PROD.SOURCE.COBOL	UPDGL2	LEDGERIN	MIXED
	GLVERFIY	PROD.SOURCE.ASM	VERIFY1	LEDGER	INPUT
PROD.HISTORY.FILE	HIST001	PROD2.SOURCE	HISTOUT	HIST001	OUTPUT
PROD.TRANS.LOG	P001DLOG	UTIL.SOURCE	LOGOUT	LOGFILE	OUTPUT
	P002ULOG	UTIL.SOURCE	LOG	LOGFILE	INPUT
	P003XLOG	UTIL.SOURCE	SYSIN	LOGFILE	MIXED

Figure 7.1
Sample environmental analysis depicts relationships between physical data and source programs. This type of information expedites research and changes involving data and program definitions.

Environmental analyzers may be batch-driven or may function in an interactive mode and should address legacy and emerging environments.

- **Batch Environmental Analyzer**

  A batch-driven environmental analyzer accepts application libraries as input and provides information on execution flow, physical system object relationships, and dependencies. Ideal requirements include the ability to rapidly parse and cross-reference system objects across multiple applications, load this information into an open repository, produce metrics and reports, and allow analysts to examine and extract information on an ad hoc basis. Results should be depicted graphically as well as in cross-reference lists.

- **Interactive Environmental Analyzer**

  An interactive environmental analyzer contains all of the features found in the batch-driven analyzer, but also provides interactive access to an underlying repository. The interactive analysis capability should include online, ad hoc query capabilities, the ability to hyperlink from one view to the next, an extensible repository, and an easy-to-use interface.

7.5 The Open Repository

Product support for a transformation repository, discussed in Chapter 5, can be any open repository that can depict an entity relationship model representing current and target system components. The transformation repository defines attributes and relationships for each object in the repository. The repository model should be flexible enough to allow an enterprise to specify any physical or logical object type required.

Flexibility for such a tool is important because the items to be defined and mapped to each other can vary dramatically due to the diversity of information environments typically found within a given enterprise. The repository should have the following capabilities.

- The repository should be able to represent any physical or logical object (entity) within the repository model.
- Analysts should be able to define attributes for each object. For example, a source program object would contain attributes such as name, language, lines of code, and complexity metric.
- The repository should ideally have the ability to parse physical application objects.
- The repository should be open to import and export capabilities. For example, the repository should be able to accept import data, including cross-reference relationships, collected by an environmental analyzer.
- Parsing or import tools should be able to recognize and update only modified components to avoid a complete reload when updating is required.
- Users should be able to run online or batch inquiries against the repository on an as-needed basis using standard query tools.
- Analysts should be able to update the repository model without having to reload all of the repository data already defined in the original version of the repository.
- Ideally, the repository will come with a transformation template model similar to the views defined in Figures 5.3 and 5.4 in Chapter 5.

In the absence of a formal repository product, transformation teams have used standard, relational database tools to mimic the repository features listed above. Difficulties with this approach include:

- Redefining the repository model without rebuilding the database.
- Having to repopulate the database from scratch because the database does not recognize the delta between what has already been captured and what is being updated.
- The lack of sophisticated parsing and inquiry tools that comes with many repositories.

Because the transformation repository represents a superset of physical, logical, and external component objects, development platforms, environmental analyzers, or other point tools are typically not designed to support transformation repository requirements.

7.6 Source Program Analyzers

Source code analysis involves the parsing of logic flow and data definition usage within a single source program. Because the source program is the basis for the maintenance, upgrade, and transformation activity associated with a legacy application, source code analyzers provide very useful information for an analyst or programmer needing to understand that source code. There are two general categories of source program analyzer.

- **Batch Static Analyzer**
  The batch-driven static analyzer can parse programs, track all logic flows through that program, assess program structure and complexity, produce additional metric summaries, generate path flow diagrams and in-line reports, and highlight any diagnostics found within the code. Figure 7.2

Program Flow–Path Analysis

```
LINE TRANSFER    TRANSFER    *--*--*--*--*--*--*--*--*--*--*--*--*--*--*--*--*--*--*--*
     FROM  TO    TYPE        1  2  3  4  5  6  7  8  9 10 11 12 13 14 15 16 17 18 19 20
                             *--*--*--*--*--*--*--*--*--*--*--*--*--*--*--*--*--*--*--*

  1 00786 00786      ENTRY SAMPLE
  2 00787 00787 NULL FALL  BEGIN-PROGRAM
  3 00788 00788 NULL FALL  BEGIN-PROGRAM-010
  4 00789 01564      PERF  GET-ENTITY-TITLE
  5 01569 01587      PERF  .  9100-LINK-TO-005
  6 01588 00000      CALL  .  .  FAM006
  7 01573 01589 COND PERF  .  9000-DISPLAY
  8 01598 00000      CALL  .  .  FAM000
  9 01575 01589 COND PERF  .  9000-DISPLAY >7
 10 01576 01593 COND PERF  .  9900-ABORT-JOB
 11 01594 00000      CALL  .  .  ILBOABN0
 12 01594 00000      STOP  .  .  NON RETURNING CALL
 13 01580 01587      PERF  .  9100-LINK-TO-005 >5
 14 01584 01589 COND PERF  .  9000-DISPLAY >7
 15 01586 01593 COND PERF  .  9900-ABORT-JOB >10
 16 00790 01519      PERF  S100-MAIN-RTN
 17 01521 00971      PERF  .  D000002-XX
 18 00974 00976      PERF  .  .  0220-PROCESS-OPT-B
 19 00977 01446      PERF  .  .  .  0600-READ-DETAIL-INPUT
 20 01448 01450 COND GO TO .  .  .  .  0685-CLOSE-DETAIL-INPUT
 21 01454 01595      PERF  .  .  .  .  .  TEST-FOR-USAM-E1
 22 01596 01596 NULL FALL  .  .  .  .  .  .  TEST-FOR-USAM-E1-A
 23 01603 01589 COND PERF  .  .  .  .  .  .  9000-DISPLAY >7
 24 01604 00000 COND CALL  .  .  .  .  .  .  ENDIT
 25 01605 01605 FALL THRU  .  .  .  .  .  .  TEST-FOR-USAM-E1-EXIT
 26 01455 01455 FALL THRU  .  .  .  .  .  0690-EXIT
 27 01449 01455      GO TO .  .  .  .  0690-EXIT
 28 00978 01489 COND GO TO .  .  .  0800-PRINT-E1-TOTALS 018
 29 01491 01526 COND GO TO .  .  .  .  0850-NO-E1S
 30 01528 01373 COND PERF  .  .  .  .  .  0610-CLEAR-STORAGE
 31 01380 01380 FALL THRU  .  .  .  .  .  .  0620-EXIT
 32 01530 01310 COND PERF  .  .  .  .  .  0550-PRINT-E1S
```

Figure 7.2
Program flow analysis allows an analyst to quickly determine the overall logic flow of a program slated for an update or transformation.

In-line Program Cross-Reference

```
    00973              MOVE 1 TO LINE-ERROR
    00974              PERFORM 8220-PROCESS-OPT-B.                                    00976
    00975    511100*


  *------------------------------------------------------------------------*
  * . GO TO CONDITIONAL FROM 00906 8181-OLD-HIST-EOF.                       *
  * . PERFORMED BY 00957 8200-F18TM-READ-NEXT, 00971 D088082-XX.            *
  * . BEGIN GO TO LOOP RETURNING FROM 81000 8258-CONTINUE.                  *
  * . PERFORM RANGE VIOLATION TO 01489 8800-PRINT-E1-TOTALS.                *
  *------------------------------------------------------------------------*


    00976    511800 8220-PROCESS-OPT-B.

    00977    512500     PERFORM 8600-READ-DETAIL-INPUT THRU 8690-EXIT.      01446 01455
    00978    513200     IF OPT-A GO TO 8800-PRINT-E1-TOTALS.                01489
    00979    513900*


  *------------------------------------------------------------------------*
  * . BEGIN GO TO LOOP RETURNING FROM 00957 8200-F18TM-READ-NEXT.           *
  * . FALL THRU FROM 00976 8220-PROCESS-OPT-B.                              *
  * . PERFORM THRU 00999 8240-EXIT BY 01038 8200-OPT-C-E1, 01052 8300-IS-V1-ON-FILE, *
  *   01470 8760-OPT-C-READ.                                                *
  *------------------------------------------------------------------------*


    00980    514600 8230-VERIFY-DETAIL-INPUT.

    00981    515300     IF DP-ID NOT = '001'
    00982    515800        MOVE 1 TO E1-NO (1)  ADD 1 TO E1-SWITCH.
    00983    516700     IF DP-SORT-CODE NOT = 'B'
    00984    517400        MOVE 1 TO E1-NO (2)  ADD 1 TO E1-SWITCH.
    00985    518100     IF OPT-B
    00986    518800        IF DP-SEQ IS NOT NUMERIC
    00987    519500           MOVE 1 TO E1-NO (3)  ADD 1 TO E1-SWITCH.
    00988    520200     IF OPT-B
    00989    520900        MOVE DP-SEQ TO CK-CRD-SEQ.
    00990    521600     IF DP-AMOUNTX = SPACES OR ZEROES          NEXT SENTENCE
    00991    522300     ELSE IF DP-AMOUNT IS NUMERIC
    00992    523000           MOVE DP-AMOUNT TO CE-PAY-AMT
    00993    523700           MOVE 1 TO AMOUNT-SWITCH.
    00994    524400        ELSE MOVE 1 TO E1-NO (8)  ADD 1 TO E1-SWITCH
    00995    525100           MOVE DP-AMOUNTX TO CE-PAY-AMTXX.
    00996    525800     MOVE DP-DOCUMENT TO CK-DOC-NO.
    00997    526500     IF DP-FILLER NOT = SPACES
```

Figure 7.3

In-line cross-reference reports ensure that source code analysis reflects all explicit or implicit references to program logic.

depicts a sample report that programmers can use to understand the overall logic flow of a program. Figure 7.3 shows a sample in-line cross-reference report that a programmer or analyst can use to determine how other points within a program access a routine.

- **Interactive Static Analyzer**

  The interactive static analyzer has the same basic features as a batch analyzer, but additionally allows a programmer to view the analysis results interactively. Interactive analyzers allow a user to see multiple views of the same information and keep those views synchronized. For example, a control flow graph would scroll as an analyst moved through an adjoining source code view within that same program.

The use of a batch versus an interactive static analysis tool is really driven by need. An interactive tool is useful for a programmer doing ad hoc research into a problem or project. A programmer may be looking for every path associated with a given transaction value and could use the interactive analysis tool to trace those paths. The programmer will probably need to trace through multiple programs and the interactive analyzer should facilitate the ability to navigate from one source program to another.

A batch analyzer, on the other hand, is more conducive to planning activities. Planning teams can use metric and summary-level information to assess the complexity of an application. The more complex a system, the more time it takes to analyze, enhance, improve, or transform. If, for example, a group of programs is highly complex, poorly structured, and utilizes a number of constructs that are hard to decipher, it would increase the time and the skills needed to extract business logic from those programs.

7.7 Application Improvement Tools

The term *application improvement* can be interpreted in a variety of ways. Within the context of a transformation project, however, improvement refers to making a program or group of programs more understandable through the structuring, splitting or slicing, or aggregation of related source logic. The goal can be as simple as improving the understandability of a program or as significant as creating a consolidated application that facilitates the collapsing of multiple business entities into a single, united functional unit.

- **Source Program Editor**

  A source program editor allows source text to be accessed and altered. This is highly useful for development, ongoing maintenance, and transformation-related work. A programmer may, for example, eliminate a runaway logic path in a program that was identified by a static program analyzer. Editing tools may also be used to select, copy, and reuse logic from one application to another application, a common activity in a consolidation project. Program editors are included with most operating environments.

  Modern editing tools, such as those used in a Java IDE, are more intelligent than their older predecessors. They can anticipate what logic a programmer plans to enter and produce the code as a result. Modern editors can also check syntaxes in real time. Similar tools are available for COBOL and other legacy languages and are typically delivered as part of a workstation product that also supports testing and related programming functions. The source program editor will remain an important tool for development, maintenance, and transformation projects.

- **Language Change/Upgrade Tool**

  The language change/upgrade tool converts source code to comply with either the requirements of a newer version of the same language or an entirely different language. Converting source code should not cause any change in functionality, although this can happen and is why converted source code should be tested thoroughly. Numerous conversion tools have been used over the years, although most of these tools have been consulting tools as opposed to off-the-shelf software products. The reason for this is the transitory nature of conversion software.

  Source code conversion is a transliteration of one language to another and not recommended when the target language is of a different architecture than the original language. For example, converting Assembler to COBOL is a legitimate translation because both languages have a procedural architecture. Converting COBOL to C++ or Java, however, is not recommended because the target languages are object-oriented. Replicating COBOL procedural flows, such as the GO TO verb, within Java would create cryptic Java code and deliver little or no value to the business unit relying on that application and the application team maintaining it.

- **Program Structuring Tool**

  A source program structuring tool can parse and analyze source code, determine all possible logic paths, and create a functionally equivalent version of the program in a structured format. The degree of flexibility in output formats and styles varies from tool to tool, but most allow the user leeway in determining the format of the resultant code.

  The underlying technology behind structuring tools involves concepts such as graph theory and other software engineering disciplines that impose a PERFORM-based structure on previously unstructured programs. These products incorporate a variety of parameters that allow analysts to customize the output to inhouse programming standards.

  The newly structured program is more easily understood and more easily maintained. This is particularly true for programmers who are unfamiliar with the original source program. Program structuring also provides a good starting point for transformation analysts who may not have a sophisticated reverse engineering tool available for the project. Structured code is also useful for "reengineering in place" projects, such as an application consolidation effort.

  Structuring tools are typically employed with program static analysis software. Static analysis identifies anomalies in code, such as runaway logic or unplanned recursion. These constructs can be "handled" by the structuring tool, but are more effectively corrected by humans who understand the intent of a given logic path. Encountering one of these anomalies in a production environment—typically triggered by unusual combinations of data—would cause a production application to fail in various ways. Production failures are extremely costly, and these anomalies should be corrected before they trigger latent application problems.

At one point, there were four COBOL structuring tools and one FORTRAN structuring tool available for license. Unfortunately, these products have fallen into disuse, even though case studies showed that they offered significant productivity gains for the maintainers of those systems. The bottom line is that structured code is a better baseline for application consolidation, migration, outsourcing, and related upgrade initiatives.

- **Code Modularization Facility**

  A code modularization facility performs code slicing to carve out segmented functions of a source program and turn the original program into a main program and series of subprograms. Code slicing is based on multiple criteria that can be established as parameters within the slicing tool.

  An analyst should be able, for example, to slice along a data usage path, a conditional path, or a control-based path. If, for example, a high-level routine dominates a certain number of low-level routines, the high-level routine becomes a candidate to be a program driver. Slicing works more effectively on structured source code. The process of aggregating programs, which combines sliced modules into common routines, uses a combination of slicing and code comparison tools coupled with various techniques, as explained in later chapters.

  Slicing technology can be acquired as a standalone software tool or it can be embedded in a business rule extraction facility. The role of slicing in the latter case is applied within the concept of the reverse engineering tool category discussed later in this chapter.

Application improvement tools have not been leveraged to the degree that they were during the 1980s and 1990s, in spite of the fact that organizations are adding 5 billion lines of COBOL code to their legacy portfolios per year. Much of this new code is unlikely to conform to structured or modular standards because legacy updates tend to adhere to whatever structure was in place in the original application. Transformation teams would be well advised to reconsider the use of these tools under a business-driven transformation strategy.

Improving the overall quality of outsourced applications, for example, would cut the cost of maintaining those applications while improving the quality of the software asset the outsourcing firm has been chartered with managing. Because legacy systems are here to stay, improving the quality of applications targeted for major enhancement, rehosting, migration, or other transformation efforts makes good sense.

7.8 Data Definition Analysis and Improvement

Data definition analysis and improvement tools address the understandability and quality of data definitions as they are defined in the legacy application architecture. These tools are subdivided into analyzer, rationalization, and expansion software categories.

- **Data Definition Analyzer**

  A data definition analyzer parses and cross-references data definitions across one or more applications as a means of providing analysts with information about the relationships, similarities, redundancy, and quality of those data definitions. Tool attributes include the ability to create a data definition cross-reference analysis based on physical data structure links, size, underlying attributes, control transfer, and record structure layouts. Data definition analysis identifies redundancies, inconsistencies, and relationships of the data definitions used across the applications being assessed.

  The ideal tool determines where program data definitions link to physical data structures on a cross-application basis. This type of tool also examines screen, data definition language, and other sources of external data references and definitions. Such a tool is useful for large-scale, cross-functional data upgrade or migration projects. Understanding, for example, the relationship between seemingly different data record structures is a very powerful capability for any teams assigned to upgrading all data defined by a common set of record definitions.

  Figure 7.4 depicts related data definitions that were defined as unique data structures yet represent the same physical data across multiple programs and applications. If a project is chartered with upgrading data related to Group 254, for example, the project team may apply the change only to the individual Copy member and neglect to update other data definitions that define that data structure. The resulting change would result in a production failure, which could cost the enterprise in lost productivity and revenue. A record grouping analysis tool identifies synonym groups and reduces research time for a project by a significant margin.

  Additional impact analysis involves element tracing, which was common in Y2K projects, and homonym analysis for data elements with the same name but with a different meaning. Certain tools provide this capability along with data definition redundancy identification via record grouping analysis. Other tools support element tracing, typically driven by a combination of name and usage analysis, as a standalone feature.

  An HIPAA project team, for example, may be inclined to use element tracing tools when they should be using a record grouping analysis tool to develop

Data Definition—Record Grouping Report

GROUP	GRP TYP	SIZE	MEMBER	RECORD NAME	PHY LEV	ORIG COPY	M T	REDEFINES
GRP0252	10	115	PROG011	CUS1-RFC	01			
	10		PROG019	CUSTOMER-REC	01			
GRP0253	10	140	PROG002	ADJUSTMENT-REC	05	MONTHREC		
	10		PROG011	MTHLY-ADJ	05			
	10		PROG012	MONTH-ADJUST-RECORD	01			
GRP0254	10	140	PROG002	CHARGE-REC	05	MONTHREC		ADJUSTMENT-REC
	10		PROG011	MTHLY-CHG	05			MTHLY-ADJ
	10		PROG012	MONTH-CHARGE-RECORD	01			MONTH-ADJUST-RECORD
	10		PROG014	MTH-C	01			
GRP0255	10	140	PROG002	CASH-REC	05	MONTHREC		ADJUSTMENT-REC
	10		PROG011	MTHLY-ADJ	05			MTHLY-ADJ
	10		PROG012	MONTH-CASH-RECORD	01			MONTH-ADJUST-RECORD
GRP0256	10	220	PROG006	TRANSACTION-INPUT	01			
	10		PROG006	TRANS-IN	01			
	10		PROG009	WS-TRANS-REC	05	TRANSREC		
	10		PROG015	WS-TRANS-REC	05	TRANSREC		
	10		PROG020	WS-TRANS-REC	05	TRANSREC		
	10		PROG031	WS-TRANS-REC	05	TRANSREC		
GRP0257	10	220	PROG017	TAPE-OUT	01			
	10		PROG031	TAPE-IN	01			
	10		PROG032	TAPE-REC	01			
GRP0258	10	500	PROG007	MASTER-HEADER-REC	05			
	10		PROG022	MAST-HEAD	01			
	10		PROG031	HDR-REC	01			
GRP0259	10	500	PROG007	MASTER-DETAIL-REC	05			MASTER-HEADER-REC
	10		PROG022	MAST-DTL	01			MAST-HEAD
	10		PROG023	MASTER-INPUT	01			
	10		PROG032	MASTER-REC	01			
GRP0260	10	625	PROG014	PRODUCT-RECORD	01			
	10		PROG016	PROD-REC	01			
	10		PROG019	PRODUCT-MASTER	01	PRODMAST		
	10		PROG024	WS-PRODUCT-AREA	01			
	10		PROG027	PRODUCT-MASTER	01	PRODMAST		
	10		PROG032	PRODUCT-MASTER	01	PRODMAST		

Figure 7.4
Data definition groupings depict redundantly defined data across applications. This reduces research time and costs for data-related projects.

a comprehensive impact analysis that links data definitions to physical data structures. If a major data upgrade or migration project is planned, a data definition analysis tool is essential to reduce the cost and time needed to deliver that project.

• **Data Definition Rationalization**
A data definition rationalization tool builds composite records from redundant record groupings, facilitates analyst-driven name standardization and field expansion, and propagates the new composite records back into the programs that use them. This final step renames the original element names

(attributes) in the source code to the new composite names. Additionally, a data name rationalization tool should be able to replace program-level data references with new names as needed.

Data definition rationalization is useful for any large-scale data upgrade, such as that required for HIPAA projects. Composite record development is also a prerequisite to data redesign projects, although the source code may not need updating, depending on the approach. Not rationalizing legacy data definitions as input to a data redesign effort, which is commonly the case, results in target data models that omit critical business data or misrepresent relationships among various data elements. No one tends to notice these problems until data migration efforts find that there is no place in the new database for critical operational data or until a business user cannot use the system. Project postmortems should track these problems back to the use of redundant, inconsistent data definitions within the redesign process.

The availability of data definition rationalization technology in the marketplace has varied over the years. Two automated rationalization tools were in one case pulled from the market and in another case never made it to market due to a lack of perceived demand for the product. As organizations gain more insight into the need for data definition rationalization, various tools are likely to mature while new tools reemerge. In the meantime, a number of analysis tools support project teams who wish to pursue this work in a semi-automated fashion.

- **Data Definition Expansion**

   A number of projects can require the identification and expansion of legacy data elements across data definition language, source programs, and physical data structures. Data definition expansion tools identify and expand field definitions within programs and related data source objects across one or more applications. The analysis is typically based on date usage (i.e., Move, Compare, etc.) and similar tracing capabilities of an individual element versus a record group. This approach works if the only goal is to correct that single element, which was typically the case with a Y2K project.

   Data definition rationalization, which deals with record structures at the group rather than the element level, is a more sophisticated and comprehensive solution because it deals with data within the context of the physically defined group. Element tracing, on the other hand, is a quick-fix solution that may be useful if there are no larger-scale transformations planned for the applications involved.

   Most of the data definition expansion software in the market emerged to support Y2K projects. Some of these tools are still available to support projects involving field expansion. Any project requiring the addition of new data to a physical file structure or other more comprehensive structural change should consider a record group-centric approach rather than an element-centric approach.

7.9 Presentation-Layer Extraction and Migration

The user view is the most visible aspect of an application environment. It also happens to be the area where IT can achieve the greatest impact. Software tools support the documentation and migration of application user views and may be used as standalone tools or in conjunction with more comprehensive transformation solutions.

- **Presentation-Layer Extraction**

  A user presentation extract tool supports presentation-layer analysis of a system by providing automated the creation of screen or report mockups based on screen and source program definitions. In addition to providing useful documentation to analysts planning upgrades to an application, user views also provide a way for transformation analysts to ascertain high-level functionality from a legacy environment. Extracted user view mockups are used to create a first-cut assessment of an application's functionality in the absence of other documentation.

  Most tools that support this capability tend to be part of more comprehensive workbenches. These products read program or screen definition source and extract a mockup of screens and reports using position and length attributes. Reports tend to be overlooked by less experienced analysts because many junior analysts tend to believe that all processing is done online. In a legacy environment, report mockups can tell as much or more about an application as online screen mockups.

  Some types of applications in the scientific or real-time arena are less likely to lend themselves to this type of analysis because their inputs and outputs may be limited. Applications that use character-based input with no screen formatting also do not lend themselves to this type of extraction process.

- **User Interface Migration**

  A first step in legacy transformation can involve the migration of legacy application interfaces. Certain integration products allow analysts to transform and integrate legacy system interfaces into Web-based or other GUI interfaces. User interface migration technology, for example, can support the transformation of mainframe or other character-based input formats to Web-based front ends. In some cases, tools support the capture and consolidation of multiple character-based screens into a single GUI or Web-based front end.

This tool category can take one of two approaches. A tool can replace the user interface but not require modifying the legacy application source code. In this case, the legacy program still believes that it is accessing, for example, a mainframe CICS menu. The interface, however, takes the CICS commands and transforms them into GUI or Web-driven front ends from the user's perspective. A second approach modifies the application source code to interface with GUI or HTML drivers. The first tool category is the more prevalent approach because it is noninvasive to the legacy source code and therefore limits the amount of modifications and testing.

7.10 Reverse Engineering and Reengineering Technology

The capture and reuse of legacy data and application functionality have been a quest for IT for many years. Portions of reverse engineering and reengineering solutions are in place. Tool-assisted data definition capture and redesign, for example, have been available for more than a decade. Other tools, particularly those that address business logic, are less mature. I will describe both tools currently in the market along with the ideal solution reflecting approaches that are still in evolutionary stages.

- **Transaction Flow Analysis Tool**

  A design import facility can capture and represent current system flows in dialog flow format. This type of tool parses and analyzes job control and screen definition source objects and, to the degree possible, depicts how a system flows from one transaction to the next. The ideal representation for depicting legacy transaction flow is within a UML sequence diagram.

  Because many online environments tend to be event-driven, the results of transaction flow analysis require analyst input to fill in missing information that the tool did not fully interpret. The output from such a tool would be highly valuable for documenting current environments as well as input to the assessment, design, and deployment of replacement environments. Tools had been created to support this type of analysis, but they relied on CASE technology that is no longer commercially available. Certain consulting tools can also support this type of analysis. Additionally, there are other products available in real-time, C-based environments to support transaction flow analysis.

- **Data Reverse Engineering and Reengineering**

  Data reverse engineering and reengineering tools capture, import, and redesign legacy data definitions with the intent of deriving or augmenting a logical model from the legacy environment. Some tools attempt to do this by evaluating the physical data as well as the application definitions. The results of such an effort produce an entity relationship (ER) model for the new system. Data analysts could then further normalize such a model. Such a tool should either reconcile data redundancies and inconsistencies prior to creating the logical model or be used in conjunction with a data definition rationalization product.

Features of a data reengineering product include the ability to capture existing data definitions and represent records such as entities and elements as attributes in a design tool. Optional but highly desirable features include the ability to automatically derive an ER model, merge multiple models, and assist in producing a normalized data model from that ER model.

Another approach to reverse and reengineering legacy data involves the transformation of legacy data records into entity beans. A reversal of this process allows entity beans to be transformed from an object orientation into a relational view using standard IDE tools. One issue that has limited transformation projects is that data reverse and reengineering tools have not been integrated effectively with business rule capture tools. These products must be synchronized to a greater degree to allow transformation teams to become more efficient over the long term.

- **Business Rule Capture and Consolidation**

A business rule capture tool identifies and slices logic paths based on specified selection criteria. Such a tool would statically or dynamically analyze logic paths across source program boundaries. It should ideally bypass or highlight implementation-dependent logic, store the extracted rules, further extract against previously extracted rules, display rules in a variation of formats, and transform extracted rules into a reusable format.

This is a difficult challenge when applied to procedural languages where the 20 to 30 percent of the source code comprising business logic is intermixed with data manipulation, user interface, and environmental logic. The ideal tool would allow an analyst to interactively select, trace, capture, tag, and migrate business rules. These features should be complemented by the ability to identify business logic in diagrammatic form based on the events that trigger that logic.

Some reverse engineering tools run dynamically, while others run in a static mode. A combined approach is ideal, and work is under way to capture business logic using both approaches. Dynamic rule capture is currently isolated to use in real-time systems using languages such as C.

Static business rule capture tools fall into two categories. Some tools run in batch mode, capture rule candidates, isolate environmental logic, and change the rest of the code into Java. This solution is limiting because it does not allow for interactive analyst query and rule refinement. Early interactive products were barely more than fancy source code editors. Today's products can capture, display, and integrate legacy business rules in a highly interactive fashion. Certain consulting tools are beginning to mature as well.

There is research and development work under way to incorporate these capabilities into a transformation workbench, but these efforts are unlikely to result in an off-the-shelf product in the immediate future. As more companies pursue transformation work, these tools should mature significantly.

Certain UML modeling tools currently support the extraction and loading of Java classes into UML models. This capability is limited to new systems that should have been model-driven in the first place. Building reverse engineering capabilities into analysis and design tools is an important step, however, in the maturation of the vendor tool community toward recognizing the ongoing need for this technology. The Java reverse engineering process is much more straightforward, because Java is developed in a highly structured environment. The more than 200 billion lines of procedural software in the world, however, were not developed in readily reverse-engineered environments.

- **Legacy Componentization**

   There are two options for component reuse currently being supported by legacy componentization products. One option is to leave the code in its native format. COBOL components, for example, can be reused under an EJB environment if they are recompiled with special compilers. This approach is effective for companies committed to COBOL as a long-term language environment, but still requires the business logic to be identified, captured, and consolidated in preparation for being turned into a component. This may be done using the previously discussed business rule capture technology or performed manually using an editing tool.

   A second approach is to convert these components into Java as a prerequisite to reusing them under a Web-enabled architecture. Certain tools facilitate the capture and transformation of legacy business logic into Java components. These are not considered language-conversion tools because they only work against an extracted business rule and not against an entire application or program. Componentization relies on architecture teams designing and creating a target architecture that transformation teams can target.

Appendix A provides a most current view of commercially available reverse engineering technology, but the capabilities of these tools are likely to continue to mature beyond where they are today.

7.11 Validation, Verification, and Testing Technology

Validating the correctness of a project deliverable is required in legacy transformation, maintenance, and new development. Transformation projects require testing at interim stages. For example, an application may be tested after a data definition rationalization phase, after a consolidation phase, and finally at the conclusion of a redesign phase. Various tools support program and application testing and quality assurance tasks as follows.

- **Change Integration Tool**

  A change integration tool detects, consolidates, and reconciles multiple versions of applications. This tool provides impact analysis capabilities for identifying versions that contain differences and identifies patterns for merging different versions of members with different names. Such a tool should also produce an audit trail of all modifications.

- **Test Coverage Analyzer**

  A typical production cycle only executes about 5 percent of a given application's source code. For this reason, project teams will want to use coverage analyzers to determine if the right functionality has been tested. This tool category includes dynamic coverage analysis, test data selection, and transaction capture and playback. Dynamic coverage analysis determines the percentage of logic or statements executed during a given test run. These tools allow analysts to refine the data being run through a given test cycle to ensure that the proper code is tested based on the test specifications for that project.

  Online transaction capture and playback tools capture a series of online transactions and allow that captured data to be run back through the system later in a controlled or batch mode. This type of tool helps ensure that comprehensive test data is available on a recurring basis to ensure that the right code is tested within an application.

- **Transaction Simulation Facility**

  A transaction simulation facility captures, packages, transmits, and receives host-based transactions to and from a client/server environment using transaction simulation software. The concept involves testing a program or application outside of its normal execution environment through a simulated execution. This can save time by allowing an application to be tested in the same environment in which it is being maintained.

- **Compiler/Preprocessor**

  A source language compiler and/or preprocessor is required to convert a source program into machine-executable instructions. This tool comes with most operating environments, although speciality compilers are available for certain situations. One example of this is a compiler that can create an executable COBOL module in a J2EE compliant architecture. Note that a number of compilers come with debugging options built into them.

- **Source and Object Code Comparison Tool**

  A comparison tool is used to compare source or data files, on a byte-by-byte basis, to determine all differences. Tool functionality includes the use of keys or indexes to allow synchronization of files and also includes the ability to mask portions of a record by specifying fields to ignore during the comparison process. This tool is useful when an application has undergone a change that can be assessed or verified against a baseline version of that system. It should also be able to distinguish between different object modules to ensure that no unintended changes have occurred. This is typically used to support validation testing and quality assurance.

7.12 Maintenance and Transformation Workbenches

A maintenance workbench incorporates interactive program analysis with additional product features such as an environmental analyzer or data definition analyzer. This environment also incorporates interfaces to a program editor, compiler, testing tools, and configuration management facilities. In some cases, a workbench might incorporate business rule capture or other transformation capabilities.

If a workbench incorporates transformation tools, it is likely that the vendor is positioning it as a transformation workbench. While maintenance workbenches are normally licensed as off-the-shelf products, consultants typically bring in a transformation workbench as part of a consulting project. The reason for this is that the transformation workbench is viewed as a transitory tool by both the vendor and the inhouse management team.

A transformation workbench may only be transitory, however, from the perspective of the application area that hired the consulting team. When viewed from an enterprise perspective, however, a transformation workbench could be applied to a variety of projects over a period of years. This is one of the reasons that a centrally coordinated software tool function should identify, procure, and deploy software technology and tools. Applying a product to a variety of projects allows for that product to be more readily cost justified on a long-term licensing basis.

Maintenance and transformation workbenches provide the opportunity to create a shared, underlying metamodel against which a variety of tools can function. This reduces the reparsing and related overhead of rerunning standalone analysis tools.

Workbenches can either provide many of the tool capabilities discussed thus far or enable various point tools to be built into a workbench environment. A workbench can also be customized to conform to the methods and processes being used within a given enterprise. The software tool center should work with the transformation team to identify, procure, and deploy this type of workbench environment.

7.13 Physical Data Analysis and Migration Technology

Tools for managing physical data analysis, migration, and related tasks tend to fall under the domain of a data management or database administration group. Data ownership determines who is responsible for maintaining data quality and consistency on an enterprise basis. The following tools support these requirements within the context of ongoing transformation efforts.

- **Data Mining Technology**

  Data mining technology is used to interrogate large cross-sections of data files or databases and discover patterns, associations, anomalies, and other user-driven data content information. The concept behind data mining is to turn information into useful knowledge that a business user can utilize more effectively in order to make decisions. Data mining is a transformation analysis activity, although it is not generally thought of as such. There are a number of data mining products available in the commercial vendor market.

- **Physical Data Analyzer and Cleansing Tool**

  The physical data analyzer is capable of automatically scanning selected data and producing a sampling of defective data. There are three common methods for determining defective data. Users can compare data to user-defined data authentication or integrity rules. Users can also compare data to hardcoded data found within the source code or values defined in a data dictionary. They can also assess data to discover inherent rules and dependencies based on related data. For example, if an employee can only be a male or female, then a contract employee can also only be a male or a female. Product features include the ability to select data samples and to produce data quality management reports.

  A data-cleansing tool, which may be part of a data analyzer, allows a user to interactively or via background processing select and change data values to conform to accepted values. Tool features include the ability to analyze data, as discussed above, as well as to effect changes to data values. Care must be taken when applying these changes, and they should be closely coordinated with application, business, and data management personnel.

- **Physical Data Design Tool**

  A physical data design tool automates the data design process by facilitating the finalization of the physical relational data model. Key features include the ability to accept a logical data model and physical data volume requirements as input to the creation of relational database tables. In addition, the tool may assist in normalizing a data model.

- **Data Migration Technology**

  A data migration tool automates the process of converting data values from one physical format to either the same or a new format. For example, a migration tool may support moving from two physical files to one file using the same format or while incorporating minor changes. Another tool could populate a relational database from a sequential file. Tool functionality includes the ability to analyze, manipulate, and convert data to meet predefined migration specifications. The tool should be able to utilize a data dictionary, repository, or other user-defined specifications to provide a source definition and a target definition for the data being converted.

7.14 EAI Technology

EAI technology includes a broad list of software categories that have two things in common. The technology should connect applications with other applications or enterprise data structures and achieve this goal using a noninvasive approach that does not require modifying the applications involved. The following categories, discussed in more depth in Chapter 9, are included in the EAI technology group.

- **Middleware**

  There are several types of middleware. A Web-based front end can use a remote procedure call, for example, to invoke a back-end legacy system running in a mainframe transaction-processing environment. At the higher end of this category is the message broker, which can queue and route a variety of messages to invoke a series of back-end legacy transactions, triggered based on certain events or at a given point in time.

  Middleware evolution has produced a tool category called the application server. Application servers allow a Java-based front-end application to invoke back-end legacy transactions within a mainframe environment. These products have grown quite sophisticated and are becoming the hub for managing new component-based applications. Middleware becomes part of the production environment that it is integrating. It is therefore more a production solution than a tool and should be considered as such.

- **Business-to-Business Integration Technology**

  B2B integration facilitates supply, distribution, and customer information exchange and collaboration. B2B integration addresses the issue of connecting processes, transactions, and data across multiple enterprises. Initially, simple B2B activity focused on point-to-point EDI solutions. Now B2B technology has grown in sophistication and includes peer-to-peer as well as hub-based technology. As with the middleware category, these B2B technology becomes a part of the environment that organizations rely on to exchange information and manage supply and distribution chain activity.

- **ERP Integration**

  Special technology is sometimes employed to integrate ERP packages with Web-based front ends. ERP systems have defined interface points and, as a result, vendors have created a special ERP integration category. To support ERP integration, a number of e-business integration vendors have created API solutions that can access published interface points within an ERP product. Most ERP vendors openly share information on these interfaces so that ERP integration middleware can access data or trigger ERP transactions as required.

- **Interface/Bridge Technology**

  Over the years, many types of ad hoc data interfaces or bridges have been created to convert data from one format to another on the fly. For example, Y2K projects used bridging tools to change data within a program to a four-digit year and change it back prior to writing it to a file or database. This technique allows for files to be selectively converted over time and eliminates the need to simultaneously convert all of the programs that use a given data structure. These bridges can occasionally turn into land mines for teams changing systems during a maintenance or transformation project. A second concern is that certain bridges, in the case of a time-dependent solution, only work for a limited period of time. Many Y2K bridges, for example, will likely fail in 20 to 30 years. Bridges should be documented during initial transformation planning and analysis efforts.

7.15 Project Management and Administration Technology

A number of software technologies support the management and administration of medium to large transformation projects, particularly those projects that span physical locations, business units, or enterprise boundaries.

- **Configuration Management**

  Configuration management tools provide the ability to manage multiple versions of an application during a transformation project. Product features include the ability to control access to libraries by defining user access rights and to change control procedures. This includes the creation of working version libraries. Cataloging features provide the user with the ability to establish libraries and data sets on the system catalog with specific characteristics, including location, read/write capability, and file duration.

- **Project Management**

  A project management tool provides the capability to define a project in terms of a series of chronological steps from inception to completion, including step-based estimates, roles, deliverables, and dependencies. It also allows project personnel to automatically track and update a project plan as steps are completed or as items are delivered.

- **Spreadsheet**

  Spreadsheet technology provides an all-purpose capability to track and record changes as well as to create working templates for projects. Transformation projects typically use forms built using spreadsheet technology.

- **Collaborative Work Environments**

  A collaborative work environment ties together project participants using Internet technology. One important feature is the ability to aggregate project management to an enterprise level for tracking progress, participation across projects, and cross-functional overlap in roles and tasks. These products also support virtual meetings and the triggering of tasks upon the delivery of a prerequisite task or deliverable. This is an important tool if an organization has many projects with shared resources at an enterprise level and should span inhouse and third-party project participants.

7.16 Creating a Software Tool Strategy

Before selecting and procuring software tools, it is important to have an overall software product strategy. A software tools strategy should be crafted by the software tool center with input from various communities within the architecture team. The transformation team should be able to determine the types of planned and ongoing projects that require access to various types of software technology.

The software tools center, working with development, maintenance, and transformation teams, should create a list of required tools based on the types of various initiatives planned. This requirements list should then be filled in with inhouse or third-party products already in place. This includes software currently in use by third-party consultants and a status on the availability of those products for use on inhouse projects. Any essential software categories that cannot be filled with available tools can signal the need for additional product acquisitions.

The software tools center should also define where various products fit within a software tools framework. A number of design and development products can play a role in certain legacy application analysis and transformation tasks. Business modeling and design tools, for example, can be used to represent legacy architectures as well as target architectures. Other examples of products that support both new development as well as redevelopment include project management software and testing tools.

Certain products, such as an IDE with reverse engineering features, may contain transformation features that no one is even using. Many organizations find themselves in a position of having tools in place that support the analysis, documentation, and transformation of legacy data and application architectures but being unaware of their availability. This is because owning a set of software tools does not guarantee their use.

For a variety of reasons, many companies have good software products sitting on the shelf. Organizations have found it difficult to convince business and IT professionals to use these products on new development efforts. These same individuals are unlikely to apply these tools to transformation-related tasks. One insurance executive, for example, would not even discuss looking at a new and powerful application analyzer because IT teams in his organization refused to use the tools they already had in place.

The real challenge for management and the software tools center involves identifying ways in which various software products can leverage the efforts of business and IT professionals for work already planned or under way. The software tool strategy should therefore include deployment plans, workbench integration, training, and tool mentor programs. General guidelines for developing such a strategy include

- Build a consensus on the need for inhouse software tool management and establish a software tool center within the architecture community.
- Assess overall transformation project requirements to determine the need for various software tools as outlined in this chapter.
- Create a list of required software tools based on anticipated project requirements.
- Determine if any of the tools that fit these requirements are already available inhouse, and verify that there is a support structure for these tools.
- Verify that vendor product licenses are current, or update them as needed.
- Incorporate third-party consulting and outsourcing vendors into these discussions to augment and leverage available consulting tools on inhouse projects.
- Focus on tool integration and incorporate tools, if possible, into a workbench environment.
- Tool integration should incorporate IDE solutions to ensure that development tools are synchronized with transformation projects.

- Establish a tool training facility and testing lab for new products that may be required on various projects if justified by enterprise tool requirements.
- Develop a deployment plan that delivers tools to the projects that need them in a timely and effective manner.
- Communicate tool options to application teams and business units as required.
- Focus on the benefits of applying transformation technology within the context of business unit and application team requirements.

7.17 Software Tool Justification, Procurement, and Integration

Management should instill one overriding principle regarding tool justification: Software tools must be justified based on business-driven initiatives. In other words, business requirements drive projects and projects drive tool requirements. This may be apparent to most people, but I have worked with clients where tool deployment became the overriding driver behind projects.

One client, for example, took me into a room that was stacked from floor to ceiling with shrink-wrapped boxes of CASE tools that management had acquired but never opened. They wanted me to help justify the use of these tools on projects—but there was no valid reason for doing so. This is the ultimate example of the tail wagging the dog and of tools driving a deployment strategy.

Tool justification begins with the definition of requirements. If six transformation projects and seven maintenance teams can benefit from an environmental analyzer, this should translate into rapid analysis, selection, and procurement of such a product. The same is true for other tool categories listed in this chapter. Tool centers should streamline justification, procurement, and deployment.

Unfortunately, IT has had a tendency to complicate technology procurement. In some cases, tool centers have turned tool selection and procurement into a long, torturous process for the vendor and the project teams that need those tools. This is totally unacceptable. If a tool is needed and cost-justified for a project, procurement of that tool must be expedited.

Cost justification is also straightforward. Software is typically the lowest cost item on a project. A million-dollar project can easily justify a $50,000 product if it enhances project productivity by 5 to 10 percent. Use of the tool on other projects further supports the business case for such a product and must be a consideration as well. A transformation tool can also be justified if it increases a team's ability to meet user requirements. A business rule capture facility, for example, would enable a project team to capture application knowledge and improve the integrity of the resulting application.

Procurement is a matter of determining the potential scope of tool deployment and negotiating a contract that supports a product's required scope of use. One option involves starting out with a limited number of product licenses and expanding the product's use as dictated by ongoing projects. A vendor may offer a special deal for a greater number of copies, something to be considered during the justification process. One special consideration involves the use of consulting tools.

Consultants tend to limit the use of proprietary technology to their own project teams. This situation may be driven by contractual limitations if that product is licensed from a software vendor. If this is the case, and if a tool has broader applicability on other projects, the tool center should negotiate a license directly with that vendor. If the consultant's tool is proprietary and the tool center wants to use it on other projects, they should negotiate directly with the consulting firm for use of that tool on those projects.

Once tools have been licensed, the software tool center should ensure that various development, maintenance, integration, and transformation software is integrated to the degree possible. In many organizations, tools that complement each other may be isolated to a given application unit without the knowledge of central coordinators.

For example, UML modeling tools can be used to depict an existing architecture, but these tools may be isolated to new development projects. In this example, the value of this technology is not being leveraged to the greatest degree possible. The software tool center is responsible for identifying, integrating, and deploying these tools on an enterprise-wide basis. This is the most effective way to ensure that tools are leveraged to achieve the greatest ROI, once implemented.

Executives should ensure that there is a coordinated effort to manage and leverage the use of transformation and related technologies across the enterprise. Ignoring this requirement is likely to mean that business-driven projects will not be delivered as effectively and efficiently as would otherwise be the case.

Enterprise and Project-Level Assessments

8

In any IT initiative, management must strike a balance between too little and too much analysis. Many organizations are leery of spending too much time in front-end assessment efforts. This reflects a backlash from the days when project teams spent years stuck in the requirements analysis phase of information engineering projects. This backlash is dangerous, however, because ignoring front-end analysis and planning results in false starts, poorly coordinated projects, haphazard architectures, and wasted time and resources.

The incorporation of selected transformation tasks within various IT initiatives relies on a comprehensive understanding of what business and IT executives are attempting to accomplish over a defined period of time. Enterprise and business unit plans, along with well-articulated information architecture requirements, are essential inputs to the development of a transformation strategy. This strategy is the result of coupling an enterprise assessment with business and IT requirements.

This chapter describes transformation assessment and planning activities that can be applied on an enterprise-wide basis as well as to an individual IT project. The enterprise assessment produces a plan that weaves selected transformation tasks into various business-driven projects. Each of these business-driven projects would incorporate transformation analysis and implementation tasks into development, upgrade, package deployment, and other "traditional" projects.

The enterprise and project-level assessment tasks described within this chapter should be performed within the context of the transformation planning and justification options discussed in prior chapters. Readers should keep in mind that transformation assessments produce documentation that provides planning, implementation and maintenance teams with invaluable intelligence on legacy information architectures.

8.1 Enterprise versus Project-Level Assessments

Enterprise assessments produce a high-level view of legacy environments and architectures. Project-level assessments produce a detailed analysis of a subset of the enterprise architecture. Project-level assessments may be performed in the absence of an enterprise assessment, but individual projects benefit significantly from the comprehensive view of legacy architectures produced by the enterprise-wide assessment.

Enterprise assessments provide planning and project teams with an aggregate view of legacy information architectures. This information, coupled with business and IT requirements, is used to develop a transformation strategy that typically includes a number of transformation-oriented projects. Various transformation projects would then initiate and leverage project-level assessment tasks to produce detailed legacy analysis results for individual project teams.

For example, a government agency created a high-level, cross-functional analysis of legacy applications. This included documenting the physical relationships among those applications and the high-level functions performed by those applications. The tax systems targeted by this assessment represented a cross-section of the enterprise. The results produced by this assessment allowed planning teams to accurately define the scope of subsequent projects. Prior to the creation of this high-level analysis, planning teams had erroneously defined the boundaries of an application replacement initiative that omitted tightly coupled subsystems.

Subsequent projects then used the high-level assessment results as the starting point for extracting additional details about the legacy applications involved. In the above example, analysts decomposed high-level functions into more detailed business rules and data definitions to ensure that the right programs and subsystems were being replaced with the correct functionality.

Executing the enterprise assessment first, as discussed in the above example, helped analysts ascertain individual project scope and boundaries. Individual project teams tend to have difficulty carving out project scope due to a lack of planning capacity, authority, and cross-functional insight. In other words, projects involving legacy architectures are at a major disadvantage if they do not have access to a comprehensive view of how those projects impact or are impacted by other business units, applications, subsystems, data, and projects.

Historically, organizations have sidestepped enterprise assessments because planning teams have had difficulty assigning responsibility and obtaining funding for comprehensive initiatives that cross multiple business units and application areas. Transformation and architecture planning teams will need to initiate and procure funding for enterprise assessments in conjunction with cross-functional business and application areas.

8.2 The Role of Metrics in Assessment Initiatives

Before discussing enterprise and project-level assessment and planning activities, it is important for readers to understand the role of software metrics within the context of the analysis and planning process. Software metrics have been around for decades and made a brief rise to prominence during the Y2K era. Metrics play an important role in the analysis and planning of transformation activities because they help define the scope and level of effort associated with assessing, upgrading, migrating, integrating, and otherwise transforming legacy environments.

Software metrics include simple counts and scores. Scores are calculated from counts. A program complexity score, for example, may be a factor of the number of lines of code, logic nesting depth, and other factors. An enterprise can use formal industry metrics, such as the Halstead or McCabe program complexity metrics, or apply their own metrics. Transformation metrics fall into a range of categories and have a foundation within industry standard methodologies [1].

Y2K drove the need for legacy application and data usage metrics and included system, source program, Copy member, line-of-code, date, and other counts for applications and data structures targeted for compliance. Many organizations accepted the need for metrics on Y2K projects because they were essential to determining the scope and difficulty of assessment and remediation projects.

For example, analysts may have known that 300,000 lines of source code required remediation, but this single metric did not provide a strong foundation for developing an accurate remediation and testing plan. Project teams also needed to know the number of job streams, screens, reports, source programs, data structures, and nonstandard application objects. These additional metrics helped managers define the number of personnel required hours associated with each task and overall project delivery schedule. Testing, for example, takes longer for 300 programs with 100 online screens and 300 reports than it does for 100 programs that produce 100 reports.

This same premise lies behind the use of metrics on transformation projects. The larger, more complex, and more diverse a legacy environment, the more time and skill it takes to analyze, enhance, integrate, and transform those applications. Transformation metrics fall into several categories and include environmental, data usage and structure, program-level, architectural, and functional metric categories.

Transformation metrics provide management with the information needed to create a project plan for a transformation project. The use of metrics, as applied to the planning steps at various points of the assessment and implementation phases of projects, can be summarized as follows.

- Creating an estimate for the enterprise assessment requires determining the number of applications, application areas, business units, physical locations, and hardware environments. These metric counts allow an assessment team to determine the number of weeks needed to complete various enterprise assessment tasks and build a subsequent transformation strategy.

- Estimating the level of effort required for a project-level assessment requires determining the total number of applications, source programs, lines of code, application areas, major data structures, environments, and physical locations.

- Building an implementation plan for an application or cross-section of applications relies on metrics derived from the project-level assessment. Based on the type of project driving the assessment, this can include one or more metric categories. Example categories include data definition grouping counts, average program complexity, physical data structure counts, percentage of functional overlap between the legacy and target architecture, and a variety of other metrics.

In other words, project teams use metrics to determine how long an enterprise assessment will take, how long a project-level assessment will take, and how long the implementation phase or phases of that project will take. Metric gathering and estimating techniques support the phased delivery of transformation projects. For example, there is typically enough data available to estimate the project-level assessment, but not enough information to accurately estimate the implementation phases of a project. Analysts can, however, create a "ball park" estimate for the implementation phase at the onset of the project-level assessment. Once the project-level assessment has been completed, analysts can then refine estimates for the implementation phase based on the detailed analysis results derived from that assessment.

Consider, for example, a project that augments a component-based design model based on legacy business rules spanning two separate applications, 50 source programs, and one major database. The project-level assessment was estimated to take two weeks and deliver a functional decomposition for the applications targeted for analysis. The initial implementation stage estimate was slated to take four to six weeks; analysts refined this down to four weeks after completion of the detailed project-level assessment.

Phased refinement of project estimates is necessary because it is very difficult to determine how long an implementation phase will take until the detailed assessment phase in completed. Fortunately, analysts can typically estimate implementation tasks within a range that should suffice for project funding purposes.

One topic that arises when discussing software metrics involves the use of function points. A function point defines a user-driven view or feature within an application. Applying function points to a transformation project may seem like a good fit. Function points, however, do not apply to most transformation projects. Functional transformation metrics reflect the degree of functional overlap between strategic requirements, legacy environments, and/or target architectures.

Degree of overlap relies on identifying one or more specific functions, data types, or business rules and determining the existence of overlapping items across legacy and target architectures. Function points, on the other hand, identify how many functions exist in a current system or in a target design. If the current architecture and the target architecture each contained 400 function points, the level of overlap between these architectures would still be unknown because these metrics probably reflect different functions. In other words, function points alone do not indicate how many legacy functions overlap with those functions defined in a requirements specification, target architecture, and/or package.

One word of caution involves the frivolous use of software metrics. Entire teams of people have been assigned to count and analyze metrics in some organizations. The process of counting became the driving factor over the need to deliver business value through projects. If metrics are not essential to a project, project teams should not gather them. Apply common sense whenever possible to avoid getting buried too deeply in metric analysis efforts.

For each major section that follows, I have listed important metric categories that can help project teams assess the level of effort associated with a project or quantify the findings from a given set of analysis tasks.

8.3 Enterprise Assessments—Examining the Big Picture

An enterprise assessment examines the "big picture" view of legacy architectures and, optionally, the legacy architecture's relationship with strategic requirements and planned target architecture. Reasons for performing an enterprise assessment include

- Defining technical and functional boundaries that allow project teams to determine the scope of a given project.
- Identifying data and functional redundancies that signal the need to reconcile and consolidate applications, data structures, and business units.
- Developing a high-level map of how various applications support specific business units and interface with third parties as input to reorganizations or related business redesign efforts.
- Creating an overall baseline from which business and application planning teams can assess and plan integration, replacement, transformation, and a variety of other near-term and long-term initiatives.

The tasks involved in such an assessment vary based on the needs of the enterprise. At a minimum, enterprise assessments produce a high-level summary of the environments, applications, shared data stores between major applications, significant third-party interfaces, and major functions performed by each application. Additional tasks can then map legacy applications, data structures, and functions to strategic requirements, target architecture models, and/or packaged applications. The following tasks comprise the enterprise assessment.

- Strategic business planning and target architecture definition.
- Current systems inventory and legacy architecture analysis.
- Current-to-target architecture mapping.
- Transformation strategy definition.

Readers should keep in mind that an enterprise assessment's main goal is to provide executives, project teams, and transformation planners with the intelligence needed to do their jobs more effectively. Delivering the maximum value with the minimal level of effort requires being selective when determining which enterprise assessment tasks and subtasks should be applied to a given situation.

This may mean documenting the legacy architecture as a first phase and delaying the mapping of the legacy architecture to a yet-to-be-defined target architecture until a later point in time. This is particularly applicable in situations where documentation of the legacy architecture is required for integration purposes, even though analysts have not fully defined the new target architecture.

8.4 Strategic Business Planning and Target Architecture Definition

The enterprise assessment provides an excellent foundation for planning teams who need to understand the structure and functional decomposition of a legacy environment. Transformation planning teams do not require strategic plans and target architecture definitions to perform a basic assessment of a legacy information environment. If such plans in place, however, and management wishes to deploy a transformation strategy to help deliver on those plans, then the transformation team should incorporate those plans into the assessment process. Unfortunately, many IT people tend to work in a vacuum as far as understanding a company's business strategy, particularly as it relates to the IT planning process and strategic architectures.

Business plans have a direct bearing on information architectures, and information architectures can thwart the most well-intended business plan. A business that sells off a business unit that IT was diligently working to integrate into its information infrastructure would have wasted time, staffing, and budgetary resources. Business executives should therefore have a general strategy that can be translated into a target set of IT requirements and architecture plans.

Businesses also rely on IT to support rapidly shifting business strategies, but IT may not be able to respond in the near term. Consider the inability of a major utility to retool its information systems to support the shift from a power producer to a power broker. IT needs to be fully engaged in these planning sessions to ensure that the enterprise will succeed with these plans.

Consider some of the business motivations behind architecture transformation initiatives. There are phone companies with redundant billing systems, healthcare providers using incompatible claims systems, banks merging across international borders, and manufacturing companies building subsidiaries in countries around the world. In order to develop an information transformation plan, IT needs to ask certain questions of the business executives involved in these decisions. For example, IT may ask business units to reply to the following questions for planning purposes.

- Is there a business unit consolidation plan? If so, which units will be consolidated first, and what are the timeframes for delivering a consolidated information infrastructure?
- After the merger, which redundant functions and related business units will be eliminated, and which ones will be retained?
- Does consolidation imply elimination of one business model in favor of another, or will the best processes of two overlapping business units be merged into one?
- Will a foreign company acquisition require the integration of Euro handling into domestic systems, or will the two business units be kept separate?

IT planning questions should consider future market expansion, divestiture, merger, acquisition, and globalization activities. For example, if a planned European acquisition is part of the strategic business plan, then create a target information architecture that incorporates globalization into the overall design. If that acquisition is a one-time thing, then ignore global issues in the target architecture plan.

In addition to these factors, the architecture integration team should consider several other business-driven issues when designing the target architecture and accompanying transformation plans. These include new markets, general expansion plans, supply chain considerations, product line obsolescence, and general industry trends.

While the transformation team is not chartered with creating business strategy or defining the target information architecture, drafting a long-term set of transformation options and plans requires these plans as input. The target information architecture defines the ideal data, functional, and technical architecture for an enterprise.

Any enterprise trying to apply widespread changes to its information environment needs such a target. Many companies have tried to acquire and deploy software packages, attempted major rewrites, or found themselves in a constant frenzy to develop new systems without a clear direction of where they want to go. The target information architecture sets this direction.

Many companies have created portions of an information architecture that reflect their business strategy. For example, a telecommunications provider seeking to become a global wireless company may have drafted an integrated customer data model to support this concept. A manufacturing firm that is globalizing independent subsidiaries into a common business model may have already completed a functional design to support this from an information perspective.

Planning teams should seek out any architectural models that may have been created to date and validate these models as the target for transformation planning purposes. Whether updating existing models or developing new ones, the resulting architecture definitions must reflect the view of the ideal enterprise information architecture. Items to identify include

- **Entity relationship diagrams.** Enterprise data models tend to be too large and too complex to be deployed in practice. Models depicting data for related business areas, such as customer management, human resources, supply chain management, and so on, can be used, however, to envision how information should be organized. ER diagrams help planning teams envision how legacy data structures, package data, data warehouse designs, and other data requirements should be organized and deployed.
- **Functional decomposition of the enterprise.** Functional hierarchies are an effective way to depict functions across a target information architecture. One functional decomposition diagram per business unit, for example, provides a target for package selection, application replacement, integration, and consolidation projects. This is particularly true when cross-functional application integration or consolidation is envisioned.
- **Business entity/business function matrix.** A business entity/business function matrix shows the intersection of business data and the functions that use that data. This can help planning teams determine data needed by certain business functions in various development or transformation initiatives.
- **Technical architecture.** Chapter 3 discussed future technical architecture options. These architectures should be augmented with a list identifying acceptable and obsolete technologies. The technical architecture helps guide project teams through package selection, integration, development, migration, and replacement projects.

As stated earlier, an enterprise may have no written strategy detailing where it is going from a business or an information management perspective and still benefit from an enterprise assessment. On the other hand, if management would like to map existing architectures against a strategic set of requirements, then defining those requirements and related information architecture should be a priority.

8.5 Current Systems Inventory and Legacy Architecture Analysis

The initial stage of the enterprise assessment involves an inventory of the enterprise-wide information environment and an analysis of the information gathered during that inventory. Performing an enterprise assessment of legacy architectures requires preliminary setup work by the planning team. This includes

- Creating a small assessment team that has the ability to collect, record, analyze, and communicate the need for the assessment and the results of the findings.
- Establishing an enterprise repository as introduced in Chapter 5. This high-level repository allows the team to represent enterprise inventory data in a cohesive model that can readily convey the information collected to business units, application teams, and executives.
- Developing a communication and collaboration infrastructure that allows the team to garner knowledge about legacy environments from business and application teams. This is essential because the assessment team cannot gather this information in a vacuum.

Understanding how the current information architecture works involves a physical and logical analysis of the data, processes, and technologies within those systems. The following guidelines apply.

- A physical systems assessment should precede efforts to develop logical models of the current environment because logical models rely on inventory information as input.
- Unless the information enterprise is small (5 to 10 million lines of code, for example), avoid trying to obtain too much detail during the enterprise-wide assessment.
- Physical inventory tools are useful in understanding which systems are currently active and how they interrelate. Be aware, however, that these tools produce details that go well beyond what is required in an enterprise assessment.
- Technical environments are never static. Analysts should use a database or repository to store legacy metadata gathered during the assessment and update that information as required over the long term.

The first step of an enterprise assessment involves creating an inventory of the existing enterprise information environment. Many organizations created a baseline inventory during Y2K projects and this may be a good starting point. Creating this inventory and documenting relationships among applications, business units, and external entities requires collecting physical inventory data and interviewing subject matter experts in IT, business units, and third parties. This process includes the following steps.

- **Document all business units and major third parties.** Record all business units and third parties that play a major organizational role in the enterprise repository. Analysts should then identify major business processes performed by each business unit or third party and record these processes, along with their relationship to various business units, in the enterprise repository. In a large organization, these processes should be kept at an abstract level so as to limit the analysis time involved.

- **Inventory the existing information environment.** Identify any existing application and data structure inventory data that may already be available. Analysts will need to inventory all major hardware and software environments used within the IT and non-IT infrastructure. This includes business units and third-party domains. One approach involves inventorying software program and job control source code, executable modules, data files and database definitions, and user interfaces across all program libraries. Analysts should categorize all system and subsystem components by business unit. In extremely large organizations, analysts will want to keep this effort to a minimum by simply identifying all major areas that own any applications and then moving on to the next step.

- **Identify and categorize major applications.** Organize the collected inventory information into categories by application. Most of this work will be based on interviews with business units, IT, and third parties. If available, categorize applications into systems and subsystems. This analysis includes all major applications on all platforms—not just the mainframe environment. The team should then work with various areas to create a brief functional description for each application and related subsystem in the inventory list. The functional description should be loaded into the enterprise repository.

- **Identify and categorize major data stores.** Analysts should identify and record all major data stores in the enterprise repository. This includes any database or permanent data structure shared between the major applications documented in the prior step. The number and diversity of data structures, availability of information, and time set aside for the project determine the level of detail analysts should pursue within this step.

- **Identify and categorize system dependencies.** This step documents critical dependencies across applications. This involves tracking the flow of major data stores and the applications that utilize them. The enterprise repository is the best place to represent this information. The second part of this step involves identifying user interfaces to major applications. These can be summarized at a high level. For example, if an order entry system had 25 to 30 user screens, analysts could identify these as "order-entry online menus."

- **Identify external interfaces and dependencies.** This step documents critical dependencies between internal applications and external interfaces. Analysts should identify applications that utilize external data interfaces. In some companies, this information can be voluminous. This information is typically available from business units and may just be a matter of recording it in the enterprise repository. If this is not the case, analysts should simply summarize the information. For example, a high-volume EDI environment would have an interface summarized as "direct supplier EDI interfaces."

- **Identify supply and distribution chain dependencies.** External dependencies include third parties that supply raw materials, component parts, end products, services of all types, infrastructure, and information. Most of this information can be collected from business analysts on the integration team. Gathering supply and distribution chain data is very useful because third parties play increasingly important roles in enterprise business and information strategies. Third parties may be requested in the enterprise repository.

Enterprise assessment metrics gathered through this initial inventory process include

- Total number of enterprise business units and functions performed by each business unit.
- Total number of applications and applications per business unit.
- Total number of major data stores and third-party interfaces (if collected in detail).
- Total number of third-party data interfaces and suppliers/distributors per business unit.

Completing the above inventory steps, at whatever level the assessment team deems necessary, establishes a baseline inventory of the enterprise information infrastructure. This information, once loaded into the enterprise repository, can be reproduced in a variety of ways for business and IT planning teams. Analysts can use this information to

- Document high-level information flows across applications and related business units.
- Assess business-unit-to-business-unit or business-unit-to-third-party process usage and flow to determine where redundant processes may be streamlined to make the enterprise more efficient and effective.
- Depict which applications support common business processes as input to a business unit/application consolidation initiative.
- Identify physical data redundancy or fragmentation by identifying all data structures that replicate or overlap with other data structures.
- Document all external dependencies as input to streamlining supply and distribution chain management.
- Identify external interfaces as a way to consolidate or otherwise upgrade aging, third-party EDI interfaces.
- Identify all nonstandard technologies that should be slated for replacement or migration.
- Use this information as input to planning a wide variety of integration, replacement, upgrade, or other transformation projects.

Creating logical views of the existing information architecture requires understanding the functions that various systems perform and the relationships among those systems. Analysts can use the captured metadata to extract and document functions performed by systems across business units. They would then load functional and data representations into hierarchy or similar documentation diagrams. In doing so, the assessment team is formalizing logical views of the information architecture. Examples of these logical views, which graphically depict enterprise architecture metadata, include

- Data flow diagrams of existing enterprise-wide data flows.
- Data store/system usage matrix.
- High-level ER diagrams.
- Current data store/existing entity matrix.
- Current systems function hierarchy diagram.
- Existing functions/current systems matrix.

Analysts can derive and create logical views of the information architecture from the information collected in the enterprise repository. Creating ER diagrams and other functional abstractions require knowledge of the applications and data involved, the ability to interpret and formalize a logical view of that information, and the use of certain modeling tools.

The decision to create these views depends on the analysis and development methodologies used within an enterprise and the need to map this information to formal views within the target information architecture. If the target architecture has been specified using the above models, then the team will want to depict the current architecture in a similar format.

8.6 Current-to-Target Architecture Mapping

Understanding how strategic requirements map to legacy information architectures is the missing link within many IT planning projects. This is due to a limited understanding of legacy environments and a lack of a perceived need to map those environments to information requirements. Transformation strategies are poorly articulated when analysts have no definitive understanding of the existing information architecture.

For example, buying a package without mapping that package to strategic requirements and legacy architectures is like trying to navigate a maze with your eyes closed. Current-to-target enterprise architecture mapping involves assessing the relationships among data, functional, and technical definitions within the legacy and target information architectures.

Current-to-target data architecture mapping identifies levels of conformance between current data usage and target data definitions. This requires comparing existing business entities with target entities as well as mapping current physical structures to required or desired logical data structures. Figure 8.1 depicts the conceptual data architecture mapping process.

Use of this information increases the integrity of the strategic data model while providing analysts with a map for various data integration, replacement,

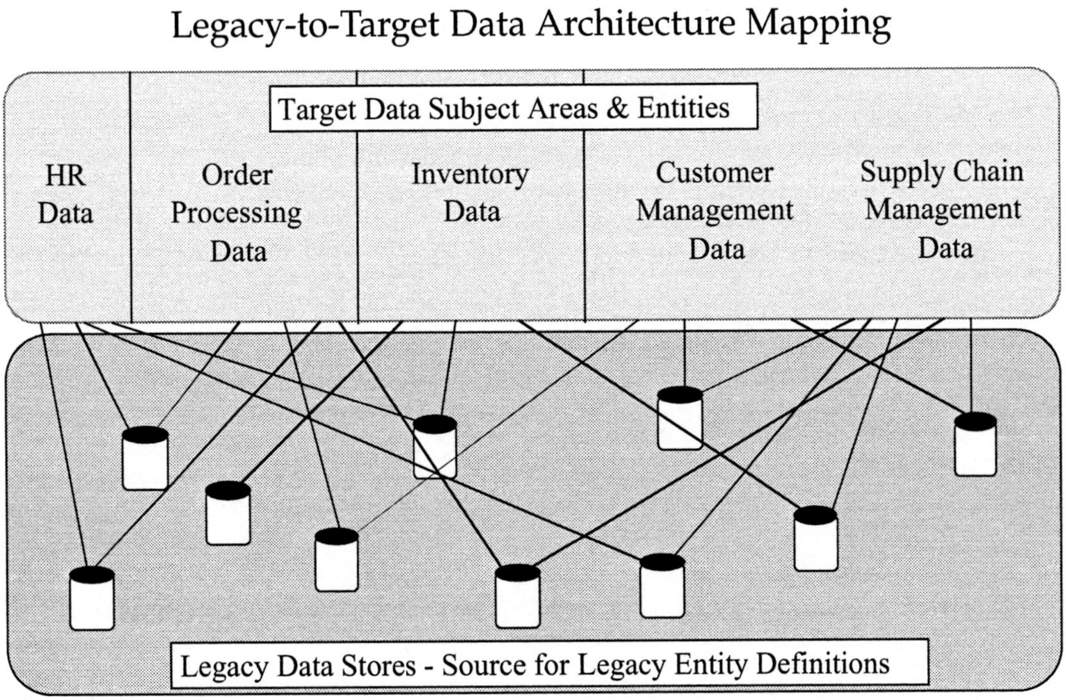

Legacy-to-Target Data Architecture Mapping

Figure 8.1
Legacy-to-target data mapping highlights redundancies, inconsistencies, and fragmentation within the legacy architecture.

and transformation projects. Environmental metrics can be used to articulate and communicate the level of overlap between current and target data architectures.

Many complexities typically surface during this type of data architecture analysis. Consider a business unit that uses the term *supplier* to mean any third-party entity. Data planning teams may erroneously limit the use of the term *supplier* to companies that sell component parts. Comparing current-to-target entity usage would be comparing homonym (same name with a different meaning) data. These discrepancies should be discovered and corrected during requirements planning based on discussions resulting from the current-to-target data mapping process.

Mapping results should be loaded into the enterprise repository, which would then allow analysts to trigger data entity (legacy) to data entity (new) comparison reports as needed. Additional metrics from the current-to-target data mapping analysis include

- Number of entities in the current model and in the target model.
- Number of entities in the current model, but not in the target model.
- Number of entities in the target model, but not in the current model.

The current-to-target functional mapping process identifies the level of conformance between the existing and the target functional architecture. This process requires creating functional hierarchies of cross-sections of the legacy architecture and mapping these to comparable functionality in the target architecture.

Planning teams can use this information in a variety of ways. If multiple occurrences of a single legacy function map to a target function, this could signal an integration or consolidation requirement. For example, a billing function replicated across three systems and three business units is likely a strong target for consolidation. Once the assessment team has recorded functional mapping information within the enterprise repository, inquiries may be run against the repository to extract current-to-target functional mapping information.

As with the data mapping process, certain metrics summarize functional discrepancies and overlap between current and target architectures. These metrics include

- Number of functions in the current model and in the target model.
- Number of functions in the current model, but not in the target model.

Current-to-Target Technical Architecture Mapping

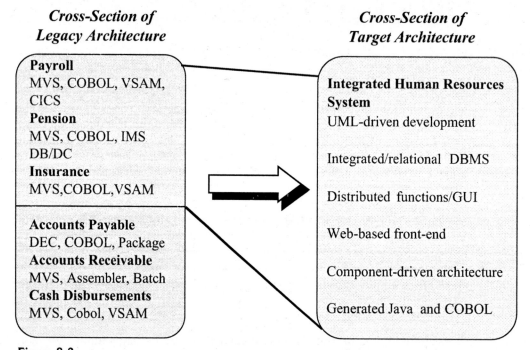

| **Cross-Section of Legacy Architecture** | **Cross-Section of Target Architecture** |

Figure 8.2
Current-to-target technical architecture mapping identifies where noncompliant technologies need to be migrated or replaced.

Legacy Architecture Laid Over Target Architecture

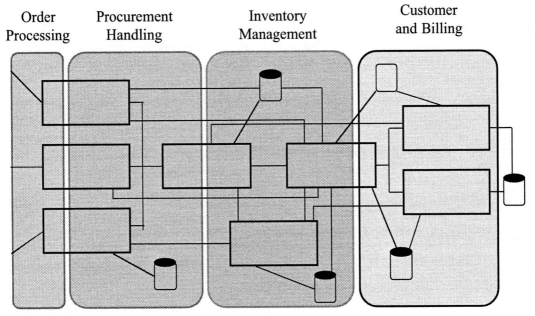

| Order Processing | Procurement Handling | Inventory Management | Customer and Billing |

Figure 8.3
Laying the legacy application architecture over the target architecture helps planning teams define project scope.

- Number of functions in the target model, but not in the current model.

Assessment teams can also create a technology mapping, shown in Figure 8.2, to ensure that technical conformance is included in redevelopment plans. Technical architecture mapping ensures that nonconforming technologies are omitted from target information initiatives. Integration, replacement, package deployment, and related projects should ensure that the target application environment conforms to strategic technology requirements.

In addition to the technical mapping, assessment teams can perform a structural mapping. A development initiative at one company, for example, tried to replace a system that overlapped with other functional areas. The implementation was doomed to fail because it lacked an understanding of the structural impact of such a project.

Structural or architectural conformance is more difficult to quantify than technical conformance, but relies on information collected during the enterprise assessment. Creating a system-to-system flow analysis, extracted from the enterprise repository, allows analysts to determine how legacy architectures were conceived. These views can then be overlaid with a set of target requirements for overlapping functions. Figure 8.3 depicts an example of one such overlay structure.

This is useful for projects involving applications that span a given logical function because it facilitates scope setting. For example, if an application spans two major functions, as defined by the target architecture, that application could not be replaced cleanly. It also may involve multiple business units and overlapping data structures. The picture in Figure 8.3 would serve notice to analysts that they should perform more research using the information in the enterprise repository.

It also provides transformation teams with an understanding of where weaknesses in the existing architecture need to be addressed in a transition plan. Understanding how how functions fit together today is key to the redesign of the business and technical architecture in emerging e-business environment.

8.7 Transformation Strategy Definition

The transformation strategy incorporates recommendations for addressing business requirements that involve legacy information architectures. These recommendations trigger various tactical and strategic projects. The enterprise assessment may also trigger new requirements based on the findings. For example, analysts may have surfaced business process and application redundancies or inconsistencies that were previously unknown in key business areas. These issues should be considered as transformation plans are developed.

Establishing a business-driven, legacy transformation strategy requires understanding changes planned or under way within the business. Analysts should therefore identify priority business initiatives and use them to drive architecture transformation and integration projects. The following example demonstrates how to map business requirements to a business-driven transformation project.

If an organization is planning an acquisition with a company that has overlapping functional units, executives must consider various information architecture consolidation requirements. The following tasks address the consolidation and migration of overlapping or redundant applications and data structures under such a scenario.

- Executives should determine which redundant business units they plan to leave as independent entities, which ones will be eliminated, and which ones will need to be integrated.
- Create a set of business-driven information requirements based on input from all relevant and affected business units and IT executives.
- Perform an enterprise assessment for the existing enterprise and the enterprise being acquired.

- Integrate the results of the enterprise assessment by mapping overlapping or common business functions and application systems within the enterprise repository.
- Deliver the assessment results to management depicting where overlapping or redundant functionality and applications can be consolidate and/or eliminated.
- Based on business unit plans, determine which applications and data structures need to survive, merge, or be eliminated.
- If applicable, determine if there is any new design work or application package software specifications required and pursue the creation of those specifications as needed.
- Review the applicability of creating an integrated data architecture that reflects key business entities captured during current-to-target data architecture analysis.
- Map candidate applications and data structures involved in the merger to corresponding applications and data structures belonging to the newly acquired business unit(s).
- Consider using one set of existing systems as a baseline and migrating selected business functions into that baseline from the business unit being merged.
- Establish a list of required near-term projects, such as creating common front ends to link disparate systems through a middleware solution.
- Develop a list of long-term objectives, such as consolidating common functions into a single application, creating modular functions unique to a given customer base, and migrating to a component-based architecture.
- Develop a phased migration strategy and timeline that address the above requirements under a common approach that delivers interim value to the business community.
- Create a list of achievable projects that deliver a phased strategy and include staffing, timelines, budget models, deliverable options, and related project requirements.

The above example utilizes the results of the enterprise assessment to craft an information strategy that supports a business acquisition plan. Based on the results of the integrated enterprise assessment, the enterprise can craft a phased approach that implements a series of projects that meet the requirements set forth by the business. Figure 8.4 depicts a cross-section of sample transformation targets and projects based on the completion of an enterprise assessment. Under this approach, each interim project deliverable serves as a building block for subsequent projects. The following sections outline various project-level assessment tasks that serve as the initial phase of a business-driven transformation project.

Summary of Transformation Strategy

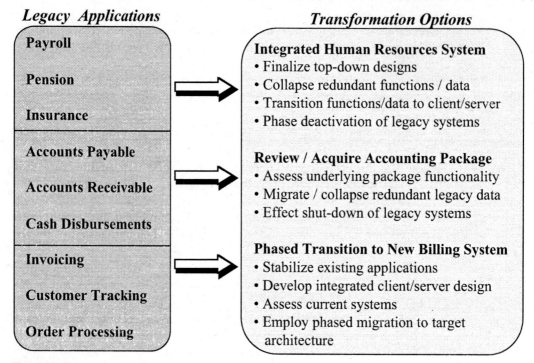

Figure 8.4
Transformation options include consolidation, migration, design, and development activities.

8.8 Transformation Projects—The Assessment Phase

The project-level assessment offers several benefits to traditional IT projects. First, it strives to determine how value can be gained by analyzing existing applications as a key component of the planning process. It also focuses on how reuse may be applied to subsequent phases of the development cycle to minimize the time, cost, and risk involved in replacing, upgrading, or otherwise transforming those applications.

Project-level assessments accommodate time-critical business requirements involving a wide variety of projects. If minor enhancements, rehosting, data upgrade, or other tactical initiatives are required, the technical assessment streamlines efforts to meet these objects. If a replacement, consolidation, package deployment, or other major architectural changes are planned, architecture and functional analysis tasks ensure that the resulting application is of high quality and delivered in the time required.

Occasionally, executives will skip assessment tasks and move directly into the implementation phase of a project. An application replacement project team at an entertainment company bypassed critical assessment work to jump into the business rule extraction and reuse phase of a project. Without the requisite high-level functional analysis, the project team lacked essential cross-functional mappings needed to perform this work.

One critical byproduct of the project-level assessment is functional and technical documentation that is useful for individuals supporting the current application environment. This documentation is also valuable for developers, planners, managers, and designers involved in any project involving legacy environments. In other words, the project-level assessment is an essential first step for any project involving legacy architectures.

The most critical aspect of this assessment requires analysts to identify the application or applications of interest. Accurate determination of project scope is critical. Omitting an application or data structure from an assessment means that the functions, data, and interfaces related to that application will be omitted from the assessment and leave a "hole" in the results. If the status of these "interface" systems is unclear, then include them with the understanding that this is the case.

Project scope is driven by business requirements. These requirements typically include cost reduction, process redesign, functional integration, business unit consolidation, and a wide range of related activities. All application systems directly impacted by these requirements should be included in the project-level assessment. For example, if a replacement system is proposed that will eliminate or replace three standalone systems, all three standalone systems must be included in the assessment.

Another important step of the assessment establishes alternative implementation approaches based on input from project participants. Approaches are considered and tested throughout the assessment and decided upon during the feasibility analysis stage of the project. The team eventually narrows the list of proposed alternatives to a single transformation plan.

The assessment uncovers as much information as possible about the legacy architecture, business strategy for that application, and cross-functional requirements. Once this information is gathered, a plan is created to address tactical and strategic business and application area requirements. Setting up and planning a project-level assessment require establishing clear objectives along with a concise plan. Project initiation tasks include

- **Developing a background description for the project.** This includes identifying the business impact of project, summarizing the functional condition of the application or applications involved, and identifying the general technical quality of the applications of interest.
- **Setting project objectives.** This includes identifying short-term maintenance or upgrade requirements, quantifying long-term or strategic requirements, and establishing alternative options for achieving these requirements.

- **Establishing overall scope of effort.** This includes determining the applications to be included in the assessment, identifying applications to be excluded from the assessment, and establishing the specific level of analysis to be performed on each application.
- **Setting up alternative options.** A business consolidation strategy may, for example, be addressed through an EAI middleware solution or through a long-term consolidation plan. These alternatives may ultimately be consolidated into single strategy with EAI solutions being applied immediately and consolidation options being pursued as a second phase of the project.
- **Identifying the activities to be performed.** This includes specifying required assessment tasks and identifying the steps to be performed within each assessment.
- **Developing a plan and supporting justification for the assessment.** This includes building a set of assessment tasks and steps, producing a work plan and cost justification for each project stage, finalizing the assessment work plan, and gaining commitment from project participants and sponsors.

The following sections discuss various phases within the project-level assessment. These phases include the technical assessment, architectural assessment, functional assessment, and implementation plan development. It is important to reiterate that project teams will need to selectively pick and choose which tasks apply to a given project. Only the assessment tasks that deliver value to the project should be included in the project plan.

8.9 The Technical Assessment

The technical assessment, summarized in Figure 8.5, inventories and documents the legacy application environment. Technical assessment tasks are typically the minimum level of analysis performed during a project-level assessment. This information serves as a basis for the architecture and functional assessments. In fact, without the information collected during the technical analysis, pursuing subsequent transformation analysis or implementation tasks would be very difficult and risky.

The technical assessment focuses on identifying all physical system components and determining the quality and interrelationships among those components. The assessment team examines the environment as a whole, cross-functional data usage and procedural logic within the application source programs. A good percentage of the analysis process is automated and utilizes tools defined in Chapter 7.

The environmental analysis task lays the foundation for all subsequent assessment steps by inventorying all physical applications components. Components are defined as any source program, object code module, or related

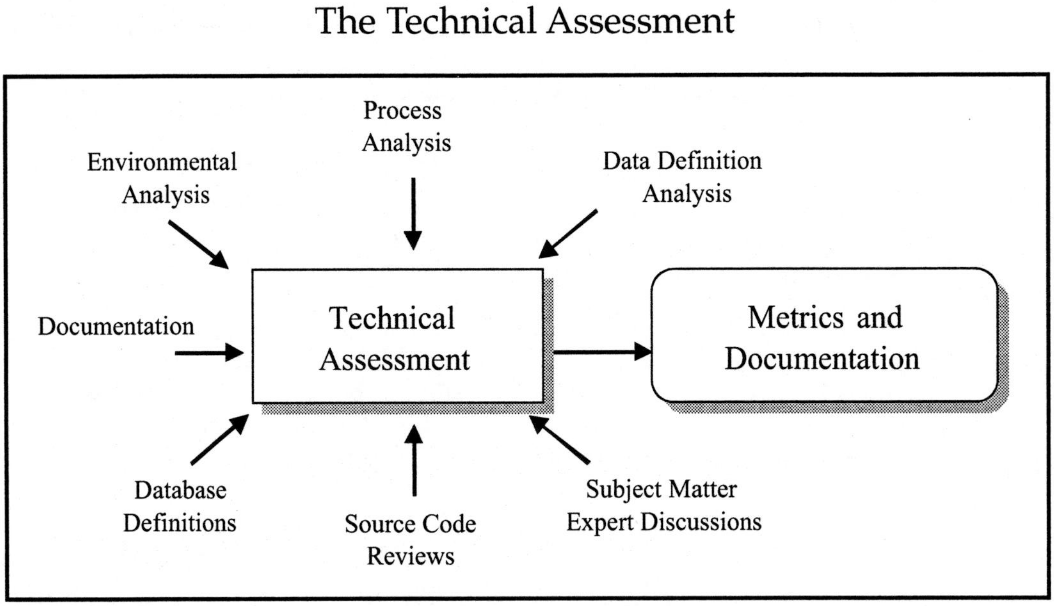

The Technical Assessment

Figure 8.5
The technical assessment inventories and documents legacy environments, data usage, and program flow.

documentation comprising an application of interest. Note that the use of the term *component* in this case does not refer to a reusable component as discussed in Chapter 3. The environmental analysis categorizes application components, determines relationships among these components, identifies missing components, and summarizes this information in the form of metrics and cross-reference reports.

Environmental analysis results include metric counts, execution flow, Call structures, cross-reference reports (see example in Chapter 7, Figure 7.1), and an updated detailed legacy transformation repository (see Chapter 5, Figure 5.3) for each component and relationship captured during the assessment. Metrics include

- Total number of program, data definition, job control, screen, and related source components.
- Total number of environmental components per application.

The environmental analysis helps determine the scope of analysis for the process flow and data definition analysis tasks. Process flow analysis assesses the complexity and structural quality of program source code. This can be applied to any project that requires an understanding of logic flow or the quality of the source code within an application. Sample projects relying on process flow analysis include any program enhancement, consolidation, modularization, or rule extraction project.

Process flow analysis examines program logic flow, structure, complexity, and quality. This information is summarized using program-level metrics derived from process flow analysis tools identified in Chapter 7. Metric results include

- Program-level keyword, construct, nesting, and defect (e.g., runaway logic, recursion, etc.) counts.
- Program-level structure and complexity scores, such as the Halstead or McCabe metrics, as well as program-level defect scores.
- Structure and complexity scores summarized by application.

Data definition analysis supports transformation projects such as systemwide migration, integration, data warehouse, consolidation, replacement, or any data redesign effort. Data definition analysis objectives include inventorying and cross-referencing systemwide data usage, determining data usage quality across applications, extracting "primary" data elements, and assessing intersystem data usage. Primary data elements are the essential, nonderived data elements that can be used to re-create a cross-section of application functionality in a target architecture.

Additional objectives include determining the level of data usage redundancy and inconsistency, assessing data usage impact based on project objectives, and providing essential information to field and record size expansion efforts. Data definition analysis uses the data definition analyzer introduced in Chapter 7. This involves the identification of redundant record groups as well as more detailed information relating to individual data element definitions. Data definition metrics include

- Total physical number of record groups (which includes redundant definitions), Copy members, and elements.
- Total logical record groups (each of which contains multiple, redundant physical definitions).

Environmental, process flow, and data definition analysis tasks provide the basic foundation for subsequent architectural and functional assessment tasks involved in an assessment project.

8.10 The Architectural Assessment

The application architectural assessment addresses the gray area between the technical assessment and the functional assessment. Architectural analysis for existing systems typically uncovers inconsistent, haphazard design infrastructures added to application infrastructures that lacked a cohesive design in the first place. The architectural assessment breaks down into general architecture analysis, data architecture analysis, and presentation layer analysis tasks.

System architecture tends to be the source of the majority of business user and customer complaints. The architectural assessment documents how a system is constructed from a procedural flow, user interface, and data structure perspective and is key to uncovering important issues relevant to data migration, user perspective, and related transformation issues. Objectives for the architectural assessment include

- Developing an overview of how the applications of interest have been constructed.
- Assessing the general flow, and implementation of that flow, of data and processes throughout the system using documentation media such as the data flow diagram.
- Summarizing application user views and relationships among those views including batch outputs and online interfaces.
- Documenting interface points to related applications and external data interchange sources.
- Highlighting the use and impact of nonstandard or obsolete technologies.
- Determining and reconstructing the underlying structure of data stores and databases.
- Assessing the impact of the existing architecture on specific project objectives.

The architectural assessment is divided into three stages. Those stages include the general analysis of application flow and construction, the extraction and analysis of user views, and the extraction and documentation of data structure designs. It requires a combined approach of technical documentation and human analytic skills to determine the nature of existing application flow, data structures, system interfaces, and interface applications. General architecture analysis deliverable items include

- Summary of batch system and online system execution flows.
- A map of application system and subsystem Call structures.
- Assessment of the effectiveness of batch versus online functionality.
- Application-to-application interfaces.
- Metric counts of system interfaces and subsystem access points.

Data architecture analysis tasks attempt to understand and reconstruct a view of how current data structures were built. Deliverables include

- A database and data file inventory by application.
- Graphical hierarchies or relationships of database structures.
- Determination of physical data redundancy, fragmentation, and consistency.
- Assessment of data integration quality.
- A summary of the level of architecture conformance to the ideal architecture envisioned in strategic requirements documents.

- Metric counts of all databases, data files, and data language definition source modules.

Presentation layer analysis tasks examine the applications of interest from the perspective of the user of the system. Deliverables include

- Identification and mockups of all batch outputs and inputs.
- Identification and mockups of all online user interfaces.
- Summary of distributed applications and user interfaces.
- Summary of any user-supported interface applications.
- Summary of how well legacy user views conform to the ideal presentation requirements in a requirements document.
- Metric counts of online and batch interfaces defined by type.

Planning teams will want to focus specific architecture analysis tasks based on need. If, for example, the project is investigating the creation of new, Web-based user interfaces, analysts will want to perform a presentation layer analysis. If, on the other hand, a project team were planning a database consolidation, redesign, or other migration project, then they would perform various data architecture analysis tasks as the foundation for such a project.

The general architecture analysis applies to any project that needed to determine the overall flow and design composition of one or more legacy applications, including the relationship those applications have with related applications. Application-to-application interface analysis allows the project team to refine the scope of a project prior to moving on to the implementation stage of that project.

8.11 The Functional Assessment Overview

The functional assessment embodies essential analysis steps needed to derive high-level functional capabilities and weaknesses across legacy applications and data structures of interest. This assessment phase includes a gap analysis between legacy environments and target architectures—which can also be applied to application package solutions. Specific objectives include

- Quantifying and reviewing business requirements for the application areas under review.
- Assessing the current functional environment and formally redocumenting the functionality for applications of interest.
- Determining functional similarities and differences between legacy applications and target architecture definitions, and documenting the findings in a formal gap analysis.
- Determining the potential for legacy design or component reuse under the target architecture.

There are two main task categories within the functional assessment. User requirements analysis reviews and categorizes business upgrade and enhancement requests. The second task category addresses the redocumentation, integration, and gap analysis of legacy data and functionality using formal planning models. This second category incorporates the extraction and analysis of high-level functional views across applications of interest.

User requirements analysis simply captures the current backlog of requirements and organizes these requirements into two groups. The first category can be addressed under the current information architecture. The second group of requirements would, by definition, force project teams to deploy those requirements under the modified information architecture.

For example, assume that multiple business units want to have a single invoice sent out to all customers across multiple regions. This single invoice would need to summarize all billing activities for a given customer for all product lines. Such a requirement could force an architectural redesign and consolidation of current legacy applications and data structures.

As a next step, analysts would map all priority user requirements to alternative project scenarios currently being considered by the assessment team. This analysis step is useful regardless of the type of transformation strategy being employed because it creates a set of working requirements that can be addressed under simple enhancement or more comprehensive transformation scenarios.

The second functional assessment category documents legacy environments and allows an application area to determine the feasibility and practicality of design and component reuse under a replacement or migration scenario. The detailed legacy transformation repository (see Chapter 5, Figure 5.3) plays an important role in this analysis because it links functional analysis findings to the physical system documented during the technical assessment.

Entity relationship, function hierarchy, and function/entity matrix business analysis models can be used to document the results of the "bottom-up/top-down" analysis. Analysts derive bottom-up versions of functional models for both the data and process components for the applications of interest. Once this derivation process has been completed, analysts can compare, contrast, and integrate bottom-up models with top-down models to augment the target architecture requirements while refining their application transformation strategy.

The depth of analysis varies depending on project objectives. If no replacement effort is planned, documentation in the form of bottom-up models provides excellent documentation for business and application planning and project teams. If a replacement or consolidations effort is planned, then these bottom-up/top-down models create the foundation for understanding which application functions should be reused, deactivated, replaced, or consolidated under the target architecture.

Performing the current-to-target mapping on a replacement or package deployment project is the first step in leveraging reuse in the deployment of new, replacement, or significantly redesigned applications. This approach allows analyst and planning teams to make strategic decisions regarding the reuse of existing functionality and removes ad hoc reuse by individual programmers with limited access to the overall strategy. This approach

- Verifies the integrity of top-down models and target specifications.
- Supports formal reuse of existing data and business rules under strategic architectures.
- Facilitates the phased transition of existing systems to new architectures.
- Supports the consolidation of legacy applications with other applications, new requirements, and package application solutions.

The functional assessment tasks summarized below include the entity type analysis and functional hierarchy analysis. These are basic redocumentation steps that allow planning teams to see what data and functionality have been deployed across the legacy architecture for planning upgrade, replacement, migration, or consolidation projects.

8.12 Functional Assessment—Entity Type Analysis

Business entity type analysis applies formal data modeling techniques to document high-level data usage across legacy applications of interest. This provides a means of determining overlap between current system data usage and target system data usage. This task derives entity types and attributes from current systems. Analysts can then link entities using an ER diagram. This approach can be expanded upon in more detail during the project implementation phase. Specific objectives for this task include

- Defining an ER diagram for each system being assessed.
- Defining an integrated ER diagram representing all legacy applications of interest.
- Mapping legacy data logical views to target requirements to determine the gap between target requirements and legacy environments.
- Summarizing similarities and discrepancies between current and target entity types and attributes.

Figure 8.6 overviews entity and attribute capture and analysis. Data definitions captured during data definition analysis are input to the data derivation process. Group-level data items are entity candidates, while elements defined within record groups become attribute candidates. For systems undergoing strategic redesign, planning teams should map legacy entities and attributes to top-down data models. This is called gap analysis and provides planning input to a variety of transformation scenarios.

Current-to-Target Data Entity Mapping

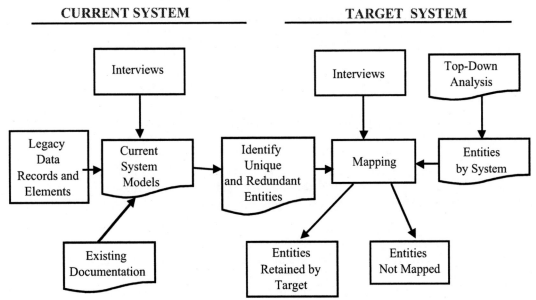

Figure 8.6
Current-to-target entity mapping extracts bottom-up entities and attributes to create or validate target data models.

For example, assume that three related, yet distinct, inventory management environments are currently running in production in a multidivisional manufacturing firm. A planning team could extract and integrate data models from each of these individual applications to create a new, consolidated target model. This model could then be refined to help build an interim data warehouse application and ultimately serve as the foundation for a consolidated inventory management application.

The benefit of this approach is that the new system would retain and reuse critical legacy data in the target design model. This would ensure that data essential to the continuity of the enterprise would be incorporated into any new design or replacement initiative. This is not always the case when project teams omit bottom-up analysis from various replacement or transformation initiatives. Entity type analysis delivers

- A list of current system entity types for each application of interest. The data grouping analysis collected during the data definition analysis performed earlier is input to this list.
- A bottom-up entity relationship diagram for each application of interest. The relationships can be developed with input from data analysts and application users.

- An integrated bottom-up entity relationship diagram reflecting a consolidated, logical view of all primary data from all applications of interest.
- A current-to-target data gap analysis. This is a list of legacy entities missing from the target architecture, target entities missing from the legacy architecture, and overlapping entities defined in the legacy and target architectures.
- An integrated ER model that incorporates all legacy and target architecture data entities. Such a model would serve as the foundation for the new target architecture.
- Updated detailed transformation repository model. This model can be used to perform the gap analysis as well as each of the other steps within this task. Producing an ER model would require an ER modeling tool.
- Summary metrics, which include the number of legacy entities missing from the target architecture, the number of target entities missing from the legacy architecture, and the total number of overlapping entities.

ER models are useful when formally specifying a new target data structure. The remaining gap analysis tasks can be performed using the repository as a mapping device. If no target data models exist, an integrated legacy data model could be used as the basis for designing a data warehouse or target application data architecture. This mapping process can target new requirements or an application package data model.

8.13 Functional Assessment—
Function Hierarchy Analysis

Function hierarchy analysis decomposes legacy application functionality using function and, optionally, process hierarchy diagrams across the applications of interest. This task documents the functionality of legacy environments and helps determine if reusing legacy business rules within the target application architecture is a viable option.

A function is a group of activities that support one aspect of the mission of the enterprise. A process is a low-level activity that has a specific effect on a data entity, falls within a subcategory of a function, and defines "what" is being done within a system. The reason for adding process decomposition to this phase of a project is pragmatic. Bottom-up analysis typically must get down to a process level prior to extracting and mapping functions back to application programs. Functions can then be derived from a series of processes. An example of a program-to-process-to-function mapping is shown in Table 8.1.

For replacement projects, the benefit of this approach is that the new system would reuse and not need to re-create critical legacy business rules. As a result, users would not be forced to adopt new and potentially disruptive business practices as defined in a vendor package or risk the recoding of these rules from

Table 8.1 Program, Process, Function Map
Current-to-target functional analysis maps legacy programs, processes, and functions to target architecture functional definitions.

Mapping Functions to Program Source Modules			
Program Source	**Current Process**	**Current Function**	**Target Function**
PU300200	Select vendor/product	Purchasing	
PU300200	Change vendor/product	Purchasing	
PU300200	Roll off vendor/product	Purchasing	
PU300200	Order supplies	Purchasing	
PU300200	Pay vendors	Purchasing	
SR774200	Track vendor shipments	Sending/Receiving	
SR600350	Disperse supplies	Sending/Receiving	
INV08040	Maintain supply stock	Inventory	
Manual	Maintain supply stock	Inventory	
INV00100	Request supplies	Inventory	
SR400100	Ship corporate products	Sending/Receiving	
SR400200	Ship corporate products	Sending/Receiving	
MA906600	Manage materials	Manufacturing	
Manual	Manage materials	Manufacturing	
MA665000	Request supplies	Manufacturing	
MA240030	Create products	Manufacturing	
MA240050	Create products	Manufacturing	

scratch. This is a major advantage of the transformation approach over a packaged solution or a from-scratch rewrite.

Bottom-up function hierarchy analysis also benefits EAI projects. Mapping application programs to legacy functions and processes allows integration teams to quickly determine which back-end application programs require integration using middleware technology. Objectives of the function hierarchy analysis include

- Documenting legacy application functionality in an easy-to-follow list or chart. This should be in a format that business users can understand.
- Decomposing current functions into processes as a way to validate which programs perform those functions. This technique bridges the knowledge

gap between a given business function and the technical implementation of that function. Table 8.1 shows an example of where this was done.

- Developing a gap analysis between legacy and target requirements to ensure that replacement projects deactivate or replace the correct application cross-sections.

- Validating target architecture analysis results using the functionality defined in the legacy applications. Omitting essential functionality in replacement applications, including packages, is common and this eliminates this problem.

- Creating a foundation for a consolidated application from the legacy application environment. Application consolidation would begin with an aggregate data and functional model that reconciles functional redundancies within the new consolidated application view.

- Assessing opportunities for reuse within the target application architecture. The high-level functional model can be further decomposed during subsequent implementation steps so that business rule reuse is approached systemically.

- Developing functional documentation to support EAI, upgrade, outsourcing, or other initiatives that need this documentation as input.

Figure 8.8 depicts the current-to-target functional mapping approach, but omits intermediate process decomposition for the sake of simplicity. This is a highly analytical task, since a function is the highest abstraction of an application and the implementation level is the most granular view of a system. The intermediate extraction of processes facilitates this analysis. The function hierarchy analysis task produces the following deliverable items.

- A mapping of legacy functions, legacy processes, and the programs that perform those processes. Table 8.1 is an example of such a hierarchy. This would be produced for each legacy application of interest.

- Consolidated function hierarchy for multiple applications of interest. The production of a consolidated chart would be limited to consolidation-oriented transformation projects.

- Mapping of legacy functions to target architecture functions, as shown in Figure 8.7. This is applicable in scenarios where validation of a strategic requirements model is needed. It is also applicable in cases where an application package is being evaluated or implemented and analysts need to determine how that package maps to the legacy environment for deactivation or integration purposes.

- Updated, detailed transformation repository model. Analysts can map legacy functions and processes along with target functions to each other and to legacy application programs. Once this information has been loaded into the repository, reports like the one in Table 8.1 can be generated as needed.

- Summary-level metrics depicting the number of legacy functions missing from the target architecture, the number of target functions missing from the

Program/Function Gap Analysis

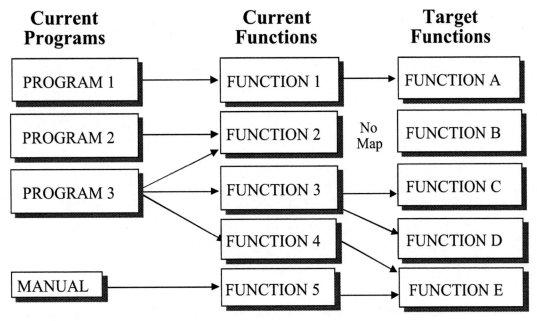

Figure 8.7
Program-to-function mapping helps determine level of legacy application conformance to target architecture.

legacy architecture, and the total number of overlapping functions. Additional metrics can summarize the number of legacy processes captured in each application.

Analysts performing a functional assessment should ensure that they only derive and/or map information that they find useful. Other bottom-up analysis options include the development of functional dependency diagrams and the creation of business entity/function practices. These steps can be performed based on the methodology or preferences of the assessment team.

Additional techniques for legacy data, process, and business rule capture and mapping are discussed in later chapters. Some of these more detailed techniques can be moved into the assessment phase of a project if time permits.

8.14 Finalizing the Project Implementation Plan

The technical, architectural, and functional assessments, in and of themselves, do not provide a complete picture of how existing applications can evolve to meet short-term and long-term information requirements. When these assessments are

integrated and used as the basis for determining the feasibility of alternative project approaches, however, they form the foundation for creating a project implementation plan. Transformation implementation planning involves selecting a
project approach from proposed alternatives through a feasibility analysis and
building a plan that delivers value through a phased approach.

The feasibility analysis task is driven by project objectives and alternatives
and is where analysts consolidate their assessment findings. This involves reviewing the original project objectives, using the findings from various assessment
steps to validate various alternatives, factoring the cost of those alternatives, and
selecting an approach. Feasibility analysis eliminates approaches that will not
work and then mixes and matches options that complement each other and can be
phased in over a period of time.

For example, extracted logical data views may be used as input to a data
warehouse over the near term and subsequently be used to create a replacement
application data model over the long term. Feasibility analysis includes

- Reviewing various alternatives set forth at the start of the assessment.
- Identifying critical success factors needed to succeed from a business-driven
  approach.
- Discussing the implications of various options based on the assessment findings. For example, if a consolidated data and functional model can serve as
  the basis for a new system and no package option matches these requirements, redevelopment of the legacy application is the best approach.
- Discussing probable timing, resource requirements, and costs for each
  approach.
- Identifying the risks of each option and considering these along with cost
  and time factors. Reuse is typically a lower-risk approach because the project can be phased in more easily than a from-scratch option.
- Working with all relevant and affected parties to rank all alternatives by desir-
  ability. Once this is done, analysts can select an approach based on the option
  that accommodates the applicable cost, risk, time, and resource criteria.

Once an approach has been selected, a phased delivery plan will need to be
developed. A phased delivery plan should apply the cost justification and related
planning considerations discussed in Chapter 6.

Unless a system is being phased out completely, there is typically some level
of support that must continue near term, regardless of the long-term plans for those
applications. For example, project planners should consider addressing issues such
as data definitions that need to be updated for a planned initiative or inadequate
front ends that can be addressed within a reasonable payback period. These activities should appear as near-term steps in an implementation plan, even if it means
that different participants will be working on different stages of the project.

It is important to remember that outputs from one stage of a project should
be leveraged wherever possible as input to a subsequent phase of a project. For

example, data definition groupings feed directly into the development of a bottom-up ER model. Additional short-term requirements tend to address data integrity, integration (i.e., EAI) and presentation issues, performance, and reliability factors. Near-term objectives should also address

- Weaknesses in current physical system that, once corrected, could leverage maintenance and outsourcing teams.
- Additional redocumentation techniques for the legacy environment based on known business requirements.
- Project cost benefit analyses for each interim deliverable—typically broken into phases of no more than two to three months each.
- An understanding of how near-term improvements can leverage strategic transformation goals.

For various reasons, some of which may be political, management may not be able to articulate a long-term strategy for an application environment. If they cannot articulate and agree upon these requirements, the plan may be limited to the near-term, tactical solutions outlined above. If a more systemic solution is needed, then more far-reaching transformation options may be required.

This can include the need to integrate or merge multiple standalone applications, deploy a more centrally defined global data architecture, move an application to a new distributed architecture, deploy a package, or rewrite an application. These projects should also be phased in so they can deliver value over interim periods of time.

The Strategy Matrix in Figure 8.8 suggests that application value be examined based on the importance to the organization as well as the technical and functional quality of that application or cross-section of application components. High-impact software should not be subject to shortcut solutions such as those options employing certain EAI middleware. Ignoring highly valued software assets as these strategic plans are developed will hurt the business capacity of the enterprise.

With this in mind, implementation planning should focus on technology migration, replacement, consolidation, package options, or other areas where transformation can help solidify and reuse valuable application and data assets. Analysts should remember that any type of project might include a mix of reuse, package software, or new development. Categorizing an initiative is not as important as establishing a plan to meet organizational information requirements. Strategic planning options should

- Address business-driven requirements identified at the beginning of the assessment.
- Avoid shortcuts that will result in more problems downstream.
- Be deployed using a phased approach.
- Produce a cost benefit analysis of the selected approach that delivers interim value over time.

Software Option Strategy Matrix

ORGANIZATIONAL IMPACT

	LOW	HIGH	LOW	HIGH
GOOD	MAINTAIN/ MIGRATE/ INTEGRATE	UPGRADE / CONSOLIDATE	MAINTAIN	MAINTAIN
POOR	PHASE OUT	REPLACE	INTEGRATE OR ENHANCE	ENHANCE / CONSOLIDATE

FUNCTIONAL CONDITION

POOR   GOOD

TECHNICAL QUALITY

Figure 8.8
High-impact software components should be enhanced, consolidated, or maintained based on business requirements.

- Incorporate transformation tasks into any alternative, given that legacy applications and/or data play a role in that project.
- Leverage near-term solutions as a way to achieve long-term results. Creating a more modular application, for example, is excellent preparation for a Web Services migration project.

Analysts should couple long-term objectives with near-term tasks and bundle these into a single, phased plan. The plan should have points where the project can be halted, based on team input, and still have delivered interim value along the way. The assessment deliverables outlined above will play a key role in implementation tasks discussed in later chapters.

Note

1. "USRM—Systems Redevelopment Methodology" [Online], Available: www.comsys.com, 2002.

Part III

TRANSFORMATION IMPLEMENTATION

This section discusses the implementation approaches and techniques commonly found in a transformation project. Chapter 9 provides a transformation-oriented perspective on various enterprise application, business-to-business, and business process integration scenarios. This includes outlining integration options and approaches that can be pursued over the interim and in conjunction with strategic transformation projects. Chapter 10 provides detailed approaches and techniques for improving application source code and data structures without the need to redesign those structures. These discussions are provided within a context of providing near-term value to the users and beneficiaries of those systems and data structures.

Chapter 11 delves into data and business rule transformation options and techniques. This chapter provides a comprehensive discussion of legacy architecture reverse engineering, reengineering, and reconstruction. This discussion incorporates current-to-target mapping, data and business rule extraction, reuse in target architectures, and related topics. Chapter 12 ties together the strategies, approaches, and techniques presented in previous chapters under case-study-oriented scenarios. These scenarios include application consolidation, multisystem integration, application package selection and deployment, middleware deployment, rehosting, data migration, and component migration. Finally, Appendix A provides a sample list of vendors that offer software and services that can help leverage transformation initiatives.

- **Chapter 9** Incorporating EAI, B2Bi, and BPI into a Comprehensive Integration Strategy
- **Chapter 10** Structuring, Rationalizing, and Upgrading Legacy Applications and Data Structures
- **Chapter 11** Logical Data and Business Rule Capture, Redesign and Reuse
- **Chapter 12** Transformation Project Strategies and Case Studies
- **Appendix A** Tool Vendor Listing

Incorporating EAI, B2Bi, and BPI into a Comprehensive Integration Strategy

Noninvasive enterprise application, data, business process, and B2B integration, which relies on various middleware and related technologies, arose out of a need to connect disparate application functionality, enterprise data, processes, and enterprises. Driven by e-business, supply chain, and related business requirements, users have demanded that IT provide front-end integration to highly segregated, back-end application functionality. These demands have been particularly resonant for applications supporting customer and supply-chain-focused business processes.

In a perfect world, noninvasive integration would not exist, because underlying information architectures would already be seamlessly integrated, but legacy architectures are far from perfect. Because few enterprises will ever achieve the ideal, homogenous information architecture, noninvasive integration is probably here to stay. EAI, for example, has proven to be a useful short-term option for linking Web-based front ends to back-end applications and data when architecture transformation would take too long. That said, many integration scenarios are best addressed on a more systemic basis over the long term.

Some organizations see EAI and related noninvasive techniques as a long-term solution to every conceivable business integration requirement. As middleware transitions into application server products, which play an increasingly important role in component-based architectures, management may be compelled to institutionalize middleware solutions as an alternative to architecture transformation. Over the long run, however, extensive use of middleware interfaces is likely to complicate already convoluted legacy architectures. Applying noninvasive integration solutions should therefore be pursued selectively and with full knowledge and understanding that alternative transformation-oriented options are available.

This chapter discusses how to incorporate EAI, B2B integration (B2Bi), and BPI options into a long-term transformation strategy. This includes summarizing available application, data, process, and B2B integration technologies, reviewing related implementation options, leveraging assessments to support integration projects, and building noninvasive integration deliverables into a transformation plan. This chapter also outlines how noninvasive integration impacts architecture redesign efforts along with ways to uncouple middleware solutions as legacy environments transition to modern architectures.

9.1 Integration—Past, Present, and Future

As discussed in Chapter 4, a Morgan Stanley survey of 225 CIOs identified application integration as a top priority. This simply means that executives want information systems to facilitate business solutions across business unit and enterprise boundaries. As pointed out in prior chapters, stovepipe architectures, functional and data redundancy, application incompatibility, and data fragmentation and inconsistency limit EAI's ability to meet business integration challenges.

The smartest middleware or most effectively deployed BPI/BPA technology will not compensate for major weaknesses in legacy architectures. In spite of this limitation, noninvasive integration solutions continue to play an important role in addressing many time-critical business integration requirements. Care must be taken, however, to not let middleware interfaces become so convoluted as to create an unmaintainable, indecipherable maze of front-end to back-end interfaces.

Examining the evolution of noninvasive integration technology will help executives position it more effectively in an overall transformation strategy. Middleware first emerged on the scene more than a decade ago in the form of remote procedure calls (RPCs). RPC technology evolved out of the need for one application to get data or trigger another application to perform a function. Programmers created custom RPCs over the years. A client/server application can, for example, trigger a CICS mainframe transaction. The RPC became a basic component in what emerged as middleware. Many of these early RPC interfaces are not well documented and therefore contribute to the complexity of legacy architectures.

Between 1999 and 2001, the middleware market grew to the point where scores of vendors began to deliver hundreds of products to enable EAI solutions. As Web-based systems proliferated and the user base for these systems grew larger and more diverse, integration requirements and solutions became more complex. Simple front end-to-back end application programming interface (API) calls matured into middleware that routes and transforms messages in real-time environments. This technology is still catching up with ever-growing e-business and related integration demands.

E-business requires cross-functional integration to link applications and data across business units, operating systems, and hardware platforms. Enterprise-wide integration must also address complex legacy, ERP, and data access requirements. Analyzing and implementing scaleable integration capabilities quickly and effectively is essential to satisfying an increasingly sophisticated user base.

E-business requirements took another leap in complexity as supplier and distributor relationships matured and drove B2Bi requirements. Early partner-to-partner EDI links could not support the growing need to streamline data and process flow across supply and distribution chains. Demand continues to grow for technology that facilitates customer relationship management (CRM), supply chain initiatives, electronic marketplaces, and industry portals.

The future of e-business integration envisions a scenario where aspects of integration products will be consolidated and coordinated through common repositories and rules-based engines. This transformation is already under way, as exemplified by the fact that simple connectivity tools are now embedded in more comprehensive integration products. Future directions will focus on consolidation across disparate applications, databases, platforms, and enterprise boundaries.

EAI and B2B solutions are rapidly merging as vendors and products continue to be acquired. In addition to this, BPI/BPA tools are increasingly being viewed as an integration option that can displace many of the application or data-level solutions on the market. I have included a BPI/BPA discussion in this chapter because these tools are being utilized to meet EAI and B2Bi requirements.

Middleware has also become a mainstay within development architectures. The application server is middleware technology that directs transaction-related traffic and performs various security, performance, and operational functions. Application server and related middleware cannot be burdened with the entire legacy integration workload, however. Legacy architecture transformation will need to play an ongoing role in migrating applications toward increasingly consolidated, component-based, and Web Services architectures. Under this approach, application server technology can focus on addressing component management and other key functions within emerging information architectures.

The challenge for an enterprise considering or using EAI technology is to ensure that middleware, in whatever form it takes long term, fits into an architectural framework from a strategic perspective. Unfettered, low-level deployment of EAI tools will eventually result in chaos. For this reason, I have positioned today's noninvasive integration solutions within the context of an overall transformation strategy.

9.2 Middleware Technology Overview

Enterprise application and data integration technology is essentially middleware-based. There are a number of variations on these technologies, but they break down into one of two types. Linear middleware can connect an application or data using a point-to-point bridge. Point-to-point solutions grab data or a message, format it, and send it to some target. A message bus or broker, on the other hand, can facilitate the flow of data or messages, or both, among multiple applications, data structures, or user interfaces [1].

Middleware can also be developed using an API or through more customized methods that require creating an interface application (i.e., a method) or special user interface. The loosely coupled API approach is preferred because it can be generalized and reapplied to multiple integration requirements [1]. Point-to-point solutions use either an RPC or message queuing technology. While common, the proliferation of point-to-point solutions complicates information environments. For example, if a project team creates 50 customized interfaces between a distributed system and a back-end database, changes to the database architecture could trigger a rewrite of all 50 customized solutions. If these point-to-point interfaces were not documented, the entire application relying on them could fail.

Message brokers, on the other hand, offer an alternative that reduces the complexity of the solution to the point where it becomes more manageable over the long term. In the case of a message broker, a single piece of software can serve as the interface point to back-end applications. However, adapter technology, which interprets front-end and back-end data formats and application functionality, can require a good deal of custom coding as well.

The industry generally agrees that middleware technology is defined as software that facilitates the communications between two or more applications [2]. Middleware allows applications running on one computer or platform to communicate with applications and data residing on other computers and platforms. Middleware is the main enabling technology underlying an EAI solution. When discussing middleware, it is useful to summarize some basic concepts.

- **Synchronous versus Asynchronous Communication**

  Synchronous communication means that an application cannot continue processing until a reply is received for the message sent to another application. Asynchronous communication implies that the sending application can continue processing after it sends a message to another application. Asynchronous processing offers clear advantages over synchronous processing because applications do not have to stop and wait for a reply after sending a message.

- **Point-to-Point Communication**

  Middleware can communicate between one point in one application to another point defined in another application. This is called point-to-point middleware, which is limited to those two applications. The many-to-many communication approach implies that there can be multiple applications on the sending and the receiving side of a middleware transaction. Many-to-many middleware is the more flexible and preferable approach because it allows for more flexibility than point-to-point middleware.

- **Direct versus Queued Communications**

  Middleware may employ either direct communications or queued communications. Direct communications means the middleware must pass information directly to the receiving program and is synchronous by nature. Queued communications uses a queue manager to receive, hold, and pass a message to its target application. The queued approach is the preferable communications model because it allows a system to send a message and continue processing.

- **Publish-and-Subscribe Capabilities**

  If middleware has publish-and-subscribe capabilities, it means that the sending application does not need to know anything about the receiving application. This requires a middleware broker to interpret and transform the information being sent. This level of sophistication increases the value of a middleware product because it saves the sending and receiving applications from having to interpret information being shared.

- **Adapters**

  Adapters sit between a message broker and an application. Adapters map differences among disparate application interfaces while hiding these complexities from the user of that system. More sophisticated adapters allow for the addition of custom code, which can increase the types and number of applications being integrated. Adapters must be easy to use as well as have the ability to scale up to support increased traffic levels found in the mid-to-large enterprise.

  An intelligent adapter should maintain knowledge of business logic within the source and target applications. This capability requires an adapter to incorporate application logic for validation of data. Many existing adapter solutions force programmers to write this logic. Emerging adapter technology should allow an analyst to generate an intelligent adapter that can automate the generation of this logic [3].

  Predictions for adapter technology indicate that it will move from dumb interfaces that simply pass information to intelligent adapters that manage application integration. These tools will evolve to incorporate rules-based processing within the adapter [4]. Care must be taken, however, to not allow adapters to become a legacy morass that turns into a maintenance nightmare.

As discussed previously, middleware has been around in various forms for many years. Early middleware was typically deployed using simple RPCs, where one program function invoked another program function on a remote machine. An RPC is tightly coupled to the application it services and uses synchronous communications.

Tight coupling, however, reduces the ability to reapply a specific instance of an RPC to subsequent integration tasks without additional custom coding. RPC technology is typically found within more sophisticated middleware products that have emerged since RPCs were first introduced.

Readers should note that while many industry participants concur on general middleware terms and functions, there are no universally agreed-upon definitions for EAI middleware categories. Any given book or article on the topic can have a unique interpretation when compared to another book or article.

The following technology categories and subcategories manifest themselves in a variety of commercially available middleware products. Note that a number of middleware tool categories could be combined to create a more comprehensive product category.

- **Communication Middleware**

  Message-oriented middleware (MOM) is not coupled to an application and can therefore send and receive messages to and from other applications without holding up processing at either end. MOM employs asynchronous communications and typically involves message-queuing products that send pieces of data from one application to another. MOM is a basic middleware function for applications exchanging information with other remote applications. RPC and MOM collectively comprise a category called communication middleware.

- **Data-Level or Data Management Middleware**

  Data-level or data management middleware allows an application to access data that is not natively defined within that application. Database-oriented middleware is a valuable facility because it allows new applications to access a multitude of data structures defined outside their immediate environment. This involves integration and transformation of data formats. For example, if two applications used incompatible data formats, then data management middleware could be used to transform that data in a real-time scenario.

  Another data middleware category synchronizes databases with overlapping data. In this case, the second database would have the capacity to reflect updates on a real-time basis. The overhead associated with this type of solution could be a problem, but it would be useful in situations where a fully redundant application and data environment needed to be maintained. The real question from an architectural perspective is why anyone would want to maintain such a redundant or overlapping environment long term.

- **Transaction-Oriented Middleware**

  Transaction-oriented middleware sends a bounded transaction, which is defined as having a beginning and an end, to perform some type of activity against a database or message queue. An early incarnation of transaction-oriented middleware was the teleprocessing (TP) monitor, which sends a stream of data via software that triggers an application to perform in a specific way.

In practice, developers have created Web-based front-end applications that fool back-end applications into thinking that it is merely processing a CICS transaction. The transaction is handled just as it would be if it were triggered by a mainframe CICS command. The user and the application remain oblivious to the activity being performed behind the scenes.

- **Platform Middleware**

  Many vendors have bundled transaction-oriented middleware, object request brokers, and related services, including resource and memory management, operating system functionality, load balancing, and error handling. These products can be broadly defined under a category called platform middleware. Platform middleware is an example of how various technologies can be bundled to create more full-function product offerings.

- **The Application Server**

  The application server is Web-enabled software that facilitates the sharing and processing of component-based application logic while connecting front-end applications to back-end, operational environments. These environments include legacy applications, ERP systems, distributed systems, and databases. Application servers can host business logic that can interpret complex data and transactions through a series of exchanges or conversations with the application receiving the information.

  Application servers represent an evolutionary step in middleware technology because they support the development of new Web-enabled applications, typically in Java. This category of middleware is typically included in the application development architecture, particularly as enterprises move toward J2EE or .Net environments. Some application server products support specific connectors to major ERP products. Overall, application server products are becoming increasingly important in an e-business integration environment.

  Object request brokers (ORBs) are technically considered middleware because they allow application-to-application communications. A distributed object contains functionality that can be triggered by another application via a standard interface and communication protocol. ORBs are also part of application development architecture. ORBs fall into the application server category because they are used within the context of emerging architectures.

- **Gateway Middleware**

  Gateway middleware is specialty middleware because it connects disparate applications and commercial software products. For example, gateway middleware can provide interfaces between IBM's mainframe CICS product and COM, Java, or Tuxedo in distributed environments.

- **Message Brokers**

  Message brokers coordinate integration services across a variety of applications, networks, and middleware. Specifically, message brokers have the capability to intelligently route and distribute messages based on rules that analysts build into the middleware using scripting languages.

  Message brokers also use the concept of message warehousing, where messages are stored in a database. This allows analysts to review the messages sent over a period of time, archive messages, and audit messages to ensure that they are being properly routed. Integration repository services support the administration, monitoring, performance checking, and message status checking.

  Directory services are an important function within a message broker because messages are being transferred across disparate computing environments that typically use a multitude of directories. These directories contain log-on identification and passwords. Directory functions involve security issues that must be handled as part of a message broker environment.

As stated earlier, other technology categories are beginning to overlap or compete with EAI middleware solutions. B2Bi technology is merging with EAI solutions, and BPI/BPA solutions continue to displace middleware as an integration strategy. In addition to this, application servers continue to evolve within development environments, and planning teams should be prepared to incorporate evolutionary changes to these technologies as application architectures continue to shift.

Ultimately, middleware will coalesce into a subset of product categories. Given that much of this technology is a moving target, organizations will need to incorporate shifting trends and emerging products into an overall legacy transformation strategy to ensure its effective deployment.

9.3 ERP Middleware Technology

Certain middleware technology has been customized to connect to back-end ERP packages that are not Web-enabled. This differs from other legacy integration middleware because ERP systems have defined interface points. Legacy applications, on the other hand, represent an endless variety of system architectures, languages, platforms, interfaces, and data structures that typically require customized adapter technology.

To support ERP integration, a number of e-busines integration vendors have created APIs that can access published interface points within an ERP product. Most ERP vendors openly share information on these interfaces so that integration middleware can access data or trigger ERP transactions as required.

Some ERP vendors conform to an open standard, such as CORBA, that would eliminate the need to have a customized interface for each ERP vendor. E-business architects should examine the integration architecture they select to interface with EPR systems. With a growing number of organizations locked into ERP vendor packages, integration middleware is likely to remain a fixture within an ERP-driven enterprise.

9.4 B2Bi Technology

B2Bi enables supply, distribution, and customer information exchange and collaboration by connecting processes, transactions, and data across enterprise boundaries. Initially, simple B2Bi tools supported point-to-point EDI solutions that became the prime avenue for exchanging information among trading partners. EDI, while still necessary, reflects a linear view of supplier and customer relationships that cannot support the level of collaboration needed to streamline and manage B2B activities.

As B2Bi business requirements and technology became more demanding and complex, a new discipline emerged called collaborative commerce. Collaborative commerce involves multidimensional synchronization of business processes, transactions, and data by streamlining interbusiness activity via the Internet. B2Bi technologies that facilitate information exchange and collaborative commerce include EDI, XML, information exchange standards, Web integration servers, trading partner technology, and Web Services.

- **EDI and XML**

  Based on the ubiquitous nature of EDI, it will continue to play a key role in supporting external data exchange for many years to come. Unfortunately, EDI typically uses proprietary data formats. XML, on the other hand, facilitates the open exchange of information, including an endless variety of data types, workflow definitions, business rule definitions, and security assurances. In spite of EDI's entrenched presence, XML has emerged as the standard technology for exchanging information with business partners as well as internally.

  XML-based data interchange formats rely on a number of different industry standards. These standards are created and managed by groups such as the World Wide Web Consortium (W3C). As industries create specific XML standards unique to their market requirements, those industries will need to adopt these standards along with those being promoted by the W3C.

  Asynchronous XML communication will grow increasingly common and become the dominant communication medium for B2Bi. XML will ultimately span the vast majority of industries and information exchange environments.

Companies should consider this as they review various middleware and other e-business integration technologies in coming years.

- **Web Integration Servers**

EAI and B2Bi technology is beginning to merge with the help of Web integration servers and related middleware technology. The reason for this is that middleware is beginning to expand to support external integration requirements based on the same premise used to support internal integration. In other words, integration technology will trigger and route messages and data without regard to where those messages and data originated.

Web integration servers offer similar functionality to external partners, as one would expect from internal middleware solutions. These products provide a unifying layer between external entities and internally focused application servers and integration brokers. A number of vendors provide B2Bi solutions, which rely on XML as a standard interface language.

The challenges facing organizations as they begin to explore the concept of triggering transactions and accessing data structures from a cross-industry perspective are significant. Information exchange formats rely on XML as a standard interface language, but standards for various industries are still being developed and adopted. Industry groups must ensure that commonly agreed-upon formats and standards are deployed and utilized. These industry groups will also need to ensure that external information exchange is as secure as possible.

- **Trading Partner Technology**

Trading partner technology facilitates collaborative efforts across distribution and supply chain communities. Many industries have created trading communities to streamline partner-related activity as a way to reduce costs and increase business opportunities through the collective management of distribution and supply chains. This approach focuses on the elimination or streamlining of intermediaries within distribution chains to increase supply chain management efficiency and effectiveness. To meet these goals, companies need to deploy e-business services to enable and integrate B2B activities.

The auto industry created an example of how to streamline distribution chain management when it established an exchange to sell vehicles directly through the Internet. The auto industry also pioneered collaborative supply chain management by creating an exchange called Covisint, where participants can exchange parts through the Internet and track the availability of those parts electronically. Software to support these exchanges must have portal capability, partner tracking facilities, buy-sell technology, and the ability to communicate with each partner participating in these trading communities.

- **Web Services**

  Web Services, driven by e-business requirements, are the result of new industry approaches to the development, sharing, and dissemination of software. Web Services will greatly facilitate B2Bi among trading partners who need to share common processing capabilities and data. Consider a situation where a group of distributors wants to utilize common sales management, tracking, and reporting capabilities. Each distributor may have its own IT environment, but could create reusable business components that perform commonly applied sales management tasks and share these components through a Web Services architecture.

  A number of vendors are working on software to help make Web Services architecture a reality. The concept of obtaining reusable components from external sources or gaining access to an application functionality via the Web is very appealing to companies that require standard solutions across a given industry. This is particularly true for small to mid-sized companies that rely on large corporations for the bulk of their revenue. Web Services will grow in popularity as B2Bi requirements continue to grow.

9.5 BPI and BPA Technology

BPI/BPA technology can be applied to system-oriented workflow or to the broader category of business processes, which include manual and automated tasks performed within and outside the bounds of the enterprise. Workflow and BPA technology provides varying degrees of value to an enterprise based on the objectives of the management and integration architecture team.

- **Workflow Management and Automation**

  A subset of business processes exists within the context of automated application systems. For example, a legacy application portfolio automates numerous functions within an enterprise. Workflow automation technology supports the integration of work-related activities linked to and performed by a given application. Workflow automation supports the integration of application-oriented tasks across standalone application environments.

  This technology is typically delivered as part of an integration middleware product suite and offers Web-enabled front ends to support workflow automation and integration. API links trigger transaction-oriented functions within various applications. Workflow automation is constrained by the application architecture defining that workflow and does not address the integration of human touch points in conjunction with these application-driven processes. While system-driven workflow management is a useful option for automating workflow within the context of a given application, such as an ERP package, this technology is a subset of BPI/BPA technology.

- **Business Process Management and Automation**

  BPI/BPA technology facilitates the integration of manual and automated processes across business unit, application, and enterprise boundaries and can be applied to internal and external process integration requirements. Because BPI/BPA software supports external process integration, some analysts believe that it overlaps with B2Bi technology. This is true, but BPI/BPA remains in a class by itself because it deals with the integration issue at the point where the user performs critical tasks.

  BPI/BPA products map the flow of manual and automated business processes and links these processes with the roles, individuals, and systems responsible for executing or invoking them. These products also enable process documentation, integration, and automation. For example, a user can create a process map showing how processes flow through and beyond enterprise boundaries. Creating such a map allows analysts to visualize how to best integrate and automate business processes. Another useful integration feature is a rules-based engine to support process tracking, evaluation, and consolidation.

  BPI/BPA products generate graphical user interfaces to automate, integrate, and trigger manual and automated processes based on the completion of a prerequisite process. Another feature allows a BPI/BPA product to generate links between manual process interfaces and back-end application systems.

  These products also allow analysts to codify business rules to define conditional, unconditional, and time-triggered business processes. Building this type of intelligence into a process management environment facilitates process integration across business units, supply chains, and distribution environments. Process reporting facilities further allow analysts to produce trend analyses and to fine-tune process integration efforts as a business evolves.

9.6 Integration Solution Architecture

Integration architecture provides the implementation infrastructure that is hidden from the users, the applications, and data being integrated. The integration architecture establishes an infrastructure that analysts can use to establish relationships among various integration products, the overall technical environment, internal and external users, data, and other factors involved in an IT environment.

It is important to differentiate the integration architecture from the enterprise information architecture. Information architectures specify the relationships among business data, applications, and business functions across an enterprise. The integration architecture, on the other hand, defines the technological "building materials" underlying, supporting, and enabling a business-specific information architecture.

An example of an integration architecture model is shown in Figure 9.1 and summarizes how business users can access applications either directly or through intermediary software. Middleware plays a key role in this architecture and coordinates access to legacy applications, ERP systems, data structures, data warehouses, a repository containing a metamodel of the overall environment, and B2B interface points.

Information within each of these architectural components would be specified in more detail to depict the underlying mechanics of such an architecture. For example, the box in Figure 9.1 entitled middleware technology would include application servers, APIs, intelligent routing tools, custom components, and other elements commonly found within a middleware environment.

Noninvasive Integration Architecture

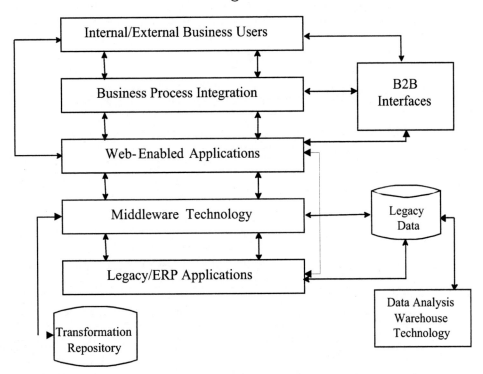

Figure 9.1

A noninvasive integration architecture defines relationships among integration disciplines, information architecture, and users.

Similarly, the box entitled Web-enabled applications would define details relating to an application development environment. This would include development languages and environments, component libraries, and design products used to specify, generate, and test Web-enabled applications.

Architecture teams will need to create an internal definition of where various tools will interface with environments, applications, data, and people for their enterprise. This depiction allows planning teams to understand where each of the enabling technologies they require for an integration project may fit together. With an ever-evolving integration technology landscape, a map of the integration architecture is essential for application and planning teams trying to apply these technology options to business-driven projects.

9.7 Noninvasive Integration Deployment Options

Noninvasive integration technology is a moving target and will continue to change as more products become increasingly integrated with development environments and related solutions. This is why it is important to have a tool-independent model for deploying noninvasive integration options. Creating an integration framework avoids a scenario where integration becomes tool-driven instead of being business-driven.

Managers, analysts, and developers have a myriad of integration solutions available. Figure 9.2 identifies various application, data, B2B, and process integration options that projects can pursue. Having such a planning framework allows an enterprise to synthesize emerging integration software solutions into existing environments to address ongoing business demands. A user-driven framework also helps categorize basic e-business integration functions into the following solution-oriented categories.

9.7.1 EAI

EAI allows users to trigger or access a series of back-end, typically standalone application functions from a common set of user interfaces and was the first major integration category to emerge. Subcategories for application integration include Web access to legacy transactions, front-end to back-end application integration, and ERP integration.

Early integration projects focused on building distributed front ends that invoked back-end transactions. This approach still has merit, although these front ends are now typically Web-based. A simple example might involve a Web-based order-processing application that needs to trigger a series of back-end procurement transactions on a mainframe system. The procurement application thinks that these transactions were triggered from mainframe interfaces, when they were really triggered from a Web-based front-end.

Noninvasive Integration Planning Framework

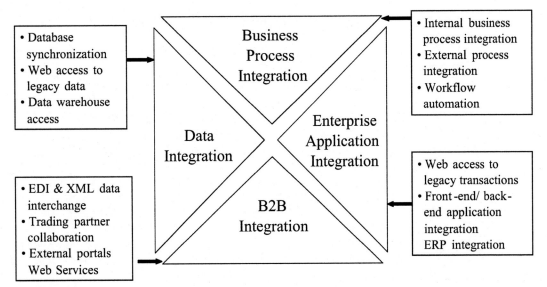

Figure 9.2

A conceptual framework for noninvasive integration allows planning teams to position integration within an overall strategy.

EAI implementation scenarios can grow very sophisticated. For example, a single distributed transaction may invoke multiple mainframe transactions to capture and build a comprehensive set of information for a distributed user. In the prior procurement example, the Web-based front-end application may trigger transactions across multiple stovepipe environments to capture the information it requires. This is a very powerful technique because it greatly streamlines the work of the user while bringing together disparate information from multiple legacy applications.

Many of these solutions do not impact the legacy application at all. Other approaches could involve modifying legacy source code, but this begins to shift into a more invasive approach because it modifies the presentation layer logic within the legacy application. Allowing distributed front ends to trigger back-end transactions is applicable in scenarios where the legacy architecture primarily supports existing transaction requirements, but needs to be accessed by Web-enabled users.

Tighter integration involves the addition of custom code to integration middleware that not only can access the legacy application but can customize the information being returned from that application. If simple Web access to legacy transactions do not meet user requirements, this custom coding supports a more sophisticated approach.

For example, if a series of transactions relied on the outcome of prior transactions, a rules-based engine could determine in real time which transactions would need to be triggered in a specific sequence. In the previous order-processing example, a transaction may return a status that would invoke a series of procurement steps. These steps would in turn trigger an inventory transaction, but only if inventory levels fell below a certain amount. This logic would be incorporated into the middleware itself.

Application servers support this more sophisticated integration approach by allowing analysts to create new application logic that extends and integrates legacy application logic. An environment deploying this type of concept is called a composite application. Composite applications are systems created through the use of new code that interfaces with legacy application logic.

When assessing and deploying application integration technology, architects should focus on the major functions required over the next one to two years with the understanding that new technology is likely to supersede existing products. In the above example, a rules-based engine that incorporates decision logic could displace extensive custom coding. This is an example of how subsequent releases of EAI technology could force application teams to build layer upon layer of application interface solutions over a period of years.

Planning teams should remember that noninvasive approaches to legacy integration are useful when the applications involved contain one or more specific transactions that can be identified and triggered to meet the needs of a Web-enabled application. Any type of noninvasive approach to legacy application integration is limited in terms of the flexibility an architect can provide to a business user. Legacy architectures typically restrict the level of cross-functional integration needed to support an e-business transaction due to interdepartmental redundancies and inconsistencies.

ERP integration may seem like an unnecessary task because it involves integrating packaged application software that an enterprise probably spent millions of dollars to acquire and deploy. In spite of the money spent on these systems, ERP applications are difficult to integrate with legacy applications, front-end applications, and other ERP systems. The need to deliver integrated views of ERP data and functionality is a result of pressure being placed on IT because of the time and cost spent on ERP systems that cannot communicate with other systems or with the Internet.

ERP integration is likely to be one area of noninvasive integration that has a degree of permanence. This is because an ERP user requiring access to other applications and to the Web is locked into using third-party integration tools to get non-ERP applications to communicate. Eventually, ERP vendors will supply direct Web interfaces, so planning teams will want to document any ERP-specific middleware deployed in the meantime so it can be deactivated when replacement technology arrives.

9.7.2 Data Architecture Integration

Legacy data is required by many newer, Web-enabled applications. Noninvasive data integration approaches involve accessing enterprise data from Web-based or distributed applications, synchronizing data usage across multiple databases, and building data warehouse solutions. Planning teams undertaking data integration projects should examine which applications require certain data, how often that data needs to be accessed, whether that data needs to be current, and the level of redundancy and fragmentation of the data involved.

Accessing legacy data directly from a Web-based application may involve transforming legacy data in real time and can be accomplished using the message queuing middleware discussed earlier. API technology facilitates this type of integration and typically involves a front-end application triggering an SQL call to a relational database. Messages can also be sent directly from a Web-based front end and, depending on the middleware, formatted appropriately for user presentation.

If an application requires data from a nonrelational data structure, which is common in a legacy environment, certain data integration products support the translation from nonrelational to relational data on a selective basis. These products are typically used to extract and convert data in an as-is format and do not always deliver ideal results unless some redesign work has been performed.

Database synchronization can occur in real time or offline. Real-time integration involves custom or rules-based integration of multiple data structures based on a front-end application inquiry. Offline integration would utilize a data warehouse solution. In either case data synchronization involves organizing data by topic, retrieving and integrating that data from multiple data sources, and presenting it in a common format to Web-based business users.

Real-time solutions consolidate data on the fly. For example, if two inventory systems maintain data on the total availability of a given product, item availability data from two disparate inventory systems would need to be accessed, added together in real time, and presented as the total available on-hand inventory. This is a useful approach to quickly ascertaining related yet segregated information across multiple data structures.

A data warehouse, which is discussed in more depth in Chapter 10, consolidates data offline. This approach is more conducive to capturing a greater cross section of data from a more diverse set of data sources. Real-time consolidation is best applied to simple data capture and consolidation, while a data warehouse facilitates more voluminous and diverse data capture and consolidation. While neither approach impacts legacy applications or enterprise data structures, real-time data integration is preferable over a data warehouse if it meets performance requirements.

If an organization is not ready to invest in large-scale invasive legacy data redesign and/or consolidation, noninvasive data integration that enables Web-based access of enterprise data should be considered as a viable alternative.

9.7.3 B2Bi

B2Bi scenarios can vary widely and are driven by the need to exchange information fluidly with business partners. This includes EDI- and XML-based interchange, trading partner collaboration, information portal strategies, and Web Services options. Because Web Services tends to impact underlying legacy architectures, it will be discussed in later chapters.

EDI provides customized data interchange with suppliers and distributors, while XML offers a more industry-standard open exchange of data with those same trading partners. EDI links are entrenched in most organizations, while XML is just beginning to make inroads. For any point-to-point interfaces with a third party, organizations should focus on XML and gradually phase out EDI interfaces. One thing that has become increasingly clear is that supply chains dictated by a few large organizations are pushing for more standard solutions for exchanging data with partners.

Trading partner collaboration utilizes hub-and-spoke-oriented and point-to-point solutions that are typically managed by trading partner consortiums. This type of technology is beginning to open up enterprise data and transactions to third parties via information portals. These portals create a situation in which external users have access to internal data and application functionality.

Consider, for example, an HR management firm that provides human resource services to third parties who need to link directly into their systems to check on 401K, pension, benefit, or related plans. In the past, the HR firm provided this information in the form of reports or over the phone through online mainframe look-ups. Customers, however, requested an information portal so they could check on their account status in real time.

This approach combines an information portal with middleware connecting the Web front end to the back-end mainframe application. This is a B2Bi solution coupled with an EAI solution to provide noninvasive integration to customers. This solution, however, may be short-lived if it cannot scale up or if the back-end architecture is limited in being able to deliver required account information in real time.

B2Bi options, like EAI options, should to be viewed as near-term solutions that will ultimately require redesign of legacy back-end applications. These requirements should be incorporated into an overall transformation strategy.

9.7.4 BPI

BPI provides an integration solution option on the one hand while exposing the need to transform underlying legacy architectures on the other hand. BPI, as discussed in prior chapters, provides the business user with the most effective point of integration—the point where a process-related decision or activity is triggered by the user. In spite of the benefits offered by the BPI approach, legacy architectures can still stifle the impact of the results.

Consider a scenario where three applications perform overlapping customer management functions for a single business unit. This business unit has had a difficult time training new users due to the complexity of manually reconciling functions across three overlapping systems. BPI could be used to create common interfaces for the universe of functions performed by that business unit.

These process-driven front ends would flow from process to process, each notifying a user to approve or perform some subsequent step in the process. Various process-driven menus could then trigger transactions against the three back-end applications. The overall environment would be easier to learn and to use, but it would still rely on a poorly integrated set of applications with conflicting data formats and functional definitions.

This solution provides two important deliverables. First, business users have streamlined their overall work environment without incurring significant application retooling costs. Second, the new process-driven environment has established a defined set of legacy transformation requirements for the eventual retooling of back-end applications. Subsequent application redesign and retooling would need to be independently cost justified. The role of process integration along with other noninvasive integration options within the context of various legacy transformation strategies is discussed in the following sections.

9.8 The Role of Legacy Assessments in Noninvasive Integration Initiatives

As with any project utilizing or impacting legacy information architectures, noninvasive integration projects should leverage enterprise- and project-level assessment results. Legacy architecture assessments provide crucial documentation on application functionality and data usage. EAI, B2Bi, and BPI projects all need to understand where and how to access application functionality and enterprise data during the course of a given project.

For example, assume that an EAI project requires a Web-based customer information application to invoke back-end customer tracking functions across redundant legacy applications. Identifying redundantly defined customer functions, linking each of those functions to a specific user interface, and determining the formats of redundant, inconsistently defined data are all standard tasks within a project-level assessment.

Legacy transaction interface development relies on identification of the user interfaces that trigger those transactions. Presentation layer analysis documents user interfaces and links those interfaces to the source programs that process them. The functional assessment ensures that all programs and user interfaces required in the creation of a given EAI implementation are included in the project.

As discussed in Chapter 8, the project-level assessment captures the above information, stores it along with related legacy metadata in the detailed legacy transformation repository, and makes it available to integration project teams. Data integration tasks can leverage legacy architecture metadata as well.

For example, assume that a data integration project needs to capture and consolidate customer billing and address information from three disparate customer databases. Analysts will need to create an integration environment in which the customer data is captured, formatted, consolidated, and presented to the business user in a standardized format. Data usage and data architecture assessment tasks identify data redundancies, relationships, and logical structure across a functional cross-section of the enterprise. This is an instance where the enterprise assessment provides the requisite information needed to cross-reference and capture data for an integration project.

Enterprise assessments also form the foundation for B2Bi and BPI projects. B2Bi relies on the identification of external data interfaces, suppliers, and distributors across business units and application areas. B2Bi project teams can access this information once it has been captured within the enterprise repository. As new B2Bi interfaces and relationships are established within the context of a given project, they should be updated within the enterprise or project-level repository as appropriate.

BPI projects rely on the identification of business processes and their relationship with business units and user interfaces. The enterprise functional assessment documents high-level processes and process flows across functional areas and third parties. Understanding these relationships is an essential component of a BPI project. As new BPI interfaces are established, project and transformation support teams should ensure that they are reflected in the appropriate repository.

Transformation assessments establish the foundation for various noninvasive integration efforts. The information gathered during these assessment projects and recorded in the enterprise and/or detailed repository ensure that implementation teams have an accurate understanding of the legacy environment. In the absence of this information, integration deployment efforts would need to gather this information using haphazard or piecemeal approaches. As a result, the metadata captured by these teams would be poorly integrated from an enterprise perspective and not reflect cross-functional redundancies and relationships essential to the success of these projects.

Integration projects, whether performed at the enterprise, individual business unit, or application level, can also trigger a project-level or even an enterprise-wide assessment if one has not yet been performed. In other words, if transformation planning teams have had difficulty justifying or launching an assessment initiative, one or more integration projects can serve as the justification for these assessments.

If, on the other hand, enterprise or project-level assessments have already been performed, integration projects can leverage legacy architecture and target architecture mapping results as required. Integration planning teams should ensure that they update or coordinate repository updates with architecture teams and application areas. It is essential that new relationships, interfaces, middleware, and related integration project deliverables are incorporated into these repositories.

Unfettered deployment of poorly documented middleware and related integration interfaces will create a legacy environment that will be difficult or impossible to decipher as legacy architectures evolve. If there is one lesson taken from this chapter, it is that integration projects must be closely coordinated with architecture transformation efforts. This will ensure that integration solutions leverage and are reflected in ongoing legacy documentation, management, and transformation initiatives.

9.9 A Multidimensional Integration and Transformation Strategy

Noninvasive integration, whether addressing EAI, B2Bi, or BPI, should be planned and delivered within the context of a broader transformation and integration strategy. EAI, B2Bi, and BPI as discussed previously all become more effective tools for delivering business value when the are combined with legacy assessment, planning, and transformation deployment tasks under business-driven scenarios.

Because virtually every aspect of the modern information enterprise is a monument to an era when data and functional segregation was the norm, a wide variety of cross-functional and external factors must be incorporated into an overall transformation strategy. Organizations attempting to meet this challenge should embrace a multidimensional integration strategy that examines and addresses the root cause of highly fragmented business and IT environments.

Such a strategy looks beyond the symptoms of poor integration and tackles the challenge of integrating infrastructures, processes, and systems under a common strategy. This requires taking a holistic look at the organizational structures, processes, data, applications, and external relationships that are the cause and the effect of poor integration. Figure 9.3 identifies how integration challenges form at the organizational level, drive into the applications and data structures within an enterprise, and are then intertwined with interim integration solutions. Interim integration solutions, in the form of middleware and related short-term options, can become part of the problem if not managed effectively.

Over the long term, tackling these issues in piecemeal fashion or purely from a front-end perspective will encumber efforts to deliver the fundamental value that business users demand. For example, creating an e-commerce Web site that can access back-end order processing, procurement, and inventory systems through message queuing or related technologies provides only the first level of an integration solution. While delivering near-term value by providing users with the illusion of integration, this approach ignores fragmented business structures and related processes, data structures, and applications.

Multiple Dimensions of Integration Challenge

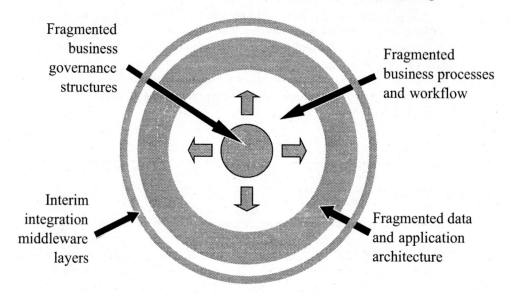

Figure 9.3

Integration solutions must assess fragmentation impacts between business units and IT while considering the impact of interim integration layers.

Even more problematic is that first-generation integration projects tend to ignore the need to address the line of business compartmentalization that gave rise to this fragmentation and redundancy in the first place. In order for companies to move beyond the first-generation integration mindset, integration planning must be undertaken at the most senior levels of the enterprise. This will ensure that internal and external business units and processes, including those performed by suppliers, outsourcing vendors, and business partners, are aligned and integrated to conform to strategic requirements.

Fortunately, the enterprise assessment delivers real value for executives and senior planning teams attempting to quantify the degree of redundancy and fragmentation across the enterprise and within supply and distribution chains. Redundantly defined functions can be quickly mapped back to unique or redundant applications, processes, business units, and third parties. Figure 9.4 shows how requirements are captured from and circulated back into the enterprise transformation repository.

For example, if analysts reviewing the repository find that a billing application links back to a redundant billing function and business unit, they will be able to determine that the integration problem is systemic and not just an IT issue. Addressing systemic business issues requires a strategy that concurrently reconciles,

Aligning Interim and Strategic Integration Options

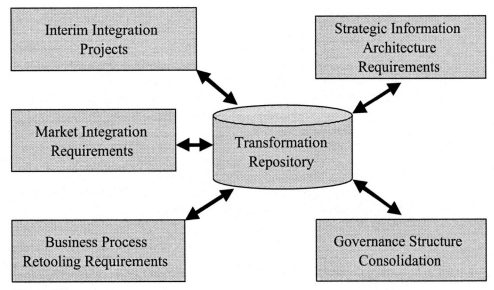

Figure 9.4
Multi-dimensional integration requires managing business unit, IT, and external integration within the transformation repository.

integrates, and/or consolidates redundant data, applications, business processes, and business units. Such a strategy should consider the following tasks.

- **Consider the business impact of integration.** Is the enterprise better served by consolidating business units over the long term and concurrently consolidating of the applications and data supporting those business units? This question must be answered at some point because the real cost savings for most integration projects can be found within the business units where redundant, fragmented information architectures originated. Business unit consolidation plans, in turn, have an impact on information-related options and decisions. Time spent creating interim EAI solutions may be better spent, for example, by focusing on a BPI approach.

- **Integrate business processes as a design strategy.** Business process definitions can be consolidated without eliminating redundant or fragmented business units. Creating a common set of business-driven front ends that automate manual processes while triggering back-end applications can serve as an excellent interim step to business unit consolidation as well as application architecture redesign. The work done to integrate common business practices, for example, would reconcile discrepancies or inconsistencies within those business units that could be incorporated into a common application architecture. BPI, therefore, offers immediate benefits by streamlining and standardizing processes across business units while providing excellent insights into design requirements for consolidating business units, applications, and data structures.

- **Examine and deploy EAI options over the near term.** EAI options, whether integrating enterprise data or back-end applications, can be a powerful way to rapidly integrate common functions across disparate legacy environments. In the billing example, application front ends can be established to trigger transactions unique to one or more redundant, back-end billing applications. Depending on the user and/or business unit, a rules-driven front-end could trigger a transaction to occur in a given back-end billing application. The data and the underlying legacy architecture in this case would remain untouched, but business users would have a common front end to access back-end systems functionality.

- **Determine strategic architecture redesign and consolidation requirements.** Based on business unit plans, consolidated business processes, and front-end application design, analysts could undertake the redesign of a consolidated billing architecture. Figure 9.5 depicts a scenario where the legacy infrastructure forms the basis for assessing existing business processes and functionality. This infrastructure is used to extract and consolidate business processes, which are then driven back down into the new design.

  This approach is based on a scenario where streamlined business processes are input to redesign requirements for a retooled application and data architecture. Creating this new design requires IT analysts to review and map revised business processes to a consolidated view of the application. Legacy business rules can then be captured, consolidated, and redeployed under a common billing architecture. The platform, language, and/or design paradigm could be left intact or utilize emerging technologies and component-based architectures.

- **Synchronize business and IT short-term and long-term integration options.** Management should synchronize each of the above project options under a common plan. Retooled business processes and integrated front-end interfaces serve as interim steps and become building blocks for longer-term integration options across the underlying information architecture. A phased approach with interim deliverables in this case provides integrated business processes across business units, Web-based front ends to multiple back-end billing applications, a common billing application and data design, and a common billing application that encompasses other customer management functions based on the new design.

  In addition to this, the enterprise could collapse redundant billing business units, teams, and locations into a single, virtual operation. The savings associated with eliminating redundant roles and responsibilities, consolidating

Legacy Reuse Should Be Built into Design and Specification Process

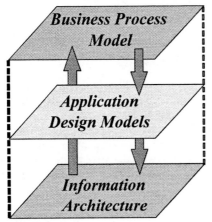

Business models represent as-is   and reengineered business processes

Design models depict business processes to be automated

Legacy systems: Input to redesign process and source of reusable data and business rules

Figure 9.5
Mapping legacy architecture to requirements and reusing legacy components in the new design and implementation increases the integrity of the resulting application.

customer contact points and invoices, eliminating redundant, inconsistent, and fragmented data, and streamlining the flow of business processing could be significant. In addition to the cost savings, such a consolidation of data and business functionality could position an organization to more effectively enter global markets and new lines of business.

Multidimensional integration, as discussed in the above example, is a significant undertaking and cuts directly to the cause and effect of the integration challenge. Attempting to address integration at the point that a user interfaces with an application addresses only the symptoms of the problem and ignores the underlying root cause. The main reason that integration has been addressed almost exclusively at such a tactical level, through the use of EAI and related tools, is that senior management has not been involved in crafting integration-related solutions.

IT analysts attempt to correct systemic integration problems the best way they know how—by throwing more technology at the problem. It is almost a given that senior executives are not involved in these discussions. Yet these same executives cannot figure out why their organization is losing customers, unable to streamline supply chain management, taking days to process an order, unable to keep accurate inventory information, or failing to meet other strategic business requirements.

To rectify this situation, executive planning teams must step to the forefront of the integration challenge and participate in crafting a multidimensional strategy to address this challenge. There is no such thing as piecemeal integration—yet that is the approach that many integration projects have pursued to date. It is not that they are doing anything wrong; it is just that the work being done to build EAI and other interfaces to legacy architectures will not ultimately solve the problem it is supposed to fix.

Phased integration, as outlined in the earlier example, will result in the delivery of interim value to the business community by leveraging the best aspects of BPI, EAI, and B2Bi over the near term while leveraging interim deliverables within an architecture transformation initiative. The upside of this strategy is that interim ROI justifies each subsequent step in the project. The downside of this approach is that executives may declare victory after having achieved a superficial level of integration—thinking the problem was solved when it was not.

Building and deploying a phased, multidimensional integration strategy will take time. A multidimensional strategy must be clarified at the onset of the project so executives can buy into a longer-term strategy. The executive team must then sustain the initiative as long as each subsequent phase can be justified. Delays in getting started will result in losses in revenue, productivity, market share, and new product and service opportunities in the decades ahead.

9.10 Documenting, Managing, and Uncoupling Integration Implementations

As middleware, connector technology, and customized adapter software proliferates, it will become part of the legacy information architecture. Over time, this will create a legacy middleware environment that will turn into a maintenance problem in the best of situations and result in indecipherable production problems in a worst-case scenario. Integration solutions must therefore be documented so that they can be debugged, maintained, and uncoupled over the long term.

Documenting integration solutions involves adding an interface object to the transformation repository along with a description of the middleware or related software. The middleware object should also identify the name of the product and custom software so that it can be identified quickly for planning and research purposes. The same type of documentation is required for any data or external third-party interfaces.

Establishing these repository objects, descriptions, and appropriate pointers will allow anyone applying changes to the underlying application or data architecture with a roadmap or warning sign that a middleware, adapter, or connector needs to be updated or deactivated depending on the changes involved.

Management should also be able to request a summary of all middleware interfaces by application, data structure, business unit, third party, or other aspect within the transformation repository. This information may be rolled up from the detailed repository to the enterprise repository for summary-level purposes.

Another benefit of establishing repository documentation of integration solutions is that a given connector can be deactivated or uncoupled quickly. Consider that changes to the underlying application or data architecture may force application teams to uncouple a middleware link. Uncoupling noninvasive integration solutions is one requirement that many integration teams are unlikely to have included in their plans.

Integration interfaces will need to be deactivated, however, in situations where more intelligent middleware is developed or where legacy transformation solutions obsolete a given integration solution. IT must be prepared to quickly find, fix, replace, or uncouple middleware and related integration software, or these interfaces will ultimately cause more problems for the enterprise than they solved.

Notes

1. "Architectural Choices for OSS Integration," Arald Jean-Charles and Suhas D. Joshi, *EAI Journal*, Sept. 2001.
2. *Enterprise Application Integration*, David Linthicum, Addison-Wesley, 2000.
3. "Adapting to Total Integration," Cheryl Traverse, *EAI Journal*, Sept. 2001.
4. "Next Generation EAI: Eight Prophecies for 2001," David S. Linthicum, *ebizq.net*, Feb. 21, 2001.

Structuring, Rationalizing, and Upgrading Legacy Applications and Data Structures

To meet ongoing business demands, organizations must maintain, enhance, or otherwise modify their installed base of legacy applications on an ongoing basis. The ability to upgrade these applications in a timely and reliable manner directly impacts an enterprise's ability to meet time-critical business requirements. Unfortunately, legacy software tends to be difficult to understand and modify with any degree of reliability or predictability. To address this limitation, maintenance, enhancement, and migration projects, whether performed inhouse or by outsourcing teams, should rationalize, structure upgrade, or otherwise stabilize legacy applications in conjunction with business-driven initiatives.

Legacy data structures, which tend to have integrity and redundancy problems, are also difficult to decipher and enhance in a timely fashion. Legacy data is rife with invalid values, redundant definitions, and conflicting semantics. Addressing these issues, along with legacy application integrity problems, should be a high priority for any management team relying on these systems to support ongoing and strategic business requirements.

Application improvement tasks provide strategic value to an enterprise. Business rule and data definition capture and reuse are significantly more difficult when inconsistent data and poorly written source code form the basis for those efforts. If planning teams intend to leverage legacy applications and data in redesign and redevelopment initiatives, rationalizing and stabilizing those systems and data structures will streamline these efforts. Improvements applied as a result of the techniques outlined in this chapter will deliver major benefits to ongoing maintenance, migration, and upgrade projects as well as to strategic redevelopment initiatives.

This chapter discusses approaches for structuring, slicing, and modularizing application source code as well as rationalizing and standardizing the data definitions defined across those applications. I have also included approaches for mining and improving the integrity of physical data structures to improve the reliability of the applications and business units relying on that data. Collectively, this chapter outlines ways to upgrade applications and related data as a way of streamlining the time and improving the reliability associated with changing, testing, and using those application environments.

10.1 Incorporating Upgrade Options into Business-Driven Projects

The tasks and techniques discussed in this chapter meet the criteria of "reengineering in place" because they do not transform the underlying application or data design paradigm. In other words, these tasks do not impose a logical redesign on legacy application environments or related architectures.

Logical application and data architecture redesign tasks are discussed in Chapter 11. The tasks discussed in this chapter have been segregated from logical redesign techniques because they can streamline the delivery of various business-driven projects without forcing the redesign of the underlying information architecture. Stabilization and rationalization tasks also position application and data structures for subsequent redesign and transformation, and can be incorporated as steps within more comprehensive initiatives.

Many of these tasks can be combined with architecture redesign techniques to increase the value of core applications to business users. For example, database redesign and redeployment may necessitate the retooling of the application architecture. Modularization tasks discussed in this chapter can be used to retool application source code that has been impacted by a logical data redesign and migration. Scenarios that synchronize application and data stabilization, architecture transformation, and business-driven scenarios are discussed in Chapter 12.

Planning teams should assess the return on investment for any application or data stabilization tasks based on the value those improvements deliver over the short term. Additional value provided to project teams who need to extract and reuse legacy data definitions or business rules, or both, should be included in the cost benefit analysis as well. I will provide a context for building various stabilization tasks into project scenarios for each of the sections contained within this chapter.

Structuring, rationalizing, and upgrading application and data structures enhance the understandability, maintainability, business responsiveness, and testability of critical information assets. Various stabilization scenarios may be driven by

- The need to make applications more understandable as the first stage of an outsourcing agreement.
- A need to increase maintenance productivity and reliability for new or less experienced programmers.
- Cross-functional data upgrades such as HIPAA or similar initiatives.
- Plans to capture and redesign data definitions for an architecture transformation project.
- Data consolidation requirements as part of an architecture consolidation or related requirement.
- Preparatory efforts to capture and redesign business logic within an application environment.
- Rehosting and redeployment project requirements.
- Any project requiring stabile, reliable application environments and/or data structures.

One concept that certain application stabilization tasks utilize as a risk reduction factor is the interim reintroduction of upgraded source code and data structures back into production over a multistep delivery window. This is a risk-adverse approach that focuses on delivering interim versions of a system or upgraded data structure to reduce the overall potential for problems commonly found in long-term, large-scale enhancements. To facilitate this approach, project teams need to ensure that version control, change management, and validation testing are coordinated effectively.

10.2 Application Staging, Quality Reviews, and Validation Testing

Certain tasks are common across the various transformation concepts outlined in this chapter and include application staging, quality reviews, and validation testing. Staging application source code, executable environments, and data structures are essential to the successful delivery of phased application and data upgrade projects. These concepts evolved from the need to have a baseline against which project teams can validate the results of their modifications and increase the reliability and integrity of their deliverables. The objectives behind application staging include

- Managing change control and source code "freeze time" within the context of a multiphased project. Applications are highly volatile, and the ongoing changes being applied to those applications must be coordinated through the use of a phased delivery cycle.
- Facilitating the phased testing and delivery of multiphased transformation projects. Interim quality reviews and validation testing, for example, require the use of staging libraries.

- Segregating structural upgrades to an application and related data from functional changes to that same application and data. Testing structural and functional changes can be accomplished more quickly when performed as separate steps.

Validation testing and quality reviews rely on the ability to freeze and control changes to application source code. Oddly, many application teams believe that applying all planned changes to an application in one pass is more time- and cost-effective than phasing in changes over a period of time. This is rarely the case, however. Transformation teams should therefore alternatively pursue a strategy that divides the work into verifiable and readily managed segments.

Consider an HIPAA project, for example, that requires a new data element to be added to multiple data structures and source code data definitions across an enterprise. If the project team rationalizes source code data definitions as a first step of the project, they could reduce the collective number of changes being applied to those data definitions. In such a project, the data structures targeted for the HIPAA upgrade could be rationalized from many hardcoded data definitions into manageable subset definitions. Analysts could then apply changes or add new data elements in a handful of places instead of in thousands of hardcoded definitions.

This scenario is most effectively accomplished by validating the rationalized code against the original application baseline, applying the HIPAA changes to the rationalized applications, and then retesting isolated functional upgrades. Project teams should review the appropriateness of this approach on a case-by-case basis. The interim, rationalized version of the application could be returned to a production status if the freeze time for that application is limited. The application staging process supporting this approach includes

- **Gaining concurrence from application and project teams on the timing and approach of the staging process.** If, for example, an application is highly volatile due to ongoing business activity, the project team may want to reduce the time that a system is frozen from production changes.
- **Identifying all system components to be included in the stabilization or rationalization effort.** This includes all programs, data structures, user interfaces, job control language structures, and related application components.
- **Establishing staging libraries for all application components involved in the project.** This minimally includes a working copy of the production system to be used for baseline testing and a second version that the project team will upgrade based on project requirements. Additional versions of the application can be established if the project team wishes to segregate manual changes from changes performed by an automated software product.
- **Applying comparison tools to highlight stabilization and rationalization upgrades for quality review purposes.** Source code comparison tools highlight differences between various versions of programs, data structures, and

object modules. This type of tool is typically included with various development workbenches or source code management environments. Quality reviews increase the reliability of the resulting application changes and ensure they meet the objectives they set out to accomplish. Such a review should focus on the differences between the baseline version of an application or data structure and the modified version of that same application or data structure.

- **Reconciling staging libraries with ongoing maintenance activities.** Because most applications must be changed on a regular basis, it may be necessary for transformation project teams to reconcile changes back into the baseline or modified source code. This is fairly simple as long as the original production copy of the application can be compared to the code modified during the maintenance upgrade using an automated comparison tool. Once these changes have been isolated, they can be reapplied to the code that has been structured, rationalized, or otherwise modified.

Comparison tools create an audit trail that analysts can use to avoid the endless confusion resulting from functional anomalies that cannot be traced back to their source. Segregating functional changes from structural upgrades facilitates rapid identification of problems resulting from a given set of changes through the quality review and validation cycle.

The purpose of validation testing is to ensure that source code and data structure upgrades did not introduce unintended functional changes or errors into the application environment. The general validation process, shown in Figure 10.1, includes

- Running the identical data through the original version of the application and the upgraded version of the application. If the data structures have been expanded, automated comparison tools can ignore the new fields within the expanded data structure.

- Verifying that no functional changes were inadvertently introduced during the upgrade process. In other words, change-control procedures must ensure that structural changes are applied independently from functional enhancements.

- Assessing, resolving, and determining the validity of any differences introduced during the project. In some cases, a new field may be introduced to the source code data definitions, data language definitions, user interfaces, and data structures being tested. These types of changes can be readily identified using automated comparison tools.

- Ensuring that intended functional changes were applied correctly. Output discrepancies found within the test comparison depicted in Figure 10.1 should be confirmed as being within the scope of the project plan.

- Checking that the upgraded application executes within some defined set of acceptable performance parameters. An application should not be noticeably slower after structural or functional upgrades and the validation process can verify this. Application performance has been a critical stumbling block for many redesigned applications. Performance testing therefore ensures that inefficiencies are identified prior to interim upgrades being deployed.

Applying application staging, quality review, and validation testing processes within the context of a multiphased project verifies the integrity of each interim deliverable. In the previous HIPAA example, the project plan would decompose into the following steps.

- Create staging libraries for the project, including one original library and one library where changes will be applied.
- Perform a data definition analysis to identify related record groups based on the data being modified. The process for performing this analysis was discussed in Chapter 8.
- Rationalize relevant data structures within the source code.
- Perform a quality review to ensure that the changes were applied properly. Source code changes should be highlighted and reviewed using an automated comparison tool. Original and upgraded object modules should be

Validation Testing Process

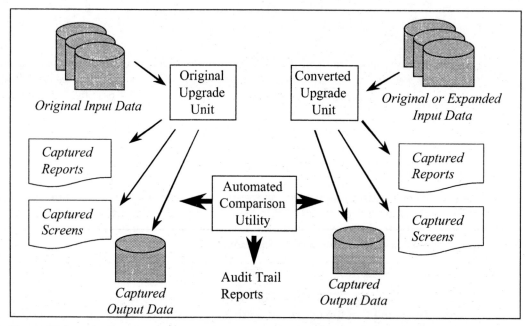

Figure 10.1
Validation testing attempts to automate as much of the process as possible.

the same as long as no new data elements were added to existing record structures and record lengths remained unchanged. Note that date and time stamps may differ.

- Run a validation test against the rationalized source code and the original production copy of that source code.
- Optionally return the rationalized source code to production and, if necessary, reapply any maintenance changes made during the period that the source code had been frozen. Comparison tools also support the code synchronization process.
- Refresh the production version of the application with the rationalized version of that same application source code.
- Apply HIPAA or other project-specific changes to the Copy (reusable record definitions) records, segments and/or tables and then recompile the affected source programs.
- Run the comparison test against the refreshed original and HIPAA-enhanced source code. Then perform a quality review of the upgraded application. The source code comparison should show that the affected record layouts now contain a new identification number.
- Use a file update utility or custom program to redefine and repopulate all physical data structures using the new record definitions. A data manipulation utility can also plug in default values into the new data structure.
- Validate the results of these changes by comparing the original application against the upgraded application. With the exception of new or expanded field definitions, output data structures, reports, and user interfaces should be identical.

Variations on this application staging, quality assurance, and validation approach should be applied to language change, rehosting, structuring, rationalization, modularization, and data structure upgrade projects as discussed in the following sections.

10.3 Language-Level Upgrade or Conversion and Application Rehosting

A language conversion translates one language to another language, while a language-level upgrade moves an application from an older version of a language to a modern or more standardized version of that same language. In both cases, the goal is to improve the portability and understandability of an application and position that application for subsequent transformation. Application rehosting, which has similar goals, moves an application from an undesirable hardware platform to a standardized platform. Rehosting typically requires a language-level upgrade as well as data and environmental migration.

Examples of a language change include Assembler to COBOL and PL/I to C. A language-level upgrade, for example, would involve moving Unisys 2200 COBOL to a distributed version of COBOL. A language change or upgrade does not include moving a procedural language to an object-oriented language, such as Java, because this requires redesigning and reimplementing the application logic.

Language change and language-level upgrade deliverables include converted source code, an upgraded runtime environment, newly compiled executable modules, test results, and audit trail results from the conversion process. A compiler upgrade, for example, could involve moving from OS/VS COBOL to COBOL 370. A user interface upgrade, on the other hand, might involve migrating from macro-level CICS to command-level CICS.

Platform rehosting moves applications and data structures from one hardware platform to another hardware platform, while minimizing changes to the application design. Rehosting typically involves a language upgrade and can serve as an intermediate step within the context of a more comprehensive transformation redesign project.

In addition to a language upgrade, rehosting requires migrating execution languages, user interface definitions, and data structure definitions. Execution language upgrades might, for example, include moving from a Unisys WFL interface to a GUI interface in a distributed environment under X-Windows. Data access-level upgrades, which require little or no redesign work, might include moving from IBM mainframe VSAM to a distributed version of VSAM.

Because conversions, upgrades, and rehosting projects tend to be one-time events, experts should be employed to plan and deliver conversion, upgrade, and rehosting projects and to identify project resources and tools. A language change or upgrade tool provides automated assistance to revise source code to comply with new language requirements. Converting source programs and related application components should not result in a change to the application's functionality. Analysts may, however, add additional functions to the converted or rehosted application after validation testing has been completed. The following steps are commonly employed within a language change or language upgrade project.

- **Migrate runtime environment.** The runtime environment provides the ancillary operating programs that allow an application, written in a given language, to execute properly. Moving from one language level to another or from one language to another may require upgrading runtime modules. Hardware or operating system vendors typically provide the runtime environment, which would then be implemented by the systems programming team with input from the project team.

- **Prepare source code for conversion.** Many conversion tools utilize an analyzer, which can tell the project team if the code will require manual conversion tasks. For example, a preprocessor for an Assembler-to-COBOL conversion would include metrics and detailed reports identifying any nonstandard macros or other constructs that necessitate manual conversion. The team uses this information to identify, eliminate, and/or convert constructs in the input or output version of the source code being converted.

- **Convert or upgrade program source code.** A conversion tool is a virtual necessity when moving from one language to a totally different language. Language-level upgrades, however, are less dependent on such a tool because there is less work involved in moving, for example, from one version of COBOL to another. If a conversion tool is available, the project team should run the source code through that tool and load the converted source code into the appropriate staging library, as discussed earlier. Language upgrade teams without access to a conversion tool can alternatively run the code through the new compiler and correct constructs that do not compile properly. In either case, the team will need to recompile the final version of the source code and correct any errors they find.

In addition to the above language migration tasks, platform rehosting projects require that the project team perform the following tasks. These tasks are typically performed on the target hardware platform because that is where the compiler and test environment resides.

- **Convert user interfaces.** The user interface, typically called a teleprocessing monitor on older mainframe systems, is the most visable aspect of a platform migration. The migration project team should employ a user interface migration tool if available. This process involves running the conversion tool against the user interface source code targeted for conversion. Some tools read the user interface definition, such as a CICS BMS map module, and convert the user view to a GUI or HTML interface. More generalized tools take screen snapshots and convert whatever they capture to the new interface. The project team should review the output and further customize the resulting interface as required.

  For example, some tools consolidate multiple character-based screens into a single GUI or HTML user interface. This may not deliver the look and feel the team desires. Modification should be minimized and only incorporate the same information that was being delivered to the user in the original system. This will reduce the time it takes to validate the results. Once the application has been rehosted and is up and running, the project team can apply additional functional or design-level enhancements. This is another example of breaking the project into interim deliverables that provide the user with short-term value while lowering project risks.

- **Migrate data structures.** Converting the data structures that are being moved to the new hardware platform involves developing conversion software that reads the old file formats and rewrites that data to a media that the new platform can interpret. The target file or database design should mimic the original data architecture as closely as possible because redesigning legacy data structures in the middle of a rehosting project would delay project delivery considerably.

Data migration may require backing up the existing data using resident utilities that can generate a sequential file format. Creating comparable data structures for the new hardware and software platform may require the use of restoration utilities native to the target software and hardware environment. Additional tasks include redefining data access routines embedded in or accessed by the source code. Planning teams must remember to convert both permanent and temporary file definitions as part of the project. The conversion team should identify and employ tools wherever possible.

- **Perform environmental migration.** The environment that executes the application, whether in batch or online, must be converted to run on the new platform. The main rule to follow is that the first version of the rehosted application should run in the same mode as the original application. In other words, batch programs in the old environment should run as background tasks in the new environment, and online programs in the old environment should run as online programs in the new environment. This avoids mixing redesign tasks with rehosting tasks, which would elongate the delivery of the rehosted application. Once the application has been moved into the new environment, validated, and returned to a production status, the project team can redesign it based on user requirements.

  Environmental migration steps involve identifying and converting batch job control language and online tables source objects, and determining how to mimic their functionality within the target environment. In many cases, this requires re-creating new execution capabilities that support batch execution, job scheduling, and/or online processes. The user interface migration may generate some of these execution capabilities as a byproduct of converting online screens. Additional steps include rewriting or incorporating runtime utilities, subroutines, or functions to support data conversion, I/O handling, access to system functions, or other features that no longer function in the new environment.

Once conversion and/or rehosting work is completed, project teams will need to compile and link all converted source components. This includes setting up all applicable user interface and execution modules as needed. The staging, quality review, and validation process outlined earlier in this chapter can be used with certain additional considerations. A rehosted application may use different utilities or function differently and, as a result, complicate a project team's ability to perform the output comparison shown in Figure 10.1. This approach, however, remains the most effective way of expediting efforts to move a rehosted application back into production as quickly as possible.

The final step involves documenting the converted and/or rehosted application within the transformation repository. This involves pointing to converted user interfaces, execution routines, programs, and data structures within the new environment. Many of these changes entail updates to transformation repository attributes.

The main point to remember when undertaking a language change/upgrade or platform migration is to convert only what is essential to get the application running in the target environment. Redesign or related transformation tasks should be applied to a validated production version of the newly converted or rehosted application. This approach delivers immediate value to the business community and reduces the risks associated with an all-or-nothing redevelopment approach.

10.4 Program Structuring and Design Improvement

Program structuring, also called restructuring, describes program-level improvements made to an application. Structuring a program does not change the architecture of the application. Rather, it takes poorly written or "unstructured" source code and transforms it into a source program that uses commonly accepted, easily understood programming techniques. Structuring can be subdivided into three distinct disciplines: the removal of program anomalies, the actual structuring of the source code, and program-level design improvement.

Candidate programs would have been highlighted in the project-level assessment discussed in Chapter 8. Structuring and design improvement candidates would typically meet several criteria. Programs that score poorly from a structural and complexity perspective, are modified frequently, and have particular value to the business community qualify as structuring candidates.

Benefits derived from program structuring and design improvement include reducing the learning curve for anyone unfamiliar with that source code, increasing the ability to apply changes more quickly and reliably, enhancing the maintenance team's ability to respond to user requests, and creating a reliable baseline for future transformation tasks. For example, structuring tools isolate and consolidate the I/O layer of a program. A subsequent modularization step could create a separate common set of I/O routines that are fully isolated from the business logic within the system.

Program structuring has been overlooked as a powerful tool for streamlining application maintenance tasks while creating a baseline application that is more malleable from a reuse and future transformation perspective. Structuring tools work primarily on COBOL and FORTRAN source programs, but structuring concepts could be applied manually to other procedural languages.

Anomaly removal involves identifying and fixing program-level flaws. Most of the code flaws addressed by this process are latent problems that have never been triggered because certain combinations of data have never been invoked. Migrating an application to a new environment, consolidating applications with overlapping systems, or reusing functional logic could trigger these latent flaws. If this occurs, it would result in a production failure and lost revenues.

Removing these flaws also prepares program source code for automated structuring. The reason for this is that a structuring tool traces all active logic paths and assumes they are all legitimate—even if they are not. Removal of recursion or runaway logic paths that could never occur in a production environment eliminates the need for a structuring tool to either plug or replicate a path that could never be taken. The end result is a source program that concisely represents the functionality of the application versus a program that has numerous "red herring" logic paths.

- **Anomaly/flaw analysis and removal.** Examples of high-risk program flaws include recursive logic, runaway paths, and a host of other potential issues. The problems vary based on the source code language and intent of the application. A programmer may plan some recursion, but this is rare and happens only in very specific programming paradigms. Runaway logic should, on the other hand, never be found in any production program. Identifying and removing these flaws typically require the use of a static analysis tool that can identify all program paths and, ideally, program flaws.

  Assuming there is a static analysis tool available, the team should run programs of interest through the tool. Many of these products provide a summary of findings—including program flaws. The most critical of these potential problems includes runaway logic paths, endless loops, recursion, and dead code.

  Dead code is program logic that can never be executed, regardless of the data values or logic paths triggered within a program. Analysts attempting to update or transform an application could mistake dead code for active business logic. Dead code can also trigger the errant capture and reuse of business logic that is never used in a real-life scenario. Static analysis tools highlight dead code. It should be removed if it is truly dead, or commented accordingly. Dynamic analysis tools can additionally determine that certain code is never executed because it is no longer applicable to the business.

  Runaway logic is relatively easy to correct. The runaway logic path example, shown in Figure 10.2, is data-dependent. In this example, the programmer forced a program to fail by dividing by zero, but this approach works only on certain hardware and software platforms. Rehosting source code containing runaway logic paths could cause an application to act unpredictably. A transformation analyst might assume that this logic was a valid business rule and reuse it in another program or design model, and this would cause that application to fail. Correcting the problem with the COBOL verb *Goback* ensures that the logic path does not continue beyond the end of the program.

  Endless loops force a program to run through the same logic over and over again. They are typically triggered by a specific data combination that would result in a production failure or cause an analyst to reuse business logic that

Runaway Logic—Program Anomaly

Runaway logic path due to forced Abend	Runaway logic path eliminated

MOVE X TO FIELD-3.
IF SEVERE-CONDITION-FOUND
    COMPUTE X = 1/0.   (*Causes Abend*)
MOVE Y TO FIELD-4.
	MOVE X TO FIELD-3.
	IF SEVERE-CONDITION-FOUND
	    COMPUTE X = 1/0
	        GOBACK. (*Terminates program*)
	MOVE Y TO FIELD-4.

Figure 10.2

Runaway logic can cause a program failure and result in the capture and reuse of errant business logic. (*Source: USRM/Comsys.*)

made no sense. Removing an endless loop requires determining why that data combination would trigger a problem and correcting the logic.

Recursion and active procedure exits are related anomalies. Most programming languages utilize a control transfer that returns control to the invoking routine when the routine hits a natural conclusion or program address. Sometimes a condition will trigger logic to transfer out of the routine prior to hitting the end of that routine. If the control logic flows back into the control verb that originally executed that routine, it becomes recursive. If it never returns, it is an active procedure exit. In either case, it is likely that a programming error is lying dormant within this code and waiting to be triggered by an unusual combination of data. These constructs can also act differently under different compiler levels or operating environments. Latent recursion and active procedure exits can also be triggered during normal maintenance or during a transformation project.

Correcting recursion involves identifying the data and related tests that trigger the recursive path. This is easily determined using a static analysis product. An analyst familiar with the code can review it and correct it, although most programmers could quickly ascertain how the recursion was triggered and remove it. Doing so creates a high-integrity baseline for any type of change planned for that application, including subsequent redesign and transformation project tasks.

There are certain constructs that are not technically programming anomalies but can complicate transformation projects. One construct, unique to COBOL, is the *Alter* verb. The *Alter* was a holdover from the early days of programming when other control transfer verbs took too much memory. The *Alter* simulates COBOL *Perform* logic as well as switches settings. There are a number of other hard to decipher constructs that are unique to certain machines or compilers. The *Exit Here* and *Unstack* commands, found in certain COBOL compilers, can complicate efforts to understand program functionality and rehost those programs to distributed platforms.

Identifying and removing these constructs, particularly if these programs are to be rehosted to a distributed platform, are important tasks that can be assisted with a static analysis tool. Program anomalies can cause application and business failures in daily operations, ongoing maintenance, rehosting, redesign, and business rule reuse projects. These constructs should be identified and, if the application is key to the business and changed with regularity, eliminated.

- **Source code structuring.** Restructuring imposes structured programming standards on source programs that did not originally conform to structured standards. Structuring upgrades the packaging and cosmetic aspects of a source program. Structuring tools parse the source program, map or graph all possible logic paths, and rewrite those logic paths using formal branch and return constructs. In COBOL, this construct is the *Perform* verb. Other languages use comparable constructs. The new program is functionally equivalent to the original program, but is easier for analysts and programmers to understand, more malleable to modification, more readily modularized, and a better candidate for rule extraction and componentization.

Management would want to structure applications being maintained by programmers who are unfamiliar with the application or who are targeted for outsourcing. An outsourcing firm would want to drive structuring efforts for the applications they plan to take over. Additional reasons for structuring applications include anticipated upgrade, consolidation, componentization, and related migration projects.

The structuring process produces cohesive, readable, and standardized source logic, imposes accepted structured standards on legacy applications, isolates and consolidates I/O logic, eliminates difficult to decipher constructs and language-specific verbs, and imposes a hierarchical structure on the program. Programs are also formatted and customized based on tool-specific parameters.

To accomplish this, project teams must choose an acceptable structuring tool (see Appendix A), correct program anomalies as discussed in the previous section, and determine how nonstandard constructs will be handled. For example, COBOL CICS programs utilize an unstructured construct called the *Handle* condition. While CICS status code checking is the accepted norm today, the *Handle* condition was the accepted approach for decades. Once structuring tools isolate the *Handle* condition, it can be removed manually.

Isolation and consolidation of CICS and other control and/or I/O logic is an excellent preparatory step for rehosting or migration projects. I/O isolation also facilitates separating data access layer and user interface layer logic from business logic for componentization or architecture migration projects. Certain preprocessors, IDMS, for example, may or may not be supported by a given structuring tool. This should be verified prior to running the application through a structuring product.

Once the preliminary review of the code has been completed, project teams should establish structuring parameters and run the application source code through the structuring tool. A review of the output code, which would be placed into a third staging library, should ensure that the results are acceptable to the project and maintenance team. Parameters, which control paragraph size, logic nesting, and other factors, may be adjusted so analysts can rerun the structuring tool to obtain the desired results.

Staging libraries for a structuring project include an original production copy, a version that has undergone manual changes as discussed above, and a version that has been run through the structuring tool. Analysts can run validation tests, as shown in Figure 10.1, against the original version of the code and the structured version of that same code. Any validation errors are almost always the result of faulty manual changes and should be identified and fixed accordingly.

- **Program design improvement.** Structuring tools cannot correct poor program design. Program-level design improvement addresses issues that were exposed by the structuring process. Correcting program-level design is a logical step toward improved maintainability, modularization, consolidation, and rule capture and reuse. Project teams should consider that correcting program-level design issues does not, however, correct system-level design issues. These will be discussed later.

Objectives include optimizing data usage, constructs, or control structures to help expose the functional intent of the program, streamlining the ability to enhance the application, and preparing the application for modularization. In some cases, these improvements can even positively impact application performance.

One simple step involves reviewing program size to determine if it is a candidate for code slicing. Unisys A Series applications, for example, tend to contain very large COBOL source programs. These large source programs would be inappropriate to redeploy in a distributed environment—although that is exactly what is being done by a number of organizations.

Slicing, discussed later in this chapter, is not the only way to shrink a program, however. Redundant paragraphs or logic, exposed by the structuring and standardization process, could be consolidated within the newly structured program. The same is true for large paragraphs, which could be reduced in size based on the functions they perform. Redundancy elimination is a phased process and facilitated through the use of business rule capture technology.

A related issue is code complexity, which can manifest itself in logical decision structures that ripple into the lower levels of the program. This concept shows up as logic "spikes" in hierarchy charts like the one in Chapter 7, Figure 7.2. "Cascading decision logic" is the underlying cause for spiking and forces a programmer to look through numerous paragraphs to decipher a business rule. Cascading decision logic also results in spreading a logical business rule across multiple paragraphs, which could be separated by thousands of lines of code. Collapsing this logic back into a single routine not only streamlines efforts to modify the legacy application, but also creates a much improved baseline for reusing that business logic in transformation projects.

Another common legacy construct is the use of switches that mask a business rule. An example of this is shown in Figure 10.3. A business rule in this case states that a processing type equal to "312" cannot be a "male." An error switch is then set and tested later in the code. If this is a one-time error test, analysts could retest the condition or conditions that caused the error to occur or eliminate the switch test entirely, since it is spurious. Error logic is considered a business rule if it changes the processing of a business function or impacts business data, and should not be taken lightly from a reusability perspective. The revised business logic on the right side of Figure 10.3 can be directly reused in a target architecture while the original logic could not.

One last design issue involves the use of hardcoded data that should be managed through a table or an external database. Common data tests that should be accessed through a table or database include day or date tests, which are normally calculated by common date subroutines, or business-specific data such as a location code or part number. This latter example involves data that was not volatile enough to have been loaded into a database by the system's designers but volatile enough to result in considerable maintenance expense or error rates when it needs to be updated. These hardcoded tests are business rules that a tool cannot recognize and redesign, but are still essential to the continued viability of the enterprise. Addressing data externalization from a system level is discussed further in Section 10.5 under program data externalization.

Switches Can Mask Business Logic

Example

Unwanted switch variable	Unwanted switch variable removed

IF PROC-TYPE = 312 AND SEX = 'M'
    MOVE 'G' TO ERR-SW
    MOVE MAST-HEADER TO ERR-HEADER
    MOVE PROC-TYPE TO ERR-REC
    MOVE SEX TO ERR-REC
ELSE
    MOVE PROC-TYPE TO MAST-PROC.
PERFORM PROCESS-REC.
PROCESS-REC.
    MOVE ...
    MOVE ...
    COMPUTE ...
    IF ERR-SW = 'G'
        PERFORM GENDER-ERR
        ELSE ...
GENDER-ERR.
    MOVE ...
    ADD 1 TO ERR-CT.
    WRITE ERR-REC.
	IF PROC-TYPE = 312 AND SEX = 'M'
	    (Switch usage and definition removed)
	    MOVE MAST-HEADER TO ERR-HEADER
	    MOVE PROC-TYPE TO ERR-REC
	    MOVE SEX TO ERR-REC
	ELSE
	    MOVE PROC-TYPE TO MAST-PROC.
	PERFORM PROCESS-REC.
	PROCESS-REC.
	    MOVE ...
	    MOVE ...
	    COMPUTE ...
	    IF PROC-TYPE = 312 AND SEX = 'M'
	        PERFORM GENDER-ERR
	        ELSE ...
	GENDER-ERR.
	    MOVE ...
	    ADD 1 TO ERR-CT.
	    WRITE ERR-REC.

Figure 10.3
Switches can mask business logic. This should be addressed in business-critical applications targeted for an upgrade or business rule reuse.
(*Source: USRM/Comsys.*)

Management may argue that correcting program anomalies, structural weaknesses, and design issues may not be justified from a near-term perspective. These issues are the very ones, however, that prevent application management teams from responding more quickly to business upgrade requests. More important, however, is the fact that program packaging and design issues must be addressed as part of strategic transformation projects. Business rule capture, consolidation, and reuse tools do not have the capacity to fully recognize and correct these issues on a real-time basis. Analysts must consider reviewing and correcting these design anomalies in preparation for strategic reuse projects, or those projects will fail to meet their ultimate objectives.

10.5 Data Definition Challenges and Options

Data definition stabilization and rationalization differ from program-level upgrades because data spans program, application, and enterprise boundaries. Identifying and correcting these issues must be considered from a systems perspective. Several data-related issues, introduced during the analysis discussion in

Chapter 8, can be addressed by applying certain structural upgrades to the existing data architecture.

The data assessment surfaces requirements for upgrading application data definitions. These include definitional redundancies, cryptic data names, related record definition inconsistencies, and misleading data usage across application areas. Planning teams can review specific business initiatives in light of data assessment findings to craft a multiphased plan to upgrade data definitions in accordance with those requirements.

A variety of projects can leverage application or cross-functional data upgrades. HIPAA, discussed in earlier chapters, requires the addition of certain identifiers across data structures. A second requirement stems from regulatory demands for U.S. financial services firms to upgrade their trading cycle window. These firms face a 2004 deadline to move to a trade-day-plus-one (T+1) cycle for processing trades. Estimates are that the industry will invest $8 billion in IT infrastructure, applications, training, development, and delivery services [1].

These are just two examples of major initiatives that rely on an accurate, rationalized understanding of cross-functional data definitions. A single data structure may be linked to dozens or even hundreds of record definitions across multiple applications. Many of these redundant data definitions define certain positions within a file in different ways. Legacy data files, for example, leave filler areas within a record for new data to be added to that file. One application team or a lone programmer may decide to use that filler for one purpose, while another application area uses it for a completely different purpose. The result is massive confusion that can only be rectified by rationalizing these data definitions across those applications. While this may trigger some reworking of that file structure, it can ultimately save an organization from experiencing costly production downtime or other major and highly visible problems.

One major obstacle to the redesign and reuse of legacy data structures is the redefinition of program data structures. There are multiple scenarios that contribute to legacy data complexity. One of the most challenging for transformation teams involves sequential master files that contain multiple record types. There are, for example, tape files that contain a dozen or more unique data formats depending on a single record type indicator. The first record may be a header record containing high-level data for a customer. The next record may contain order information, while subsequent records contain related information. This is an example of how legacy design teams mimicked database structures using sequential file formats.

Another issue involves homonyms, which are data definitions that have the same names but mean entirely different things. Homonyms cause major confusion in situations where analysts are trying to decipher, consolidate, capture, and reuse business rules. Business rule analysis tools have difficulty differentiating between data elements that appear to be the same but in reality refer to totally different business data.

Hardcoded business data, buried in legacy source program logic, can stifle efforts to respond to time-critical change requests. Plant codes, part numbers, customer authorization codes, and a host of other data are intertwined with business logic. This data should be externalized into user-modifiable data structures. Embedded data can stall enhancement efforts, introduce risks related to improper management of that data, and confuse business rule capture and reuse efforts.

One last data definition challenge involves field and record size limitations and inconsistencies. Early Y2K field expansion efforts were displaced by temporary bridging and century workaround options. So while management may believe that field and record size expansion is second nature to IT teams, most Y2K projects took shortcuts that avoided date field expansion. Future expansion efforts are more likely to involve entire record definitions that require new data elements, such as is the case with HIPAA or similar industry-driven efforts.

Data definition upgrade and stabilization tasks include data definition rationalization, homonym analysis and elimination, hardcoded data externalization, and field and record size expansion.

- **Data definition rationalization.** Data definition rationalization, which is the consolidation and redeployment of application data definitions, is most effectively applied at the front end of projects relying on consistent, succinct representations of application data. The goal is to reduce the number of physical record groups and data names in a system to a minimal subset to achieve a one-to-one correlation between physical data and application definitions.

  Record grouping analysis should use an environmental analyzer to relate physical data definitions back to source code, user interface, data definition language, and Copy (Include, etc.) definitions. This analysis is typically performed during data definition analysis, discussed in Chapter 8, and can begin with either the physical data, Copy member, or program-level record definitions. In other words, analysts can trace a physical data structure of interest to find program data definitions or use a Copy member to trace physical data back to related program data.

  This involves reviewing record groups captured during the data definition analysis step discussed in Chapter 8, collapsing those definitions into logical subsets, reconciling naming and definitional discrepancies, and propagating rationalized definitions back into the application source code. Because any data structure type, including databases, can be defined redundantly within an application, data grouping definitions can include file records, hierarchical or network database segments, and relational table definitions. Deliverables include rationalized Copy members, upgraded source programs that deploy these Copy definitions consistently across application boundaries, consolidated data definition language maps, and upgraded data names within application procedural logic.

  To accomplish this, analysts must obtain or produce a record grouping analysis, as shown in Figure 10.4. In this example, multiple record definitions define the same physical data. Note the way in which one record subdivides the name and birth date fields, while a second record group is totally unaware of

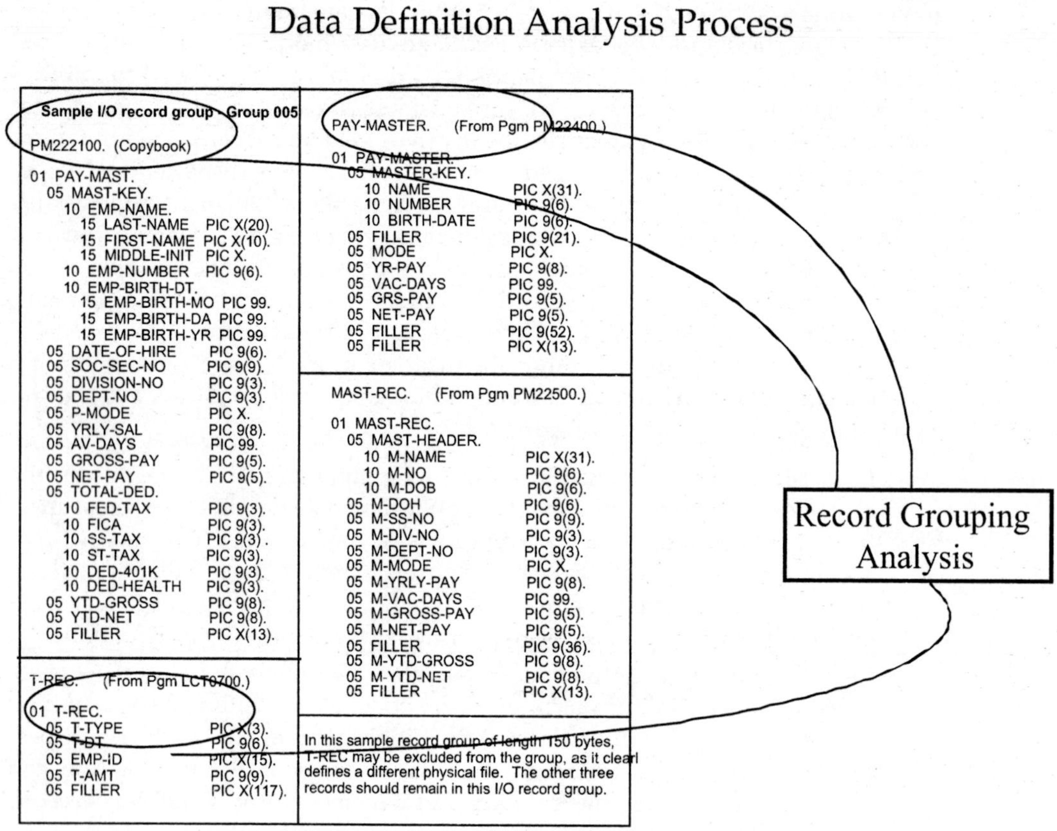

Data Definition Analysis Process

```
Sample I/O record group   Group 005

PM222100.  (Copybook)

01 PAY-MAST.
   05 MAST-KEY.
      10 EMP-NAME.
         15 LAST-NAME    PIC X(20).
         15 FIRST-NAME   PIC X(10).
         15 MIDDLE-INIT  PIC X.
      10 EMP-NUMBER      PIC 9(6).
      10 EMP-BIRTH-DT.
         15 EMP-BIRTH-MO PIC 99.
         15 EMP-BIRTH-DA PIC 99.
         15 EMP-BIRTH-YR PIC 99.
   05 DATE-OF-HIRE       PIC 9(6).
   05 SOC-SEC-NO         PIC 9(9).
   05 DIVISION-NO        PIC 9(3).
   05 DEPT-NO            PIC 9(3).
   05 P-MODE             PIC X.
   05 YRLY-SAL           PIC 9(8).
   05 AV-DAYS            PIC 99.
   05 GROSS-PAY          PIC 9(5).
   05 NET-PAY            PIC 9(5).
   05 TOTAL-DED.
      10 FED-TAX         PIC 9(3).
      10 FICA            PIC 9(3).
      10 SS-TAX          PIC 9(3).
      10 ST-TAX          PIC 9(3).
      10 DED-401K        PIC 9(3).
      10 DED-HEALTH      PIC 9(3).
   05 YTD-GROSS          PIC 9(8).
   05 YTD-NET            PIC 9(8).
   05 FILLER             PIC X(13).


T-REC.   (From Pgm LCT6700.)

01 T-REC.
   05 T-TYPE             PIC X(3).
   05 T-DT               PIC 9(6).
   05 EMP-ID             PIC X(15).
   05 T-AMT              PIC 9(9).
   05 FILLER             PIC X(117).
```

```
PAY-MASTER.   (From Pgm PM22400.)

01 PAY-MASTER.
   05 MASTER-KEY.
      10 NAME            PIC X(31).
      10 NUMBER          PIC 9(6).
      10 BIRTH-DATE      PIC 9(6).
   05 FILLER             PIC 9(21).
   05 MODE               PIC X.
   05 YR-PAY             PIC 9(8).
   05 VAC-DAYS           PIC 99.
   05 GRS-PAY            PIC 9(5).
   05 NET-PAY            PIC 9(5).
   05 FILLER             PIC 9(52).
   05 FILLER             PIC X(13).


MAST-REC.   (From Pgm PM22500.)

01 MAST-REC.
   05 MAST-HEADER.
      10 M-NAME          PIC X(31).
      10 M-NO            PIC 9(6).
      10 M-DOB           PIC 9(6).
   05 M-DOH              PIC 9(6).
   05 M-SS-NO            PIC 9(9).
   05 M-DIV-NO           PIC 9(3).
   05 M-DEPT-NO          PIC 9(3).
   05 M-MODE             PIC X.
   05 M-YRLY-PAY         PIC 9(8).
   05 M-VAC-DAYS         PIC 99.
   05 M-GROSS-PAY        PIC 9(5).
   05 M-NET-PAY          PIC 9(5).
   05 FILLER             PIC 9(36).
   05 M-YTD-GROSS        PIC 9(8).
   05 M-YTD-NET          PIC 9(8).
   05 FILLER             PIC X(13).
```

In this sample record group of length 150 bytes,
T-REC may be excluded from the group, as it clearly
defines a different physical file. The other three
records should remain in this I/O record group.

Record Grouping
Analysis

Figure 10.4
Redundant data definitions require review prior to consolidation.

the social security number, date of hire, and related information. Some analysts have argued that an application that does not need this information and could just leave it as filler area, but that application then runs the risk of having a programmer overwrite essential employee information. A data architecture redesign and migration effort might not even recognize this information and miss critical data within the new database design.

After analysts have reviewed the record grouping results, they can proceed with selective record group reconciliation on any data they plan to enhance or reuse in a migration project. This reconciliation process creates a single "composite" record and can be done manually or through the use of tools. Tool support for composite record creation is somewhat limited, but vendors are working to enhance this capability. If no tools are available, project teams should limit their rationalization efforts to records directly related to their business objectives. For an HIPAA project, for example, the team would consolidate only patient records into a single Copy definition.

Composite records should be reviewed to ensure that they reflect the most detailed level of data decomposition possible for all original record definitions used to create that composite. Redefining inconsistent data redefinitions accommodates different data views within a common set of record groupings. One application may, for example, require an employee name to be subdivided into last name, first name, and middle initial, while another application may not.

Analysts should also review all names being used within the composite record to ensure that they are meaningful to the majority of applications using the new common definition. Figure 10.5 depicts the creation of a composite record and also shows the old name/new name mapping.

Once the composite record or records are created, the rationalization team can deploy them in several ways. Transformation teams needing accurate, comprehensive data for a redesign and migration project can use composite

Original Source to Composite Record Mapping

Example

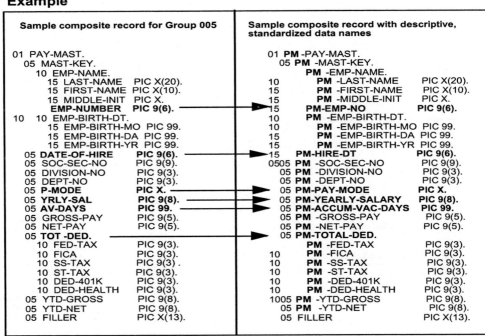

Figure 10.5
Composite records should use descriptive data names.
(*Source: USRM/Comsys.*)

records defining primary business data as input to a logical redesign process. This process is discussed further in Chapter 11. Similarly, data warehouse teams can use the new composite records as an accurate source of legacy data without worrying about the redundancies and inconsistencies found in the original program data definitions. A more tactical use for composite records is to propagate them back into the applications that rely on them.

This process involves replacing old record definitions with the common (i.e., Copy) composite definition and renaming the old element/attribute names within each program with the element names from the composite record. Figure 10.6 depicts this process and shows how data names from the newly defined composite record definition are propagated across source program logic. Selected tools support limited program propagation, but these tools are continuing to evolve.

Post-Rationalization Code View

Example

Composites propagated into programs

```
PROGRAM PRP4030.

COPY ....

01 PM-PAY-MAST.
   05 PM-MAST-KEY.
      10 PM-EMP-NAME.
         15 PM-LAST-NAME      PIC X(20).
         15 PM-FIRST-NAME     PIC X(10).
         15 PM-MIDDLE-INIT    PIC X.
      10 PM-EMP-NO            PIC 9(6).
      10 PM-EMP-BIRTH-DT.
         15 PM-EMP-BIRTH-MO   PIC 99.
         15 PM-EMP-BIRTH-DA   PIC 99.
         15 PM-EMP-BIRTH-YR   PIC 99.
   05 PM-HIRE-DT              PIC 9(6).
   05 PM-SOC-SEC-NO           PIC 9(9).
   05 PM-DIVISION-NO          PIC 9(3).
   05 PM-DEPT-NO              PIC 9(3).
   05 PM-PAY-MODE             PIC X.
   05 PM-YEARLY-SALARY        PIC 9(8).
   05 PM-ACCUM-VAC-DAYS       PIC 99.
   ......
```

```
01 WS-P-MODE                PIC X.
   88 BIWEEKLY              PIC X VALUE 'B'.
   88 MONTHLY               PIC X VALUE 'M'.
01 WS-YRLY-SAL              PIC 9(8).
01 WS-AV-DAYS              PIC 99.
.....
```

Program references changed to correspond

```
PROGRAM PRP4030.

MOVE P-MODE TO WS-P-MODE.
IF BIWEEKLY
   PERFORM CHECK-WEEK
   ADD .385 TO WS-AV-DAYS.
IF MONTHLY
   PERFORM CHECK-MONTH
   ADD 1.25 TO WS-AV-DAYS.
MOVE WS-AV-DAYS TO AV-DAYS.
...
```

↓

```
MOVE PM-PAY-MODE TO WS-P-MODE.
IF BIWEEKLY
   PERFORM CHECK-WEEK
   ADD .385 TO WS-AV-DAYS.
IF MONTHLY
   PERFORM CHECK-MONTH
   ADD 1.25 TO WS-AV-DAYS.
MOVE WS-AV-DAYS TO
   PM-ACCUM-VAC-DAYS .
...
```

Name replacement list for related subordinate references which are locally defined

ORIGINAL	PROPOSED
...	
WS-P-MODE	WS-PAY-MODE
WS-YRLY-SAL	WS-YEARLY-SALARY
WS-AV-DAYS	WS-ACCUM-VAC-DAYS
...	

Figure 10.6

Composite propagation ensures that all programs use consistent definitions for a given physical record, segment, or table.

(Source: USRM/Comsys.)

When rationalizing multirecord layout files, as discussed above, analysts should consider creating a separate composite for each unique record type. This will increase data usage understandability from an application management perspective and streamline efforts to redesign these data structures if a logical data redesign project is planned.

Planning teams should note the risks inherent in element-level versus group-level rationalization. Past efforts to rationalize application data usage have at times focused on rationalizing a single element or, in relational terms, an attribute. Elements exist only within the context of the records, segments, or tables that define them. Element-level rationalization meets few near-term or strategic business objectives and is more time-consuming and error-prone than group-level rationalization. Element-level rationalization also runs the risk of misinterpreting homonyms because the context for the element is not apparent. This can have serious business consequences.

- **Homonym reconciliation.** Homonyms surface during the data definition rationalization process. For example, multiple records used to create a new composite record may contain fields called ACCT-NO, as shown in Figure 10.7. The referential context of these fields within their respective records shows, however, that these elements refer to different physical data. These findings allow analysts to identify and correct homonyms.

  If homonyms are defined across different composite record definitions, analysts should research and assess the source of these data elements to ensure that they refer to different data. Correcting and assigning unique names to homonyms assure that maintenance programmers and outsourcing teams will avoid becoming confused during upgrade efforts. Project teams performing cross-functional data upgrades, including HIPAA, T+1, and similar industry initiatives, will also avoid tracing elements that seem to be the same while they actually define different data.

  Redesign and migration teams will benefit significantly from not having to struggle with homonyms that could ultimately taint new designs and result in serious implementation delays or user confusion within strategic application replacement and transformation projects.

- **Program data externalization.** Hardcoded literals represent data that should be stored in tables, files, or user-accessible databases. Exposing hardcoded data and moving it into a more maintainable format are key objectives of this task. The process involves identifying and grouping all hardcoded program literals, determining their relationship to external data and to each other, externalizing the data in new or existing data structures, and changing the source code to access this externalized data.

  For example, consider a situation where 25 plant codes have been hardcoded into a program data structure that is being tested for location validity. The addition or removal of a plant location would cause a user to request a

Homonym Identification and Correction

Example

```
Homonym analysis list


NAME              DEFINITION        TIMES USED


...
ACCT-NO           PIC X(8)              8  ◀─────────── Correct unique definition
ACCT-NO           PIC 9(8) COMP-3   1                   of ACCT-NO
ACCT-NO           PIC X(4)          1


ACCT-TYPE         PIC X(3)              3  ◀─────────── Correct unique definition
ACCT-TYPE         PIC X             1                   of ACCT-TYPE
...
```

```
Homonym replacement list


ORIGINAL NAME     DEFINITION          PROPOSED NAME      DEFINITION


...
ACCT-NO           PIC 9(8) COMP-3     CLIENT-ACCT-NO     PIC 9(8) COMP-3
ACCT-NO           PIC X(4)            SERVICE-ACCT-NO    PIC X(4)


ACCT-TYPE         PIC X               ACCT-MODE          PIC X
...
```

Figure 10.7
Data elements having the same name but referring to different physical data should be corrected as part of the rationalization process.
(Source: USRM/Comsys.)

programming update, which could take days to complete, test, and return to production. Ideally, the user should be able to go online and update this information in a database in just a few minutes.

Correcting this problem involves using tools to highlight and cross-reference all hardcoded data across applications of interest. Analysts can then determine where the significant business data has been hardcoded and review options for externalizing that data. Even if the user does not want to take over the updating of certain data, the IT department could still save time by externalizing that data and updating it whenever a user requests such a change.

Migration projects also benefit from this approach because the hardcoded data is not entangled with the business logic they are trying to extract. In addition to this, externalizing this data allows it to be incorporated into new logical data models to be used within a new or reengineered data model.

- **Field and record size expansion.** Field size expansion increases the capacity of all occurrences of a logical element to hold larger data values. This accommodates business issues such as an increase in the number of customers, patients, or constituents and also can address regulatory changes such as a zip code change. Another common application of this task is to accommodate inflationary trends in monetary fields. Record size expansion results from field size expansion or from the addition of a new field to a record that has no discretionary filler space remaining.

  Selective expansion can also be used to reconcile field or record size mismatches, which has a direct impact on system reliability. Field or record size mismatches are typically identified and rectified during a data definition rationalization project.

  If data definitions have been rationalized as discussed previously, field or record size expansion is a matter of expanding or adding fields within the Copy member, recompiling the source code, correcting field size mismatches found by the compiler, and reformatting physical data files. If targeted data definitions have not been rationalized, I strongly suggest that project teams consider rationalizing record groups linked to the physical data to be expanded.

  If project teams choose not to rationalize data definitions, then the same type of record group analysis performed for the rationalization process should be applied to the expansion project. Related record groups should then be adjusted to reflect new fields and/or expanded field definitions. Program-level fields can be checked with a data usage-tracing tool or with a compiler. This approach map can be applied to any large-scale, cross-functional data upgrade project.

Data definition rationalization and related data upgrade tasks can be driven by an immediate data upgrade requirement or by data warehouse, business rule capture, or other logical data redesign initiatives. Application consolidation is a prime example of where the reconciliation of data definitions is an essential first step in reconciling application functionality. Modularization, whether used for consolidation or similar application projects, is one such initiative that benefits from rationalized data definitions.

10.6 Modularization

Splitting up large programs, reaggregating programs along functional boundaries, and consolidating applications are tasks that should all be driven by specific business objectives. Modularization projects build upon structuring and data definition upgrade tasks, and should be deployed under a phased transformation plan. Basic staging and validation techniques outlined earlier in this chapter apply to each modularization task, but may require adjustments if multiple programs are consolidated across application boundaries.

- **Code slicing.** Code slicing, also known as code splitting, involves moving select data and procedural logic from one source program into a new source module. Code-slicing benefits include eliminating code that no longer has business value, reducing how long it takes to change a source program, and allowing very large source programs to be moved to a distributed platform.

  The resulting modules typically remain in the original language and, at least initially, will be functionally equivalent to the original source program. Resulting modules may be turned into subroutines within the same object module or run as separate standalone modules. Code slicing can be performed manually, but analysts should utilize slicing tools to expedite the process wherever possible. Table 10.1 depicts five criteria for slicing code out of a source module.

  The most basic slicing options, typically driven by the need to create subroutines out of a larger program, include transaction-based or report-based slicing. Analysts can use static analysis tools to identify the dominance (where a routine triggers other routines) and reach (the depth of triggered routines) of high-level paragraphs. Dominance and reach analysis determines the number of resulting paragraphs in the subroutine and original routine and allows analysts to reduce replication of sliced code. Replicated code should be reconsolidated as separate subroutines.

  Once slicing analysis has been completed, slicing tools can be used to slice out subroutines based on the criteria shown in Table 10.1. If slicing tools are not available, analysts could structure a source program, apply static analysis to determine which paths they want to slice out, and use the structuring tool to slice out the code paths. This works only on structured code and requires analysts to truncate invocation logic for the routines they want to remove (i.e., slice) from the program.

  Repeating this process by rerunning the structuring tool to remove unwanted paths creates a subroutine with nontruncated logic remaining active. Analysts also must establish calls to each subroutine from the original routine and create program entry points within each subroutine. Slicing tools are available only for COBOL, but manual slicing will work on other programs based on this approach.

Table 10.1
Business, I/O, or data access layer logic can be isolated based on a variety of criteria, which in turn are driven by a business objective.

Slicing Criteria	Objectives
1. Execution Range Criteria (Structured code is required)	Large module size reduction
	Creation of shared business logic routines to develop usable code
2. Report Criteria	Online migrations
	Reusability of report logic
	Creation of independent I/O layer
	Functional segregation
	Reusable routine isolation
3. Computation Variable Criteria	Functional isolation
	Reusable routine isolation
	Functional segregation/transformation preparation
4. Transaction Criteria	Functional reaggregation support
	Reusable routines
	Creation of independent I/O layer
	Creation of independent data access layer.
5. Statement Selection Criteria	Reusable routine isolation

(Source: USRM/Comsys.)

- **Application reaggregation.** Reaggregation applies code slicing, as outlined above, along with consolidation techniques to create functionally cohesive source programs. This task is driven by the need to align an implementation view of a system with a more functionally cohesive view of that system. Figure 10.8 shows how functions can be sliced out of certain modules and then recombined into new models.

  Reaggregation realigns program logic within the current technical architecture and moves, eliminates, and recombines application source logic based on the functions performed by that code. Reaggregation does not, however, address cross-application consolidation, which is described in the next section.

System Reaggregation

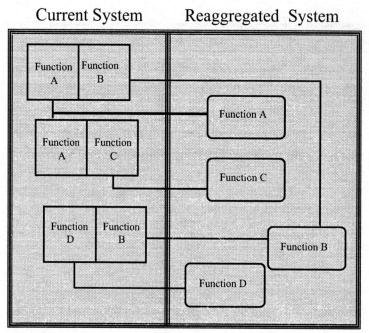

Figure 10.8
Functions can be split out and recombined to reaggregate application functionality.

Specific objectives include realigning program logic along functional boundaries, combining functions to streamline application upgrade projects, establishing a basis for component reuse and migration, and segregating business logic, data access logic, and presentation layer. This includes facilitating source code upgrades linked to a relational database migration.

For example, if a database for an application has been migrated to a relational structure from a hierarchical structure, reaggregation can isolate I/O logic used to transverse the hierarchical database. New I/O routines could then replace the old calling structures as needed.

In general, this task relies on analysts identifying functions to be sliced out and recombined. This information should reside in the transformation repository, assuming that planning teams have completed a functional assessment of the application involved. Analysts should apply slicing techniques outlined in the prior section to segregate logic related to certain transaction types, computations, or other criteria, as outlined in Table 10.1.

As logic is sliced out of a routine, analysts will need to create subroutines or standalone programs. This typically involves moving transaction data, I/O routines, and user interface definitions into these routines. Slicing tools take all the data needed for the new routine, but analysts will likely need to streamline this data into an essential subset prior to finalizing the upgraded application. Additional work includes changing online transaction and batch job control routines as needed to execute the newly reaggregated application.

- **Application consolidation.** Application consolidation is an extension of application reaggregation, but with the added task of consolidating functionality across multiple applications. The goal is to create a single application from multiple applications by slicing, reaggregating, and consolidating redundant logic. The code consolidation portion of this project involves the use of business rule capture logic that can identify redundant logic candidates for consolidation. I will outline a project-based approach for application consolidation in a Chapter 12 case study.

10.7 User Presentation Migration Scenario

There are multiple approaches to Web-enabling legacy application interfaces. I discussed middleware front-end integration options in Chapter 9, but there are other options that provide planning teams with the means to Web-enable legacy applications. These approaches include migrating "green screens" to GUI or HTML interfaces, XML-enabling legacy applications, and migrating screens in conjunction with an application rehosting project.

- **Dynamic user interface migration.** This approach applies legacy-driven versus middleware-driven user interface migration. This approach, as with other user interface migration options, is tool-dependent. For example, migration software can interpret character-based user interfaces and create graphical views on the fly based on a predetermined new interface design. This differs from most middleware options because it GUI-enables the legacy application and is not driven by the development and integration of a new Web-based application.

  Project teams apply interface migration technology that pattern-matches data found within the character interface to create dynamic GUI interfaces. This can be applied to a variety of platform interfaces to produce distributed GUI and HTML user interfaces. The benefits include Web-enablement of legacy applications as a means of increasing user productivity and linking legacy applications to the Internet.

Dynamic user interface migration is recommended if analysts do not want to minimize changes to legacy application source code, but wish to control the logic behind the GUI or Web-enabled application. A limitation of this scenario is that the resulting application remains locked into the stovepipe legacy architecture.

- **XML-enabled legacy application interface.** Another user interface migration approach modifies the data access interface within the legacy application to Web-enable the source code. The benefit of this approach is that it provides the application team with the ability to directly affect changes to the Web-enabled interface through a special source code preprocessor.

In other words, if the application team chooses to modify data related to an interface, they can immediately make that change. This avoids coordination and ripple effect problems inherent in traditional middleware where legacy support teams are segregated from Web development and integration teams.

This approach XML-enables legacy interfaces, using special code that is run through a preprocessor prior to being compiled. The application can remain on its native platform and in its native language. Once these links have been activated, XML will send and receive encapsulated messages to and from an Internet browser. This allows the legacy application source code to deploy HTML-based user interfaces [2].

Applying this concept facilitates the phased migration of applications to Web-enabled environments. It does require the use of very specific technologies, which are covered in Appendix A, and this may not be in accordance with an architecture team's technical architecture plans.

- **User interface migration and rehosting.** Combining user interface migration with application rehosting generates a new HTML front end from data found within a legacy COBOL source program. This alternative, like previous user interface migration options, is supported by industry software products, which are discussed in Appendix A. Rehosting the application to a distributed environment incorporates an extra series of steps not found in other user interface migration options. This technique, however, provides greater long-term flexibility for planning teams.

The migration/rehosting option moves the application into a distributed environment and derives new HTML front ends from COBOL linkage data. Project teams then use this same technology to generate a Web server program to facilitate communication between the COBOL application and the new HTML front end. This technique creates a hybrid application of COBOL, HTML, and a Web interface.

Pursuing this option leverages legacy applications, data access capabilities, and the knowledge of the legacy application analysts who understand the business functions of the application. Very little redesign work is involved in this approach, but it does provide a stepping stone toward future redesign efforts.

User interface migration can be combined with other transformation projects or can stand alone. The path taken by planning teams and management should be part of an overall strategy to ensure that projects are not pursuing dead-end options but employing interface migration as part of a business-driven end goal. Such a plan moves application architectures into a flexible environment that supports long-term business requirements.

10.8 Physical Data Mining, Cleanup, and Integration

The concept of knowledge reclamation from enterprise data structures has been gaining a great deal of attention as companies struggle to recapture business intelligence scattered across a plethora of legacy data structures. Much of this data is hard to access or update, is redundantly defined across platforms and data architectures, and is riddled with invalid content. Redesigning major cross-sections of the enterprise data architecture, which is discussed in Chapter 11, can be too complex of a challenge to be undertaken in the near term. If this is the case, tactical alternatives to data-related issues should be pursued. These alternatives include data validation and cleanup, data mining, and physical data structure consolidation.

- **Data validation and cleanup.** Many years ago, a legacy application research project kept turning up asterisks in the "sex code" field of an employee file. It appeared to be an anomaly because no one could determine why the field did not have an "M" or an "F" as the value. A woman who appeared to be near or past retirement age overheard the analyst team discussing this issue and said she knew what the asterisk meant. Users entered an "*" to designate that the employee was a summer intern. Since the field had no validity check in the user interface, users could create their own codes.

  This story is just one example of how seemingly invalid data may be perfectly valid to the business community. Legacy data structures are loaded with invalid or questionable data that can trigger failures in applications that do not screen for that data. Most legacy applications contain edit and validation logic to prevent a phone number, for example, from being displayed if it contains invalid letters or special characters. Web-based or other emerging applications, however, may not contain these safeguards, and this can result in errant data being exposed to customers, suppliers, distributors, users, and employees.

  To address these issues, analysts can target certain data structures for a validation check and subsequent cleanup. Targeted data structures should include any data involved in a redesign and/or consolidation effort, being accessed directly by internal or external Web-based interfaces, or serving as an EDI exchange with a business partner. Data cleanup involves running an integrity check using data analysis tools and, if applicable, replacing invalid data with valid data.

This process involves determining validation rules for data within the targeted data structures and using software products or inhouse-developed routines to validate data against the rules. Rules can be derived from users, legacy applications via rule abstraction, IT analysts, or for the best results, a combination of these sources. The validation test would typically produce a dump of the field and records in violation of these rules that can then be reviewed by the appropriate parties.

The correction process involves replacing invalid data with valid data. This can be complex given that users or analysts may not know which data should replace the invalid data. Justifying the correction process may be time-consuming and should be connected to a highly visible migration, redesign or consolidation initiative.

One last step involves ensuring that good data is kept clean. This typically requires reviewing all data input sources, including user interfaces, EDI exchange points, and automated data transfers from other programs or systems. Data interface points should be defined within the project- or application-level repository. If this information was not captured during a prior analysis step, analysts should update the repository with relevant information during the data cleanup effort. Ensuring that validation checks are in place for Web-enabled applications that input and display enterprise data will further ensure that data integrity is maintained over the long term.

- **Data mining.** "Understanding and wisdom are largely forgotten as we struggle under the avalanche of data and information" [3]. This maxim is very applicable to the modern enterprise where information systems flood users with data that they can no longer absorb, process, and convert into understanding and wisdom. Information systems arguably produce too much data and too little intelligence as far as many users are concerned. Data mining is the process of distilling data down to the point where business analysts and executives can use it to derive the wisdom needed to set a correct course of action in motion.

Data mining seeks to find knowledge buried in a flood of data. As I have discussed in earlier chapters, enterprises have created an overwhelming amount of inconsistent, fragmented, redundant, and even invalid data across legacy architectures. Data mining seeks to make sense of that information based on a business-driven objective by uncovering patterns in data that can tell an organization something of value. For example, a retailer may be looking for patterns in people who buy milk and discover that "75 percent of people buy wheat bread if they buy 2 percent milk" [4].

Data mining may be performed as a standalone project or in conjunction with a data and/or application architecture project. If the above information was required on an ongoing basis, an application may be created to support this type of analysis. Data mining project teams should consider that most "real-world data tends to be dirty" [5]. This means that integrity checking must be incorporated into a mining effort.

Mining tasks include identifying the class of data that the business wishes to research, the relationships with other classes, classification rules for how to deal with data once it is uncovered, value predictions or validation rules as discussed above, and how data may be grouped or clustered [6].

A number of papers suggest collecting data in a warehouse as a repository for related data. This will simplify the search process and knowledge-capture effort because the data will be in one place under a common format. Data warehouse development is discussed further in Chapter 11.

- **Data redundancy consolidation.** Consolidating physical data redundancies can be accomplished within the current physical data architecture or in conjunction with a logical data redesign effort. The physical consolidation of data from related structures is discussed here; logical data redesign is discussed in Chapter 11. Physical data redundancy consolidation combines existing physical structures into a single structure and may need to reconcile format discrepancies.

  The business drivers behind this concept involve the reconciliation of redundant systems that were split apart or have been running in parallel. The data may overlap 80 to 90 percent or more in this situation, and the business community may have decided to combine the applications. Physical data structures will need to be identified using data definition analysis and rationalization techniques. Data definition rationalization is a prerequisite to data consolidation and defines new, consolidated formats where discrepancies existed in the original data. Where applicable, unique data will need to be added to an expanded definition of the composite file or database being created.

  Project teams will need to map and resolve redundancies and inconsistencies along with file or database keys based on the new composite application. Data manipulation tools can then be used to merge the data. It is very likely that a data consolidation project will also involve application consolidation, which is discussed in more depth in Chapter 12.

10.9 Performance Improvement

One last issue in the stabilization of legacy applications involves performance improvement. In the early days of computing this meant using lower-level languages, such as Assembler, or avoiding certain database or programming constructs. Today, with incredibly fast machines at IT's disposal, performance issues are typically linked to architectural weaknesses.

For example, consider a sequential customer information file with millions of records that is updated on a nightly basis. Such an archaic structure is not the most efficient means of processing this data, but the massive volume of data and complexity of the applications that access that data has been too daunting to redesign. If, however, an enterprise reaches the point where it cannot continue processing information in this manner from an efficiency perspective, phased redesign of the data architecture may be justified. Normally a business decision will force this issue, particularly if these types of file structures no longer facilitate effective customer service or hinder the effective delivery of products or services.

Any performance reviews should focus on architecture issues as a high priority because this is where major efficiency impediments are most likely to surface. Performance tuning, optimization, and other techical factors have probably been tuned to the point where there is little opportunity left to squeeze more speed out of an application without making changes to how it works. Issues to consider include data architecture, an application's access to data, factors related to sequential processing requirements, and user access to an application.

Many performance improvement opportunities may be highlighted and even improved by the stabilization efforts defined within this chapter. Chapter 11 discusses various logical redesign and redeployment options that can additionally be applied to application environments as a way to address architecturally constricted performance limitations.

Notes

1. "Straight-through Processing for Competitive Advantage," Stanley Young and John Moran, *ebizQ.net*, Dec. 10, 2001, *http://www.messageq.com/real_time/accenture_1a.html*.
2. "Legacy.NET," Don Estes, *Cutter IT Journal*, Vol. 14, No. 1, Jan. 2001.
3. *Birth of the Chaordic Age*, Dee Hock, Berrett-Koehler, 1999.
4. "Mining Multiple-Level Association Rules in Large Databases," Jiawei Han and Yongjian Fu, *IEEE Transactions on Knowledge and Data Engineering*, Vol. 11, No. 5, Sept./Oct. 1999.
5. "Fault-Tolerant Frequent Pattern Mining: Problems and Challenges," Jiawei Han, Jian Pei, and Anthony K. H. Tung, Proc. 2001 ACM-SIGMOD International Workshop on DMKD '01, May 2001.
6. "The Quest Data Mining System," R. Agrawal, M. Mehta, J. Shafer, R. Srikant, A. Arning, and T. Bollinger, Proceedings of 1996 International Conference on Data Mining and Knowledge Discovery, Aug. 1996.

Logical Data and Business Rule Capture, Redesign, and Reuse

Architecture transformation extends the analysis, reuse, redesign, and redeployment concepts discussed thus far into the detailed capture, redesign, and redeployment of legacy data and business rules. Projects employing these techniques must be business-driven and have clear objectives and deliverables. If applied in the proper context, architecture transformation fulfills the strategic needs of organizations with a significant installed base of legacy applications and data structures.

The general goal, which varies based on the type of project involved, is to extract and redesign the data and business rules within legacy applications of interest. Extracted as-is models can be used to document the existing architecture, validate target design models, or establish the foundation for logically redesigning and reconstructing the existing architecture.

This chapter discusses logical data and business rule abstraction as a means of documenting the as-is architecture, validating target specifications, and reconstructing new applications and data structures that conform to strategic business requirements.

11.1 Architecture Transformation Objectives

Documenting the as-is architecture, validating target requirements, and reconstructing legacy architectures can be accomplished independently or in combination with each other. Capturing legacy data and/or business logic is the first step in pursuing each of these initiatives. Business-driven scenarios must be the overriding motivation

317

when employing any of the concepts discussed within this chapter. Without a specific goal in mind, data and business rule extraction efforts run the risk of delivering little value to the enterprise.

Documenting the as-is architecture extends the analysis work that began in the assessment phase discussed in Chapter 8. Analysts and technicians can use legacy architecture metadata captured during the assessment phase to plan subsequent transformation initiatives based on various business requirements. The detailed or project-level repository is the central source for storing and sharing this information and should be viewed as an ongoing resource for business, IT, and third-party analysts who require metadata about legacy information architectures.

Validating target architecture requirements against as-is application and data models ensures that new applications and databases do not omit essential business functionality. The mapping process can be applied to target data and object models, databases, technical designs, or application packages. At a minimum, analysts can use legacy abstractions to verify the validity of target requirements. Taken further, analysts can actually incorporate legacy data and business logic into the new design where that design has been determined to be lacking in functionality.

Reconstructing a new application and data environment based on the legacy architecture is an alternative approach to validating target requirements. This concept captures, consolidates, and redesigns functional flows, legacy data, business rules, and user views as the basis for a new application. This process applies logical redesign concepts to normalize data and business rules and redeploy those rules within retooled architectures. Analysts can add new functionality and data to the new architecture during the redesign process or after the new application has been redeployed.

Figure 11.1 shows various transformation paths a project can take. Data definition capture, consolidation, and abstraction are common to most projects. Business rule capture and consolidation are tasks unique to projects needing to document, reuse, and/or validate business rules against a set of target requirements. Synchronization of data abstractions and business rules validates the bottom-up data view and ensures that rules are classified or ignored based on the data they reference and/or modify. Architecture redesign validates strategic requirements or, in the absence of such requirements, serves as the basis for the redesigned target architecture. Redeployment of the new architecture requires deactivation of application functionality, migration of legacy data structures, and activation of redesigned application functionality.

Tasks along the transformation path in Figure 11.1 may be applied selectively or as a collective strategy. Such a strategy can incorporate package selection or implementation options, data warehouse deployment, component-based architectures, Web Services, or other business-driven scenarios. The remainder of this chapter discusses these concepts in more depth.

Transformation Path Options

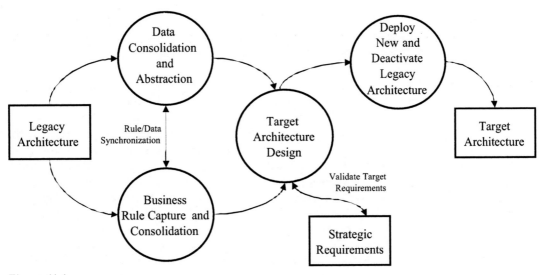

Figure 11.1
Transformation path options include data and business rule capture, consolidation, redesign, validation, and redeployment.

11.2 Leveraging Assessment and Stabilization Deliverables

The enterprise and project-level assessments captured high-level data and business functionality, documented this information in logical and physical models, mapped logical views to the physical environment, performed a high-level gap analysis, and built an implementation plan based on the business scenario. The repository metadata collected at the enterprise and at the project level serves as the foundation for subsequent and more detailed data and business rule analysis efforts.

One common mistake involves analysts who jump into detailed analysis and implementation tasks without having segregated application functionality from a high-level perspective. For example, analysts at one company attempted to extract business rules within one application without determining that two other applications contain related and overlapping business rules. Determining the applications and data structures of interest is based on an enterprise assessment and subsequent project level assessment. By the time a project team moves into the implementation stage of a given project, the scope of the detailed analysis should be well defined.

Essential work products delivered as a result of the project-level assessment include the project-level repository, generated cross-reference relationships from the repository, various logical models, and a project plan outlining subsequent implementation tasks. The deliverables produced by the assessment phase of a project are driven by the business requirements for that project. If, for example, a business or application unit plans to redesign an application, various data and functional mappings, high-level functional decompositions, and data models are required deliverables for the implementation phase of the project.

If, on the other hand, a project is solely focused on data redesign and consolidation, then the identification of legacy data entities and relationships along with the current-to-target data mapping, if applicable, are key deliverables from the assessment phase. Similarly, if the team is evaluating a package offering, the initial mapping process should be applied against that package's functional capabilities.

Stabilization project tasks deliver additional value to a logical redesign and migration project. Rationalized data, structured programs, and modularized source code deliver a more viable application baseline for projects requiring primary data inputs to a logical redesign process or a modularized view of application source code for business rule analysis and extraction.

The most important consideration is to avoid launching a data and business rule capture, mapping, and redesign process without performing the requisite analysis and related application preparation work defined in prior chapters. Skipping essential setup tasks will result in yet another failed project statistic.

As plans are finalized, remember to apply common sense when identifying architecture transformation techniques outlined in this chapter. Care should be taken to apply only essential data and business rule mining and redesign techniques to the project. For example, a project seeking to build a data warehouse would not require business rule capture, with the possible exception of data validation logic. Similarly, a project focused on comparing legacy functionality to a target functional model would not need to consolidate and componentize legacy business rules. The best way to adhere to the minimalist principle of transformation projects is to question the value and applicability of every deliverable throughout each phase of a project.

11.3 Data Architecture Transformation

One task that is common to the vast majority of transformation projects involves the capture, consolidation, and redesign of legacy data structures. This process involves capturing a cross-section of data definitions from legacy applications and data structures and consolidating that data within a relational data model that becomes the basis for a relational database. Relational databases are desirable because they make data more responsive to ongoing and ad hoc user requests, are the data structure of choice for data warehouses, and can be accessed directly by component-based applications developed in Java or other object-oriented languages.

Project teams can use an abstracted bottom-up data model, derived from the legacy data architecture, as the foundation for creating an integrated database for a replacement system or as the basis for a data warehouse. Another option involves validating or optionally merging a target top-down data model with the abstracted bottom-up data model. Finally, the bottom-up data model can be used to validate the compatibility of an ERP package.

Project teams should maintain mappings among legacy data definitions, abstracted logical entities, and attributes captured from the legacy environment with data entities and attributes in target requirements. Maintaining these relationships allows the migration team to quickly identify the physical data sources needed to populate target data structures. Current-to-target mappings also facilitate the creation of a gap analysis between the existing data architecture and target data architecture. Finally, tracking legacy data definitions and derived logical entities in the transformation repository allows analysts to map that data to legacy business rules.

The tasks involved in data architecture transformation include legacy data capture and abstraction, current-to-target mapping and reconciliation, and data architecture refinement and redeployment. Each task builds on deliverables created during prior tasks as well as work completed during the project-level assessment and related stabilization efforts. The transformation repository is central to this process, which applies reverse engineering, consolidation, and redesign techniques to achieve a target data model that accurately reflects strategic business requirements.

11.4 Legacy Data Definition Capture and Abstraction

To capture and transform legacy data definitions, the project team must ensure that data definition sources reflect all applications and data structures of interest. Analysts must also verify that redundant definitions are reconciled prior to being loaded into the logical data model so that populated data definitions lend themselves to subsequent normalization. Project teams must additionally set clear objectives based on the business goals of the project.

For example, a project team may want to abstract and represent legacy data in a relational data model for the sole purpose of building a data warehouse. This does not necessarily require mapping the bottom-up data model to a set of strategic requirements, but would necessitate understanding exactly which data is required for the users and customers accessing the data warehouse. If, on the other hand, a new database is required to support an application redesign project, then analysts may need to enhance the normalized data model to incorporate additional data based on user-driven requirements.

The process of developing a bottom-up entity relationship model began during the project-level assessment, but analysts may choose or need to begin this process from scratch. This decision may be based on changes that have taken place since the initial assessment process. The first step involves capturing primary (i.e., non-derivative) data representations from legacy applications, loading this data into a logical data model, and specifying logical relationships among that data. Analysts should use a data modeling tool to expedite this process. Some of these tools support the capture and reengineering of program or hierarchical data definitions into a relational model.

Prior data definition analysis and rationalization tasks, as defined in Chapter 10, created a set of nonredundant data definitions in the form of standardized record structures and subordinate elements. Each rationalized data record forms the basis for a logical entity within the data model. Each subordinate data element within those records forms the basis for a logical attribute within that entity. Non-business data, such as a record type indicator, should not be loaded into the logical data model.

This data model load process continues for each rationalized record definition. Analysts must verify that redundantly defined attributes are reconciled during the data model creation process. Even if project teams rationalize legacy data definitions prior to loading them into the relational data model, it does not guarantee that cross-functional redundancies will be fully eliminated. Overlapping data may still exist across business units and application data structures. For example, a conflicting customer file may overlap with 70 percent of the customer file data found in a second business unit. This would not be resolved during record group rationalization. These redundancies should therefore be reconciled during the load process.

Establishing entity relationships requires help from skilled data analysts. Analysts' efforts can be augmented through the use of intelligent reengineering tools that can derive data relationships from legacy data structures. Data analysts should use standard data modeling practices when building these relationships. For example, a tape file with multiple order record types may create a relationship called "Item is part of Order." Project teams can also leverage data reverse engineering tools that take a hierarchical or network database schema as input and produce a relational database. These tools are highly recommended if the project team is reengineering a legacy database environment.The process of capturing, consolidating, and abstracting legacy data definitions produces a bottom-up data model that becomes the basis for data architecture transformation. If the strategic architecture team created a target data model, they can use legacy data representations to validate data and relationships within that target data model.

11.5 Current-to-Target Mapping and Reconciliation

The process of validating a target data architecture against legacy data representations runs along a spectrum and depends on the depth of completeness of the target model. If a strategic design team has developed a comprehensive target data model, transformation analysts can use rationalized data definitions to ensure that essential entities and attributes are included in that new data model. If, on the other hand, planning teams only have a rudimentary data model or no target data model at all, the derived, bottom-up data model takes on much greater significance.

The availability and maturity of the strategic model dictates the approach taken within this task. For example, assume that a strategic planning team has developed a customer information data model that consolidates requirements for each billing unit across a multidivision enterprise. The approach the planning team can take in this case is to bypass the development of a bottom-up data model and simply validate the top-down model against the legacy data definitions. This approach involves rationalizing prime record definitions for each customer management application across multiple business units and using these rationalized data definitions to verify that existing entity types and attributes are fully incorporated into the new, top-down data model.

The transformation repository helps track and manage multiple, complex, legacy-to-target data mappings. The repository supports complex data mappings in situations where record groups across applications differ in structure. Not validating target data structures runs the risk of missing critical data in the new system. If missing data is discovered during implementation, the project would be delayed significantly and costs to deliver the new application would likely skyrocket.

Another scenario involves planning teams that have had difficulty creating a top-down data model because they do not fully understand complex data requirements for the business. In this case, project teams will want to expedite the development of a high-integrity data model by merging a bottom-up data model with a partially defined top-down model. Project teams can use tools that support merging multiple data models or perform this task manually with standard data modeling tools.

Model merging requires establishing the top-down data model as a baseline and merging the bottom-up model into this baseline, as shown in Figure 11.2. Analysts may need to reconcile data names between the top-down and bottom-up models, although the bottom-up model should have applied standard data naming conventions that were derived from rationalized record definitions. These rationalized data names should in turn have been based on standard business naming conventions. This process includes reconciling missing entities from the target data model and investigating entities defined in the target model but missing from the legacy environment. In some cases, data attributes may have been assigned to different entity types. These discrepancies will need to be rectified during the merge process. Analysts should also reconcile homonyms, attribute names, and field lengths where appropriate.

The other end of the reconciliation spectrum involves a scenario where planning teams have no top-down data model and need to use the bottom-up model as the foundation for a new strategic data model. The starting point for the

Building a High-Integrity Data Architecture

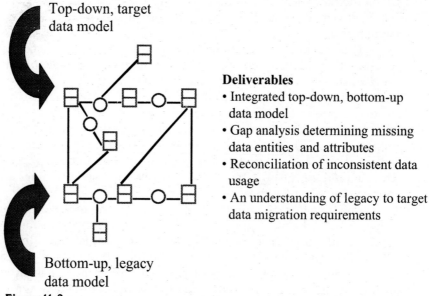

Top-down, target
data model

Deliverables
• Integrated top-down, bottom-up
  data model
• Gap analysis determining missing
  data entities and attributes
• Reconciliation of inconsistent data
  usage
• An understanding of legacy to target
  data migration requirements

Bottom-up, legacy
data model

Figure 11.2
Consolidating top-down and bottom-up data models produces a higher-quality data architecture and increases likelihood of project success.

new data model is the consolidated data model derived from rationalized record definitions in the prior step. Under this scenario, cross-functional business and data analysts will need to carefully scrutinize the bottom-up data model to ensure that it conforms to strategic planning requirements. The process of redesigning and refining a bottom-up or merged bottom-up/top-down data model is discussed in Section 11.6.

11.6 Data Architecture Refinement and Redeployment

Refinement and redeployment prepare the consolidated data model for use within the target architecture. This target may be an operational data environment, relational database for new Web-based applications, or a data warehouse. Project teams meet this requirement by reviewing the newly created data model with business units, data analysts, application teams, and applicable third parties. Note that several of these refinement steps may be applied as a prerequisite step to merging the bottom-up data model with the top-down data model. This is a judgment call by the data design team.

As a first step, analysts must verify that the data model synchronizes missing, overlapping, or redundant entities and attributes from multiple business units. For example, data definition rationalization may have reconciled conflicting names and substructures within identical physical record definitions, but other sources of this data may exist that can be used to refine a given entity or attributes. Additional customer information, for example, may reside within secondary file structures. These data definitions should be used to augment the initial entity definitions derived from billing master files. This secondary level of refinement ensures that all essential legacy data views are incorporated into the new data model.

Once analysts have loaded essential data definitions into the data model, they must ensure that the data model defines enterprise data according to a common set of conventions. Data attribute lengths, data types, and data names should be agreed upon across all affected business units and third parties relying on the data defined within this model. A customer problem-reporting number, for example, may need to be expanded to accommodate the most complete definition of that number.

As legacy data discrepancies are reconciled and an agreed-upon data model emerges, the project team will need to normalize the model. This normalized data model will ultimately be transformed into a relational database that can be accessed by various applications or front-end, user-driven environments. Project teams will need to apply data design techniques to the initially derived entity relationship model, which is typically in first normal form, to create a "normalized" data model. Normalization was developed by data design pioneers decades ago and is based on mathematical models that ensure the usability and integrity of the resulting relational database.

Most data analysts agree that a viable relational database should be deployed in third normal form, although databases can be in first, second, third, fourth, or even fifth normal form. Once legacy data has been accurately loaded into the data model, with discrepancies reconciled as needed, data design analysts who understand the desired level of normalization and the process for achieving it should normalize the model. The following is a quick overview of high-level normalization guidelines. These guidelines are not meant to replace more detailed techniques, tools, or skilled analyst support.

The first step in achieving a normalized data model involves finding and eliminating all repeating attributes under a given entity. This typically means turning repeating groups into a new entity definition. A second step determines if any non-key attributes depend on only part of the key to ensure uniqueness. If so, that portion of the key should be broken out into a new entity. A subsequent step would move all attributes dependent on that new entity into that new entity. This essentially separates entities into separate tables in the relational database produced from this modeling exercise. From a practical perspective, the process of looking up data based on a key field value, such as a customer number, is greatly streamlined in a normalized database.

Analysts will also need to verify that each non-key attribute within an entity does not depend on another non-key attribute. If it does, analysts will need to create a new entity that uses this attribute as the key along with all other non-key attributes that rely on this new key field. This rule, for example, ensures that a secondary telephone number, which identifies backup contact information, could be established as a key within a unique entity called "Backup Contact."

Various data modeling tools support the normalization process with an "intelligent assist" capability. These tools may be used to augment data analyst skills on the project. Readers should note that certain vendors promote data transformation shortcuts that produce relational database from nonrelational data structures, but bypass the refinement and normalization steps outlined here. This concept is discussed in Section 11.7.

11.7 Quick and Dirty Data Migration Projects

Moving from a nonrelational to a relational data environment can stem from motivations other than improved data accessibility. For example, some organizations want to eliminate a proprietary database environment because of poor support, high maintenance fees, or a lack of individuals who understand how these data structures work. In some cases, management's main goal is to eliminate an old data structure as quickly as possible to cut annual licensing fees. In these situations, "quick and dirty" data conversions tend to be the migration pattern of choice.

The quick and dirty data migration typically involves using a tool, coupled with a vendor service, to read program source and data definition language code and convert database call structures to embedded SQL. SQL is the standard access mode used to read and update data within a relational database. Such an approach sacrifices comprehensiveness, quality, and integrity within the resulting relational database for the sake of time. The result is a database that is poorly designed, limited in its accessibility and flexibility, and detrimental to the business units relying on this data.

A second limitation of this approach is that it is driven by the applications being converted as opposed to a comprehensive view of data requirements across the business units that rely on that data. For example, if I were a manager who commissioned a network-to-relational database conversion for my billing application, the service vendor might convert my system and accompanying database to DB2 (the IBM relational database) without considering a second billing system that defines common or related billing data.

In this situation, a good deal of time and effort may have been wasted on a database migration that will need to be repeated along with significant redesign work. In other words, an opportunity to improve data integration and user accessibility will have been missed because of a quick and dirty migration.

Management should carefully consider the goals of these projects and broaden their scope and related approach to ensure that the resulting solution delivers business value to the enterprise. This will ensure that a project driven by the perceived need to reduce vendor maintenance fees does not result in reduced user responsiveness, lost revenues, or increased costs over the long term.

11.8 Object Derivation: Issues and Options

One aspect of creating component-based architectures involves object-oriented analysis. The object derivation approach discussed here is one option for a project team wishing to migrate to an object-oriented environment. Deriving objects from a legacy environment involves deriving a relational data model and transforming this model into an object model.

The reason for creating a relational data model as an interim step is that commercial, object-oriented applications use relational databases as their data repository for speed and accessibility. In other words, because legacy data will need to be migrated into a relational database for deployment, a relational data model is a required step in the process.

Various software products support objectification of legacy environments as well as the derivation of objects from relational database designs. One such product facilitates the reengineering of legacy data structures to an object-oriented database using artificial intelligence. This type of product, which is listed in Appendix A, allows analysts to derive object-oriented databases from relational databases, hierarchical databases, such as the IBM IMS product, and IBM VSAM file structures. A number of other products also support the reengineering of relational database definitions into object representations.

These types of software products are typically bundled into Java development environments and have the ability to create relational views from object views and object views from relational views. Assuming the availability of this type of technology, I have provided some general guidelines geared at providing a basic understanding of the process for management teams.

Object derivation incorporates the transformation of entities within a relational environment into objects, further refines this object model based on a series of techniques, and encapsulates business rules along with the data defined within these objects [1]. Table 11.1 depicts some of the differences between data entity types and object types. These rules should help analysts who need to understand the bi-directional translation between entities and objects. In reality, entity and object types are similar except for the fact that objects encapsulate processing rules along with data within a given object.

Regardless of one's position on object orientation, planning teams should keep in mind that any transformation task should be driven by business requirements

Table 11.1 Entity Types Differ from Object Types

Entity Type	Object Type
Represents a data view only	An object type has encapsulated process
Simple, no internal structure (all attribute types relate only to the identifier	Simple or complex, can have internal structure (composite relationships)
Must have at least on attribute	Can have not attributes; the existence of an instance is meaningful in itself
Must have identifying attribute or attributes	Object types require no identifiers
Singular entity types (only one instance) are not used	A singular object type is possible
Interacts with processes (must be established and then modified or used)	Has process encapsulated in it (each process encapsulated with one object type)

(Source: USRM/Comsys.)

and not by the desire to use a specific development paradigm or technology. The synchronization of objects with legacy data and business rules can be managed through the transformation repository but requires an object modeling tool to create the object model. A UML diagramming tool is well suited for such a task.

11.9 Data Warehouse Considerations

"A data warehouse is a single, enterprise-wide collection of data that is subject-oriented, integrated, nonvolatile, and time variant" [2]. A data warehouse is a place where operational data can be loaded and synchronized as a source of ongoing information for users and customers who need to see that information consolidated and packaged under a common set of readily accessible views.

The data warehouse does not impact existing operational data structures, but rather creates an extracted relational view of operational data. This consolidated data view can then be used for customer inquiries and other functions that would be impossible to obtain from the operational data. Operational data tends to be too fragmented and splintered across disparate physical file structures, hardware platforms, formats, and locations to support this requirement.

As previously discussed, legacy data capture and the derivation of a bottom-up relational data model provide the necessary foundation for the creation of a data warehouse. Project teams pursuing the development of a data warehouse will want to ensure that they incorporate all data structures of interest in the initial data analysis and capture process. For example, if billing data is being loaded into a data warehouse so that customer hotline personnel can have access to this information in one place and in a common format, all essential billing data should be included in the bottom-up data derivation portion of this project.

The subsequent implementation steps for a data warehouse project differ from an operational data transformation project because legacy application and data structures remain untouched. Warehouse project teams will need to create or license software that can perform ongoing data capture, integrity checking, consolidation, format reconciliation, and warehouse data population.

Rationalized, composite data definitions provide the basis for the operational data extraction process. Extract programs can use rationalized record definitions to obtain an accurate view of legacy data that may be unclear when viewed through a single Copy member definition. Analysts can then use these same record definitions as input to the creation of a relational data model and subsequently define a database as the repository for the warehoused data. Integrity checking routines can apply the data cleanup process discussed in Chapter 10.

Data warehouse tools and third-party expertise should be leveraged to streamline the development, deployment, and management of the data warehouse environment. The metadata repository plays a critical role in tracking and synchronizing operational and warehouse data and should be incorporated into these projects as an ongoing tool.

11.10 Data Architecture Redesign: A Strategic Opportunity

Legacy data tends to be stored in very large file structures and databases. Because of this, it may be inconceivable to consider moving this data into a relational environment for reasons such as performance or the magnitude of the effort. Legacy data architectures, however, tend to be the source of poor performance as well as the inability of a business to respond quickly to time-critical requests from users and customers. Management should reconsider data architecture transformation based on the need to provide more flexible and accessible information for users and customers.

I was speaking recently with a data management analyst who wondered how a Java application could ever process millions of customer records on a nightly basis. This individual, however, was asking the wrong question. Regardless of whether the application he referred to remained in COBOL or was re-architected into Java, redesigning the data and application architecture could yield significant benefits for the enterprise. Because modern databases and hardware are becoming increasingly efficient, the data in the large customer master file might be a legitimate redesign target if business requirements warrant such a project. It might be possible, for example, to replace the nightly batch processing with an application that performs real-time updates to a DB2 database residing on a mainframe. The business goals for such a project would need to be very concise, and management would need to balance performance with data accessibility requirements.

Data architecture redesign can address a wide variety of integration, integrity, performance, accessibility, and business agility requirements if addressed by a collaborative team of cross-functional business and IT analysts. The continued patching or ignoring of these issues, however, will only make the problem worse and harder to correct over the long term.

The process for redesigning an operational data architecture utilizes the approaches discussed in Sections 11.4 through 11.6. Such an effort would need to be closely coordinated with the functional architecture redesign and redeployment approaches outlined in Sections 11.11 through 11.19. Chapter 12 provides a case-study-oriented discussion on how a project team would approach a comprehensive data, functional, and technical architecture redesign and redeployment initiative.

11.11 Business Rule Transformation

"Business rules embody the fundamental business practices and policies of the enterprise" [3]. Business rule capture, redesign, and reuse are driven by changes in business practices and policies that in turn impact the applications containing these business rules. The benefits can be significant depending on the context of the project under which rule extraction is being performed. One thing is generally agreed upon by most IT analysts: The business rules embedded in legacy applications perform vital tasks that are critical to the business continuity of the enterprise.

The challenge involves knowing which rules are relevant and how to extract them from the implementation-dependent environment in which they are entangled. If this can be accomplished, business rules, along with relevant enterprise data, can be redeployed in agile architectures that allow an enterprise to respond to highly dynamic business environments.

Rule identification and reuse can fulfill a wide range of business requirements. For example, a project team may wish to upgrade inhouse financial applications, but not know where certain processes are defined or performed. This is particularly challenging when business rules are redundantly defined across a spectrum of applications and environments. Rule identification and capture, under this scenario, fulfills a documentation role.

The project-level repository links business rule objects back to the program or programs that implement those business rules. This type of documentation, given that it is updated on a regular basis, provides an excellent guide to analysts who need to maintain or enhance an application. Repository maintenance, under this scenario, becomes part of the application documentation process.

Using business rule analysis in this way may seem like overkill, but this is not the case. If application support teams apply business rule documentation on an ongoing basis, they would simply update the transformation repository on a target-of-opportunity basis. This means that any change or research applied to an application would result in an update to the business rule documentation within the repository. A business rule object in the transformation repository has a name, description, and relationship pointer to the program(s) and paragraph(s) (i.e., procedure object) in which it has been implemented.

Other applications of business rule extraction are more strategic. Management may wish to implement an ERP package but be unclear as to which business rules map to the business functionality defined within that package. Business rules captured within the transformation repository facilitate the mapping of existing business logic that may be defined within the package or missing from the package. If functionality is missing from the package and important to the business community, then the program or programs defining that logic should be retained in the post-implementation environment. Today, this type of analysis is applied haphazardly at best.

Analysts may additionally want to integrate related applications containing overlapping functionality and the transformation repository facilitates this process. Tracking rules within and across various projects is an essential part of the transformation approach. Specifically, business rule identification and mapping ensure that redundant rules are recognized, consolidated, or discarded within the context of phasing the transformation of the application architecture. As rules are consolidated, analysts would update the repository accordingly. The level of complexity of large commercial applications demands this level of formality during the phased retooling of legacy applications.

Additional projects that benefit from business rule extraction include application integration, component migration, and any project that requires the understanding or reuse of legacy applications. The following sections discuss business rule definition, categorization, setup work, requirements tracing, capture, consolidation, and reuse.

11.12 Business Rule Definition

What exactly is a business rule? There has been some industry debate as well as meetings of industry groups that have sought to define a business rule. Business rules can exist in paper format, in source code, or even in the head of a senior manager. Based on the stated objectives of this book, I am limiting our discussion to those business rules that can be found within production computing environments. The following definitions are adopted from the Object Management Group (OMG) [4].

1. Rules are declarations of policy or conditions that must be satisfied.
2. Business rules are rules that govern the way a business operates.

For purposes of legacy business rule identification and extraction, I have refined the OMG definitions to say that

A business rule is a combination of conditional and imperative logic that changes the state of a business object or business data element.

Note the phrase "business object or business data element." Much of the source code currently running in organizations has countless tests of switches, status code indicators, and similar environmental elements. These elements do not constitute globally defined business data, at least from a user's or customer's perspective. Confining business rules to logic that acts on business data, therefore, draws a line in the sand that analysts can use as a litmus test for what is and is not a business rule. An example clarifies the above definition. In the English language, a rule might appear as follows.

- If account balance is zero, deduct two times total monthly charges.
- If account balance turns negative, calculate a penalty.
- If account balance is positive, deduct the total monthly charges.
- If account balance turns negative after deducting monthly charges, calculate a penalty.
- Output the account balance to a posting file.

The above rule seems simple enough—at least when written in English. Note that "calculate penalty" is a separate business rule that is triggered by an event in which an account balance drops below zero. Another version of this business rule can be viewed in its COBOL source code format in Figure 11.3. This example shows how a business rule can evolve into a format that is less understandable than the above English version. The source code in Figure 11.3 has undergone modification since it was first implemented as shown by the in-line comments.

Other source code languages would implement a business rule differently, but still require logic to test account balance value conditions and take action as a result of these tests. Tests can be complex. In other words, multiple conditionals may require testing during the implementation of a business rule. In Figure 11.3, for example, the logic uses multiple tests to determine if an account balance is zero or less than zero. It tests the balance again to see if it goes below zero. This style was largely a result of the preference of the programmer who wrote the code.

Note that legacy program logic can be confusing. The formatting of source code logic, for example, is left to the whim of the individual programmer. Poorly aligned If/Else logic, shown in Figure 11.3, is ignored by compilers, code analyzers, and reverse engineering tools—but can confuse analysts. Code structuring tools can, however, clean this logic up.

Transformation teams may not agree on the OMG or other industry definitions of a business rule. This is not important as long as the team can agree upon

Business Rule Candidate

```
 B9000-POST-8000.
* CALCULATE CURR AND OUTPUT ACCOUNT BALANCE TO POSTING SUSPENSE VSAM
     PERFORM B9050-CALC-MONTHLY-CHARGES THRU B9050-EXIT.
     IF DDACCT-ACCT-SRVC-CHG-FL NOT = "W" AND "G" AND "X"
          IF HEA1010A-ACCT-BAL = ZERO
             COMPUTE HEA1010A-ACCT-BAL = DDACCT-ACCT-BAL - (WS-TOT-MONTHLY-CHARGES * 2)
             IF HEA1010A-ACCT-BAL < ZERO
                 PERFORM U8010-CALC-PENALTY        THRU U8010-EXIT
                 MOVE "Y" TO HEA1010A-PENALTY-FL
             COMPUTE HEA1010A-ACCT-BAL = HEA1010A-ACCT-BAL - WS-TOT-PENLTY-CHG
          ELSE NEXT SENTENCE
          ELSE
             COMPUTE HEA1010A-ACCT-BAL = DDACCT-ACCT-BAL - WS-TOT-MONTHLY-CHARGES
             IF HEA1010A-ACCT-BAL < ZERO
                 PERFORM U8010-CALC-PENALTY        THRU U8010-EXIT
                 MOVE "Y" TO HEA1010A-PENALTY-FL
             COMPUTE HEA1010A-ACCT-BAL = HEA1010A-ACCT-BAL - WS-TOT-PENLTY-CHG
          ELSE NEXT SENTENCE
     ELSE IF DDACCT-ACCT-SRVC-CHG-FL = "W"
             MOVE WS-TOT-MONTHLY-CHARGES TO HEA1010A-SRVC-CH-DFR-HLD.
**** DISABLED 05/03/89 BY BGG - HANDLED DIFFERNTLY NOW
***       ELSE IF DDACCT-ACCT-SRVC-CHG-FL = "G"
***          MOVE WS-TOT-MONTHLY-CHARGES TO HEA1010A-SRVC-CH-GIC-HLD.
     PERFORM B9100-FILL-SGMENT                THRU B9100-EXIT.
     PERFORM B9200-OUTPT-POST                 THRU B9200-EXIT.
 B9000-EXIT. EXIT.
```

Scope of business rule candidate

Figure 11.3
COBOL logic block is a rule candidate, but output logic should be segregated from account balance calculation, depending on reuse objectives.
(Source: © Netron, Inc. Hotrod Product 2002. Reprinted with permission.)

a common definition of a business rule that can be applied to business rule identification and extraction efforts within the enterprise The most important consideration is to keep the definition of a business rule as simple as possible. More information can be obtained on the topic of business rules from the Business Rules Group [5].

The rule categorization and extraction discussions that follow should further clarify the definition of business rules within the context of finding and reusing those rules on transformation projects.

11.13 Business Rule Categorization

Not all business rules are equal. While constraining the definition of a business rule by stating that it should test and modify business data is valid, not everyone agrees on the precise definition of business data versus non-business data. To alleviate this issue, project teams should have a rule classification or categorization scheme that they can use to identify, organize, classify, and discard rules during the scope of a project.

Rule classification schemes vary, and this is why transformation analysts should agree upon a scheme that works best for their enterprise. Once a scheme has been identified, any project attempting to identify and extract business rules should adhere to that scheme. The classification category should become an attribute within the business rule object defined in the transformation repository.

As one embarks on rule classification, consider that only about "20% to 30% of the source code within a given system can be linked to actual business rules. The remaining code tends to deal with the physical constraints of the environment" [4]. This statistic alone is reason enough to remember that wholesale conversion of applications to Java, C++, or other object paradigms will result in unnecessary and extraneous procedural logic being imported into an object-oriented environment. This logic would then become meaningless and the resulting application would be useless to the object programming team.

One step toward avoiding this problem is to classify the type of logic that should not be reused. Consider the following business rule classification scheme as one way to meet his goal.

- **Presentation rules.** Specifies a user interface rule. These rules tend to be embedded in user interface macros or in source code. Presentation rules include display, validation, and other user-facing rules that govern the acceptance, format, and existence of a given data field on a screen or on a report. EAI interfaces complicate an analyst's ability to determine where interfaces exist and how they are being used because external interfaces are being governed by EAI software and not by the application itself. EAI middleware may therefore need to be included in the rule analysis process.

- **Data validation rules.** These rules constrain a data element's type, value, and contents. Data validation rules can be found in menu management routines as well as in program source code. For example, a rule may state that a telephone number must be numeric or that a data must fall within a given range.

- **Condition/imperative rules.** The condition/imperative forms the basic foundation for a business rule. A condition tests the state of a data value, which in turn can trigger certain imperative actions. Imperative statements transfer data from one element to another, compute or calculate a value, invoke another rule, update permanent (also known as persistent) data structures, or deliver information back to the user. The condition portion of a rule is also known as an event because it triggers a rule to be invoked.

Other business rule categorization schemes can get more complex. Most notably, the condition/imperative concept can be decomposed into more categories, depending on the nature of the imperative. For example, if an imperative statement computes a value, then this would translate into a derivation rule because data is "derived" from a calculation of related business data [6].

As stated earlier, I kept this classification scheme simplistic for purposes of analysis within the context of reuse. The three-part classification scheme above is also in keeping with the concept of an application having a presentation layer, data access layer, and business rule layer.

Within this categorization scheme, logic may be a valid target for reuse or it may be deemed irrelevant. This is up to the team evaluating that logic, but if rules are going to be referenced in the transformation repository or reused, they should have direct business value. Table 11.2 depicts a list of rule types that may be excluded from the category of business logic, depending on the goals of a given business rule analysis task.

Much of the logic shown in this table is implementation-dependent, but that does not mean it should automatically be discarded. Each logic category defined within this table should be reviewed by the project team at the onset of the project to determine what type of application program logic to capture or ignore during the business rule analysis process.

For example, dead code and extraneous logic are rarely useful in any type of transformation project. Unless the team is directed to save specific dead code, it should be ignored. Extraneous logic, which tests a conditional situation and invokes a path that could not possibly be taken based on data, should also be discarded—unless this is a coding error.

Table 11.2 Identifying and Discarding Non-Business Logic

Non-Business	Logic Non-Business Logic Identification
Syntactically dead code	Logic never executed regardless of data values.
Semantically dead code	Logic not executed based on setting of data values.
Program initialization	Logic that initializes element or record area values.
Input/output logic	Code accessing physical data. Includes call, read, write, and other I/O statements.
Output area build	Logic that moves data to screen and report work areas.
Status checking	Tests directly after I/O commands, checking communication or other status codes.
Error handling	Imperative logic that invokes exception reporting or module termination based on status code results.
Data manipulation	Database or file manipulation logic.
Environmental logic	Manages security, homegrown technology, date handling, or similar routines.
Extraneous logic	Redundant conditionals, mutually exclusive tests, or similar routines.

Certain non-business logic may be worth capturing and saving, depending on the type of project being undertaken. For example, data manipulation logic retains a high degree of value if the data architecture is not going to change. If the application is being transformed from a hierarchical to a relational database, however, then data manipulation logic loses its intrinsic value.

Other logic categories listed in Table 11.2 may also retain their value or be discarded from a reuse perspective. Error-condition testing, environmental status code checking, or program initialization logic are all likely to be handled automatically in the target technological environment. If not, then this logic should be retained and categorized accordingly.

Analysts should clarify a rule classification scheme and guidelines for retaining or ignoring non-business logic within the context of the project as a prerequisite for any transformation project involving business rule identification and reuse.

11.14 Business Rule Extraction—Setup Requirements

Business rule extraction requires certain preparation work. This setup work includes placing the rule extraction process within the context of a business-driven project and transformation initiative, identifying tool options, establishing the transformation repository, assessing related data usage, and performing a high-level assessment of the business units and applications of interest.

Project context is very important for any effort that plans to leverage business rule capture and reuse. If the goal is to document cross-functional applications to streamline planned upgrades, the project will likely require less effort than a project that plans to reuse business rules within a component-based environment. Reuse requires identifying rules, discarding extraneous rules, logging them in a repository, consolidating overlapping or redundant rules, and repackaging them for reuse. It is also important to know which rules to ignore and which ones to capture and reuse.

I discussed how environmentally dependent logic, such as error checking for a TP monitor, can be ignored assuming that user interfaces are being rebuilt in HTML or a distributed GUI interface. These rules cannot be ignored, however, if the project is merely rehosting the application and reusing the interface logic. Project planning teams must therefore clarify the goals of the project and related impact on the business rule extraction process at the onset of the project.

Planning teams will also need to ensure that they have the right software tools to help identify, capture, and track business rules. Because there are countless business rules, many of which are redundant and do not adhere to any predefined structure or format, project teams should make every effort to automate the capture and analysis of those rules. A business rule extraction tool should ideally bypass or highlight implementation dependent logic, store extracted rules, signify when a rule invokes another rule, display a rule, interface with a rule tracking repository, and transform extracted rules into reusable formats.

While automated tools simplify the rule extraction process, analysts can also apply source code edit and slicing tools to this task. A standing guideline to tool use for business rule extraction is to use a tool if one is available for the language and platform you are working on. If a rule extraction tool is not available for the computing languages involved in the project, analysts should use source code edit or code slicing tools where available.

Most business rule analysis and capture technology uses an internal repository to store captured business logic. This tool-specific repository is in addition to the more generalized transformation repository referenced earlier. Business rule capture tools may be static or dynamic, as discussed in Chapter 7. Figure 11.4 shows a screen view of how one business rule capture product (i.e., the Netron Hotrod product) automatically isolates business logic extracted from a COBOL application. Figure 11.4 also depicts a program-level process flow analysis facility that depicts the flow of a program. This feature assists in the rule analysis process.

Automated Flow and Rule Capture

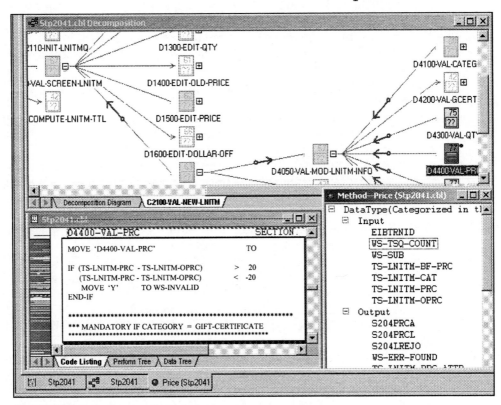

Figure 11.4

Automated business rule capture also depicts process flow and data element usage.

(Source: © Netron, Inc. Hotrod Product 2002. Reprinted with permission.)

While static rule capture tools are available for COBOL, dynamic analysis tools are more commonly found for languages such as C, C++, and various real-time languages and environments. One reason to use dynamic analysis tools as an alternative to static rule capture technology involves the type of application being analyzed. Certain real-time systems have very few output screens or reports. This lack of user interfaces limits the use of reverse requirements tracing (see Section 11.15) and other functional segregation and decomposition techniques. For example, a FORTRAN application that determines new oil drilling locations may run for hours and produce only a few numbers. Dynamic analysis traces logic during execution, identifies live logic paths, and forms the basis for business rule candidate extraction.

A hybrid tool category involves a static rule capture tool that can simulate the flow of potential data values through a program or an application. This type of product, which is still in the evolutionary stages from a commercial perspective, combines the ability to statically identify rules but constrains the analysis to logic paths invoked based on viable data that is simulated through the system. The user of the tool would be able to trigger, query, and review this analysis in real time.

Because many commercial environments have thousands of rules spread across hundreds of applications, the complexity of the rule classification process could quickly overwhelm a manual tracking process. In other words, business rule analysts can get lost in the details. The team should therefore extend the use of the transformation repository to log and record rules, rule location within an application, and the relationship of those rules to enterprise data and the physical environment. For ease of reference, Figure 11.5 shows the project-level transformation repository originally introduced in Chapter 5.

The transformation repository must be able to represent, define, and map these rules to logical definitions. As business rules are found, analysts log them in the repository and link them to the system component that physically defines them. Redundant rules are represented by mapping the rule object to itself and defining additional relationships that link a rule in various programs and applications.

The transformation repository grows in importance as project teams begin to map these rules to target functions defined in requirements specifications or packaged applications. This can involve adding attributes to the business rule object, including description, rule type (i.e., legacy, target, or both), and rule classification type. A relationship pointer links a rule to the exact source program and paragraph (i.e., procedure object) or other physical application object that defines that actual rule.

Data usage analysis, which ranges from record grouping analysis on the one hand to the creation of a bottom-up data model on the other hand, leverages business rule extraction projects. The bottom-up data model can serve as a place to represent data validation rules that are captured from the legacy environment. Even if the project did not require the creation of a bottom-up, logical data model,

Detailed Legacy Transformation Repository

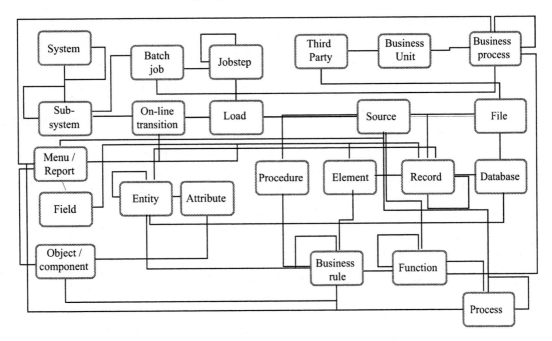

Figure 11.5
Detailed transformation repository depicts legacy and target system components and relationships to support transition planning and management.

analysts should minimally perform cross-functional record grouping analysis for all applications involved in a rule capture project.

A clear understanding of cross-functional data usage allows the project team to more effectively decipher certain business rules. They will also be able to identify redundant rule candidates more effectively when a project spans multiple applications that use variations of the same data with different data names. For example, an order validation rule may use a field called ITEM-NO when a similar rule uses a field called I-NUM. Record grouping analysis results would identify these two fields as defining the same data within a common record group. If the data definitions have been rationalized, rule analysis would be further simplified. Some rule extraction tools can recognize application-wide data element relationships, but most do not.

One critical preparatory step requires analysts to segment applications by performing a high-level assessment of all applications of interest. This requires performing a functional assessment as outlined in Chapter 8. This preliminary analysis also ensures that the scope of the business rule extraction effort is well defined and does not leave out critical applications or programs. Other relevant

assessment tasks include identifying shared data among applications and exter-
nally shared interfaces.

As the project team segments enterprise applications into interrelated subsets, they should reflect the results of these analysis tasks in the transformation
repository. The rule extraction process then extends the preliminary analysis, performed during the project-level assessment, to the business rule level.

Project assessment tasks may have identified flaws or weaknesses in the
applications of interest that should be reviewed and optionally corrected prior to
rule extraction. Removal of code flaws, structuring convoluted logic, and slicing
cumbersome modules simplifies rule extraction. Data name rationalization, as discussed earlier, also streamlines rule analysis and consolidation. Code improvement
techniques must of course be justified as a separate item by the project planning
team. Code improvement is applicable where portions of the existing application
will continue to run in production in their current technological format.

11.15 Reverse Requirements Tracing and Process Flow Analysis

The first level of business rule analysis involves a process called reverse requirements tracing. This process, which is based on user views of an application, augments the high-level functional assessment discussed earlier. Reverse requirements tracing is useful in situations where analysts have a limited functional
understanding of the applications of interest. It is also useful in situations where
the targeted applications are large and cross multiple functional units.
Applications of interest are considered large if they represent more than a million
lines of code.

Reverse requirements tracing requires user presentation views captured
during the presentation layer analysis outlined in Chapter 8. If this analysis was
not performed, analysts should refer back to that discussion in Chapter 8. These
user views, which include online screens and offline reports, should be linked
back to the programs that use them inside the transformation repository. This
allows analysts to map a given function back to a specific source program, which
becomes important when mapping applications to target specifications.

There are two levels of reverse requirements tracing, although the tasks
involved overlap. Figure 11.6 depicts the highest level of reverse requirements
tracing, which involves reviewing header information on screens and reports to
discern the functionality being performed by a given source program that is
linked back to that report. This level of analysis may already be in place based on
work performed during the functional assessment. If not, analysts should validate
captured functions with business analysts, record them in the transformation
repository, and link them back to their respective user interfaces. User interfaces

Reverse Requirements Tracing of Functions

FORM 004 - Create current function / process hierarchy - establish current functions

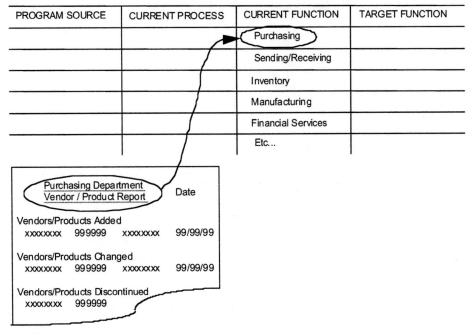

PROGRAM SOURCE	CURRENT PROCESS	CURRENT FUNCTION	TARGET FUNCTION
		Purchasing	
		Sending/Receiving	
		Inventory	
		Manufacturing	
		Financial Services	
		Etc...	

Purchasing Department
Vendor / Product Report   Date

Vendors/Products Added
xxxxxxxx   999999   xxxxxxxx   99/99/99

Vendors/Products Changed
xxxxxxxx   999999   xxxxxxxx   99/99/99

Vendors/Products Discontinued
xxxxxxxx   999999

Figure 11.6
Reverse requirements tracing determines application functionality by tracking user views back into the source code.
(Source: USRM/Comsys.)

are automatically linked back to source programs based on the environmental analysis defined in Chapter 8.

The next level of reverse requirements tracing is shown in Figure 11.7 and documents application processes. I discussed processes earlier in two contexts. A business process occurs outside an automated system but may invoke an automated system to support that process. A process within an automated system is very similar and is a subset of a high-level function. In the example in Figure 11.7, the analyst discovered three processes involving vendor products. In this case, the program or programs that use this interface support the vendor and product selection, change, and roll-off processes.

Process flow analysis is a derivative of reverse requirements tracing. When a process is uncovered, analysts should log that process in the transformation repository. The discovery of redundant processes triggers the creation of a relationship back to the process object and a new relationship to the interface defining that process. A process should also be linked to the high-level function it

Reverse Requirements Tracing of Logical Processes

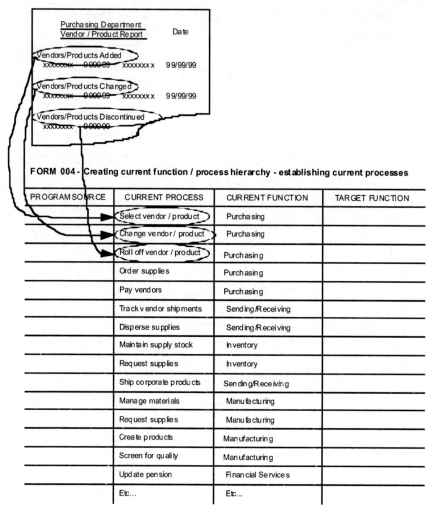

Figure 11.7
Reverse requirements tracing identifies detailed processes within functions by tracking user views back into the source code.
(Source: USRM/Comsys.*)*

belongs to, the user interface where it originated, and, as I will discuss below, the business rule that implements that process.

The transformation repository, which can be used to generate the forms shown in Figures 11.6 and 11.7, creates a framework for subsequent business rule capture. If analysts are seeking business rules relating to vendor selection, they now know where to look. The reverse requirements tracing process is also an excellent way to quickly document large applications. Reverse requirements tracing works well for business systems, but not as well for real-time applications that have limited user interfaces.

The repository can be used to generate a process flow analysis to support subsequent architecture transformation. Process flow analysis is based on the ability to track the execution sequence of a batch or online application and reflect that sequence in the "process invokes process" relationship within the repository. Process invocation analysis, which should be completed as each process is loaded into the repository, is based on batch job flow and user analysis of transaction flows.

11.16 Business Rule Identification and Logging

Finding business rules is not the only rule identification and capture task. Determining where a rule begins and ends, declaring its purpose, logging it, mapping redundant rules, and determining which rules to ignore are all challenging, related tasks. When undertaking rule identification and capture, analysts should use the high-level function/process decomposition discussed above as a guide to seeking out specific rules or general categories of rules.

Analysts should additionally ensure that they have secured business rule capture software, preloaded the transformation repository with environmental and related metadata, and have access to assessment results performed up to this point. The data definition analysis and, if applicable, bottom-up data model should also be used as a guide to deciphering rules as needed.

Two rules of thumb should be considered when identifying rules. "A good business rule is atomic and declarative" [6]. Being atomic means that complex rules can be decomposed into more simplistic rules. The business rule shown in Figure 11.3 was decomposed into four, more simplistic rules. A declarative rule means that a rule should only state what the rule is and not state how a rule is implemented. Using a declarative approach to logging a business rule is a good guideline for specifying the description of a rule within the transformation repository.

For example, the business rule in Figure 11.3 would be described in the transformation repository as "Calculate Account Balance." The initial discovery of this rule requires an analyst to add a new business rule object to the transformation repository along with a relationship to the procedure (i.e., paragraph) and, via the procedure link, to the source program defining this rule. The procedure name in this case is "B9000-POST-8000." Analysts may optionally omit procedure identification and link the business rule directly to an application source program object.

Analysts should also link each business rule object to the element referenced by that business rule, as shown in Figure 11.5. This is important because legacy elements map back to data attributes, which in turn link back to entities in the bottom-up data model. These mappings will be used during architecture reconstruction.

If the project team discovers additional logic that performs a similar, yet slightly different, function, an existing rule may require further qualification. For example, the "Calculate Account Balance" could be further qualified by renaming it "Increment Account Balance by Monthly Charges." In many cases, business rule identification uncovers logic that implements the same business rule in other programs and applications. When this occurs, analysts should update the business rule object in the repository by adding a relationship link to the programs or procedures that contain additional implementations of that rule.

To track the sequence of business rule invocation, analysts should link business rule objects in the repository to the business process that the rule implements. This is accomplished by linking the rule object to a process object, which in turn is linked to a business process. Business analysts can assist with this effort, or the project team can leverage the repository itself to determine invocation sequences. If the transformation repository was updated throughout the assessment stage of the project, it likely contains enough information to draw the connection between a rule and an abstract business process. Each process is linked to a user interface (i.e., menu or report) that has been linked to a source program. The source program is in turn linked to a business rule. Following paths through the repository provides analysts with a good overview of business process and rule flow through an application and the enterprise.

The importance of creating a link between an application process and a business rule becomes more evident as we examine the architecture reconstruction and event synchronization later in this chapter. In short, the process execution sequence dictates the sequence in which rules are applied to support a given application function. This sequence provides guidance on how to specify and reconstruct these rules in the context of the target architecture.

One caution when identifying business rules involves the tendency to concatenate rules. Transformation analysts should consider that a rule in a legacy environment could invoke other rules. In the Figure 11.3 example, the rule "Calculate Current Account Balance" invoked a rule called "Calculate Penalty." Tracing rule imperative statements into other rules and, as a result, creating an overly complex or concatenated rule, could hinder rule identification and capture.

Confusion stems from a common question among transformation analysts. If a rule invokes another rule, does the invoked rule become a part of the invoking rule? The guideline for this situation is fairly simple. If different business data is tested and/or modified in the subsequent set of conditional/imperative logic, that logic should be considered a unique business rule. In this situation, an analyst would identify and log a new rule in the repository. For example, a condition may trigger invocation of a subroutine that contains four data transfer statements that are related directly to the conditional test. In this case the conditional and the data transfer logic may be considered a single rule.

11.17 Business Rule Capture and Redundancy Identification

Now that we have discussed how to identify and log business rules, I want to outline various guidelines and techniques for capturing and consolidating business rules. This process involves identifying the type of rules needed for the project and using automated tools, analysis techniques, and prior assessment results to extract and consolidate business rules. Analysts can use tools specifically designed to capture business rules or, if business rule capture technology is not available, apply interactive edit, code slicing, static analysis, or dynamic analysis technology to trace and capture business rules.

Prior to embarking on this effort, analysts should establish constraints on the types of rules to be captured. This involves reviewing project objectives to determine what is essential to the delivery of a successful project. For example, if a project is attempting to capture all rules related to a purchasing function across multiple applications, all purchasing programs and applications will need to be included in the applications of interest. Under this scenario, analysts should ignore any business rules not related to purchasing functions and processes.

The project team will also require guidance on how to distinguish which rules are to be kept and which rules should be ignored. Criteria for finding rules within the previously introduced purchasing example include

- Capturing business rules that use a reference or modify data defined within a specific record group category. In this case, any data defined within any purchasing master file, update file, or database, along with any locally defined data related to that data, would tell an analyst to capture that rule.
- Capturing derivative business rules that are triggered by a purchasing rule. If, for example, logic is triggered to notify accounting of a purchase transaction, that logic would constitute a rule candidate for purposes of this analysis.
- Ignoring logic linked to the manipulation of physical data structures used to store purchasing data. Any logic, for example, that contains error tests or triggers a database search should be ignored. The reason for ignoring data manipulation logic is that the new database will be relational and not require logic to traverse a hierarchical data structure.
- Ignoring logic linked to the status or error checking of the CICS interface for the application.
- Ignoring dead code, extraneous logic, and initialization routines that do not directly impact purchasing data or functionality.

Business rule analysis should follow a logical sequence because rules make more sense when reviewed and captured in context. For example, an order-processing rules sequence receives an order, checks inventory levels, reduces inventory levels, triggers a shipment, and so on. Logging business rules in their natural sequence simplifies the process for the analyst team because they will need to link each rule to process flows within the transformation repository.

In situations where an application veers from any detectable processing sequence, analysts should begin at the point where a user or a batch processing cycle begins and then proceed from that point forward. This includes following subroutine invocations into source program logic where applicable. Analysts can meet this objective by

- Reviewing execution sequences with business users.
- Identifying all source programs linked to the processes uncovered during the reverse requirements tracing stage of the project.
- Sequencing the review of these programs based on the batch execution flow derived during the environmental analysis phase of the project.
- Further sequencing the program reviews by using the logical sequence of online transactions defined in the transformation repository.
- Performing rule extraction beginning with the first source program in the sequence and proceeding through each program until all relevant rules have been captured and logged.

In many cases, applications will divert from what might be perceived as a logical sequence. This is particularly true with online applications that function on an event-driven basis. Even online systems, however, were designed to run in some anticipated sequence, and analysts should follow the application flow as closely as possible when extracting rules within an event-driven environment.

Within a single source program, analysts should perform rule isolation and extraction by tracing logic paths based on various selection criteria. This includes tracing logic that leads to the creation of a given output variable, logic linked to a specific condition or variable test, and logic associated with a given input or output transaction type. The rule isolation process is very similar to the code slicing criteria outlined in Chapter 10. As analysts track a logic path, various rules will emerge. Rules should be selected based on

- The fact that certain logic references business data elements within condition/imperative logic.
- Identified transaction types or related criteria established at the onset of the project.
- Logic is tied to a path that is targeted for capture and not on the rule omission list.

In a given program module, for example, logic flow may split down three unique paths based on a processing indicator. In the case of an insurance claim processing program, three major functions may be triggered by a three-way transaction variable that signals the program to verify a claim, process a claim, or reject a claim. Each path contains unique as well as shared business logic. Analysts should categorize various rules under the processes that flow down each functional path based on their project objectives.

The project team should view each conditional and related imperative statement as a business rule candidate based on previously defined criteria. One challenge involves identifying and linking conditional tests that are physically remote from the imperative statements they trigger. Because business rules do not limit themselves to the confines of a source program, the extraction process should analyze logic across program boundaries. Figure 11.8 depicts the tracing of logic constituting a business rule that spans multiple modules. In this insurance example, a common condition and related business data establish this logic as a cohesive business rule.

Business rule extraction tools greatly simplify and streamline this process. As shown in Figure 11.4, tools can capture and isolate business rule candidates, catalog them, map rules to required input and output data elements, and repackage them in a user-friendly format. Tools can reduce the time it takes to isolate business rules by as much as 500 percent over manual approaches. Rule extraction tools can also help reconcile redundant business rules.

Business Rule Tracing and Extraction

Legacy Insurance System

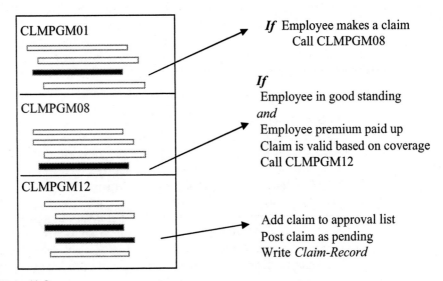

Figure 11.8
Business rule tracing supports rule capture of logic crossing physical program boundaries. This example works backward from output statements.

Redundant rule recognition and consolidation are important requirements for many organizations. Over the years, programmers and entire business units have cloned application source code in an effort to shortcut development project timeframes. This was an unfortunate attempt at reuse that was poorly managed because it used physical replication of modifiable source code rather than the reuse of executable components.

Using the transformation repository, analysts have the ability to determine if a similar or redundant rule is already defined within the application architecture. This is accomplished by interrogating all business rules previously linked to a common set of business data or business processes. This may take some investigation if the code is not identical, but certain rule extraction tools can help identify redundant business logic through a clone detection capability. Redundancy identification is extremely important for a number of reasons.

Anyone changing an application that impacts redundant business logic should know where these redundancies exist and a simple inquiry against the repository meets this need. The process of identifying redundant rules is also essential to application consolidation projects, which are discussed in more depth in Chapter 12. Business rule consolidation, within the context of current-to-target architecture mapping, is discussed further in Section 11.18.

11.18 Business Rule: Current-to-Target Mapping, Reuse, and Reconciliation

The reuse of captured business rules, which requires reconciling redundant as well as similar business rules, streamlines the overall design and development cycle for project teams. Business rule reuse facilitates the componentization of legacy business logic in its original language or in a target language such as Java. This section discusses rule reuse and consolidation within both legacy and component-based architectures.

The transformation repository facilitates mapping legacy business rules to target business rules as well as to redundant business rules defined within the legacy environment. This is an important capability given that a wide variety of transformation projects need to address business rule redundancy consolidation, target architecture mapping, and reuse.

If a set of formal target requirements has not been defined for a given project, business rule consolidation can still play a vital role within a project. Consider a "reengineering in place" initiative that needs to consolidate multiple applications into a single application. Business rule consolidation is a key element in such a project. As analysts trace business rules among various applications, they will want to consider the following issues.

- Begin the rule abstraction process by focusing on the application with the "richest" set of application logic. This will create a business rule baseline within the repository against which to map other applications.
- Verify retention requirements for implementation-dependent logic, including user interface, data access, I/O management, and related environmental logic.
- Identify redundant business rules that contain identical logic constructs to be consolidated.
- Identify similar logic that may optionally be consolidated after review and modification by analyst teams.
- Seek specific opportunities to consolidate I/O logic in order to create shared modules that manage presentation and data access layer logic.
- Within the transformation repository, define each logical rule one time and map it to the procedure and source program in the application that implements that rule.
- Collapse redundant rules from various applications into the baseline application. This will isolate unique rules and eliminate redundant functionality.

While projects using the reengineering-in-place approach can benefit from business rule extraction and consolidation, projects seeking to transform the underlying data and application architecture can derive even greater benefits. For example, assume that a business unit has committed to developing new applications in Java with a focus on Web Services and component reuse. To meet this objective, the project team wants to create target components based on business rules that have been extracted from the legacy environment. To accomplish this, the project team will want to consider the following.

- Business rule identification, extraction, and reuse should encompass all applications that contain any functionality related to the development project. Understanding the scope of the project requires current-to-target functional mapping, outlined in Chapter 8.
- Only the business rules that contribute value to a given project should be targeted for capture and reuse. This means that most implementation-dependent logic, along with business logic that does not enrich the target architecture, will need to be ignored. Analysts should verify that any logic not mapping to the target architecture is not missing from the new application design. The functional assessment results provide a good indication of whether or not this is the case based on a high-level view of the current-to-target architecture mapping.
- Deactivating business rules within the legacy environment will ensure that replication of business functionality is not propagated across new and legacy applications. This may be difficult, however, if only a portion of a function is activated in the new application. Rule capture efforts must extend

across all applications containing rules related to the new application. Section 11.19 discusses this in more depth.

- Multiple physical implementations of legacy business logic may map to a single target application function or process. This would suggest there are conflicting implementation options for a single business rule, which is extremely important to know if you plan to develop reusable application components. A development project might implement this rule incorrectly and cause additional confusion to users of the application.

- The need to transform reusable business rules from one language type to another (e.g., COBOL to Java) should be well defined at the onset of the project.

The initial current-to-target functional mapping performed during the functional assessment and the process decomposition performed during reverse requirements tracing provide a framework for mapping current-to-target business rules. The mapping and redundancy reconciliation process is outlined as follows.

- Review each function/process defined within the target architecture specifications.

- Trace the relationships between the target function and/or process object and the current function and/or process object within the transformation repository.

- For each rule linked to a legacy process, determine the applicability of reusing that business rule within the target application architecture.

- Review each legacy logic implementation linked to each legacy process, including any redundantly defined legacy rules. Redundant legacy business rules appear as a single legacy business rule object linked to multiple occurrences of a procedure/source program.

- Where one or more redundant business rules exist in a legacy application, and where those rules map to a business rule requirement in the target architecture, analysts will need to review the implementation logic to determine if it is identical.

- If the redundant business logic is found to be identical, the rules should be consolidated using the new logical data names from the redesigned data model. If the logic differs slightly, analysts will need to reconcile business rule logic discrepancies and create a new composite business rule.

- Each legacy business rule used to create a target architecture rule or component will need to be marked for deactivation in the repository. Deactivation is discussed further in Section 11.19.

- Legacy business logic will need to be transformed into either an implementation-independent business rule or into a language-specific component. Figure 11.9 depicts the mapping of legacy logic to generic business rule implementation.

- Legacy data definitions, defined within the legacy business logic, should be mapped to the new relational data names used within the target data model. Current-to-target data usage mappings are traceable through the transformation repository based on the data architecture redesign work outlined earlier in this chapter.

The above approach assumes that legacy business rules are being moved into a newly defined, model-driven application architecture. Regardless of the target language environment, formalization and componentization of business rules require the identification of both the business logic and the data used by that business logic. Business rule extraction tools support this encapsulation capability, as shown in Figure 11.10. The logic and the rules would need to be carried over into the target component environment.

A variation on this approach involves the componentization of COBOL source code using XML as the communication interface between COBOL components and the applications needing to access those components. This approach is a hybrid solution that leverages legacy application logic to form Web Serviceable components without migrating those components to Java. This option is based on the decision by the architecture team to maintain existing business rules in their current language environment versus moving those rules into a Java format.

Validating target specifications against legacy functions and processes ensures that the target architecture does not omit essential user requirements.

Business Rule Tracing and Extraction

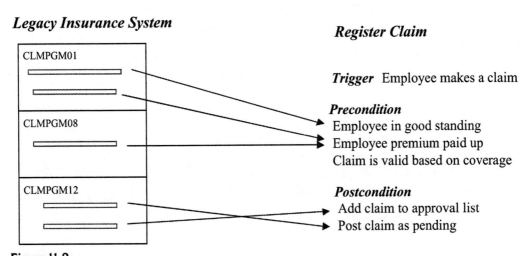

Figure 11.9
Legacy business rule reuse reduces delivery time and increases the integrity of replacement applications.
(Source: Martin/Odell, Intellicorp.)

Automated Mapping of Rules and Data Elements

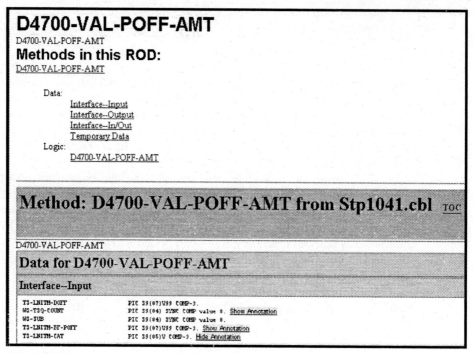

Figure 11.10
Business rule/data mapping forms baseline for component creation.
(Source: © Netron, Inc. 2000. Reprinted with permission.)

Reusing legacy business rules, on the other hand, ensures that the new application does not change critical functionality that users have come to depend on. This is essential in environments where users rely on tax calculations, employee benefits, pricing structures, contract terms, and a host of business functions that must remain consistent in the target architecture.

Automating business rule reconciliation requires the use of a business rule extraction tool that can identify, highlight, and cross-reference redundant rules captured from legacy environments. Complex projects must still track current-to-target function and process mappings in the transformation repository. Rules should be mapped to components in the target architecture. Large-scale rule reuse and deactivation become manageable using this approach.

Project teams should also remember to apply the predetermined rule classification scheme to legacy business rules as they are captured. This will allow analysts to review or discard entire classes of business rules if the objectives of the project change. For example, if the project planned to keep the original legacy data architecture intact, data manipulation logic would need to be reused in the target application. If this decision was reversed in favor of moving to a new relational database environment, these rules could readily be ignored.

Analysts will also need to maintain links between legacy business rules and the legacy data elements they reference. This relationship will allow analysts to tie a legacy rule back to the record, file, and/or database it references and, secondarily, back to target data entities and attributes. This is important for projects that redesign the data architecture and need to synchronize legacy source code with the newly defined data structure.

11.19 Architecture Transformation and Reconstruction

The question of architecture transformation and reconstruction is not an easy one. In most cases, there will not be a clean cut over from the monolithic legacy architecture to a Web Services architecture. Most commercial business environments are too large and intertwined to accommodate wholesale migration. The exceptions to this might be found in real-time environments or smaller organizations where an application is isolated and therefore can be migrated into a new architecture in its entirety.

The following statement summarizes the relationship between business rule capture and shifting information architectures. "In the new approach to e-business development, the current application portfolio is assessed to determine which programs or functions can be modularized, which can be accessed as is, and which can be maintained in place. Then, the business logic for applications that need to be externalized is mined and migrated from the current system to new business components in a Web Services framework. In almost all instances, some back-end databases and entire applications may continue to reside and run on the host platform, even as the business rules of other applications are mined and moved to a middle-tier in the new n-tier architecture" [7].

The value in a transformation approach that utilizes a generic repository is that management can change the development technology and target architecture requirements as often as they like. This is because the rule definitions in the repository are implementation-independent and can be reused under different project scenarios and implementation technologies. In other words, once the legacy environment has been captured and is being maintained in the transformation repository, the target architecture can shift and project teams have the ability to rapidly adjust. This is in sharp contrast to the failed projects of the past, where a shift in direction resulted in a project team tossing out all of its work and having to start over.

The bottom line is that architecture targets, management dictates, and project objectives will continue to change, and organizations need to be prepared to deal with this reality. The following suggestions will help planning and architecture teams address the architecture transition and reconstruction process.

- **Recognize paradigm the shift.** Any organization with a desire to move legacy applications into an object-oriented language such as Java or C++ should avoid transliteration and focus on rule capture, redesign, and redeployment under a component-based architecture. According to one methodologist, "The most difficult problem in teaching object-oriented programming is getting the learner to give up the global knowledge of control that is possible with procedural programs, and rely on the local knowledge of objects to accomplish their tasks. Novice designs are littered with regressions to global thinking: gratuitous global variables, unnecessary pointers, and inappropriate reliance on the implementation of other objects" [8].

  The problem described above would also manifest itself if a project performed a straight conversion from a procedural language to Java or other object-oriented languages. This problem can be avoided, however, by redesigning data and business rules and redeploying redesigned data and rules in a component-based architecture. Management must recognize the paradigm shift. If anyone approaches your organization and says he or she wants to convert COBOL to Java, simply reply "No thank you."

- **Create a Web Services architecture.** "Although legacy business rules are not object-oriented by nature, they can provide for a high degree of reuse, modularity, and encapsulation of a specific business function, as well as a solid foundation for the individual Web Services" [3]. This statement implies that encapsulated business rules are the key to making Web Services a reality. This means that applications can access services from within or from outside the enterprise as required. The benefits of this concept were discussed in Chapter 3.

  One aspect of a Web Services architecture is the ability to manage components, reuse, internal and external service interfaces, and a rules-based environment. The transformation repository becomes that rule base, and components can be drawn from the repository and enabled under the Web Services architecture. As this occurs, the move to Web Services will be streamlined and become easier over time.

- **Synchronize event mapping.** At a simplistic level, applications are comprised of process flows, business rules, and environmental components. We examined high-level functional flows in the project-level assessment and documented this information in the transformation repository. Flow analysis was decomposed further during reverse requirements tracing. In many cases, existing process flows could be mimicked under a Web-based architecture to ensure the continuity of the business processes that legacy process flows currently support.

  Figure 11.11 depicts an event flow that was derived from a legacy environment but recast using newer design techniques. Recasting process flows in a formal, reusable format is important because it places business rules within

Application Area Event Analysis

"Event Dependency Diagram"

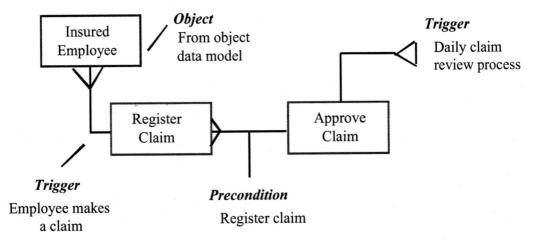

Figure 11.11
Event dependency diagram can be used to model legacy event flow and transform those events into a strategic design model.
(Source: Martin/Odell, Intellicorp.)

a context in which they can be reused effectively. Synchronizing legacy application process flows with target architecture process flows is a key element of the transformation process. This should be a focus for any project involving architecture reconstruction and data and business rule reuse.

- **Separate business, presentation, and data access layer.** Separating business logic, presentation logic, and data access logic is valid for a wide variety of project scenarios. Business rule extraction as well as more basic code slicing technology can facilitate the separation process. Layering legacy architectures makes them more adaptable to changes in user views, data access upgrades, and a wide variety of functional upgrades. The separation process will also streamline ongoing migration to new architectures, including Web Services.

- **Emphasize legacy deactivation.** The reason for the tremendous amount of functional redundancy in legacy environments is the inability or unwillingness to deactivate applications, programs, or embedded logic that has been made obsolete or redundant by another project. The transformation repository makes legacy deactivation manageable, while redundancy analysis and extraction tools make the identification of obsolete logic viable. Management should plan to shrink applications down to a primary subset and place a special emphasis on deactivating legacy source code that has been redeployed in a new architecture or environment.

- **Address functional splintering.** Legacy architectures are splintered because functions are performed across platforms and applications. Making functions more cohesive would radically streamline IT's ability to respond to business change. Consider options for building more cohesive, not less cohesive, application and data solutions. This does not run counter to the "loose coupling" of business logic under a Web Services environment. It does, however, reflect the need for HR, order processing, financial management, and other project teams to consolidate control over the applications and programs that perform these functions.

- **Focus on data migration and consolidation.** Most of the problems with legacy environments stem from data inconsistency and inaccessibility. Management should place a high degree of emphasis on addressing this issue. This includes migrating legacy data to relational environments while merging redundant or splintered physical data structures wherever possible. If an inventory application has six "part management" databases of differing formats across six business units, a project should be launched to fix this problem. This can be accomplished by reconciling these databases to create a combined view of the aggregate data. This type of project can be combined with the data definition rationalization and data cleanup scenarios. While there are quick and dirty approaches to data redesign and reconciliation, they are not recommended because they decrease data flexibility and increase data inaccessibility, which are the source of these problems.

- **Consider fast-path transformation options.** Some project teams may find the level of repository mapping and interim analysis steps burdensome. If a project team is seeking to shortcut transformation project steps, certain options are available. One approach eliminates the procedure (i.e., paragraph) and process objects and relationships from the repository. Analysts would map business rules directly to source programs on the one hand and functions on the other hand. A second option, which accompanies the elimination of process tracking, involves tracking process flows outside the repository through various process flow diagrams. A third option involves allowing the business rule extraction tool to perform as much of the extraction and clone detection analysis as possible. For small systems, analysts may want to avoid using the project-level repository all together. Project teams should use common sense when taking shortcuts and avoid eliminating essential steps in the process.

Legacy business rule extraction and reuse are as integral to systems upgrade, integration, migration, and interface projects as are the people and computers used to implement those projects. Launching a rule extraction effort requires a commitment from management and a willingness to deal with legacy systems as opposed to sidestepping them. Legacy transformation is not that complex, but it takes focus and commitment. It is particularly important to synchronize the redesign of data, business rules, and process flows throughout the transformation process. Architecture transformation will ultimately separate who will effectively leverage information assets from those who will continue the failed policies of the past. Those that continue chasing silver bullet solutions while ignoring the installed base of legacy systems will lose out on the potential power of Web Services and a host of emerging technologies and opportunities.

Notes

1. "USRM—Systems Redevelopment Methodology" [Online], Available: www.comsys.com, 2002.
2. *Building and Managing the Meta Data Repository,* David Marco, John Wiley & Sons, 2000.
3. "Web Services: Turning Lead into Gold?" Len Erlikh, *ZDNet,* Feb. 12, 2002.
4. "Knowledge Mining: Business Rule Extraction and Reuse," William Ulrich, *Cutter IT Journal,* Vol. 12, No. 11, Nov. 1999.
5. Business Rules Group [Online], Available: www.businessrulesgroup.org.
6. "Automated Business Rule Mining for eBusiness Transformation," SEEC, Inc. [Online], Available: www.seec.com, 2000.
7. "A Web Services Framework for Enterprise Agility," SEEC, Inc. [Online], Available: www.seec.com, 2000.
8. "A Laboratory for Teaching Object-Oriented Thinking," Kent Beck, Special Issue of *SIGPLAN Notices,* Vol. 24, No. 10, Oct. 1989 [Online], Available: http://c2.com/doc/oopsla89/paper.html.

Transformation Project Strategies and Case Studies

The success of a legacy transformation strategy is measured by the value delivered to the business community on an ongoing basis. Ensuring the success of transformation projects requires tying together the concepts, approaches, and techniques discussed to this point. This chapter ties together various transformation options and solutions by reviewing specific strategies through a case-study-oriented approach.

Case studies outlined within this chapter include projects that address application consolidation, multi-application integration, package assessment, application rehosting, EAI and Web-enabling, logical data redesign, and component-based migration. Each case study makes extensive use of the transformation strategies and techniques discussed in prior chapters.

Readers should note that while the basic premises for these case studies were borrowed from real-life scenarios, they are primarily amalgamations of situations that have arisen or have been implemented within various organizations. In some cases, a given case study decision, strategy, or result was modified based on the fact that certain projects were halted due to a change in management or other political factors. I have also included a discussion on how to avoid major project failures based on some of these experiences. This discussion encapsulates many of the lessons learned over the course of this book and my career.

12.1 Application Consolidation Project

Throughout this book, I have discussed many of the approaches and techniques that facilitate application consolidation projects. This application consolidation case study discusses various background, justification, planning, and implementation issues underlying this type of project. The background motivating this consolidation project involved a business that had grown through a regional expansion strategy that involved the acquisition of similar companies within the same industry. Each company had a common business infrastructure and relationship with its customers.

Consolidation of business units and information delivery capabilities had been stymied, however, because each acquired business unit had its own unique information infrastructure, applications, and data structures. Each organization was also large, servicing millions of customers within its respective region. Internally facing applications, such as HR and accounting, were easy enough to consolidate because the payroll, insurance, and accounting functions were highly interchangeable across the enterprise infrastructure. Customer-facing applications, data structures, and business units were another story.

Because each region supported unique regulatory requirements, it was impossible to simply cut all customers over to a single customer information system. Size was another issue. Each application incorporated dozens of subsystems, each of which was fairly significant in terms of size and the number of customers supported. Billing was just one of the complex components of this application, which also included customer information and service-related functions.

The business driver behind this project was a desire to reduce business unit overhead, increase customer responsiveness, and create a customer management baseline from which to launch other business initiatives. Without addressing these issues, the organization would become less competitive in prime markets and be held back from leveraging a consolidated customer view needed to launch new products and services.

A secondary issue involved the time and difficulty involved in having three different maintenance teams coordinate customer-related enhancements across multiple applications. Most enhancements had to be applied and tested at least three times over. The following planning, justification, and implementation options were used to address these critical business challenges.

- **Project strategy and mobilization.** A small team was assembled to examine options for how to address the three-pronged challenge the organization was facing. The core team quickly focused on expanding participation to include representatives from all relevant and affected parties across a variety of business units and IT functional areas. They knew a diverse team was needed to undertake this project because it was a cross-functional challenge that involved data, application, and customer ownership issues. A subcommittee was selected to identify, refine, and present various project options.

  Any proposed solution would need to address the business unit and application redundancy issues that were driving up operational costs. The project would also need to consolidate customer management information to support strategic business initiatives. Replacement was not an option because the individual applications involved in this project took decades to evolve and contained rules and data that were essential to business continuity. Replacing these applications would be too time-consuming, expensive, and, most important, risk-prone. Most people did not even know what the existing applications did at any level of detail; they just knew that they were essential to business operations.

A package was also out of the question. The functionality of these applications was unique and mirrored business processes across the enterprise. There was no package that came close to the richness of functionality provided by these applications.

Other options were considered as well. One suggestion involved deleting two of the three applications, migrating data into the format used by a third application, and moving customers to that third application. This was interesting, but each of the applications contained unique business functionality unique to the regulatory and regional customer requirements for a given line of business. This approach would essentially shut down two-thirds of the company.

Another option involved creating a common EAI front end to the three back-end applications. This approach, the reasoning went, allowed the enterprise to consolidate business users through a common front end. While this addressed some user integration requirements, it did not address back-end data integration, which was required if the business was to leverage customer data to launch new products and services. EAI also did not address conflicting and redundant business rules that resulted in the inconsistent handling of common requirements. The same customer in different regions, for example, received different invoices that were calculated inconsistently because the underlying applications differed. Another complexity was the fact that most of the processing was in batch mode. These factors collectively meant that the integration of business functionality and enterprise data needed to go well beyond what an EAI solution could offer.

One approach that met the requirements outlined for this project involved the phased consolidation of the three applications into a single application that would service all customers across the enterprise. This would reconcile redundantly defined business rules, maintain unique regional rules as required; consolidate data, including redundantly defined customers; streamline maintenance, management, and operations of these applications; and facilitate the consolidation of billing and related customer business units. This approach would also create common customer data structures across the enterprise.

- **Project planning and justification.** The executive team understood the criticality of the business requirements because business unit and application redundancies were costing the company over $100 million per year in excess management overhead. While support for a solution was in place, the approach to addressing this challenge needed to be justified and sold to the executives and the board. The justification process involved creating a report that outlined each of the above options along with the pros and cons associated with each alternative. Assuming that the executive committee grants approval for the consolidation approach, the team needed to provide more detail on the approach, a feasibility analysis, and cost estimates for each phase. The general approach underlying the consolidation alternative can be summarized as follows.

1. Develop an estimate for a performing a consolidation project assessment. The assessment included reviewing business user consolidation requirements, building an inventory and data definition analysis for all three major applications, mapping major data stores and functionality across all three applications, and determining the percentage of functional overlap and uniqueness across these applications.

2. Based on the assessment results, the team needed to determine project feasibility, create a phased implementation plan, develop cost estimates by phase, draft deployment timeframes, and define project resource requirements. The plan needed to include business unit commitments and impacts as well as IT commitments and impacts. Resource requirements needed to address the use of internal as well as external project resources.

3. The assessment cost estimate was $500,000. Project implementation cost estimates were broken down by phase and totaled $25 to $30 million. The implementation plan broke down as follows.

   • Clarification of detailed project requirements and implementation plans.

   • Rationalization of data definition usage across all three applications. This provided application analysts with a common view of data usage across business units.

   • Isolation and consolidation of data and user interface logic. This step prepared source programs for subsequent consolidation of user interfaces and application source code.

   • Application consolidation and modularization. This step created common routines from overlapping business rules across the three major applications.

   • Isolate and incorporate special routines based on business rules that were found to be unique across all three applications. Specialized routines included regional processing logic along with related business rules that were unique to a given application or business unit.

   • User interface consolidation. This phase allowed the business units to begin planning consolidation efforts.

   • Data structure and data access layer consolidation. This phase consolidates physical data and access to that data.

   • Interim and ongoing testing. Testing would occur over the life of the project, including after each of the above phases.

- Consolidation of business units, call centers, equipment, application teams, and facilities. This final phase consolidates physical locations, hardware, operational facilities, and personnel.

4. The delivery of this project was to be phased in over a three-year window, with interim deliverables slated every three to six months. Each interim deliverable provided value to the enterprise by either moving the business closer to its overall goal or streamlining applications in preparation for the next phase.

5. The process of justifying the project was broken down by phase as well as considered as a whole. Each of the above phases was justified based on the value delivered to the ongoing management of the applications involved. For example,

   - Data definition rationalization facilitated cross-functional data enhancements by reducing the time needed to add new elements to customer and billing data structures.

   - Data and presentation-layer access logic consolidation streamlined common changes across all customer management applications.

   - Consolidation of common routines allowed all future customer information and related billing changes to be applied in fewer places, more quickly and reliably.

   - The consolidation of user interfaces created common views that allowed selected business users to begin to reorganize into common teams.

   - Data structure and related data access layer consolidation established a foundation for managing customers across regions and under a common data architecture. This facilitated subsequent business unit consolidation as well as reducing IT support and operational expenses.

- **Project infrastructure and implementation considerations.** A phased application consolidation project demanded a great degree of coordination and collaboration. Project communities had to be established for planning, business unit consolidation, data-related tasks, application consolidation, quality assurance, testing and validation, performance certification, and production integration. Each team worked in parallel with other teams while synchronizing tasks across the project.

  Ongoing functional enhancements had to be interspersed with application, user interface, and data structure consolidation. The quality assurance, testing, and production integration teams needed to closely coordinate change control and application certification. One of the challenges involved integrating user enhancement requests across three business units and application teams. The business unit consolidation team coordinated ongoing enhancement requests and related business integration tasks.

  This project involved numerous political hurdles. Consolidating business units, operational functions, and application teams were all major challenges. The leadership on this project kept focused, however, and continued to drive the solution forward even when a midstream change in management raised questions about the investment.

Certain post-implementation upgrades were incorporated later for the sake of implementation expediency. Creating a stabile baseline that supported core customer information processing capabilities was the main goal of the project. Post-implementation enhancements included the addition of Web-driven front ends, table-based management of regional business logic, and new user functionality. Other plans included the addition of data warehouse accessibility and redesign of back-end data handling routines. The project ultimately allowed the enterprise to enter new markets because all customer information could now be managed through a single environment in common formats.

12.2 Multi-Application Integration: Rebuilding an HR Application

The government entity involved in this project processed the payroll, pension, and insurance for hundreds of thousands of employees across a wide geographic area. The applications had evolved over the course of two decades, functioned as standalone entities, and had very rudimentary data exchange capabilities. Tape files, for example, were used to pass data from one application to another. Employee names were stored in up to a dozen redundant physical file structures. This was the classic stovepipe application and data architecture, strewn with fragmented data. Data redundancy and inconsistency were rampant.

In addition to the above challenges, the applications were difficult to support. Reconciling changes across the HR environment was becoming almost impossible. One of the unique factors about the application environment was that business rules had been highly customized around various payroll and pension functions. Because of the diversity of the employee base and the uniqueness of the business rules governing payroll, pension, and insurance functions, these applications could not be replaced by an HR application package.

As a result, management decided to examine alternative options for transforming these critical applications into a single, more cohesive application. The new application would need to share data through a common data architecture, synchronize changes to any personnel data and make these updates immediately available to all HR functions, and basically function as a fully integrated application. To accomplish this, the executive team launched a strategic planning effort to review various options and outline an implementation plan for the selected alternative.

- **Strategy development and mobilization.** A small team was chartered with crafting high-level alternatives for this project. The team wanted to eliminate unworkable options prior to expanding the team to incorporate additional business and IT participation. As stated earlier, no one believed that a package presented a viable option to this challenge. The business rules were unique, and if an unintended functional change was deployed in the new application, it could throw off payroll, pension, and insurance payments to thousands of people.

The basis for needing to retain business rule functionality stemmed from the fact that pay amounts were initially determined by legislation but implemented at the source code level. While a given payee calculation may not always be in full compliance with legislative dictate, the amounts being paid out were agreed to be correct by the paying department and the payee. In other words, the business rules embedded in the application source code were deemed to be correct by default—even in cases where the source code did not adhere to the letter of the law as it was originally crafted. Just as a footnote, this situation is more common than most business executives would ever admit to or even begin to believe.

This scenario created a challenge for the planning team. Rewriting this application from scratch, according to the letter of the law, would deliver a system that was technically correct but would not meet the needs of the ultimate beneficiaries of the application—the employees. Nevertheless, the planning team wanted to keep their options open, so a from-scratch rewrite was one proposed option. A second option to be explored involved building an EAI front end and using middleware to synchronize payroll, pension, and insurance functions. A third option was to transform the existing applications into a common, fully integrated application.

To explore these options further, the initial planning team needed to expand to include representatives from various functional areas and IT units. Participants included senior business managers from the payroll, pension, and insurance teams and their IT counterparts. Additional participants included a senior data analyst, an application architect, an outside transformation specialist, and the chief technologist. The team spent two weeks reviewing the three proposed options to determine a best approach. The strategy involved crafting a high-level approach for each option along with a list of the pros and cons of pursuing each option.

The EAI option did not meet the needs of creating the ideal consolidated data architecture, although it was also discussed as an interim option that could be synchronized with one of the other alternatives. The EAI limitation was that most of the functionality across the three applications involved in this project was batch-oriented and not easily triggered through a middleware solution. EAI was therefore dismissed on a long-term and on an interim basis.

Rebuilding the application from scratch had a good deal of support from a number of analysts. The business community, however, continued to question the wisdom of attempting to rewrite business functionality that was so entrenched in their core business processes. The team continued to come back to the point that suggested a from-scratch rewrite would not be suffi-cient to meet the core requirements of the agency. If any of the thousands of business rules governing employee payroll, pension, and insurance func-tions were modified in a way that changed a payee amount, the project would be deemed a failure.

Reengineering the three existing applications had merit, but detractors believed that a bottom-up approach to this project would omit critical new data or functionality. Supporters of the reengineering approach suggested that a bottom-up approach could be used if the design models derived from the existing application were refined based on a set of strategic HR require-ments. After much deliberation, the team reached a compromise project strategy that included the following characteristics.

- The existing applications would be used to form the basis for an initial integrated data model.
- The project-level transformation repository would be used throughout the process, as discussed in Chapters 10 and 11.
- Legacy application functionality, extracted from all three applications, would form the foundation for the functional decomposition of the new application.
- The project team would refine the bottom-up data model and functional decomposition based on a set of strategic requirements received from the business community. These new requirements were anticipated to be more architectural in nature as opposed to forcing changes in how the existing business rules functioned.
- The project would apply a phased migration approach to move from the current stovepipe architecture into a new, integrated HR environment.
- Phased migration would deploy the new database, populated with employee data, along with the application functionality to manage per-sonnel information. Additional payroll, pension, and insurance functions would be deployed under the new application and data architecture in subsequent phases.

The overall strategy for this project is shown in Figure 12.1. The concept involved extracting, refining, and redeploying a new, integrated data model from the existing applications. Subsequent steps phased in functionality under the new application architectures. This phased approach was geared at reducing the risks of an all- or-nothing implementation. This would help alleviate concerns of the project sponsors. They were concerned about this project because the agency had attempted to replace this application before and failed after spending millions of dollars.

Project communities were established to address the assessment and plan-ning phase, functional consolidation, data model development, technical architecture design, application consolidation, quality assurance, testing and

Multi-Application Integration Strategy

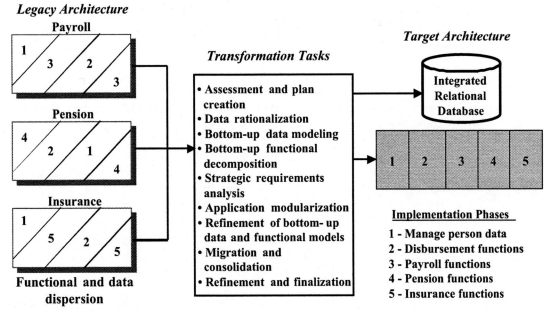

Figure 12.1

In the multi-application integration approach, bottom-up models form the basis for the target information architecture.

validation, and phased production integration. With the team mobilized and an overall strategy selected, the project team moved on to the planning and justification stage.

- **Project planning and justification.** Project justification was not a major issue in this initiative because the commitment to move forward was solid and based on an inability to manage employee information effectively. The approach, however, did require some justification. The plan, along with the background for each task, included the following major tasks.

1. Establish a time and cost estimate for an initial assessment of the feasibility of a bottom-up application integration project and gain authorization to proceed with the assessment. The assessment findings provided the decision point for proceeding with the implementation plan.

2. Develop and deploy a cross-functional assessment plan to determine the feasibility of the bottom-up approach to the redevelopment of a new HR application. This assessment provided a high-level functional decomposition of the applications, mapped application functions against each other, examined data integration and redesign requirements, and finalized a deployment plan.

3. Based on the assessment results, the project team would launch a phased implementation plan. The implementation plan included the rationalization and modularization of the existing application, development of bottom-up data and functional models, refinement of those models, phased migration of the legacy data structures and application architecture, and finalization of the new application.

4. Rationalizing legacy data definitions ensured that the same physical data names and structures were defined consistently across applications. This step created composite data structures that became data entity and attribute candidates to be input to the bottom-up data modeling effort. It also resolved homonyms across business units.

5. Developing a bottom-up data model established the as-is logical view of the legacy data architecture reflecting the applications of interest. Rationalized record groups were used as the initial entity/attribute definitions for the bottom-up data model, beginning with payroll and moving through the pension and insurance applications. Payroll data served as the baseline for the model because it contained the richest decomposition of personnel information. Data entities and attributes not defined in the payroll application were used to enrich the bottom-up data model until all prime legacy data definitions had been accounted for in the target model. The transformation repository played a key role in mapping data usage across legacy applications, among application data definitions and physical data structures, and among legacy records and elements and target data model entities and attributes.

6. Strategic requirements were determined during the assessment phase of the project. This step deserves special mention because of the nature of this project. Long-term requirements were largely unclear, other than that the team needed to create a common application from three standalone applications. Extracting views of the legacy data and application architecture, however, helped business analysts envision how they would like to see the architecture evolve. In other words, the bottom-up views of the legacy environment created a straw-man architecture that users could modify.

7. Bottom-up functional decomposition derived a functional view of the current application architecture. Figure 12.1 depicts a high-level view of this decomposition for managing personnel data, disbursement, payroll functions, pension processing, and insurance tasks. The project team mapped redundant functions, processes, and business rules to source programs, procedures, and related legacy application objects. The results produced a functional view of legacy applications along with mapping redundant or overlapping processes and rules to the source code that defined those rules. This step was essential to the development of an integrated HR application.

8. Data model redesign and refinement efforts focused on streamlining the previously derived bottom-up data model. This included refining the data model to reflect a business-driven view of logical HR data and adding new data based on user-driven requirements. The refinement step also eliminated

legacy data that could be derived in other ways or was no longer essential to the business.

9. Functional redesign involved examining bottom-up functional decompositions, including process flows, and retooling these definitions to address the business needs of the collective user community. One caution was taken, however. Opportunities to add new functionality were logged, but identified as post-implementation tasks. This approach was in keeping with the concept of creating a functioning application first and phasing in enhancements later.

10. Isolation of common routines and unique application functions was the next step. The refined functional decomposition identified how new application functionality would be distributed within the new architecture. This step isolated and consolidated common routines based on refined user views of functional requirements.

11. User interface capture and redesign involved mirroring the existing interfaces, but consolidating or eliminating screens and reports where possible. The redesign of user interfaces was minimized to ensure that the migration process was as streamlined as possible. Batch outputs would be converted to online interfaces as a post-implementation task.

12. Phased migration of legacy data structures and applications, as shown in Figure 12.1, involved moving multiple versions of the application into production over a phased period of time. This would require keeping data and applications functioning concurrently across two separate environments for a brief period of time. This synchronization process is discussed further in the next section.

13. The team established an ongoing quality review, testing, and validation process whereby various versions of the application could be checked out and certified prior to being moved into production.

14. Users began to employ the new application in phases. Users responsible for adding or updating employee information, for example, were the first to begin using the new application. Additional users moved to the new application as legacy functionality was populated into the target architecture. Because the application's technical platform was initially unchanged, very little user retraining was required. As users began using the application, redundant user roles were consolidated and/or eliminated—which was a major cost saving for the enterprise.

15. Refinements to the new integrated application were treated as post-implementation tasks. The objective, as stated earlier, was to ensure that a functioning application was deployed as quickly as possible with the understanding that subsequent enhancement were planned at the back end of the project.

Project justification was based on four factors: functional integrity, risk management, user role consolidation, and time criticality. Functional integrity implied that the business rules implemented in the new application worked the same way as those rules performed in the existing, fragmented applications. Risk management referred to the fact that the project was being phased in and that core functions were not radically altered so as to cause business continuity problems.

User roles were consolidated when tasks such as updating employee data could be performed in a single location by a small team of users. This task was previously split across three business units and multiple locations. Finally, executives approved of the approach because it did not require extensive user interviews to tell the team what the legacy applications already could tell them. In other words, it took less time to extract and reuse core functionality in the new application than it did to re-create an application from scratch—which would have delivered incorrect functionality anyway.

- **Project infrastructure and implementation considerations.** To deliver this project as efficiently as possible, project communities relied on deliverable dependencies as a way of timing project tasks. As soon as a given project community received a prerequisite deliverable, they could proceed with their piece of the project. For example, the bottom-up data modeling team relied on rationalized record groups as input to their analysis effort. This allowed various project teams to remain loosely coupled so that they could perform related tasks concurrently.

Data cleanup and standardization was a major challenge with this project. Much of the data had been around for years, and one application had different data validation and integrity concepts from another application. The data had to be cleansed during the migration process so that it conformed to the highest standard of integrity set by the project team.

Another challenge was the interim synchronization of legacy and target applications and data. For example, the manage-person function was implemented in the new architecture, which utilized the integrated relational database. Each business unit had to begin using the new interface and related application to add or update employee information. This data was then reconciled on a nightly basis with legacy data files.

The project team migrated disbursement, payroll, pension and insurance functions, and data into the new architecture in subsequent migration phases. This process is depicted in Figure 12.1. The team could have chosen to consolidate these tasks, but chose this approach as the most risk-adverse. While user interface changes were minimized throughout the integration project, significant consolidation occurred for overlapping or common functions.

Planned post-implementation enhancements included the addition of new functionality and Web-based interfaces. There were also plans to further integrate

HR with other applications within the agency and with outside agencies. The project was deemed a success and delivered in a two-year window. A from-scratch rewrite, on the other hand, would have never been implemented at all based on the unique business requirements.

12.3 Package Assessment and Implementation

Applying transformation analysis techniques, particularly as it applies to mapping business rule logic, to an application package assessment and deployment project can dramatically reduce the time, cost, and risk of performing such a project. An insurance company obtained a 500 percent ROI by using a business rule extraction tool to map legacy functionality against functions contained within an application package [1]. The following case study outlines ways in which an enterprise can apply transformation techniques to reduce the time, costs, and risks associated with selecting and implementing an application package.

The background for this case study involved a multinational corporation that was looking for ways to upgrade and modernize the applications within its manufacturing division. The current application environment was comprised of inhouse-developed application software and databases. These systems did not share information effectively and were not integrated with accounting, order handling, or purchasing. Because most of the applications in these areas were aging as well, management wanted to investigate replacing the bulk of the inhouse applications with an ERP package.

- **Strategy development and mobilization.** Management had a specific application package in mind but wanted to assess two additional package offerings just to be sure they considered a range of options. The goal of the project was to explore the viability of acquiring one of three ERP packages by determining which package mapped to their overall requirements and to their legacy applications. Mapping each package to strategic requirements and to legacy applications was a way for management to validate their requirements as well as their package options. If the legacy applications contained significantly greater functionality than a given package, management felt that the package would have a hard time replacing existing applications—which was their main goal.

  To meet this objective, the team needed to map the selected package in more detail against strategic requirements and the legacy environment in an effort to finalize a detailed implementation plan. This plan would guide the team in their package implementation and legacy application integration and deactivation efforts. Implementing the package and ensuring that the right legacy software was retained and/or deactivated would be the final test of success for the project.

Mobilizing the team involved identifying participants from business units, including manufacturing, inventory management, order handling, purchasing, and accounting. IT participants included representatives from the strategic planning, architecture, transformation, data management, application management, and operations areas. The transformation team had already performed a high-level assessment of the legacy application environment and loaded that information into the enterprise transformation repository, shown in Figure 12.2.

The enterprise repository had also been preloaded with functions and entities defined in the strategic requirements document development by the strategic planning team. This version of the enterprise repository was expanded to include function and entity objects based on the level of mapping requirement for this project. These are shown in Figure 12.2.

The project team planned to obtain the software and/or documentation for each application package and then map the functionality of each package against the requirements and legacy functionality that had been preloaded into the repository. This would require three teams and three copies of the preloaded enterprise repository.

Multi-Application Integration Strategy

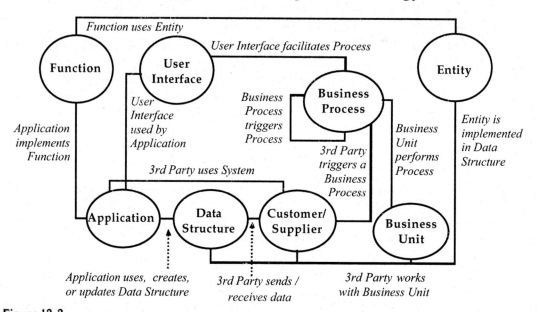

Figure 12.2

Transformation repository maps data and application architecture to business units, business processes, and third parties.

The reason behind using the enterprise transformation repository as opposed to the project level transformation repository was purely pragmatic. The functional assessment applied in this project crossed various application areas and took a broad-based look at the enterprise application environment. Mapping this large cross-section of the application and data architecture would require unnecessary effort by the package assessment team. Driving the analysis down to the business rule level for three packages was not required for the selection phase of the project.

In other words, obtaining a high-level functional mapping for all three packages fulfilled the requirements of the project because it allowed analysts to determine which strategic and/or legacy functions were addressed by each package. The detailed implementation planning and deployment team would, however, need to use the project-level repository to map legacy business rules and data as they moved into the implementation phase of the project.

Cost justification for this project was based on risk aversion. It would initially be cheaper to license a package without determining how well that package mapped to requirements and inhouse applications. This would defer some upfront costs, but most organizations that pursue this option experience a 90 percent package implementation failure rate. As I pointed out in Chapter 4, only 10 percent of package deployment projects come in on time and on budget, and 35 percent of all package implementation projects are canceled outright.

To avoid coming out on the losing end of these statistics, organizations should spend more time in the upfront analysis and selection process. This project scenario has been divided into a package assessment and selection phase and a deployment planning, implementation, and integration phase.

- **Package assessment and selection.** The package assessment and selection process involved breaking the planning team into three groups, each of which examined one of the application packages. Executives were careful to exclude individuals with a predisposition toward a given package option. Individuals that had already made up their mind as to which package they wanted would have had difficulty being objective during this assessment effort. The following tasks were involved in the package assessment and selection process.

1. **Project planning.** The planning task finalized the package assessment plan for the first phase of the project. It involved establishing three teams, each of which compared the functionality and related compatibility of each package to strategic requirements and to legacy environment. The steps defined in the package assessment plan are listed in the remaining task descriptions.
2. **Project setup.** This step required obtaining copies of the software and documentation for each package. In cases where the software could not be installed, a full set of documentation was obtained. This included data models, functional decomposition models, technical specifications, and user documentation.

User documentation typically included screen and report samples. The technical documentation included an application hierarchy chart, execution flow diagrams, a list and a description of each source model, database requirements, and related platform and environmental requirements. The second portion of this step established the three assessment teams—one for each package—and three copies of the transformation repository.

3. **Technical assessment and architecture mapping.** The technical assessment determined if a package conformed to the technical specifications of the environment. This included determining the type of languages used to develop the software, the use of tables as a way to manage decision logic, database, user interface, and other specifics related to running the package. In situations where a package had incompatible technology, a note was made to include this in the final analysis.

4. **Data assessment and architecture mapping.** A package application data model was used to ascertain the data entities used within the package, load these into the repository, and map each entity to a strategic target and legacy entity. Data mapping results were summarized using metrics. Metrics included the number of legacy entities missing from the package but found within the legacy data architecture and/or strategic requirements. Metrics also defined the number of entities found in the package that were missing from the legacy data architecture and from the requirements documentation. Other analyses included an assessment of the structure and relationships unique to a given package database. This analysis was performed for each package.

5. **Functional assessment and architecture mapping.** The planning teams needed to obtain a functional decomposition of each package. If a functional decomposition was unavailable for a given package, a functional decomposition was derived using reverse requirements tracing of functions from user interface views. This process was discussed in Chapter 11. The functions within each package were mapped to the functions in the legacy environment and the requirements documentation. The results included metrics that quantified the percentage of functions found in the legacy environment or requirements specification but that were missing from the package. A second metric category included functions found within the package but missing from the legacy environment and from the strategic requirements.

6. **Findings review, consolidation, and recommendations.** Entities missing from the package signaled an incomplete vendor solution. Entities in the package, but missing from the legacy environment or strategic requirements, signaled a potential mismatch in vendor requirements. The same analysis held true for the functional mapping metric results. The team consolidated its functional findings in a chart like the one shown in Figure 12.3. Each function was mapped between the strategic requirements, the legacy environment, and each package. A similar chart was created for data entities defined within each package, the legacy environment, and the strategic requirements. Package acquisition recommendations were based on how closely a package mapped

to the data and functional requirements of the enterprise as well as on the technical compatibility of each package. One package contained 90 percent of the data and 80 percent of the functionality defined within the requirements documentation and the legacy environment. This was significantly better than the other packages that were reviewed, and it simplified the selection process.

- **Package deployment planning, implementation, and integration.** The deployment planning process required driving the results from the package selection process down to greater level of detail. Based on the initial assessment results, the project team was able to develop a detailed analysis and implementation plan for the package. This plan involved more detailed analysis, migrating and integrating legacy data, deploying the package, deactivating legacy functionality, testing the results, and adding post-implementation enhancements. The team needed to implement the following tasks across the applications being targeted for replacement by the package.

1. **Detailed package deployment analysis.** The step provides the underlying detail required to fully implement the newly licensed package. This task expanded the initial data and functional mapping completed during the package evaluation process. The team needed to port the metadata loaded into the enterprise repository into a more detailed transformation repository. Analysts mapped user interfaces found within the package to each functionally equivalent user interface in the legacy environment. This allowed the team

Mapping Legacy Functionality to Business Requirements and Package Applications

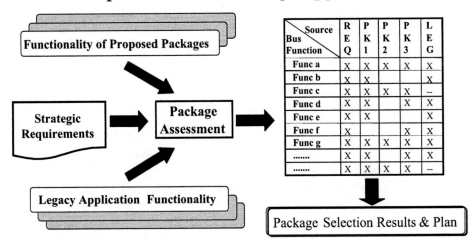

Source Bus Function	R E Q	P K 1	P K 2	P K 3	L E G
Func a	X	X	X	X	X
Func b	X	X			X
Func c	X	X	X	X	--
Func d	X	X		X	X
Func e	X	X			X
Func f	X			X	X
Func g	X	X	X	X	X
....	X	X		X	X
....	X	X	X	X	--

Figure 12.3

Multipackage assessment defines how packages map to requirements (REQ) and to legacy (LEG) functions.

to build a deployment/replacement plan for all user front ends and reports. Logical and physical data usage mapping, as discussed in Chapter 11 under Section 11.5, helped analysts identify missing, overlapping, and inconsistently defined data definitions. Data record grouping analysis was applied to the application package source to verify record structures, lengths, naming conventions, and links back to physical data structures. This analysis provided the basis for the data migration and integration phase.

The team also expanded the functional mapping down to the source code and business rule level, as discussed in Chapter 11 under Section 11.18, and recorded this information in the project-level repository. This information formed the basis for determining which legacy functions to deactivate or keep as well as identifying which package components to implement or ignore. Ignoring a component of the package would be an option if the strategic requirements document indicated that a function was not required in the target environment. Figure 12.4 depicts the detailed conceptual mapping process and the action to be taken based on the findings.

2. **Data migration and integration.** The data migration process required using the data definition analysis and repository mappings to define the exact data migration requirements for the package. This involved mapping existing data to package data structures, creating data cleanup, reformatting and migration routines, migrating the data, and accommodating physical data that is not defined in the package. This last step was addressed by redefining the package database to accommodate new data from the legacy environment. In cases where entire legacy data structures were not defined by the package, these data structures along with the source programs that processed them were left intact. Special programs had to be created to integrate the legacy functions and data into the package environment.

3. **Package deployment and legacy deactivation.** Deploying the application package required using the functional mappings created during the detailed assessment. Based on the functions to be deployed and legacy functions to be retained, revised, or deactivated, the project team identified specific source programs and subsystems that would be reused under the new architecture. The result was a hybrid set of applications that crossed manufacturing, inventory, order processing, and related areas.

The hybrid application was a result of identifying the exact functions that were essential to the business continuity and ensuring that they were in place upon final implementation. A phased deployment approach installed the manufacturing modules first, followed by inventory management, order processing, and purchasing. In each phase, selected legacy source code was retained in part to perform very specific functions that the user community deemed strategic, but that the package did not support. Each interim phase required temporary bridging between legacy and application data formats. The retention of legacy source code in each case required reconciling data

Package Assessment and Implementation

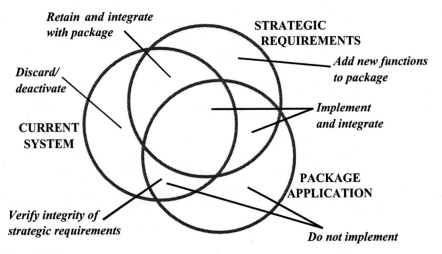

Figure 12.4
Mapping requirements, legacy applications, and the package provides an implementation and deactivation roadmap.

definitions, which was possible due to the legacy-to-package data mappings created during the detailed assessment. Legacy source code was always kept and maintained in separate source programs to simplify future vendor application upgrades. If the vendor produced new modules that replaced the functionality in the retained legacy source programs, the legacy modules could then be deactivated with little effort.

Deactivation of various legacy source code functions was a matter of implementing the new package, along with retained legacy functions, and deactivating various legacy systems and subsystems. In some cases, entire legacy subsystems needed to be retained intact, as discussed previously. This required saving certain user interfaces and data structures unique to those subsystems. One decision the team had to make involved whether to build middleware interfaces to the retained legacy subsystems or to convert legacy subsystems to use the new database formats as dictated by the package. The team decided to modify the legacy data formats within each retained legacy subsystem so that those programs could access the package database directly.

Figure 12.4 depicts one functional category defined in the strategic specifications, but not defined within the package application or the legacy application. The team decided to incorporate these "missing" functions as part of a post-implementation upgrade to the package once it had been fully implemented. This coincided with the team's goal of deploying the package as quickly as possible and enhancing it later.

One last step included unhooking and relinking external interfaces, including EDI functions. Each legacy application had a number of external data linkages that were documented during the assessment process in the repository shown in Figure 12.2. The new hybrid application architecture was reflected in updates to the repository, which continued to serve as a source of ongoing documentation for the package, related data structures, retained legacy functions, and interfaces to external data sources.

4. **Acceptance testing and validation.** The testing process for the package deployment effort was greatly streamlined by the functional and data decomposition defined in the transformation repository. The team created a test plan that targeted each function, process, user interface, and external interface across the business units and functional areas impacted by the new application. This approach created a business-driven test plan that was phased in along with each application package module.

Eliminating the politics and guesswork from an application package selection process avoids many of the problems inherent in the implementation of licensed software. Given that the requirements have been drafted in advance, an assessment like the one described here would only take a couple of months, depending on the size of the enterprise and scope of the package. To date, it appears that the majority of enterprises are unwilling to invest the time involved in front-end analysis—and end up paying dearly for that decision later.

12.4 Application Rehosting Project

An insurance company had a financial processing and claims handling application running on a hardware platform that had grown obsolete. This application was limiting the business's capabilities to integrate accounting and other functions. Management needed to take action to address technological obsolescence and the inability to respond to ongoing business requirements. Their goals included

- Creating an application that would be more flexible from a user and accessibility perspective.
- Establishing a business intelligence system that would allow executives to assess the state of the business.
- Moving away from an obsolete computing environment.
- Making the application Web-accessible while avoiding user retraining.
- Not being forced to rewrite a complex application from scratch.
- Improving data integrity through improved validation of front-end data entry.

There are typically a variety of reasons behind rehosting an application, and this situation was no exception. The system was running on obsolete Wang hardware, used character-based front ends, was difficult to upgrade due to the technological platform, and did not integrate well with other applications because it was isolated on an aging platform. Consulting support and integration tools from Micro Focus, a vendor described in more depth in Appendix A, provided support for the rehosting project [2].

The plan was to keep the application in the original COBOL dialect and port it into a distributed computing environment. A language-level upgrade would, however, be needed to adopt the source code to a new compiler. The project planning effort took two months and included a newly designed technical architecture. The following tasks were involved in this project.

1. Defined a new distributed technical architecture, which employed a 32-bit Windows NT environment.
2. Moved the application data from a Wang, indexed sequential file structure to a relational database built using Oracle. This improved user access to data and the ability to perform ad hoc inquires to that data.
3. Migrated character-based front ends to a graphical user interface that could be deployed using browser technology the Web.
4. Redeployed the application, along with new enhancements, in a distributed, Web-accessible environment.

From a justification perspective, the insurance company needed to pursue this project and considered it an essential project from a business perspective. They created a baseline environment that could be built upon for the future.

Support for rehosting projects like the one discussed in this case study is growing. One analyst recently wrote, "We must compare the total cost of legacy renewal (typically in the range of 50 cents to $2 per line of code) to the total cost of a rewrite. If Java and Oracle, with or without lean methodologies, can get the cost down into this range, then the assertion is false, and Java is the future. If the total cost is more on the order of $5 to $10 per line of code or more (adjusted for differences in bulkiness of language), then the assertion is plausible, and COBOL has a significant future side by side with Java" [3].

This case study was completed in a period of 18 months. This timeframe demonstrates that legacy applications can be reengineered in a very reasonable period of time. A rewrite of this application would have taken significantly longer, cost a good deal more, and not delivered the bottom line business value to the enterprise.

12.5 EAI Case Study

A government defense agency found itself in a difficult situation. Central command discovered that coordinating logistics activity across more than 30 locations worldwide had become almost impossible. The agency was responsible for delivering everything from food to equipment to field-support personnel. The information architecture was comprised of scores of applications, hundreds of user interfaces, and a dozen databases, each with its own unique view of critical logistical data.

The situation had grown to problematic proportions because there were increasing delays in coordinating cross-agency activities and delivering field support. The head of the agency felt that action needed to be taken. The challenges, however, were immense. The applications were old, the data formats were defined inconsistently, and no one was quite sure how they functioned as a collective. In addition to these underlying issues, the user interfaces that supposedly performed similar or identical functions across various locations were based on varying designs and, in some cases, different software and hardware configurations.

Various solutions were discussed as a way to address the situation. Replacing the applications, which were loaded with unique business rules and critical data definitions, was not a consideration due to the inherent complexity of the applications. These systems had been in place for over three decades, and no one was sure how they worked at any level of detail. There were no commercial packages available to address the type of procurement, distribution, and logistical coordination required. Several packages had been reviewed and quickly discarded as not providing the functionality required.

A large-scale application consolidation project had been discussed and viewed by most of the team as the correct solution, but this would take a minimum of three years to fully implement in a best-case scenario. Given the procurement delays common in government environments, no one could foresee even beginning such a major initiative for at least a year. The executive committee, made up of civilian and senior officers, needed a solution implemented well in advance of these timeframes.

The IT team assigned to review requirements and come up with a solution wanted to leverage the Internet to enable a new, common front end across this environment, but no one was sure how to go about this task. Some of the team felt that a middleware solution could address a number of near-term requirements, so they decided to commission an assessment to determine the best approach to delivering an interim solution to the logistics management issue.

- **Logistical project assessment.** The assessment had several goals. These included assessing the functionality deployed across various locations and units, determining the overlap and uniqueness of user interfaces, assessing data commonality across these environments, and crafting a common solution to address the most critical of the logistics issues. The approach involved documenting high-level functions, interfaces, applications, and data structures across these applications. The task involved identifying redundancies and determining opportunities to tie various functions together via middleware and Web-based front ends. The following steps were involved in this assessment.

1. Develop a high-level inventory. The team inventoried all logistical applications, major data stores, user interfaces, and external interfaces. They loaded the information into the high-level repository shown in Figure 12.2. Data structure analysis was limited to major databases or file structures that stored essential logistical data.

2. Document high-level functionality. Using the physical inventory as the baseline, the team identified major functions and business processes across each functional unit within the agency. The Figure 12.2 repository was used to record relevant functional (i.e., logistical) units, functions, and business processes. Documenting cross-functional business processes was deemed critical to the development of common Web-based interfaces. A business process could, for example, invoke a common interface and trigger back-end functions across various applications.

3. Document relevant user interfaces. User interfaces were the main integration target for this project, so each interface needed to be identified and linked to its respective application. In addition, redundant, overlapping, or similar interfaces needed to be mapped to each other in the repository using an "Interface is similar to Interface" relationship. These mappings provided a roadmap to implementation teams designing Web-based front ends.

4. Develop an integration plan. The findings from this assessment determined that the complexity and diversity of the legacy environment did not allow for direct access of data from a Web-based front-end application. The most expeditious approach to achieving management's goal was to develop Web-based front ends using Java, HTML, and XML, and to use middleware to trigger back-end transactions.

- **Logistical project deployment.** The implementation project involved mobilizing the team, creating Web-based front ends, middleware deployment, integrating front ends and back ends across relevant applications and business units, and testing.

1. Mobilize the project implementation team. The team was comprised of business analysts, Web designers, legacy analysts, middleware specialists, and testing expertise. They synchronized their activities to coincide with a phased, cross-functional deployment schedule.

2. Develop Web-based front ends. Tools were used to abstract data views from legacy user interfaces and create prototype Web-based front ends. Edit and validation logic embedded in the old user interface had to be redeployed in the new user interfaces. The main challenge in this portion of the project was to identify overlapping or similar user interfaces as identified in the repository and create a common interface across disparate applications. Legacy application analysts, business analysts, and Web designers needed to collaborate on this process. The resulting front ends had to be linked to middleware to trigger a given transaction based on the user type, functional unit, and data required.

3. Implement a middleware solution. The middleware selected allowed Web-based messages to be converted to mainframe messages that triggered legacy transactions. The legacy applications required no modification. Each program thought it was being invoked by a legacy user interface even though it was a Web-based message that mimicked a given legacy transaction.

4. Perform phased deployment of new front ends. The replacement of legacy user interfaces was delivered over a phased period of time. Each functional unit was slated to begin using the new interfaces in a sequence that began with the most functionally rich environment and proceeded across subsequent environments. Old interfaces were deactivated as the new interfaces were brought online. Because every user already had Internet access, no additional hardware or software was required for users to access the new Web-enabled front ends.

5. Update repository documentation. The project team needed to reflect new Web-based interfaces and relationships to the program it triggered in the repository. Analysts also needed to deactivate the old user interface objects in the repository.

6. Perform validation testing. Validating the results involved running tools to capture legacy input and output transactions as well as new Web-generated transactions. The transaction messages entering and leaving a given program were checked to ensure that the data and formats matched. Users also performed additional acceptance testing for the Web-based front end.

The EAI solution in this case study was ideal for the time-constrained environment. The project team developed and deployed new front ends over a period of several months once the initial analysis and tool procurement work had been completed. The team also planned to use the new front ends as input to the functional design of a planned replacement application.

12.6 Logical Data Redesign Project

A retailer found that accessibility to customer data had grown increasingly complex and burdensome to users across various business units. In particular, data had become "trapped" inside a very large master file and scattered across a series of localized files. Marketing needed to access information on a much more flexible basis for research purposes, while other areas needed more effective access to data on a real-time basis. The applications in question were written in COBOL and used a combination of sequential and indexed file structures.

Management was very conservative in their thinking and not ready to commit to rewriting their legacy applications or to acquiring and deploying an application package. Management was also not eager to move toward component-based application environments and willing to adopt new technology only after it had moved into the mainstream. The IT organization, on the other hand, felt that moving to Web Services would be ideal for the business because they could begin to leverage reusable components through business partner consortiums.

A team of senior IT and business personnel was assembled to examine the situation. An outside facilitator worked with the group to outline their collective goals and try to reach a compromise. The situation grew tense, but everyone felt they were making progress. The facilitator got the team to agree to address the immediate goals of marketing and other business units under a plan that would eventually move the information architecture toward a shared component technology.

The approach that was settled upon defined a very specific project to address data accessibility on a cross-functional basis. This approach also served as a launch point for subsequent componentization and architecture migration. The immediate project was a relational database migration effort that involved redesigning the existing data architecture and redeploying that data within the retooled legacy environment. This initial project did not entail a change in hardware or application software and continued to leverage the installed base of legacy applications and related functionality. The project planning and deployment strategy is discussed below.

- **Data migration project plan.** The project assessment phase consisted of an inventory of the environment and an analysis of the current data and application architecture as follows. The planning phase took about three months.

1. Inventory applications and related data structures. The planning team performed an environmental analysis on all major applications requiring access to core customer data. These areas included marketing, sales, order processing, billing, and related customer management functions. The inventory consisted of identifying major data stores used by the applications of interest along with the source programs comprising those applications. This information was loaded into a detailed transformation repository.
2. Extract application program data definitions. The team performed a data definition analysis that linked major data stores back to application record definitions. These record definitions would be used as input to the bottom-up data modeling effort.
3. Determine feasibility of creating a consolidated database. The team used extracted data definitions created in the prior step to create a high-level logical data model. This model represented a cross-section of data from major record definitions across the applications of interest. The team determined that creating and redeploying a relational database across the applications of interest were feasible and would not require a major rewrite of the current application.
4. Determine application retooling and redeployment requirements. Application retooling in this project required isolating I/O routines, converting those routines to access a relational database, and making other adjustments to the application. For example, routines that were used to sort data could not be eliminated because the data was accessible upon request through an SQL call.

5. Develop a data migration strategy and implementation plan. The implementation strategy the team crafted involved a parallel approach to the data redesign, record rationalization, and application upgrade. For example, the application upgrade team could rationalize data definitions and isolate I/O routines while the data architecture team was creating and populating the new relational database.

- **Data migration project deployment.** Upon completion of the assessment, the team launched an implementation project to build and deploy a customer management, relational database environment. The assessment process loaded the project-level repository with data and program cross-reference information that formed the baseline for the database implementation and application retooling tasks described below. To the degree possible, the team performed these tasks in parallel.

The overall implementation, due to the nature of replacing a shared data structure, was implemented in one pass. Multiple dry runs and other tests were performed as a prerequisite to full-scale deployment. The implementation phase of the project, which involved five applications and roughly 250 programs, took close to 10 months.

1. Rationalize record definitions of interest. This step consolidates and standardizes record definitions that had been extracted from the program source code into a concise subset. This was an important step in the project because it created a consistent baseline for creating the bottom-up data model and simplified the replacement of legacy record definitions with relational database segment definitions. Rationalization was carried through to the point where records group and program-specific (i.e., local) element names were standardized and propagated back into the source code. This step was taken because various applications used different data names to refer to the same physical data, and this confused the design team.

2. Create bottom-up data model for the customer data structures. The collective set of customer data that was currently stored in large master files was taken as the basis for the new data model. High-level data entities were stored and cross-referenced in the repository during the assessment phase of the project. In this step, the design team transformed each rationalized record group into a logical data entity and subordinate elements into logical attributes within those entities.

3. Redesign and normalize the bottom-up data model. Refining the bottom-up data model involved consolidating redundant record and element definitions across major data files. This process ensured that the database could be used by the broadest possible set of applications. The data architecture team then refined and normalized the data model according to the process defined in Section 11.6 in Chapter 11.

4. Isolate and modify data access logic across the applications of interest. Analysts used the repository to identify each source program referencing a redesigned record definition. Application analysts used slicing technology to isolate all relevant I/O and data manipulation logic into called subroutines. These routines were consolidated to the degree possible in preparation for replacing them with calls to the new relational database.

5. Redeploy new relational database definitions back into the applications. The team replaced all relevant source program record definitions with the data definition layouts for new relational database tables. This step involved further data name adjustments and related changes to the source code so that it could access a relational data structure.

6. Upgrade the source code as required to accommodate the new data design. The team eliminated much of the I/O processing logic in the source code, but the introduction of the relational database made certain logic obsolete. Sort routines and other obsolete data manipulation logic had to be eliminated because it no longer applied to the new relational environment.

7. Validate the application changes. Validation testing was premised on the fact that much of the program logic should be identical to the original application. Interface files, reports, online data streams, and other outputs should not have been impacted by the database migration effort. Automated comparison tools were used where applicable to ensure that the application outputs were identical—or as close to identical as possible. In cases where data updates were now being performed within a relational data structure, more traditional user acceptance testing was applied.

Post-implementation recommendations involved taking advantage of the new relational data environment. One option included creating Web-accessible, front-end applications that could access relational data structures on an as needed basis for queries and updates. Over time, analysts planned to pursue a phased migration to a component-based architecture and this project provided an excellent stepping stone toward this goal.

12.7 Component-Based Migration

Component-based development projects rely on enterprise data and legacy functionality. This project picked up where the last project, outlined in Section 12.6, left off. Just to recap, the retailer had migrated major data structures to a relational database and modified five applications to use the data defined within this new relational data structure. The applications in this previous scenario remained in their original language and on the same platform. The data structures and I/O logic, however, had been rationalized and consolidated to the greatest degree possible under the current application architecture.

Management was pleased with the increased data accessibility the database migration project provided. They had grown increasingly interested in seeing if the company could begin to bring more functionality into a Web-based environment. Management asked the project team to investigate ways in which they could bring increased functionality to the Web while leveraging reusable components from retail partners. These components included pricing models, supply chain functionality, and other capabilities from a retail consortium the enterprise recently joined. The project included the following feasibility and implementation phases.

- **Component migration feasibility analysis.** The assessment team examined the current environment and repository data and determined that a feasibility assessment was warranted. The assessment, which leveraged the information gathered during the relational database migration project, took two months.

1. Obtain and verify repository metadata. This step ensured that all the information loaded into the project-level repository during the last project was current and accurate. This included logical and physical data usage as well as an inventory of physical application components.
2. Perform a functional assessment. The team needed to obtain a functional decomposition of the legacy environment to assess where certain functions were implemented and how those functions overlapped with related application areas.
3. Design a component-based management strategy. The team needed to create a component-based management environment to ensure they had the ability to coordinate component development and deployment. This included selecting an environment, which in this case was J2EE, and implementing this environment in a controlled setting.
4. Develop a phased component migration approach and plan. The team needed to create a phased plan to deliver components on an ongoing basis. One major decision involved the implementation language for new components. It was decided that components could be deployed in either COBOL or Java. The implementation of the component-driven environment, which was based on a long-term, evolutionary approach, is outlined below.

- **Component migration.** The component migration strategy involved establishing a team that could be deployed on an as-needed basis to facilitate the migration of legacy applications to components. This process broke down as follows.

1. Expand the functional assessment to the business rule level. This process involved mapping legacy business rules through the repository to the source code that implemented those rules. This was done on a case-by-case basis and driven by the business requirements of a given project, business unit, and application area.

2. Establish guidelines for business rule componentization and legacy deactivation. These guidelines were aimed at helping application teams understand what they were undertaking from a componentization perspective. Application teams had the option to componentize legacy business rules, but to leave them active under the legacy application architecture. They also had the option to componentize the application and deactivate the legacy components. If the first option was selected, the repository would point to the fact that a rule had been replicated under the component architecture. As a rule, however, project teams were encouraged to componentize an application so that the legacy architecture would eventually be deactivated and migrated into the component architecture.

3. Expand componentization into the Web Services arena. The team needed to deploy standards, such as ebXML, for application teams planning to incorporate Web Services into their business model. In addition to this, teams needed to be trained to understand the object-oriented design process for new applications.

4. Map legacy process flows to the target architecture. This technique, discussed in Chapter 11, leveraged legacy process flows to support the event-driven nature of the target architecture.

5. Apply the componentization process to a first project. The first project in this case was an effort that involved working with retail partners to exchange Web Services in relation to the procurement process. Components were service-enabled for exchange with suppliers collaborating in the supply chain management area.

Web Services and componentization were pursued on an opportunistic and ongoing basis as additional business units began to find uses for moving in this direction. This provided the organization with the ability to phase in the new architecture and phase out the legacy environment as business requirements dictated.

12.8 Ending a Pattern of Failure Requires Changing Behavior

Executives have historically seemed comfortable with handing over $20 million for a systems replacement project. There are countless examples in both the private and public sector of projects that were chartered by senior executives, ran for years, cost millions of dollars, and delivered nothing. With a history of replacement project failures, IT organizations face a major challenge. Many subject matter experts have retired, legacy systems expertise is dwindling, business users want instant access to information, and IT executives are pursuing options that no longer work.

Because a large percentage of the functionality in replacement applications already exists within legacy environments, analysts should not need to respecify replacement rules from scratch. History suggests that this is counterproductive because the first couple of years after implementing a new system are spent putting missing business rules back into the application. The fact that programmers go into old systems to obtain code and related business logic seems lost on senior executives.

Transformation formalizes the reuse of data and business rules in a way that makes these assets available to requirements, design, and development teams across an enterprise. Even when the new application is on a distributed platform or written in a new language, reuse still has great value. Failed projects could be avoided if the time spent specifying new requirements were spent creating a "straw man" specification based on business data and rules captured from legacy systems. This would ensure that replacement projects meet the core business requirements of the enterprise.

The business justification for legacy transformation is the same whether rebuilding, licensing, or integrating legacy applications. Every project needs to understand core business requirements. Rule extraction and reuse facilitates this understanding, reduces respecification time, cuts down on the coding process, and lowers testing time. Reducing testing requirements is a byproduct of getting the solution correct in the first place.

Some day, executives will look back at the pattern of failed application projects and find it bewildering. Repeating the exact same behavior over and over again and expecting the results to change will appear highly irrational in retrospect. My assertion is that executives are simply unaware that there are alternatives for addressing a wide variety of legacy information challenges. This should no longer be the case now that transformation options are emerging as a viable way to address critical information requirements.

Notes

1. "How to Avoid Risk and Reduce Cost Using Technology-enabled Gap Analysis," Netron Web Seminar [Online], Available: www.netron.com, Jan. 22, 2002.
2. "PMA Reinsurance Management Company: Brings Legacy COBOL Application to the Web" [Online], Available: www.microfocus.com, 2001.
3. "Legacy.NET," Don Estes, *Cutter IT Journal*, Vol. 14, No. 1, Jan. 2001.

Appendix

Sample Tool Vendor Listing

Appendix A identifies a sample set of software products and vendors that support various transformation tasks. This appendix is broken into two sections. The first section lists various vendor software products by the tool category discussed in Chapter 7. Organizations looking to leverage various software tools within the context of a given project can quickly identify the tool or tools available through this categorized tool section. Some of the tools listed may be delivered as part of a service. In order to be listed in this section, however, the tool must be reasonably well packaged and have a product name. Each tool is accompanied by the name of the vendor or vendors that market that tool.

The second section of this appendix identifies the same software tools listed in Section 1, only each vendor is listed by name in alphabetic order. All tools listed in Section 1 are listed in Section 2 under the vendor that markets those tools. Vendor contact information is included along with comments about that vendor. For each tool listed in Section 1, I have included a brief overview in Section 2. Section 2 also includes references to selected consulting organizations that can assist with a legacy transformation project.

Note that I have not included comprehensive information for every tool listed in Section 2. The best source for this information should always be the vendor that markets a given product or service. Also note that this appendix lists a "representative sampling" of software tools and was not meant to be an all-inclusive list. Software tools evolve, are acquired, or are discontinued on a regular basis. It is possible that a given tool or vendor listed in this appendix may have been acquired, renamed, or shut down after the publication date of this book. If this is the case, information may still be listed on the vendor's Web site.

Finally, this appendix is not meant to endorse any or all of these software tools. Anyone licensing such a tool or service does so at his or her own risk. As with any product or service procurement process, analysts must perform the requisite due diligence prior to licensing technology or securing a service from any third party. All products mentioned in this appendix are trademarks or registered trademarks of their respective companies.

Section 1: Software Tools by Tool Category

Each tool category listed below was defined in Chapter 7. For further information on the background or applicability of tools within each category, readers should refer to Chapter 7. Each software tool in this section is listed first and followed by the name of the vendor of that product.

Business Modeling Technology

The following tools support business modeling, business process modeling, and business process integration.

Business Analysis and Knowledge Management

- Gadrian – Enterprise Analytics, Inc.
- Fuego Business Designer – Fuego, Inc.
- StarBEAM – Entreon Corporation

Business Process Integration and Automation

- Fuego Component Manager – Fuego, Inc.
- Fuego Execution Engine – Fuego, Inc.
- Fuego Task Manager – Fuego, Inc.
- Fuego Business Analyzer – Fuego, Inc.

Analysis and Design Modeling Tools

The UML and data modeling tools are used by business and IT analysts to build, design, and redesign application and data models.

UML Modeling Tools

- Rational Rose – Rational
- System Architect – Popkin Software
- AllFusion Component Modeler – Computer Associates
- NeuArchitect – NeuVis

Data Modeling Technology

- System Architect – Popkin Software
- SILVERRUN – Magna Solutions
- AllFusion ERwin Data Modeler – Computer Associates
- NeuArchitect – NeuVis

The Environmental Analyzer

Batch environmental analysis tools run in a background view and produce reports. Interactive analysts perform the initial parsing and loading of information in the background, but enable analysts to view the information interactively through various query facilities.

Batch Environmental Analyzer

- ASG-Alliance – ASG Software Solutions
- PM/SS – Adpac Corporation

Interactive Environmental Analyzer

- Revolve Enterprise Edition – Micro Focus
- Hotrod – Netron
- Application Mining Suite – CAST
- Mosaic Studio – SEEC
- WebSphere Studio Asset Analyzer – IBM
- RescueWare – Relativity

The Open Repository

The open repositories below can store platform-independent metadata about an information management and related business environment. Project teams can also use standard relational databases for this purpose, but the repositories provide more flexibility, reporting, and metadata accessibility.

- PLATINUM Repository – Computer Associates
- ASG-Rochade – ASG Software Solutions

Source Program Analyzers

Source program analysis tools examine logic flow and produce metrics, summary flow analyses, and detailed reports, depending on the specific tool.

Batch Static Analyzer

- ASG-Recap – ASG Software Solutions
- VISION:Inspect – Computer Associates
- McCabe Reengineer – McCabe & Associates

Interactive Static Analyzer

- ASG-Insight – ASG Software Solutions
- VISION:Assess – Computer Associates
- XPEDITER – Compuware Corporation
- RescueWare – Relativity

Dynamic Analysis

- McCabe Reengineer – McCabe & Associates
- XPEDITOR – Compuware Corporation

Application Improvement Tools

The tools in this category facilitate the process of converting, structuring, slicing, or otherwise improving the overall packaging of legacy applications.

Source Program Editor

- ASG-SmartEdit – ASG Software Solutions
- Mainframe Express – Micro Focus
- VISION:Assess – Computer Associates

Language Change/Upgrade Tool

- ASG-SmartEdit – ASG Software Solutions
- CCCA – IBM

Program Structuring Tool

- VISION:Recode – Computer Associates

Code Modularization Facility

- ASG-Encore – ASG Software Solutions
- McCabe Reengineer – McCabe & Associates
- VISION:Recode – Computer Associates
- VISION:Assess – Computer Associates

Data Definition Analysis and Improvement

These tools analyze and help visualize cross-application data usage and facilitate the rationalization and standardization of those data definitions.

Data Definition Analyzer

- Revolve Enterprise Edition – Micro Focus
- Hotrod – Netron
- Mosaic Studio – SEEC
- XPEDITER – Compuware Corporation

Data Definition Rationalization

- Revolve Enterprise Edition – Micro Focus
- Hotrod – Netron
- Mosaic Studio – SEEC
- WebSphere Studio Asset Analyzer – IBM

Data Definition Expansion

- Revolve Enterprise Edition – Micro Focus
- Reasoning5 – Reasoning Systems

Presentation Layer Extraction and Migration

These tools help visualize and migrate the presentation layer of an application system.

Presentation Layer Extraction

- WinFast & GUI – Visual Legacy Group
- eXtremeVista – Open Connect

User Interface Migration

- WinFast & GUI – Visual Legacy
- Screen Component Adapters – Transoft

Reverse Engineering and Reengineering Technology

Tools in this category assist with the reverse engineering and redesign of legacy applications.

Transaction Flow Analysis

- Hotrod – Netron
- Mosaic Studio – SEEC
- AssetMiner – Micro Focus
- RescueWare – Relativity

Data Reverse Engineering and Reengineering

- NeuArchitect – NeuVis
- SILVERRUN – Magna Solutions
- Migration Solutions – Forecross

Business Rule Capture and Consolidation

- Hotrod – Netron
- AssetMiner – Micro Focus
- Application Mining Suite – CAST
- Mosaic Studio – SEEC
- RescueWare – Relativity

Legacy Componentization

- Hotrod – Netron
- AssetMiner – Micro Focus
- Application Mining Suite – CAST
- Mosaic Studio – SEEC
- RescueWare – Relativity
- Webification Service – Forecross

Validation, Verification, and Testing Technology

The tools listed in this section support change management, quality assurance, and testing within the context of a transformation project.

Change Integration Tool

- ChangeMan – Serena

Test Coverage Analyzer

- ASG-SmartTest – ASG Software Solutions
- EXPEDITOR – Compuware
- *QA*Hiperstation – Compuware

Transaction Simulation Facility

- Mainframe Express – Micro Focus
- Illuma – Reasoning Systems

Compiler/Preprocessor

This category is platform and operating system dependent. Project teams should therefore identify products resident within the environment in which the project is being performed.

Source and Object Code Comparison Tool

- Comparex – Serena
- XPEDITER – Compuware

The Maintenance and Transformation Workbench

The tools listed here allow an analyst to interactively examine, select, and/or edit applications and components within applications for purposes of reengineering or enhancing that application.

- Hotrod – Netron
- AssetMiner – Micro Focus
- Application Mining Suite – CAST
- Mosaic Studio – SEEC
- RescueWare – Relativity

Physical Data Analysis and Migration Technology

The data analysis and migration tools support the analysis, cleanup, redesign, and migration of physical enterprise data.

Data Mining Technology

- ETI EXTRACT – Evolutionary Technologies International
- CleverPath Predictive Analysis Server – Computer Associates

Physical Data Analyzer and Cleansing Tool

- Evoke Axio Product Suite – Evoke Software
- Advantage Data Transformer – Computer Associates
- Advantage InfoRefiner – Computer Associates
- ETI EXTRACT – Evolutionary Technologies International

Physical Data Design Tool

- SILVERRUN – Magna Solutions
- Evoke Axio Product Suite – Evoke Software
- ERwin – Computer Associates

Data Migration Technology

- File-Aid products – Compuware Corporation
- File-Manager – IBM
- Startool – Serena Software
- INSYNC – Macro4
- InfoObject – Noonetics
- Advantage InfoRefiner – Computer Associates

EAI Technology

There are a significant number of integration tools in the market today—too many to list here. I have selected a handful of tools from vendors that have an appreciation for the complexities of legacy applications and that have related capabilities in deciphering these environments.

Integration and Middleware Tools

- VisualAge for Java Enterprise Access Builder – IBM
- WebConnect – Open Connect
- Integration Broker Engine – Mercator
- EnterpriseLink – Micro Focus
- Integration Adapter – Transoft
- Application Integration Adapter – Transoft
- Data Component Adapters – Transoft
- Data Junction Integration Suite – Data Junction Corporation

Business-to-Business Integration Technology

- NeuXchange – NeuVis
- Integration Broker – Mercator

Interface/Bridge Technology

- ASG-Bridge – ASG Software Solutions

Project Management and Administration Technology

I have provided a short list of tools that support transformation project from a project management and coordination perspective.

Configuration Management

- Integrated Software Engineering Platform – Digité
- Flashline CMEE – Flashline

Project Management Tool

- Microsoft Project – Microsoft
- Integrated Software Engineering Platform – Digité

Collaborative Work Environments

- Integrated Software Engineering Platform – Digité
- Rational Suite AnalystStudio – Rational

Transformation Methodology

The methodology listed here facilitates the planning and deployment of transformation projects through a formal process.

- USRM – Comsys Information Services, Inc.

Section 2: Software Tools by Vendor

This section lists each of the vendor products listed in Section 1, by vendor. I have provided contact information, a vendor summary and relevant product summaries for each product listed in Section 1.

Adpac Corporation
425 Market Street, Suite 400
San Francisco, CA 94105
T: 800-797-8439
F: 415-284-1125
www.adpac.com

PM/SS is a systemwide inventory and analysis tool that accepts production source and generates reports on system structure, data structure, and data flow.

The product processes IBM mainframe COBOL, PL/I ,and Assembler along with JCL, CICS, and IMS objects.

ASG Software Solutions
1333 Third Avenue South
Naples, FL 34102
T: 941-435-2200
F: 941-263-3692
www.asg.com

ASG provides businesses with software and professional services for applications management, operations management, performance management, and information management. Through its various technologies, developed inhouse and through acquisitions, ASG helps mainframe clients boost productivity and enhance performance through the use of technology.

ASG-Insight is the COBOL understanding component within the ASG-Existing Systems Workbench (ESW), an integrated life-cycle solution for managing your existing systems. Insight populates the Application Knowledge Repository (AKR) with Analytical Engine to provide you with the tools for navigating and deciphering COBOL application programs. Insight enhances the understanding of COBOL program flow and data usage for more intelligent application maintenance.

ASG-Rochade, the leading metadata repository, provides a central point for collection, control, management, and reuse of information assets.

ASG-Recap is a program-level, quality measurement tool for existing systems. Recap uses Analytical Engine to populate the AKR, giving IS professionals an automated tool for conducting a portfolio analysis of COBOL applications. Recap presents measurement data in a format that dramatically improves your organization's decision support process, and it enables you to align business and technical goals.

ASG-AutoChange is the COBOL automated mass-change component of ESW. AutoChange uses application information added to the AKR.

ASG-SmartTest is the interactive tester and debugger for the ESW. SmartTest populates the AKR and provides source-level debugging for COBOL, Assembler, and PL/I application programs. With SmartTest, programmers can set up, execute, and log an application test session.

ASG-Encore is the COBOL reengineering component of ESW. Encore uses the Analytical Engine to populate the AKR, so that code segments can be extracted based on business logic, user interface, and database access. From these code segments, Encore creates reusable COBOL components.

ASG-SmartEdit is the COBOL-intelligent editor for ESW. SmartEdit uses the Analytical Engine to provide COBOL program intelligence to the ISPF editor, facilitating changes to COBOL application programs. SmartEdit increases an organization's comprehension of COBOL programs, which enables programmers and analysts to quickly apply changes return programs back into production.

ASG-Bridge is the real-time, data-bridging component of ESW. Bridge supports database conversion projects. It has proprietary facilities for intercepting file and database access in order to supply dynamically translated data to your application programs.

blackboxIT LTD
30 Christchurch Road
Bournemouth bh1 3pd, England
T: 44 (0) 1202 438344
F: 44 (0) 1202 438388
www.blackboxit.com

BlackboxIT addresses the legacy extension market and offers innovative and flexible solutions based on unique technology to enable application understanding, restructuring, migration, integration, and Web-enablement.

evolveIT is software for legacy application design discovery and redocumentation. It supports the maintenance and evolution of existing systems, helping reduce maintenance costs and releasing programming staff to perform other tasks.

emergeIT is software that assists in capturing information from existing systems. It makes application functionality available for reuse under new business architectures and Web interfaces.

exportIT is software for migrating and transforming existing systems to alternative or new environments and technologies.

CAST
500 Sansome Street, Suite 601
San Francisco, CA 94111
T: 415-296-1300
F: 415-296-1313
www.castsoftware.com

CAST provides software that helps simplify the complexity of application engineering through application mining solutions for distributed and Internet applications. CAST Software is a French software development company, whose focus is on the application mining market. For developers using modern databases and development languages such as C++, Java, and VB, CAST provides analysts with the information they need to make sense of their applications.

With the **CAST Application Mining Suite**, IT teams can extract the knowledge hidden in the millions of lines of code. CAST Analyzers mine the source code of the application and populate the Application Warehouse. CAST technology applies to Internet and client/server applications that use Visual Basic, PowerBuilder, Internet Scripting languages, Java, Forms, Oracle PL/SQL, SQL, and major 3GLs. AppViewer exploits these findings to provide developers with features such as graphical representations, automated impact analysis, and online reports.

Computer Associates International, Inc.
One Computer Associates Plaza
Islandia, NY 11749
T: 631-342-6000
F: 631-342-6800
www.ca.com

Computer Associates markets and supports hundreds of products for managing computer environments. The products listed here include the CA component and data modeling tools as well as the legacy analysis and structuring products.

The **AllFusion ERwin Data Modeler** helps you visually determine the proper structure, key elements, and optimal design for your database. ERwin Data Modeler is a database development tool that can automatically generate tables and stored procedures as well as trigger code for leading databases. The "Complete-Compare" technology allows iterative development, which keeps models synchronized with physical databases. ERwin Data Modeler integrates with the CA AllFusion ERwin Model Manager, allowing database designers, developers, and users to share model information.

The **AllFusion Component Modeler** is a robust UML modeling tool for visualizing, designing, and maintaining enterprise components for e-business. Through extensive support for collaborative modeling and component reuse, developers are able to share expertise and reuse components to eliminate redundant development efforts. AllFusion Component Modeler helps organizations deliver strategic multitier applications and evolve with today's e-business needs.

PLATINUM Repository serves as a central point of control, enabling organizations to manage, maintain, and access vast amounts of corporate data, applications, and systems in a heterogeneous environment. Mainframe-centric businesses can implement PLATINUM Repository as a DB2-based repository, accessible through a variety of user interfaces, including Windows, Web browsers, and ISPF. Distributed-computing businesses can implement PLATINUM Repository as a scaleable, client/server solution using Windows and Web browsers for the user interface. All implementations support Internet access, allowing business users to research metadata in read-only format from any standard Web browser.

VISION:Assess measures the quality of an entire COBOL application's portfolio, presenting industry-standard scientific measurements based on syntax, complexity, structure, and errors. Composite score reports provide objective decision support information in five categories and over 150 different metrics covering all major areas of COBOL programs.

VISION:Inspect speeds application analysis. This PC-based static analysis tool graphically represents all the components of an application and how they interact. Applications are viewed from a systems, files, source code, code flow, data, inventory, metrics, and screen view perspective. It interfaces with other applications management tools to provide a comprehensive maintenance environment. This product runs under Windows.

VISION:Redocument accelerates software maintenance by providing online documentation for in-depth analysis, detailed measurements of complexity and quality, and program control flow within the body of the source code. This product runs on the IBM mainframe.

VISION:Recode reduces the complexity and improves the quality and maintainability of programs. Unstructured code has all the COBOL anomalies, such as GO TO logic, fall-through logic, active exits, and dead code, eliminated while leaving the program with 100 percent equivalent functionality. Guidelines for subsequent remodularization of the program are provided. Standards for consistent representation of code can be implemented across an organization. This product runs on the IBM mainframe.

Advantage Data Transformer is a transformation, replication, and integration tool that includes a flexible and comprehensive application development environment. The product's programming language enables analysts to define simple and complex data movement tasks, join data from multiple sources, cleanse data, synthesize new data, and synchronize two or more databases on mixed platforms. All of the complexities of accessibility to source and target databases are hidden.

Advantage InfoRefiner is an enterprise data transformation and migration tool that extracts and transforms large volumes of mainframe data from DB2, IMS, and VSAM, and distributes it to your DB2 and leading client/server databases. Your data warehouses and e-business data stores can be populated with full data sets, subsets, summarizations, and aggregations, turning data into accessible information. This advanced solution also performs data cleansing, normalization, data-type conversion, and translations without requiring complex programming.

CleverPath Predictive Analysis Server analyzes and extracts business knowledge from data. This allows analysts to reveal significant factors that can impact organizational success, which allows you to predict future outcomes and achieve the business results needed to stay ahead of the competition. This solution delivers real-time monitoring, detection, and predictions that enable you to offer individualized service to your customers, partners, suppliers, and employees, enhancing user satisfaction.

Compuware Corporation
31440 Northwestern Highway
Farmington Hills, MI 48334
T: 800-521-9353
www.compuware.com

Compuware Corporation has been marketing software and services since the 1970s. Its products include mainframe and distributed computing management and testing software.

XPEDITER helps analyze, segment, build, test, and extend applications for large maintenance and development projects. Speed application and component development with advanced analysis. Developers can easily access detailed testing and analysis information on specific complex programs and systems. They can also receive detailed code coverage reports for risk assessment prior to production, view impact of an application change at a glance, and query the data dictionary showing all fields defined in multiple programs across a system.

File-Aid is a file manipulation utility designed to give users direct access to data in records too big to edit under ISPF or in VSAM, ISAM, and BDAM files. Additional versions of the product address IMS, CICS and distributed environments.

QAHiperstation is a capture/playback testing tool that automates the testing of online and batch applications. For S/390-based applications, QAHiperstation automates test creation and execution, test results analysis and documentation. QAHiperstation's functions and features enhance unit, concurrent, integration, migration, capacity and performance testing.

Comsys Information Services
10220 South West Greenburg Road, Suite 301
Portland, OR 97223

T: 503-293-2499
F: 503-293-3898
www.comsys.com

Comsys Project Services' offerings are scaleable to the needs of large or small enterprises. Comsys teams can work directly with inhouse teams, independently, or at its Technology Center. Comsys services are divided into manageable groups or service lines. The transformation services team is responsible for the USRM transformation methodology.

USRM is a complete transformation blueprint for organizations with a large installed base of existing systems. USRM includes detailed techniques on transformation planning, application upgrades, business rule extraction, data integration, and a host of other redevelopment techniques that companies need to support integration and migration efforts.

Data Junction Corporation
2201 Northland Drive
Austin, TX 78756-1117
T: 512-452-6105
F: 512-459-1309
www.datajunction.com

Data Junction was founded in 1985 by Greg Grosh. It specializes in data integration products and services and has a unique approach to integration, which includes the ability to model business processes.

Data Junction Integration Suite is a collection of visual design tools for building and testing integration projects that involve a wide variety of data formats and applications. The suite offers visual design tools to help map information across various data formats. This product would be useful in situations where an organization had a wide disparity of legacy data that needed to be delivered to a user in a real-time scenario.

Digité
888 Saratoga Avenue
San Jose, CA 95129
T: 408-260-6930
F: 408-260-6950
www.digite.com

Digité, founded in 1999, offers a Web-based service to the software development community. The solution is based on Digité's unique ProcessBazaar methodology and provides instantly available infrastructure to facilitate comprehensive software life cycle management.

Integrated Software Engineering Platform is Digité's next-generation platform for software life-cycle management. The solution platform incorporates a range of tools, content, and processes to successfully convert user requirements to software solutions. Functions include requirements management, analysis and design, quality assurance, resource management, process improvement, project planning, and change management.

Enterprise Analytics, Inc.
401 South LaSalle Street
Chicago, IL 60605
T: 312-786-4766
F: 312-786-4767
www.eanalytics.com

Enterprise Analytics is a software company that offers knowledge management and business analysis productivity tools as a desktop portal for managing work.

Gadrian is a business analysis tool that was built for business users. Unlike the complex tools used to develop UML or other IT-oriented models, Gadrian allows business users to document and retool business processes and related requirements.

Entreon Corporation
10901 Red Circle Drive, Suite 370
Minnetonka, MN 55343
T: 952-939-6037
F: 952-939-9032
www.entreon.com

Entreon makes software that helps companies understand and manage their business model; communicate it to their employees, partners, and customers; and apply it within their business applications.

StarBEAM is a business analysis tool that allows business professionals to document, model, and visualize their business processes.

Evoke Software, Inc.
832 Folsom Street, Suite 1000
San Francisco, CA 94107
T: 415-512-0300
F: 415-512-0302
www.evokesoft.com

Evoke Software is a provider of data profiling software for Global 2000 enterprises. Evoke Software enables companies to identify and subsequently correct inconsistencies, redundancies, and inaccuracies in corporate databases before they cripple applications such as SAP, Siebel, PeopleSoft, and others.

Evoke Axio Product Suite is a database analysis and design tool used to migrate from legacy data, design new databases, optimize existing databases, and rationalize multiple databases. Evoke software helps to eliminate this age-old problem. By quickly providing a complete, 100 percent accurate picture of your data through an automated process called Data Profiling, the Evoke Axio Product Suite helps ensure that there are no surprises, so your valuable IT initiatives can proceed on time, on budget, with reduced risk.

Evolutionary Technologies International (ETI)
816 Congress Avenue, Suite 1300
Frost Bank Plaza
Austin, TX 78701
T: 512-383-3000
F: 512-383-3300
www.eti.com

ETI provides customers with software solutions that help them address data integration needs. ETI's software solutions integrate, transform, and deliver data for your CRM, e-business, ERP, EAI, and data warehouse initiatives.

ETI EXTRACT moves data between a wide range of systems, including legacy databases, data warehouses, operational data stores, enterprise resource planning (ERP) applications, CRM systems, and Web sites. ETI EXTRACT is a data-driven framework of rules, models, and templates for the access and manipulation of data in a specific environment. This includes parameters, grammars, and templates that instruct the ETI EXTRACT software how to generate programs for data bridging to or from a particular database, file structure, or format.

Flashline, Inc.
1300 East 9th Street, Suite 1600
Cleveland, OH 44114
T: 800-259-1961
F: 216-861-1861
www.flashline.com

Flashline is the industry leader in providing enterprise software reuse solutions that facilitate the rapid development of software systems for business. Flashline's flagship product is Flashline CMEE. As information technology evolves, Flashline will continue to pioneer new reuse development tools and services so organizations can more quickly deliver quality products to market.

Flashline CMEE provides a comprehensive software reuse solution that enables, promotes, and measures reuse of components, Web Services, and other assets. Flashline offers reuse support services, an extensive online marketplace of world-class JavaBeans, Enterprise JavaBeans, and COM components, quality assurance testing, auction-based outsourcing, and related resources.

Forecross Corporation
90 New Montgomery Street
San Francisco, CA 94105
T: 415-543-1515
F: 415-543-6701
www.forecross.com

Webification Service can XML-enable a legacy application by inserting a tailored XML directly into the legacy source code or by using a CICS-supplied exit. Forecross offers either a native code or a middleware solution, but the middleware solution requires a 3270 bridge in CICS, while the native code solution has no restrictions as to platform or language. The result is a browser interface without the limitations and costs of screen scraper solutions because the presentation is contained in an XSL stylesheet. More importantly, the data and presentation have been separated so that each transaction becomes a Web component. These components can be mixed and matched to improve user workflow and to provide application integration solutions.

Migration Solutions. Forecross has the most comprehensive migration solutions technology available today. Our fully automated Factory technology automates up to 100 percent of the conversion of the programming language, user interface, and DBMS. This includes migrating from IDMS or other proprietary databases to relational databases.

IBM
555 Bailey Avenue
San Jose, CA 95141
T: 408-463-4012
http://www.software.ibm.com

CCCA (COBOL and CICS/VS Command Level Conversion Aid) converts both CICS and non-CICS programs from one level of COBOL to a higher level of COBOL. If you are planning to convert source code from OS/VS COBOL or VS COBOL II to COBOL/370 or COBOL for MVS and VM, CCCA will identify the required changes, and in most cases, convert them automatically in a standard fashion.

VisualAge for Java Enterprise Edition has a feature called the Enterprise Access Builder (EAB). EAB allows developers to create connectors to enterprise server products such as CICS Transaction Servers, IMS, MQSeries, CORBA, Java components, C++, and SAP Release 3 applications. The underlying connector technology isolates developers from having to deal with low-level communication APIs and data type conversions. Visual Age for Java is part of IBM's Application Framework for e-business: a unified end-to-end architecture based on Java technology, and EJB component programming model. In addition to being integrated with the WebSphere environment, VisualAge for Java works with several other IBM products. Specifically, the EAB connector technology provides links to IBM's CICS, IMS, and MQSeries products.

WebSphere Studio Asset Analyzer parses, stores, and cross-references source code and executable environments in OS/390 and z/OS operating environments. In addition to the basic inventory capabilities found in other environmental analysis tools, Asset Analyzer also helps find and assemble information needed to build connectors among applications. The metadata can be browsed through a Web browser.

Legacy Reserves
Campbell, CA. 95009-1382
T: 408-371-9064
www.legacyreserves.com
Payson@COBOLwebler.com

Legacy Reserves is a large and growing corps of veteran (over 35) Information Technology professionals with skills in legacy systems. These individuals are available for independent contract consulting assignments in connection with the Web Enabling of COBOL-based business data.

Magna Solutions
One Springfield Avenue, Suite 300
Summit, NJ 07901
T: 800-361-0528
new-jersey@magna-solutions.de

Magna Solutions is a worldwide provider of business modeling, data management, and Java-based, e-commerce-oriented products and services used by IS organizations to redocument, design, build, and migrate complex, distributed IT systems. Magna Solutions also supports customers within the evolutionary process from legacy systems to Web-based, multitier applications using object-oriented techniques and standards.

SILVERRUN ERX is a conceptual modeling tool that enables analysts to define un-normalized models and provides assistance in creating normalized models. You can automatically create normalized entity relationship models from data structures, existing file definitions, and business rules. Alternatively, design ER models directly or reverse-engineer database schemas from a variety of sources. SILVERRUN ERX offers an embedded expert system that helps both novices and experienced modelers create correct, normalized data models from data structures, existing file definitions, and business rules.

SILVERRUN RDM is a data modeling tool that enables database designers and administrators to produce and maintain high-quality, enterprise-strength relational data models. RDM is very adaptable and can be used at virtually any stage in the development life cycle. RDM models can be built from scratch, reverse-engineered from a variety of sources (RDBMS as well as non-relational sources), and created from conceptual data models built in SILVERRUN ERX. SILVERRUN RDM provides enterprise-level functionalities in a fully graphical point-and-click interface with the ease of use of a desktop tool.

McCabe & Associates
9861 Broken Land Parkway, 4th Floor
Columbia, MD 21046
T: 800-638-6316; 410-381-3710
F: 410-995-1528
www.mccabe.com

McCabe & Associates provides products and services that enable companies to deliver better applications through analysis technologies for a multitude of legacy environments. This technology is built upon the groundbreaking work in software complexity and structured testing methodologies.

McCabe Reengineer provides a graphical environment in which code can be analyzed, dissected, and modified using advanced visualization techniques and proven methods of analysis. McCabe Reengineer provides detailed graphical structure charts to document complex systems and objectively measures software quality based on industry-standard metrics. The product also identifies and pinpoints duplicate code to reduce the system's complexity and size. McCabe Reengineer also monitors the execution of a system to highlight business-critical functions.

Mercator
T: 800-234-5566
Outside North America: +44 (0) 20 7314 9600
www.mercator.com

Mercator Software's intelligent business integration solutions unify any internal operations and connect them with partners and customers while leveraging current technology investments.

For the mainframe environment, Mercator offers OS/390 Batch and OS/390 CICS execution to support a wide range of integration scenarios. Integration objects created with Mercator Design Studio are ported to a mainframe format and then moved via any file transfer mechanism to the OS/390 system, where they are stored in an object library. For batch execution, maps are invoked via standard JCL. **Mercator Integration Broker Engine** accesses and reads the source file or files, validates and converts the data, and creates any number of output files according to your specifications.

Unlike Web integration tools developed around XML, **Mercator Integration Broker** delivers best-of-breed integration power that can be leveraged across both Web-based and traditional e-commerce applications. It supports the complete transformation of content between any e-business document and existing applications without programming.

Micro Focus
701 East Middlefield Road
Mountain View, CA 94043
T: 650-938-3700
F: 650-404-7217
www.microfocus.com

Revolve Enterprise Edition is an application-understanding environment for central analysis teams involved in estimating, assessing, and managing inventory-wide mass change initiatives. It allows you to adapt more quickly to change, delivering comprehensive high-quality results in a fraction of the time of alternative approaches.

Mainframe Express is a workstation-based development environment for IBM mainframe business applications. Programmers are more productive with this alternative to host-based development, which allows them to edit, compile, debug, and test applications on workstations by utilizing a suite of mainframe emulators and specialized mainframe connectivity technology.

AssetMiner is a software inventory and analysis tool used to provide environmental as well as detailed code analysis information using several different views (source text, graphic display, etc.) and an ad hoc query language. This tool also has the ability to capture, track, consolidate, and present legacy business rules from COBOL applications. AssetMiner and Netron's Hotrod product are the same tool.

EnterpriseLink with Component Generator supports legacy presentation layer integration and componentization. EnterpriseLink includes both a Presentation Integration Server that provides a universal interface layer for new and existing applications and a Component Generator to build robust component interfaces to drive your legacy applications.

Netron, Inc.
99 St. Regis Crescent North
Toronto, Ontario, Canada M3J 1Y9
T: 416-636-8333
F: 416-636-4847
www.netron.com

Netron is a provider of IT transformation solutions focused on accelerating change and making systems transformations easier, cost-effective, and low-risk. With over 20 years of experience in legacy systems, software reuse, and application development, Netron provides methods and tools to transform proven logic and move the business forward. Offerings range from enabling legacy replacement and large-scale data migration to Web-enabling existing systems.

Hotrod is a software inventory, analysis, and business rule extraction and consolidation tool used to provide environmental as well as detailed code analysis information using several different views (source text, graphic display, etc.) and an ad hoc query language. This tool also has the ability to capture, track, consolidate, and present legacy business rules from COBOL applications. Micro Focus's AssetMiner product and Netron's Hotrod product are the same tool.

NeuVis
6 Armstrong Road
Shelton, CT 06484
T: 203-402-2000
F: 203-929-7961
www.neuvis.com

The **NeuArchitect** rapid application development (RAD) platform is the centerpiece of NeuVis's e-business platform. It is used to design and construct all aspects of an e-business application with unmatched speed, quality, and flexibility. The Modeling System includes selected UML models and RAD extension beyond current UML concepts to create a detailed, end-to-end model of your entire application. The Constructor option can access IMS and VSAM and relational databases. One important feature allows developers to capture and reverse-engineer object databases from relational systems as well as IMS hierarchical systems and VSAM systems. This is a major competitive advantage over companies limited to doing this with just relational systems. The knowledge engine capable of doing this leverages certain AI capabilities. The RunTime System consists of a set of runtime components supporting basic application, messaging, and integration functionality.

NeuXchange is a set of components that can be used to accelerate the development of buyer, seller, and exchange commerce applications. NeuXchange is an extensive set of prebuilt and easily customized integrated e-business components and is uniquely suited for building buyer, seller, exchanges, and other multi-stakeholder online business environments.

Noonetics
152 W. 58th Street, Suite 3D
New York, NY 10019
T: 212-307-6717
F: 212-315-2206
www.noonetics.com

Noonetics is a New York software start-up dedicated to the development and marketing of innovative e-business products. Noonetics started its operations in 1998. The company is privately owned by Home Information Services, which funded Noonetics' product development.

InfoObject integrates any mix of data sources into a single, virtual source of aggregated and normalized Web/e-commerce content. Information integration is done on the fly, without the need for an expensive data warehouse. The content is always fresh, and there is no limit on the size of the data sources that can be harvested. On-demand, model-driven content aggregation is the most effective solution. It maximizes content quality while minimizing infrastructure costs, even under rapidly changing business requirements.

Open Connect
2711 LBJ Freeway
Dallas, TX 75234
T: 972-484-5200
F: 972-484-6100
www.openconnect.com

Open Connect offers middleware and related tools to help analysts create nonintrusive connections between Web front ends and legacy back-end applications.

eXtremeVista provides a nonintrusive approach to capturing and transforming legacy user interfaces to GUI, Web-like front ends.

WebConnect offers Web-to-host interface capabilities so that a user can access legacy functionality through a Web browser. This is a nonintrusive approach to front-end to back-end integration.

Popkin Software
T: 212-571-3434
F: 212-571-3436
www.popkin.co.uk

Popkin Software has moved aggressively to provide state-of-the-art features in the System Architect suite, including extensive business process modeling, simulation, UML support, database modeling, code generation, and Web publishing capabilities. Since introducing System Architect in 1988, the company has unveiled a steady flow of major enhancements to the product, including schema generation for all major databases, reverse data engineering, screen painting, project documentation, and links to development environments.

System Architect is a comprehensive and powerful modeling solution designed to provide all of the tools necessary for development of successful enterprise systems. It is the only tool to integrate, in one multi-user product, industry-leading support for all major areas of modeling, including business process modeling, object-oriented and component modeling with UML, relational data modeling, and structured analysis and design. All functionality is harnessed within System Architect's extensible repository with native support for Microsoft VBA.

Rational Software Corporation
18880 Homestead Road
Cupertino, CA 95014
T: 408-863-9900; 800-728-1212
www.rational.com

Rational Software provides a software development platform that improves the speed, quality, and predictability of software projects. This integrated, full life-cycle solution combines software engineering best practices, market-leading tools, and professional services. Products include design, collaboration, and testing tools to support distributed and Web-based development.

Rational Rose software is a visual modeling tool. Business analysts can use Rational Rose to model and visualize business processes and highlight opportunities to increase efficiency. Data analysts can model databases designed in Rational Rose, improving their communication with developers. And when you model Use Cases in Rational Rose, you can be sure your solution is being built for the user. Rational Rose unifies business, systems, and data analysts by enabling them to create and manage models in one tool with one modeling language.

Rational Suite AnalystStudio package helps you solve the right problem and define the right solution by integrating a powerful combination of tools for visual modeling, requirements, and Use Case management, defect and change request tracking, and best-practice process guidelines. It also includes the Rational Suite Team Unifying Platform, an integrated platform for the cross-functional team.

Reasoning, Inc.
700 East El Camino Real
Mountain View, CA 94040
T: 650-429-0350
F: 650-429-0222
www.reasoning.com

Reasoning is the provider of automated software inspection services that enable major technology companies to dramatically reduce the time, effort, and cost required to produce quality software.

Illuma helps C and C++ development teams produce reliable software by uncovering bugs conventional testing methods often miss, finding defects early in the development process, and providing defect metrics and benchmarks. Unlike conventional code testing, Illuma is hardware-independent, does not require running code or test cases, and does not affect code size or execution speed. Reports identify the sections of the code with the greatest risk, enabling analysts to focus QA and testing resources where they're most needed.

Reasoning5 is a software reengineering environment. This is not an advertised product, so those individuals interested should contact Reasoning for further information. The product supports code analysis and language translation.

Relativity Technologies
P.O. Box 14766
Research Triangle Park, NC 27709
T: 919-484-9390
www.relativity.com

RescueWare is a service-based software solution. It is a fairly comprehensive offering that includes application understanding, business rule capture, and migration. Relativity requires the offering to include services with the software.

SEEC
Park West One, Suite 200
Cliff Mine Road
Pittsburgh, PA 15275

T: 412-893-0300
F: 412-893-0417
www.seec.com

SEEC develops component-based enterprise applications by fully exploiting the ongoing value of your existing systems. SEEC defines and builds your new systems using rule-based component development (following EJB and XML standards), business rule mining and reuse, plus flexible integration with your current systems of record.

Mosaic Studio can accelerate business change via rule-based component development, enable real-time collaboration using a Web Services framework, leverage existing policies and best practices through business rule mining and connectors to back-end applications, and build dynamic, collaborative applications.

SERENA Software, Inc.
500 Airport Boulevard, 2nd Floor
Burlingame, CA 94010-1904
T: 650-696-1800
F: 650-696-1849
www.serena.com

StarTool provides data manipulation support to teams that need to extract or convert data from one format to another.

Comparex is a comparison tool that performs one-step comparisons of the contents of any two libraries, directories, files, or databases of like or dissimilar content. It helps developers find values that reside in separate locations across multiple files.

ChangeMan helps manage changes across enterprise-wide applications from a single point. Serena offers integrated ChangeMan for all major operating environments—mainframe, distributed systems, and the Web. ChangeMan provides a single point of control to manage software code and Web content changes throughout the enterprise, from the mainframe to the Web.

Tactical Strategy Group, Inc.
2901 Park Avenue, Suite D-3
Soquel, CA 95073
T: 831-464-5344
F: 831-464-5348
www.systemtransformation.com

Tactical Strategy Group, Inc. (TSG) is a management consulting firm specializing in information architecture transformation strategies. Founded by William Ulrich, TSG has been servicing corporate clients and government agencies since 1990. TSG offers information planning services and custom seminars in the area of systems transformation.

Transsoft, Inc.
2000 River Edge Parkway, Suite 450
Atlanta, GA 30328
T: 770-933-1965
F: 770-933-3464
www.transoft.com

Transoft Application Transformation solutions include automated migration paths for COBOL applications running on a wide variety of proprietary hardware platforms, including HP 3000, Data General MV, NCR, Bull, Unisys, Wang, Prime, and many others. Transoft Application Transformation solutions provide the unique approach of blending new technologies such as Java, COM, and XML with existing application core business functions, enabling an evolutionary path to application extension and modernization, while dramatically reducing project risk, cost, and time.

Application Integration Adapter (AIA) provides high-performance transaction transformation and routing for application-to-application integration projects. Transoft AIA can be used to integrate newly developed applications or packages with mainframe legacy applications.

Transoft Data Component Adapters provides reusable SQL services, with interfaces direct to legacy relational and nonrelational data. The Transoft Data Component Adapters facilitate building tightly coupled, standards-compliant, reusable Web and e-business services for your new applications from your existing COBOL, RPG, C, BASIC, and other legacy systems.

Transoft Screen Component Adapters turn 5250, 3270, VT100, UNIX, or NT legacy application screens into reusable Web or application services that can be integrated into new applications as Enterprise Java Beans, XML data streams, COM objects, and CORBA objects. This is a nonintrusive means of connecting to terminal-based screens-flows to provide component-based services. The adapters give all the advantages of component architectures, including performance and scaleability, without the disadvantages of traditional screen-scraping. The product achieves this by means of a combination of Transoft's unique intelligent screen processing and component broker middleware.

Transsoft Component Builder, supporting ACUCOBOL, Micro Focus COBOL, and RM COBOL compilers, will automatically generate complete components for a number of commonly used services, such as "Get," "Update," and "Delete." No coding is required, and the services can be generated in a matter of minutes. Transsoft Component Builder also allows the user to customize and expand these generic services by adding standard COBOL code, enabling them to provide any required functionality. Analysts may add COBOL routines to create either generic or common services.

Visual Legacy
43 Washington Street, Suite 11
Conway, NH 03818
T: 800-491-0734; 603-447-8406
www.visuallegacy.com

Visual Legacy delivers character to GUI migration software and services to organizations that wish to migrate to modern interfaces.

WinFast transforms legacy UNIX, LINUX, minicomputer, and Windows front ends to GUI and Web-enabled front ends.

GUI transforms IBM mainframe and AS400 character-based front ends to GUI and Web-enabled front ends.

Index

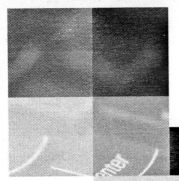

informIT

YOUR GUIDE TO IT REFERENCE

Articles

Keep your edge with thousands of free articles, in-depth features, interviews, and IT reference recommendations – all written by experts you know and trust.

Online Books

Answers in an instant from **InformIT Online Book's** 600+ fully searchable on line books. For a limited time, you can get your first 14 days **free**.

POWERED BY
Safari
TECH BOOKS ONLINE

Catalog

Review online sample chapters, author biographies and customer rankings and choose exactly the right book from a selection of over 5,000 titles.